NOBEL PRIZE WINNERS

1997–2001 Supplement

Biographical Titles from The H.W. Wilson Company

Electronic
Biography Reference Bank
Current Biography
World Authors
Junior Authors and Illustrators

Print
American Authors 1600–1900
British Authors Before 1800
British Authors of the 19th Century
European Authors 1000–1900
Greek and Latin Authors 800 B.C.–A.D. 1000
Spanish American Authors
World Authors 1900–1950 (4 volume set)
World Authors 1950–1970
World Authors 1970–1975
World Authors 1975–1980
World Authors 1980–1985
World Authors 1985–1990
World Authors 1990–1995

The Junior Book of Authors
More Junior Authors
Third Book of Junior Authors
Fourth Book of Junior Authors
Fifth Book of Junior Authors
Sixth Book of Junior Authors
Seventh Book of Junior Authors
Eighth Book of Junior Authors

World Musicians
Composers Since 1900
Musicians Since 1900

World Artists 1950–1980
World Artists 1980–1990

American Reformers
American Songwriters

World Film Directors

Nobel Prize Winners
Nobel Prize Winners, 1987–1991 Supplement
Nobel Prize Winners, 1992–1996 Supplement

NOBEL PRIZE WINNERS

1997–2001 Supplement

An H. W. Wilson Biographical Dictionary

Editor
Mari Rich

Assistant Editor
Martha Hostetter

Staff Contributors
Dimitri Cavalli
Andrew Cavin
Kathleen A. D'Angelo
Christopher Mari
Olivia J. Smith
Brian Solomon

THE H.W. WILSON COMPANY

NEW YORK · DUBLIN

2002

Library of Congress Cataloging-in-Publication Data

Nobel Prize winners. 1997–2001, supplement : an H.W. Wilson biographical dictionary / editor, Mari Rich ; staff contributors, Dimitri Cavalli . . . [et al.].
        p. cm.
    ISBN 0-8242-1018-2
    1. Nobel Prizes. 2. Biography—20th century—Dictionaries. 3. Biography—21st century—Dictionaries. I. Rich, Mari. II. Cavalli, Dimitri. III. Nobel Prize winners.

AS911.N9 N59 2002 Suppl.
001.4'4'0922–dc21
[B]

                                                                                2002028855

PRINTED IN THE UNITED STATES OF AMERICA

CONTENTS

List of Biographical Sketches

NOBEL PRIZE WINNERS
BY PRIZE CATEGORY AND YEAR, 1901–2001

Nobel Prize for Chemistry

1901	Jacobus van't Hoff
1902	Emil Fischer
1903	Svante Arrhenius
1904	William Ramsay
1905	Adolf von Baeyer
1906	Henri Moissan
1907	Eduard Buchner
1908	Ernest Rutherford
1909	Wilhelm Ostwald
1910	Otto Wallach
1911	Marie Curie
1912	Victor Grignard
	Paul Sabatier
1913	Alfred Werner
1914	Theodore W. Richards
1915	Richard Willstätter
1916	Not awarded
1917	Not awarded
1918	Fritz Haber
1919	Not awarded
1920	Walther Nernst
1921	Frederick Soddy
1922	Francis W. Aston
1923	Fritz Pregl
1924	Not awarded
1925	Richard Zsigmondy
1926	Teodor Svedberg
1927	Heinrich Wieland
1928	Adolf Windaus
1929	Hans von Euler-Chelpin
	Arthur Harden
1930	Hans Fischer
1931	Friedrich Bergius
	Carl Bosch
1932	Irving Langmuir
1933	Not awarded
1934	Harold C. Urey
1935	Frédéric Joliot
	Irène Joliot-Curie
1936	Peter Debye
1937	Walter N. Haworth
	Paul Karrer
1938	Richard Kuhn
1939	Adolf Butenandt
	Leopold Ružička
1940	Not awarded
1941	Not awarded
1942	Not awarded
1943	George de Hevesy
1944	Otto Hahn
1945	Artturi Virtanen

1946	John H. Northrop
	Wendell M. Stanley
	James B. Sumner
1947	Robert Robinson
1948	Arne Tiselius
1949	William F. Giauque
1950	Kurt Alder
	Otto Diels
1951	Edwin M. McMillan
	Glenn T. Seaborg
1952	Archer Martin
	Richard Synge
1953	Hermann Staudinger
1954	Linus C. Pauling
1955	Vincent du Vigneaud
1956	Cyril N. Hinshelwood
	Nikolay N. Semenov
1957	Alexander Todd
1958	Frederick Sanger
1959	Jaroslav Heyrovský
1960	Willard F. Libby
1961	Melvin Calvin
1962	John C. Kendrew
	Max Perutz
1963	Giulio Natta
	Karl Ziegler
1964	Dorothy C. Hodgkin
1965	R. B. Woodward
1966	Robert S. Mulliken
1967	Manfred Eigen
	Ronald Norrish
	George Porter
1968	Lars Onsager
1969	Derek Barton
	Odd Hassel
1970	Luis F. Leloir
1971	Gerhard Herzberg
1972	Christian Anfinsen
	Stanford Moore
	William H. Stein
1973	Ernst Fischer
	Geoffrey Wilkinson
1974	Paul J. Flory
1975	John W. Cornforth
	Vladimir Prelog
1976	William N. Lipscomb
1977	Ilya Prigogine
1978	Peter D. Mitchell
1979	Herbert C. Brown
	Georg Wittig
1980	Paul Berg
	Walter Gilbert

NOBEL PRIZE WINNERS BY PRIZE CATEGORY AND YEAR, 1901–2001

	Frederick Sanger		Gunnar Myrdal
1981	Kenichi Fukui	1975	Leonid Kantorovich
	Roald Hoffmann		Tjalling C. Koopmans
1982	Aaron Klug	1976	Milton Friedman
1983	Henry Taube	1977	James Meade
1984	R. Bruce Merrifield		Bertil Ohlin
1985	Herbert A. Hauptman	1978	Herbert Simon
	Jerome Karle	1979	W. Arthur Lewis
1986	Dudley R. Herschbach		Theodore Schultz
	YuanT. Lee	1980	Lawrence Klein
	John C. Polanyi	1981	James Tobin
1987	Donald J. Cram	1982	George Stigler
	Jean-Marie Lehn	1983	Gerard Debreu
	Charles J. Pedersen	1984	Richard Stone
1988	Johann Deisenhofer	1985	Franco Modigliani
	Robert Huber	1986	James M. Buchanan
	Harmut Michel	1987	Robert M. Solow
1989	Sidney Altman	1988	Maurice Allais
	Thomas R. Cech	1989	Trygve Haavelmo
1990	Elias James Corey	1990	Harry M. Markowitz
1991	Richard R. Ernst		Merton H. Miller
1992	Rudolph A. Marcus		William F. Sharpe
1993	Kary B. Mullis	1991	Ronald H. Coase
	Michael Smith	1992	Gary S. Becker
1994	George A. Olah	1993	Robert W. Fogel
1995	Paul Crutzen		Douglass C. North
	Mario J. Molina	1994	John C. Harsanyi
	F. Sherwood Rowland		John F. Nash
1996	Robert F. Curl Jr.		Reinhard Selten
	Harold W. Kroto	1995	Robert E. Lucas Jr.
	Richard E. Smalley	1996	James A. Mirrlees
1997	Paul D. Boyer		William Vickrey
	John E. Walker	1997	Robert C. Merton
	Jens C. Skou		Myron S. Scholes
1998	Walter Kohn	1998	Amartya Kumar Sen
	John A. Pople	1999	Robert Mundell
1999	Ahmed H. Zewail	2000	James Heckman
2000	Alan J. Heeger		Daniel McFadden
	Alan G. MacDiarmid	2001	George A. Akerlof
	Hideki Shirakawa		A. Michael Spence
2001	William S. Knowles		Joseph E. Stiglitz
	Ryoji Noyori		
	K. Barry Sharpless		

Nobel Prize for Literature

1901	René Sully-Prudhomme
1902	Theodor Mommsen
1903	Bjørnstjerne Bjørnson
1904	José Echegaray
	Frédéric Mistral
1905	Henryk Sienkiewicz
1906	Giosuè Carducci
1907	Rudyard Kipling
1908	Rudolf Eucken
1909	Selma Lagerlöf

Nobel Memorial Prize in Economic Sciences

1969	Ragnar Frisch
	Jan Tinbergen
1970	Paul Samuelson
1971	Simon Kuznets
1972	Kenneth Arrow
	John Hicks
1973	Wassily Leontief
1974	Friedrich A. von Hayek

1910	Paul Heyse		1962	John Steinbeck
1911	Maurice Maeterlinck		1963	George Seferis
1912	Gerhart Hauptmann		1964	Jean-Paul Sartre
1913	Rabindranath Tagore		1965	Mikhail Sholokhov
1914	Not awarded		1966	S. Y. Agnon
1915	Romain Rolland			Nelly Sachs
1916	Verner von Heidenstam		1967	Miguel Asturias
1917	Karl Gjellerup		1968	Yasunari Kawabata
	Henrik Pontoppidan		1969	Samuel Beckett
1918	Not awarded		1970	Aleksandr Solzhenitsyn
1919	Carl Spitteler		1971	Pablo Neruda
1920	Knut Hamsun		1972	Heinrich Böll
1921	Anatole France		1973	Patrick White
1922	Jacinto Benavente y Martinez		1974	Eyvind Johnson
1923	William Butler Yeats			Harry Martinson
1924	Władysław Reymont		1975	Eugenio Montale
1925	George Bernard Shaw		1976	Saul Bellow
1926	Grazia Deledda		1977	Vicente Aleixandre
1927	Henri Bergson		1978	Isaac Bashevis Singer
1928	Sigrid Undset		1979	Odysseus Elytis
1929	Thomas Mann		1980	Czesław Miłosz
1930	Sinclair Lewis		1981	Elias Canetti
1931	Erik Karlfeldt		1982	Gabriel García Márquez
1932	John Galsworthy		1983	William Golding
1933	Ivan Bunin		1984	Jaroslav Seifert
1934	Luigi Pirandello		1985	Claude Simon
1935	Not awarded		1986	Wole Soyinka
1936	Eugene O'Neill		1987	Joseph Brodsky
1937	Roger Martin du Gard		1988	Naguib Mahfouz
1938	Pearl S. Buck		1989	Camilo José Cela
1939	Frans Sillanpää		1990	Octavio Paz
1940	Not awarded		1991	Nadine Gordimer
1941	Not awarded		1992	Derek Walcott
1942	Not awarded		1993	Toni Morrison
1943	Not awarded		1994	Kenzaburo Oe
1944	Johannes Jensen		1995	Seamus Heaney
1945	Gabriela Mistral		1996	Wisława Szymborska
1946	Hermann Hesse		1997	Dario Fo
1947	André Gide		1998	José Saramago
1948	T. S. Eliot		1999	Günter Grass
1949	William Faulkner		2000	Gao Xingjian
1950	Bertrand Russell		2001	V. S. Naipaul
1951	Pär Lagerkvist			
1952	François Mauriac		**Nobel Prize for Peace**	
1953	Winston Churchill		1901	Henri Dunant
1954	Ernest Hemingway			Frédéric Passy
1955	Halldór Laxness		1902	Élie Ducommun
1956	Juan Jiménez			Albert Gobat
1957	Albert Camus		1903	William Cremer
1958	Boris Pasternak		1904	Institute of International Law
1959	Salvatore Quasimodo		1905	Bertha von Suttner
1960	Saint-John Perse		1906	Theodore Roosevelt
1961	Ivo Andrić		1907	Ernesto Moneta

NOBEL PRIZE WINNERS BY PRIZE CATEGORY AND YEAR, 1901–2001

	Louis Renault	1947	American Friends Service
1908	Klas Arnoldson		Committee
	Fredrik Bajer		Friends Service Council
1909	Auguste Beernaert	1948	Not awarded
	Paul d'Estournelles	1949	John Boyd Orr
	de Constant	1950	Ralph Bunche
1910	International Peace Bureau	1951	Léon Jouhaux
1911	Tobias Asser	1952	Albert Schweitzer
	Alfred Fried	1953	George C. Marshall
1912	Elihu Root	1954	Office of the United
1913	Henri La Fontaine		Nations High
1914	Not awarded		Commissioner for Refugees
1915	Not awarded	1955	Not awarded
1916	Not awarded	1956	Not awarded
1917	International Committee of	1957	Lester Pearson
	the Red Cross	1958	Georges Pire
1918	Not awarded	1959	Philip Noel-Baker
1919	Woodrow Wilson	1960	Albert Luthuli
1920	Léon Bourgeois	1961	Dag Hammarskjöld
1921	Karl Branting	1962	Linus C. Pauling
	Christian Lange	1963	International Committee of
1922	Fridtjof Nansen		the Red Cross
1923	Not awarded		League of Red Cross Societies
1924	Not awarded	1964	Martin Luther King Jr.
1925	J. Austen Chamberlain	1965	United Nations
	Charles Dawes		Children's Fund
1926	Aristide Briand	1966	Not awarded
	Gustav Stresemann	1967	Not awarded
1927	Ferdinand Buisson	1968	René Cassin
	Ludwig Quidde	1969	International Labour
1928	Not awarded		Organization
1929	Frank Kellogg	1970	Norman Borlaug
1930	Nathan Söderblom	1971	Willy Brandt
1931	Jane Addams	1972	Not awarded
	Nicholas Murray Butler	1973	Henry Kissinger
1932	Not Awarded		Le Duc Tho
1933	Norman Angell	1974	Sean MacBride
1934	Arthur Henderson		Eisaku Sato
1935	Carl von Ossietzky	1975	Andrei Sakharov
1936	Carlos Saavedra Lamas	1976	Mairead Corrigan
1937	Robert Cecil		Betty Williams
1938	Nansen International	1977	Amnesty International
	Office for Refugees	1978	Menachem Begin
1939	Not awarded		Anwar Sadat
1940	Not awarded	1979	Mother Teresa
1941	Not awarded	1980	Adolfo Pérez Esquivel
1942	Not awarded	1981	Office of the United Nations
1943	Not awarded		High Commissioner for
1944	International Committee		Refugees
	of the Red Cross	1982	Alfonso García Robles
1945	Cordell Hull		Alva Myrdal
1946	Emily Greene Balch	1983	Lech Wałesa
	John Mott		

NOBEL PRIZE WINNERS BY PRIZE CATEGORY AND YEAR, 1901–2001

1984	Desmond Tutu
1985	International Physicians for the Prevention of Nuclear War
1986	Elie Wiesel
1987	Oscar Arias Sánchez
1988	United Nations Peacekeeping Forces
1989	Dalai Lama
1990	Mikhail Sergeyevich Gorbachev
1991	Aung San Suu Kyi
1992	Rigoberta Menchú
1993	Nelson Mandela F. W. de Klerk
1994	Yasir Arafat Shimon Peres Yitzhak Rabin
1995	Joseph Rotblat The Pugwash Conferences on Science and World Affairs
1996	Carlos Felipe Ximenes Belo Jose Ramos-Horta
1997	International Campaign to Ban Land Mines (ICBL), Jody Williams
1998	John Hume David Trimble
1999	Doctors Without Borders
2000	Kim Dae Jung
2001	United Nations (U.N.), Kofi Annan

Nobel Prize for Physics

1901	Wilhelm Röntgen
1902	Hendrik Lorentz Pieter Zeeman
1903	Henri Becquerel Marie Curie Pierre Curie
1904	J. W. Strutt
1905	Philipp von Lenard
1906	J. J. Thomson
1907	Albert A. Michelson
1908	Gabriel Lippmann
1909	Ferdinand Braun Guglielmo Marconi
1910	Johannes van der Waals
1911	Wilhelm Wien
1912	Nils Dalén
1913	Heike Kamerlingh Onnes
1914	Max von Laue
1915	W. H. Bragg

	W. L. Bragg
1916	Not awarded
1917	Charles G. Barkla
1918	Max Planck
1919	Johannes Stark
1920	Charles Guillaume
1921	Albert Einstein
1922	Niels Bohr
1923	Robert A. Millikan
1924	Manne Siegbahn
1925	James Franck Gustav Hertz
1926	Jean Perrin
1927	Arthur H. Compton C. T. R. Wilson
1928	Owen W. Richardson
1929	Louis de Broglie
1930	Venkata Raman
1931	Not awarded
1932	Werner Heisenberg
1933	P. A. M. Dirac Erwin Schrödinger
1934	Not awarded
1935	James Chadwick
1936	Carl D. Anderson Victor F. Hess
1937	Clinton J. Davisson G. P. Thomson
1938	Enrico Fermi
1939	Ernest O. Lawrence
1940	Not awarded
1941	Not awarded
1942	Not awarded
1943	Otto Stern
1944	I. I. Rabi
1945	Wolfgang Pauli
1946	P. W. Bridgman
1947	Edward Appleton
1948	P. M. S. Blackett
1949	Hideki Yukawa
1950	Cecil F. Powell
1951	John Cockcroft Ernest Walton
1952	Felix Bloch Edward M. Purcell
1953	Frits Zernike
1954	Max Born Walther Bothe
1955	Polykarp Kusch Willis E. Lamb Jr.
1956	John Bardeen Walter H. Brattain William Shockley

NOBEL PRIZE WINNERS BY PRIZE CATEGORY AND YEAR, 1901–2001

1957	Tsung-Dao Lee		Kai Siegbahn
	Chen Ning Yang	1982	Kenneth G. Wilson
1958	Pavel Cherenkov	1983	Subrahmanyan Chandrasekhar
	Ilya Frank		William A. Fowler
	Igor Tamm	1984	Simon van der Meer
1959	Owen Chamberlain		Carlo Rubbia
	Emilio Segrè	1985	Klaus von Klitzing
1960	Donald A. Glaser	1986	Gerd Binnig
1961	Robert Hofstadter		Heinrich Rohrer
	Rudolf L. Mössbauer		Ernest Ruska
1962	Lev Landau	1987	J. Georg Bednorz
1963	J. Hans D. Jensen		K. Alex Müller
	Maria Goeppert Mayer	1988	Leon M. Lederman
	Eugene P. Wigner		Melvin Schwartz
1964	Nikolai Basov		Jack Steinberger
	Aleksandr Prokhorov	1989	Hans G. Dehmelt
	Charles H. Townes		Wolfgang Pauli
1965	Richard P. Feynman		Norman F. Ramsey
	Julian S. Schwinger	1990	Jerome I. Friedman
	Sin-itiro Tomonaga		Henry W. Kendall
1966	Alfred Kastler		Richard E. Taylor
1967	Hans A. Bethe	1991	Pierre-Gilles de Gennes
1968	Luis W. Alvarez	1992	Georges Charpak
1969	Murray Gell-Mann	1993	Russell A. Hulse
1970	Hannes Alfvén		Joseph H. Taylor Jr.
	Louis Neel	1994	Bertram N. Brockhouse
1971	Dennis Gabor		Clifford G. Shull
1972	John Bardeen	1995	Martin L. Perl
	Leon N. Cooper		Frederick Reines
	J. Robert Schrieffer	1996	David M. Lee
1973	Leo Esaki		Douglas D. Osheroff
	Ivar Giaever		Robert C. Richardson
	Brian D. Josephson	1997	Steven Chu
1974	Antony Hewish		Claude Cohen-Tannoudji
	Martin Ryle		William D. Phillips
1975	Aage Bohr	1998	Robert B. Laughlin
	Ben R. Mottelson		Horst L. Störmer
	James Rainwater		Daniel Chee Tsui
1976	Burton Richter	1999	Gerardus 't Hooft
	Samuel C. C. Ting		Martinus J. G. Veltman
1977	Philip W. Anderson	2000	Zhores I. Alferov
	Nevill Mott		Herbert Kroemer
	John H. Van Vleck		Jack St. Clair Kilby
1978	Pyotr Kapitza	2001	Eric A. Cornell
	Arno A. Penzias		Wolfgang Ketterle
	Robert W. Wilson		Carl Wieman
1979	Sheldon L. Glashow		
	Abdus Salam	**Nobel Prize for Physiology or Medicine**	
	Steven Weinberg	1901	Emil von Behring
1980	James W. Cronin	1902	Ronald Ross
	Val L. Fitch	1903	Niels Finsen
1981	Nicolaas Bloembergen	1904	Ivan Pavlov
	Arthur L. Schawlow	1905	Robert Koch

NOBEL PRIZE WINNERS BY PRIZE CATEGORY AND YEAR, 1901–2001

1906	Camillo Golgi		1946	Hermann J. Muller
	Santiago Ramón y Cajal		1947	Carl F. Cori
1907	Charles Laveran			Gerty T. Cori
1908	Paul Ehrlich			Bernardo Houssay
	Ilya Metchnikoff		1948	Paul Müller
1909	Theodor Kocher		1949	Walter R. Hess
1910	Albrecht Kossel			Egas Moniz
1911	Allvar Gullstrand		1950	Philip S. Hench
1912	Alexis Carrel			Edward C. Kendall
1913	Charles Richet			Tadeus Reichstein
1914	Robert Bárány		1951	Max Theiler
1915	Not awarded		1952	Selman A. Waksman
1916	Not awarded		1953	Hans Krebs
1917	Not awarded			Fritz Lipmann
1918	Not awarded		1954	John F. Enders
1919	Jules Bordet			Frederick C. Robbins
1920	August Krogh			Thomas H. Weller
1921	Not awarded		1955	Hugo Theorell
1922	Archibald V. Hill		1956	André Cournand
	Otto Meyerhof			Werner Forssmann
1923	Frederick G. Banting			Dickinson W. Richards
	John J. R. MacLeod		1957	Daniel Bovet
1924	Willem Einthoven		1958	George W. Beadle
1925	Not awarded			Joshua Lederberg
1926	Johannes Fibiger			Edward L. Tatum
1927	Julius Wagner von Jauregg		1959	Arthur Kornberg
1928	Charles Nicolle			Severo Ochoa
1929	Christiaan Eijkman		1960	Macfarlane Burnet
	Frederick Gowland Hopkins			P. B. Medawar
1930	Karl Landsteiner		1961	Georg von Békésy
1931	Otto Warburg		1962	Francis Crick
1932	Edgar D. Adrian			James D. Watson
	Charles S. Sherrington			Maurice H. F. Wilkins
1933	Thomas Hunt Morgan		1963	John C. Eccles
1934	George R. Minot			Alan Hodgkin
	William P. Murphy			Andrew Huxley
	George H. Whipple		1964	Konrad Bloch
1935	Hans Spemann			Feodor Lynen
1936	Henry H. Dale		1965	François Jacob
	Otto Loewi			André Lwoff
1937	Albert Szent-Györgyi			Jacques Monod
1938	Corneille Heymans		1966	Charles B. Huggins
1939	Gerhard Domagk			Peyton Rous
1940	Not awarded		1967	Ragnar Granit
1941	Not awarded			H. Keffer Hartline
1942	Not awarded			George Wald
1943	Henrik Dam		1968	Robert W. Holley
	Edward A. Doisy			Har Gorbind Khorana
1944	Joseph Erlanger			Marshall W. Nirenberg
	Herbert S. Gasser		1969	Max Delbrück
1945	Ernst B. Chain			Alfred Hershey
	Alexander Fleming			Salvador Luria
	Howard W. Florey		1970	Julius Axelrod

	Ulf von Euler	1985	Michael S. Brown
	Bernard Katz		Joseph L. Goldstein
1971	Earl W. Sutherland Jr.	1986	Stanley Cohen
1972	Gerald M. Edelman		Rita Levi-Montalcini
	Rodney R. Porter	1987	Susumu Tonegawa
1973	Karl von Frisch	1988	James Black
	Konrad Lorenz		Gertrude B. Elion
	Niko Tinbergen		George H. Hitchings Jr.
1974	Albert Claude	1989	J. Michael Bishop
	Christian de Duve		Harold E. Varmus
	George E. Palade	1990	Joseph E. Murray
1975	David Baltimore		E. Donnall Thomas
	Renato Dulbecco	1991	Erwin Neher
	Howard M. Temin		Bert Sakmann
1976	Baruch S. Blumberg	1992	Edmond H. Fischer
	D. Carleton Gajdusek		Edwin G. Krebs
1977	Roger Guillemin	1993	Richard J. Roberts
	Andrew V. Schalley		Phillip A. Sharp
	Rosalyn S. Yalow	1994	Alfred G. Gilman
1978	Werner Arber		Martin Rodbell
	Daniel Nathans	1995	Edward B. Lewis
	Hamilton O. Smith		Christiane Nüsslein-Volhard
1979	Allan Cormack		Eric F. Wieschaus
	Godfrey Hounsfield	1996	Peter C. Doherty
1980	Baruj Benacerraf		Rolf M. Zinkernagel
	Jean Dausset	1997	Stanley Prusiner
	George D. Snell	1998	Robert Furchgott
1981	David H. Hubel		Louis J. Ignarro
	Roger W. Sperry		Ferid Murad
	Torsten Wiesel	1999	Günter Blobel
1982	Sune Bergström	2000	Arvid Carlsson
	Bengt Samuelsson		Paul Greengard
	John R. Vane		Eric R. Kandel
1983	Barbara McClintock	2001	Leland H. Hartwell
1984	Niels K. Jerne		R. Timothy Hunt
	Georges Köhler		Paul Nurse
	César Milstein		

NOBEL PRIZE WINNERS
BY COUNTRY OF RESIDENCE, 1901–2001

In this listing, the editors have attempted to reflect all recent geopolitical changes.

Algeria

Claude Cohen-Tannoudji

Argentina

Bernardo Houssay
Luis F. Leloir (Born in France)
César Milstein
Adolfo Pérez Esquivel
Carlos Saavedra Lamas

Australia

Macfarlane Burnet
John W. Cornforth
John C. Eccles
Jose Ramos-Horta (Born in East Timor)
Patrick White (Born in United Kingdom)

Austria

Robert Bárány
Alfred Fried
Karl von Frisch
Victor F. Hess
Eric R. Kandel
Richard Kuhn
Otto Loewi (Born in Germany)
Konrad Lorenz
Fritz Pregl
Erwin Schrödinger
Bertha von Suttner
Julius Wagner von Jauregg

Belgium

Auguste Beernaert
Jules Bordet
Christian de Duve (Born in United Kingdom)
Corneille Heymans
Henri La Fontaine
Maurice Maeterlinck
Georges Pire
Ilya Prigogine (Born in Russia)

Bosnia

Ivo Andrić

Canada

Frederick G. Banting
Bertram N. Brockhouse

Gerhard Herzberg (Born in Germany)
Robert Mundell
Lester Pearson
John C. Polanyi (Born in Germany)
Myron S. Scholes
Michael Smith (Born in United Kingdom)
Richard E. Taylor

Chile

Gabriela Mistral
Pablo Neruda

China

Daniel Chee Tsui
Gao Xingjian

Colombia

Gabriel García Márquez

Costa Rica

Oscar Arias Sánchez

Czechoslovakia

Jaroslav Heyrovský
Jaroslav Seifert

Denmark

Fredrik Bajer
Aage Bohr
Niels Bohr
Henrik Dam
Johannes Fibiger
Niels Finsen
Karl Gjellerup
Johannes Jensen
August Krogh
Ben R. Mottelson (Born in United States)
Henrik Pontoppidan
Jens C. Skou

East Timor

Carlos Felipe Ximenes Belo

Egypt

Naguib Mahfouz
Anwar Sadat
Ahmed H. Zewail

NOBEL PRIZE WINNERS BY COUNTRY OF RESIDENCE, 1901–2001

Finland

Frans Sillanpää
Artturi Virtanen

France

Maurice Allais
Henri Becquerel
Henri Bergson
Léon Bourgeois
Aristide Briand
Louis de Broglie
Ferdinand Buisson
Albert Camus (Born in Algeria)
Alexis Carrel
René Cassin
Georges Charpak (Born in Poland)
Claude Cohen-Tannoudji (Born in Algeria)
Marie Curie (Born in Poland)
Pierre Curie
Jean Dausset
Paul d'Estournelles de Constant
Anatole France
Pierre-Gilles de Gennes
André Gide
Victor Grignard
François Jacob
Frédéric Joliot
Irène Joliot-Curie
Léon Jouhaux
Alfred Kastler
Charles Laveran
Jean-Marie Lehn
Gabriel Lippmann (Born in Luxembourg)
André Lwoff
Roger Martin du Gard
François Mauriac
Frédéric Mistral
Henri Moissan
Jacques Monod
Louis Néel
Charles Nicolle
Frédéric Passy
Jean Perrin
Saint-John Perse
Louis Renault
Charles Richet
Romain Rolland
Paul Sabatier
Jean-Paul Sartre
Claude Simon (Born in Madagascar)
René Sully-Prudhomme

Gao Xingjian (Born in France)

Germany

Kurt Alder
Adolf von Baeyer
Emil von Behring
Friedrich Bergius
Gerd Binnig
Heinrich Böll
Max Born
Carl Bosch
Walther Bothe
Willy Brandt
Ferdinand Braun
Eduard Buchner
Adolf Butenandt
Johann Deisenhofer
Otto Diels
Gerhard Domagk
Paul Ehrlich
Manfred Eigen
Rudolf Eucken
Emil Fischer
Ernst Fischer
Hans Fischer
Werner Forssmann
James Franck
Günter Grass
Fritz Haber
Otto Hahn
Gerhart Hauptmann
Werner Heisenberg
Gustav Hertz
Hermann Hesse
Paul Heyse
Robert Huber
J. Hans D. Jensen
Wolfgang Ketterle
Klaus von Klitzing
Robert Koch
Georges Köhler
Albrecht Kossel
Herbert Kroemer
Max von Laue
Philipp von Lenard (Born in Austria-Hungary)
Feodor Lynen
Thomas Mann
Otto Meyerhof
Harmut Michel
Theodor Mommsen (Born in Denmark)
Rudolf L. Mössbauer
Erwin Neher

Walther Nernst (Born in West Prussia)
Christiane Nüsslein-Volhard
Carol von Ossietzky
Wilhelm Ostwald (Born in Latvia)
Wolfgang Pauli
Max Planck
Ludwig Quidde
Wilhelm Röntgen
Ernst Ruska
Nelly Sachs
Bert Sakmann
Albert Schweitzer
Reinhard Selten
Hans Spemann
Johannes Stark
Hermann Staudinger
Horst L. Störmer
Gustav Stresemann
Otto Wallach
Otto Warburg
Heinrich Wieland
Wilhelm Wien (Born in East Prussia)
Richard Willstätter
Adolf Windaus
Georg Wittig
Karl Ziegler
Richard Zsigmondy

Ghana

Kofi Annan

Greece

Odysseus Elytis
George Seferis (Born in Turkey)

Guatemala

Miguel Asturias
Rigoberta Menchú

Holland

Tobias Asser
Christiaan Eijkman
Willem Einthoven (Born in
Dutch East Indies, now Indonesia)
Heike Kamerlingh Onnes
Hendrik Lorentz
Simon van der Meer
Jan Tinbergen
Gerardus 't Hooft
Jacobus van't Hoff
Johannes van der Waals
Martinus J. G. Veltman
Pieter Zeeman

Frits Zernike

Iceland

Halldór Laxness

India

Venkata Raman
Amartya Kumar Sen
Rabindranath Tagore
Mother Teresa (Born in
Ottoman Empire [now Macedonia])

Ireland

Samuel Beckett
Seamus Heaney (Born in Northern Ireland)
Sean MacBride (Born in France)
George Bernard Shaw
Ernest Walton
William Butler Yeats

Israel

S. Y. Agnon (Born in Austria-Hungary)
Menachem Begin (Born in Poland)
Shimon Peres (Born in Poland,
now Belarus)
Yitzhak Rabin

Italy

Daniel Bovet (Born in Switzerland)
Giosuè Carducci
Grazia Deledda
Enrico Fermi
Dario Fo
Camillo Golgi
Guglielmo Marconi
Ernesto Moneta
Eugenio Montale
Giulio Natta
Luigi Pirandello
Salvatore Quasimodo
Carlo Rubbia

Japan

Leo Esaki
Kenichi Fukui
Yasunari Kawabata
Ryoji Noyori
Kenzaburo Oe
Eisaku Sato
Hideki Shirakawa
Sin-itiro Tomonaga
Susumu Tonegawa

Hideki Yukawa

Mexico

Alfonso Garcia Robles

Octavio Paz

Myanmar (formerly Burma)

Aung San Suu Kyi

Nigeria

Wole Soyinka

Northern Ireland

Mairead Corrigan

John Hume

David Trimble

Betty Williams

Norway

Bjørnstjerne Bjørnson

Ragnar Frisch

Trygve Haavelmo

Knut Hamsun

Odd Hassel

Christian Lange

Fridtjof Nansen

Sigrid Undset (Born in Denmark)

Pakistan

Abdus Salam

Palestine

Yasir Arafat (Born in Egypt)

Poland

Günter Blobel (then East Germany)

Władysław Reymont

Henryk Sienkiewicz

Wisława Szymborska

Lech Wałesa

Portugal

Egas Moniz

José Saramago

Russia

Zhores I. Alferov

Nikolai Basov

Ivan Bunin

Pavel Cherenkov

Ilya Frank

Mikhail Sergeyevich Gorbachev

Leonid Kantorovich

Pyotr Kapitza

Lev Landau

Boris Pasternak

Ivan Pavlov

Aleksandr Prokhorov

Andrei Sakharov

Nikolay N. Semenov

Mikhail Sholokhov

Aleksandr Solzhenitsyn

Igor Tamm

South Africa

F. W. de Klerk

Nadine Gordimer

Albert Luthuli (Born in Rhodesia [now Zimbabwe])

Nelson Mandela

Max Theiler

Desmond Tutu

South Korea

Kim Dae Jung

Spain

Vicente Aleixandre

Jacinto Benavente y Martinez

Camilo José Cela

José Echegaray

Juan Jiménez

Santiago Ramón y Cajal

Sweden

Hannes Alfvén

Klas Arnoldson

Svante Arrhenius

Sune Bergström

Karl Branting

Arvid Carlsson

Nils Dalén

Ulf von Euler

Hans von Euler-Chelpin (Born in Germany)

Ragnar Granit (Born in Finland)

Allvar Gullstrand

Dag Hammarskjöld

Verner von Heidenstam

George de Hevesy (Born in Austria-Hungary)

Eyvind Johnson

Erik Karlfeldt

Pär Lagerkvist

Selma Lagerlöf

NOBEL PRIZE WINNERS BY COUNTRY OF RESIDENCE, 1901–2001

Harry Martinson
Alva Myrdal
Gunnar Myrdal
Bertil Ohlin
Bengt Samuelsson
Kai Siegbahn
Manne Siegbahn
Nathan Söderblom
Teodor Svedberg
Hugo Theorell
Arne Tiselius
Torsten Wiesel

Switzerland

Werner Arber
J. Georg Bednorz (Born in Germany)
Élie Ducommun
Henri Dunant
Richard R. Ernst
Albert Gobat
Charles Guillaume
Walter R. Hess
Paul Karrer (Born in Russia)
Theodor Kocher
K. Alex Müller
Paul Müller
Wolfgang Pauli (Born in Austria)
Vladimir Prelog (Born in Bosnia)
Tadeus Reichstein (Born in Russia)
Heinrich Rohrer
Leopold Ružička (Born in
Austria-Hungary)
Carl Spitteler
Alfred Werner
Rolf M. Zinkernagel

Tibet

Dalai Lama

Trinidad

V. S. Naipaul

Ukraine

Ilya Metchnikoff

United Kingdom

Edgar D. Adrian
Norman Angell
Edward Appleton
Francis W. Aston
Charles G. Barkla
Derek Barton
James Black

P. M. S. Blackett
John Boyd Orr
W. H. Bragg
W. L. Bragg (Born in Australia)
Elias Canetti (Born in Bulgaria)
Robert Cecil
James Chadwick
Ernst B. Chain (Born in Germany)
J. Austen Chamberlain
Winston Churchill
John Cockcroft
William Cremer
Francis Crick
Henry H. Dale
P. A. M. Dirac
Alexander Fleming
Howard W. Florey (Born in Australia)
Dennis Gabor (Born in Hungary)
John Galsworthy
William Golding
Arthur Harden
Walter N. Haworth
Friedrich A. von Hayek (Born in
Austria)
Arthur Henderson
Antony Hewish
John Hicks
Archibald V. Hill
Cyril N. Hinshelwood
Alan Hodgkin
Dorothy C. Hodgkin (Born in Egypt)
Frederick Gowland Hopkins
Godfrey Hounsfield
R. Timothy Hunt
Andrew Huxley
Niels K. Jerne
Brian D. Josephson
Bernard Katz (Born in Germany)
John C. Kendrew
Rudyard Kipling (Born in India)
Aaron Klug (Born in Lithuania)
Hans Krebs (Born in Germany)
Harold W. Kroto
W. Arthur Lewis
John J. R. MacLeod
Archer Martin
James Meade
P. B. Medawar (Born in Brazil)
James A. Mirrlees
Peter D. Mitchell
Nevill Mott
V. S. Naipaul (Born in Trinidad)
Philip Noel-Baker

NOBEL PRIZE WINNERS BY COUNTRY OF RESIDENCE, 1901–2001

Ronald Norrish
Paul Nurse
Max Perutz (Born in Austria)
John A. Pople
George Porter
Rodney R. Porter
Cecil F. Powell
William Ramsay
Owen W. Richardson
Robert Robinson
Ronald Ross (Born in Nepal)
Joseph Rotblat (Born in Poland)
Bertrand Russell
Ernest Rutherford (Born in
New Zealand)
Martin Ryle
Frederick Sanger
Amartya Sen (Born in India)
Charles S. Sherrington
Frederick Soddy
Richard Stone
J. W. Strutt
Richard Synge
G. P. Thomson
J. J. Thomson
Niko Tinbergen (Born in Holland)
Alexander Todd
John R. Vane
John E. Walker
Maurice H. F. Wilkins
(Born in New Zealand)
Geoffrey Wilkinson
C. T. R. Wilson

United States

Jane Addams
George A. Akerlof
Sidney Altman (Born in Canada)
Luis W. Alvarez
Carl D. Anderson
Philip W. Anderson
Christian Anfinsen
Kenneth Arrow
Julius Axelrod
Emily Greene Balch
David Baltimore
John Bardeen
George W. Beadle
Gary S. Becker
Georg von Békésy (Born in Hungary)
Saul Bellow (Born in Canada)
Baruj Benacerraf (Born in Venezuela)
Paul Berg

Hans A. Bethe (Born in Germany)
J. Michael Bishop
Günter Blobel (Born in former
East Germany, now Poland)
Felix Bloch (Born in Switzerland)
Konrad Bloch (Born in Germany)
Nicolaas Bloembergen (Born in
Holland)
Baruch S. Blumberg
Norman Borlaug
Paul D. Boyer
Walter H. Brattain (Born in China)
P. W. Bridgman
Joseph Brodsky (Born in Russia)
Herbert C. Brown (Born in United
Kingdom)
Michael S. Brown
James M. Buchanan
Pearl S. Buck
Ralph Bunche
Nicholas Murray Butler
Melvin Calvin
Thomas R. Cech
Owen Chamberlain
Subrahmanyan Chandrasekhar
(Born in India)
Steven Chu
Albert Claude (Born in Belgium)
Ronald H. Coase (Born in United
Kingdom)
Stanley Cohen
Arthur H. Compton
Leon N. Cooper
Elias James Corey
Carl F. Cori (Born in Austria-Hungary)
Gerty T. Cori (Born in Austria-Hungary)
Allan Cormack (Born in South Africa)
Eric Cornell
André Cournand (Born in France)
Donald J. Cram
James W. Cronin
Paul Crutzen (Born in the Netherlands)
Robert F. Curl Jr.
Clinton J. Davisson
Charles Dawes
Gerard Debreu (Born in France)
Peter Debye (Born in Holland)
Hans G. Dehmelt (Born in Germany)
Max Delbrück (Born in Germany)
Peter C. Doherty (Born in Australia)
Edward A. Doisy
Renato Dulbecco (Born in Italy)
Vincent du Vigneaud

Gerald M. Edelman
Albert Einstein (Born in Germany)
Gertrude B. Elion
T. S. Eliot
John F. Enders
Joseph Erlanger
William Faulkner
Richard P. Feynman
Edmond H. Fischer (Born in China)
Val F. Fitch
Paul J. Flory
Robert W. Fogel
William A. Fowler
Jerome I. Friedman
Milton Friedman
Robert Furchgott
D. Carleton Gajdusek
Herbert S. Gasser
Murray Gell-Mann
Ivar Giaever (Born in Norway)
William F. Giauque (Born in Canada)
Walter Gilbert
Alfred G. Gilman
Donald A. Glaser
Sheldon L. Glashow
Joseph L. Goldstein
Paul Greengard
Roger Guillemin (Born in France)
John C. Harsanyi (Born in Hungary)
H. Keffer Hartline
Leland H. Hartwell
Herbert A. Hauptman
Seamus Heaney (Born in Northern
Ireland)
James Heckman
Alan J. Heeger
Ernest Hemingway
Philip S. Hench
Dudley R. Herschbach
Alfred Hershey
George H. Hitchings Jr.
Roald Hoffmann (Born in Poland)
Robert Hofstadter
Robert W. Holley
David H. Hubel (Born in Canada)
Charles B. Huggins (Born in Canada)
Cordell Hull
Russell A. Hulse
Louis J. Ignarro
Eric R. Kandel (Born in Austria)
Jerome Karle
Frank Kellogg
Edward C. Kendall

Henry W. Kendall
Wolfgang Ketterle (Born in Germany)
Har Gorbind Khorana (Born in India)
Jack St. Clair Kilby
Martin Luther King Jr.
Henry Kissinger (Born in Germany)
Lawrence Klein
William S. Knowles
Walter Kohn
Tjalling C. Koopmans (Born in Holland)
Arthur Kornberg
Edwin G. Krebs
Herbert Kroemer (Born in Germany)
Polykarp Kusch (Born in Germany)
Simon Kuznets (Born in Ukraine)
Willis E. Lamb Jr.
Karl Landsteiner (Born in Austria)
Irving Langmuir
Robert B. Laughlin
Ernest O. Lawrence
Joshua Lederberg
Leon M. Lederman
David M. Lee
Tsung-Dao Lee (Born in China)
Yuan T. Lee (Born in Taiwan)
Wassily Leontief (Born in Russia)
Rita Levi-Montalcini (Born in Italy)
Edward B. Lewis
Sinclair Lewis
Willard F. Libby
Fritz Lipmann (Born in Germany)
William N. Lipscomb
Robert E. Lucas Jr.
Salvador Luria (Born in Italy)
Alan G. MacDiarmid
Rudolph A. Marcus (Born in Canada)
Harry M. Markowitz
George C. Marshall
Maria Goeppert Mayer (Born in
Germany)
Barbara McClintock
Daniel McFadden
Edwin M. McMillan
R. Bruce Merrifield
Robert C. Merton
Albert A. Michelson (Born in Germany)
Merton H. Miller
Robert A. Millikan
Czesław Miłosz (Born in Poland)
George R. Minot
Franco Modigliani (Born in Italy)
Mario J. Molina (Born in Mexico)
Stanford Moore

NOBEL PRIZE WINNERS BY COUNTRY OF RESIDENCE, 1901–2001

Thomas Hunt Morgan
Toni Morrison
John Mott
Hermann J. Muller
Robert S. Mulliken
Kary B. Mullis
Robert Mundell (Born in Canada)
Ferid Murad
William P. Murphy
Joseph E. Murray
John F. Nash
Daniel Nathans
Marshall W. Nirenberg
Douglass C. North
John H. Northrop
Severo Ochoa (Born in Spain)
George A. Olah (Born in Hungary)
Eugene O'Neill
Lars Onsager (Born in Norway)
Douglas D. Osheroff
George E. Palade (Born in Romania)
Linus C. Pauling
Charles J. Pedersen (Born in Korea)
Arno A. Penzias (Born in Germany)
Martin L. Perl
William D. Phillips
John A. Pople (Born in United
Kingdom)
Stanley Prusiner
Edward M. Purcell
I. I. Rabi (Born in Austria-Hungary)
James Rainwater
Norman F. Ramsey
Frederick Reines
Dickinson W. Richards
Theodore W. Richards
Robert C. Richardson
Burton Richter
Frederick C. Robbins
Richard J. Roberts (Born in United
Kingdom)
Martin Rodbell
Theodore Roosevelt
Elihu Root
Peyton Rous
F. Sherwood Rowland
Paul Samuelson
Andrew V. Schalley (Born in Poland)
Arthur L. Schawlow
Myron S. Scholes (Born in Canada)
J. Robert Schrieffer
Theodore Schultz
Melvin Schwartz

Julian S. Schwinger
Glenn T. Seaborg
Emilio Segrè (Born in Italy)
Phillip A. Sharp
William F. Sharpe
K. Barry Sharpless
William Shockley (Born in
United Kingdom)
Clifford G. Shull
Herbert Simon
Isaac Bashevis Singer (Born in Poland)
Richard E. Smalley
Hamilton O. Smith
George D. Snell
Robert M. Solow
A. Michael Spence
Roger W. Sperry
Jack St. Clair Kilby
Wendell M. Stanley
William H. Stein
John Steinbeck
Jack Steinberger (Born in Germany)
Otto Stern (Born in Germany)
George Stigler
Joseph E. Stiglitz
Horst L. Störmer (Born in Germany)
James B. Sumner
Earl W. Sutherland Jr.
Albert Szent-Györgyi (Born in Hungary)
Edward L. Tatum
Henry Taube (Born in Canada)
Joseph H. Taylor Jr.
Howard M. Temin
E. Donnall Thomas
Samuel C. C. Ting
James Tobin
Charles H. Townes
Daniel C. Tsui
Harold C. Urey
Harold E. Varmus
John H. Van Vleck
Martinus J. G. Veltman (Born in
Holland)
William Vickrey (Born in Canada)
Selman A. Waksman (Born in Ukraine)
Derek Walcott (Born in St. Lucia)
George Wald
James D. Watson
Steven Weinberg
Thomas H. Weller
George H. Whipple
Carl Wieman
Eric F. Wieschaus

NOBEL PRIZE WINNERS BY COUNTRY OF RESIDENCE, 1901–2001

Elie Wiesel (Born in Romania)
Eugene P. Wigner (Born in Hungary)
Jody Williams
Kenneth G. Wilson
Robert W. Wilson
Woodrow Wilson
R. B. Woodward

Rosalyn S. Yalow
Chen Ning Yang (Born in China)
Ahmed H. Zewail (Born in Egypt)

Vietnam

Le Duc Tho

NOBEL PRIZE WINNERS WHO HAVE DIED
SINCE LAST SUPPLEMENT

Derek Barton (*Chemistry*, 1969)
d. March 16, 1998

Konrad Bloch (*Physiology or Medicine*, 1964) d. October 15, 2000

Camilo José Cela (*Literature*, 1998)
d. January 17, 2002

Allan Cormack (*Physiology or Medicine*, 1979) d. May 7, 1998

John C. Eccles (*Physiology or Medicine*, 1963) d. May 2, 1997

Gertrude Belle Elion (*Physiology or Medicine*, 1988) d. February 21, 1999

Odysseus Elytis (*Literature*, 1979)
d. November 18, 1996

Kenichi Fukui (*Chemistry*, 1981)
d. January 9, 1998

Tryge Haavelmo (*Economics*, 1989)
d. July 26, 1999

John C. Harsanyi (*Economics*, 1994)
d. August 9, 2000

Alfred D. Hershey (*Physiology or Medicine*, 1969) d. May 22, 1997

Gerhard Herzberg (*Chemistry*, 1971)
d. March 3, 1999

George H. Hitchings Jr. (*Physiology or Medicine*, 1988) d. February 27, 1998

Alan Lloyd Hodgkin (*Physiology or Medicine*, 1963) d. December 20, 1998

Charles B. Huggins (*Physiology or Medicine*, 1966) d. January 12, 1997

Henry W. Kendall (*Physics*, 1990)
d. February 15, 1999

John C. Kendrew (*Chemistry*, 1962)
d. August 23, 1997

Halldor Laxness (*Literature*, 1955)
d. February 8, 1998

Wassily Leontief (*Economics*, 1973)
d. February 5, 1999

Merton H. Miller (*Economics*, 1990)
d. June 3, 2000

Nevill Mott (*Physics*, 1977)
d. August 8, 1996

Daniel Nathans (*Physiology or Medicine*, 1978) d. November 16, 1999

Louis Neel (*Physics*, 1970)
d. November 17, 2000

Octavio Paz (*Literature*, 1990)
d. April 19, 1998

Max Perutz (*Chemistry*, 1962)
d. February 6, 2002

Vladimir Prelog (*Chemistry*, 1975)
d. January 7, 1998

Edward M. Purcell (*Physics*, 1952)
d. March 7, 1997

Frederick Reines (*Physics*, 1995)
d. August 26, 1998

Martin Rodbell (*Physiology or Medicine*, 1994) d. December 7, 1998

Abdus Salam (*Physics*, 1979)
d. November 23, 1996

Arthur L. Schawlow (*Physics*, 1981)
d. April 28, 1999

Theodore Schultz (*Economics*, 1979)
d. February 26, 1998

Glenn T. Seaborg (*Chemistry*, 1951)
d. February 25, 1999

Herbert A. Simon (*Economics*, 1978)
d. February 9, 2001

Michael Smith (*Chemistry*, 1993)
d. October 4, 2000

Mother Teresa (*Peace*, 1979)
d. September 5, 1997

James Tobin (*Economics*, 1981)
d. March 11, 2002

Alexander Todd (*Chemistry*, 1957)
d. January 10, 1997

George Wald (*Physiology or Medicine*, 1967) d. April 12, 1997

Geoffrey Wilkinson (*Chemistry*, 1973)
d. September 26, 1996

Preface

The original edition of *Nobel Prize Winners* appeared in 1987 and contained biographical sketches of the 566 men, women, and institutions awarded the Nobel Prize from 1901 through 1986. The first supplement to that book, published in 1992, encompassed biographies of the 40 prize winners from 1987 through 1991. A second supplement, containing 55 biographical essays and published in 1997, profiled the winners from 1992 through 1996. This latest supplement–with 58 articles–examines the laureates from 1997 through 2001. These volumes are intended for students and the general reader, as an introduction to the lives and achievements of the winners. Special emphasis has been given to the body of work for which each received the Nobel Prize.

The biographical profiles are arranged alphabetically. Each article traces the development of a laureate's work and assesses its significance. Because the work is often highly technical and has not always been discussed in secondary sources, factual accuracy has been a particular concern. To address this situation, many laureates graciously offered to assist in the preparation of their profiles. Also, with the permission of the Nobel Foundation, the preparers of this volume have made use of autobiographical materials from several of the prize winners, as published on the Nobel e-Museum Web site. Additionally, some of the profiles included here appeared originally in another H. W. Wilson Company publication, *Current Biography*, and have been updated or condensed where appropriate.

In most cases each laureate has been given a separate profile, even when a prize has been awarded to two or three persons, as is often the case with the science prizes. While a certain amount of repetition therefore occurs in descriptions of joint work, the reader finds in one place a comprehensive account of an individual laureate's work. As leading members of the scientific, literary, and political communities, the Nobel Prize winners have shared in a wide network of mutual influence. To help the reader follow these connections, the names of other laureates appear in small-capital letters when first mentioned in profiles other than their own. This cross-referencing device encourages the reader to explore related profiles, thereby making it possible to trace the development of related ideas.

Within the profiles, foreign titles are given with an English translation–in italics or quotes if the work has been translated and published under that title or in roman type if the editors have supplied the translation. The preparers of this volume have included a short biography of Alfred Nobel as well as a history of the Nobel Prizes and Nobel institutions. A list of laureates who have died since the publication of the last supplement is included, as are lists allowing the reader to locate subjects by prize category, year of award, and country of residence.

The editor wishes to thank the staff writers who prepared these essays for their diligence and devotion to accuracy, Martha Hostetter for her hard work and keen eye, Clifford Thompson and Miriam Helbok for their invaluable guidance, and Willie Gin and Olivia J. Smith for their contributions. Thanks also to Gray Young and his entire production staff for their unsparing efforts on behalf of this supplement.

—Mari Rich
June 2002

ALFRED NOBEL

by Alden Whitman

Alfred Nobel, the Swedish chemical experimenter and businessman who invented dynamite and other explosive compounds and whose will established the prizes that have brought him lasting fame, was a person of many paradoxes and contradictions. His contemporaries in the last half of the nineteenth century often found him perplexing because he did not quite fit the mold of the successful capitalist of his expansionist era. For one thing, Nobel was fonder of seclusion and tranquility than of ostentation and urban life, although he lived in cities most of his life and traveled widely. Unlike many contemporary barons of business, Nobel was spartan in his habits; he neither smoked nor drank, and he eschewed cards and other games. While his heritage was Swedish, he was a cosmopolitan European, comfortable with the French, German, Russian, and English languages as well as with his native tongue. Despite the heavy demands of his business and industrial affairs, he managed to build a well-stocked library and was well acquainted with the works of such authors as Herbert Spencer, the British philosopher and exponent of social Darwinism; Voltaire; and Shakespeare. Of nineteenth-century men of letters, he most admired a number of French writers: the Romantic novelist and poet Victor Hugo; Guy de Maupassant, the short story craftsman; Honoré de Balzac, the novelist whose keen eye pierced the human comedy; and the poet Alphonse de Lamartine. He also liked to read the works of the Russian novelist Ivan Turgenev and the Norwegian playwright and poet Henrik Ibsen. The naturalism of the French novelist Émile Zola, however, left him cold. Above all, he loved the poetry of Percy Bysshe Shelley, whose works inspired in him an early resolve to embark on a literary career. To that end, he wrote a considerable number of plays, novels, and poems, only one of which was published. He then turned instead to a career in chemistry.

Likewise puzzling to his fellow entrepreneurs was Nobel's reputation for holding advanced social views. The notion that he was a socialist was, in fact, quite undeserved, for he was actually an economic and political conservative who opposed suffrage for women and expressed grave doubts about democracy. Nevertheless, as much as Nobel lacked confidence in the political wisdom of the masses, he despised despotism. As an employer of many hundreds of workers, he took a paternalistic interest in their welfare, without wishing to establish any personal contact. Shrewdly, he realized that a work force with high morale is more productive than a crudely exploited one, which may well have been the basis for Nobel's reputation as a socialist.

Nobel was quite unassuming and even reticent about himself. He had few confidants and never kept a diary. Yet at dinner parties and among friends, he was an attentive listener, always courteous and considerate. The dinners given at his home in one of the most fashionable neighborhoods of Paris were convivial and elegant, for he was a well-informed host able to call upon a fund of small talk. He could strike off words of incisive wit when the occasion arose, for instance once remarking, "All Frenchmen are under the blissful impression that the *brain* is a French organ."

He was a person of medium height, dark and slender, with deep-set blue eyes and a bearded face. In the custom of the time, he wore a pair of pince-nez (for nearsightedness) attached to a black cord.

Largely because his health was not robust, Nobel was sometimes capricious, lonely, and depressed. He would work intensely; then, finding it difficult to relax, he would often travel in search of the curative powers of various spas, at that time a popular and accepted part of a healthy regimen. One of Nobel's favorites was the spa at Ischl, Austria, where he kept a small yacht on a nearby lake. He was also fond of Baden bei Wien, not far from Vienna, where he met Sophie Hess. At their introduction in 1876, she was twenty years old, petite, and good-looking; he was forty-three. There appears to be no doubt that Nobel fell in love with "Sophieschen," a clerk in a flower shop, for he took her to Paris with him and provided her with an apartment. The young woman called herself Madame Nobel, but with time she is said to have become financially demanding. The relationship ended around 1891, only a few years before Nobel's death.

Despite his physical frailty, Nobel was capable of bursts of concentrated work. He had an excellent scientific mind and loved to tackle problems in his chemistry laboratory. Nobel managed his decentralized industrial empire through the board of directors of his many companies, which operated independently of one another and in which Nobel typically owned a 20 to 30 percent interest. Despite his limited financial interest, Nobel personally oversaw many of the details of decision making in the companies that bore his name. According to one of his biographers, "Apart from his scientific and business activities, much of Nobel's time was taken up by voluminous correspondence and paperwork, every detail of which he coped with entirely alone, from duplicating to keeping his private accounts."

In early 1876 he attempted to engage a housekeeper and part-time secretary by advertising in an Austrian newspaper: "A wealthy and highly educated old gentleman living in Paris seeks to engage a mature lady with language proficiency as secretary and housekeeper." One respondent was thirty-three-year-old Bertha Kinsky, then working in Vienna as a governess. Daringly, she came to Paris for an interview and impressed Nobel by her personality and language fluency, but after a week or so, homesickness overtook her and she returned to Vienna to marry Baron Arthur von Suttner, the son of her former employer in Vienna. She and Nobel met again, and in his last ten years they corresponded about her projects for peace. Bertha von Suttner became a leading figure in the European peace movement and through her friendship with Nobel was able to gain from him substantial financial support for the cause. She received the 1905 Nobel Prize for Peace.

In his final three years, Nobel worked with a private assistant, Ragnar Sohlman, a Swedish chemist in his twenties and a person of great tact and patience. Sohlman functioned as both a secretary and a laboratory aide. Nobel liked and trusted the young man enough to name him chief executor of his will. "It was not always easy to be his assistant," Sohlman recalled. "He was exacting in demands, plainspoken, and always seemingly in a hurry. One had to be wide awake to follow his swiftly leaping thought and often amazing whims when he suddenly appeared and vanished as quickly."

During his lifetime, Nobel often exhibited uncommon generosity toward Sohlman and other employees. When the assistant got married, Nobel impulsively doubled his salary; and, earlier, when his French cook married, he gave her a gift of 40,000 francs, a large sum in those days. Nobel's generosity also often went beyond the realm of personal and professional contacts. For instance, although he was not a churchgoer, Nobel frequently gave money for the parish work of the Swedish church in Paris, whose pastor in the early 1890s was Nathan Soderblöm, later the Lutheran archbishop of Sweden and the recipient of the 1930 Nobel Prize for Peace.

Although he was often called the Lord of Dynamite, Nobel strongly opposed the military uses to which his inventions were frequently put. "For my part," he said three years before his death, "I wish all guns with their belongings and everything could be sent to hell, which is the proper place for their exhibition and use." On another occasion, he stated that war was "the horror of horrors and the greatest of crimes" and added, "I should like to invent a substance or a machine with such terrible power of mass destruction that war would thereby be impossible forever."

Alfred Nobel's distinguished career is all the more remarkable considering his humble origins. The Nobel family came of peasant stock, emerging from obscurity with the surname of Nobelius only late in the seventeenth century. Alfred's grandfather, a barber-surgeon, shortened it to Nobel in 1775. His eldest son, Immanuel (1801–1872), was Alfred's father. Immanuel, an architect, builder, and inventor, had a precarious business life for several years until the family began to make its fortune in the oil fields of Baku, Russia. He married Caroline Andriette Ahlsell (1803–1879) in 1827; the couple had eight children, only three of whom survived to adulthood: Robert, Ludvig, and Alfred.

Born October 21, 1833, in Stockholm, Alfred Bernhard Nobel was the couple's fourth child. From his first days, he was weak and sickly, and his childhood was marked by chronic illness. Both as a young man and as an adult, Alfred enjoyed an especially close and warm relationship with his mother. No matter how busy he was as an older man, he managed a yearly visit and kept in frequent touch by letter.

After trying his hand at a business making elastic cloth, Immanuel fell on hard times and in 1837, leaving his family in Sweden, moved first to Finland and then to St. Petersburg (now Leningrad), where he manufactured powder-charged explosive mines, lathes, and machine tools. In October 1842, when Alfred was nine, he and the rest of the family joined his father in Russia, where his now prosperous family was able to engage private tutors for him. He proved to be a diligent pupil, apt and eager to learn, with a special interest in chemistry.

In 1850, when he was seventeen years old, Alfred took an extended trip, traveling in Europe, where he visited Germany, France, and Italy, and the United States. He pursued his chemical studies in Paris, and in the United States he met John Ericsson, the Swedish inventor of the caloric engine who later designed the ironclad warship, the *Monitor*.

Returning to St. Petersburg three years later, Nobel was employed in his father's growing business, by then called Fonderies & Ateliers Mécaniques Nobel & Fils (Founderies and Machine Shops of Nobel and Sons), which was producing material for the Crimean War (1853–1856). At the end of the war, the company shifted to the manufacture of machinery for steamboats plying the Volga River and the Caspian Sea. Its peacetime production, however, was not enough to offset the loss of military orders, and by 1858 the company fell into financial trouble. Alfred and his parents returned to Stockholm while Robert and Ludvig remained in Russia to salvage what they could. Back in Sweden, Alfred became engrossed in mechanical and chemical experiments, obtaining three patents. This work sharpened his interest in further experimentation, which he conducted in a small laboratory his father had established on his estate near the capital.

At that time, the only usable explosive for powder-charged mines—either for military or for peaceful uses—was black gunpowder. It was known, though, that the substance nitroglycerin was an extraordinarily powerful explosive compound, which posed extraordinary risks because of its volatility. No one had yet figured out how to control its detonation. After several small experiments with nitroglycerin, Immanuel Nobel sent Alfred to Paris in search of financing in 1861; he succeeded in raising a 100,000-franc loan. Despite some initial failures by Immanuel, Alfred became actively involved in the project. In 1863 he invented a practical detonator, which used gunpowder to set off the nitroglycerin. This invention was one of the primary foundations of his reputation and his fortune.

One of Nobel's biographers, Erik Bergengren, has described the device in this fashion:

In its first form, . . . {the detonator} is so constructed that initiation of the liquid nitroglycerin explosive charge, which is contained in a metal cap by itself or in a blocked-up borehole, is brought about by the explosion of a smaller charge let down into this, the smaller charge consisting of gunpowder in a wooden cap by itself, with a plug, into which a fuse has been inserted.

In order to increase the effect, the inventor altered various details of this construction several times, and as a final improvement in 1865 he replaced the original cap with a metal cap charged with detonating mercury. . . . With the inventions of this so-called blasting cap, the Initial Ignition Principle was introduced into the technique of explosives, and this was fundamental to all later developments in this field. It was this principle which made possible the effective use of nitroglycerin and later other violent explosives as independent explosives; it also made it possible to study their explosive properties.

In the process of perfecting the invention, Immanuel Nobel's laboratory was blown up, an explosion that resulted in the loss of eight lives, including Immanuel's twenty-one-year-old son Emil. Shortly thereafter, the father suffered a stroke, and remained bedridden until his death eight years later in 1872.

Despite the setback caused by the explosion and the resulting public hostility to the manufacture and use of nitroglycerin, Nobel persevered, and in October 1864 he persuaded the Swedish State Railways to adopt his substance for the blasting of tunnels. In order to manufacture it, he won the financial backing of a Stockholm merchant; a company, Nitroglycerin, Ltd., was set up and a factory built in the Swedish countryside. In its first years, Nobel was the company's managing director, works' engineer, correspondent, advertising manager, and treasurer. He also traveled extensively to demonstrate his blasting procedure. Among the company's customers was the Central Pacific Railroad in the American West, which used Nobel's nitroglycerin in blasting the line's way through the Sierra Nevadas. After obtaining patents in other countries for his device, Nobel established the first of his foreign companies—Alfred Nobel & Co. in Hamburg—in 1865.

Although Nobel was able to solve the major problems of manufacture, his explosives were sometimes carelessly handled by their purchasers. There were accidental explosions and deaths and even a ban or two on imports. Nonetheless, Nobel continued to expand his business. He won a United States patent in 1866 and spent three months there raising money for his Hamburg plant and demonstrating his blasting oil. Nobel also decided to found an American company that, after some maneuvering, became the Atlantic Giant Powder Company; following Nobel's death, it was acquired by E. I. du Pont de Nemours and Company. The inventor felt badly treated by American businessmen who were eager to float shares in his blasting oil companies. "In the long run I found life in America anything but agreeable," he later wrote. "The exaggerated chase after money is a pedantry which spoils much of the pleasure of meeting people and destroys a sense of honor in favor of imagined needs."

ALFRED NOBEL

Although blasting oil, correctly used, was an effective explosive, it was nevertheless so often involved in accidents (including one that leveled the Hamburg plant) that Nobel sought some way to stabilize nitroglycerin. He hit upon the idea of mixing the liquid nitroglycerin with a chemically inert and porous substance. His first practical choice was kieselguhr, a chalklike, absorbent material. Mixed with nitroglycerin, it could be fashioned into sticks and placed into boreholes. Patented in 1867, it was called "Dynamite, or Nobel's safety blasting powder."

The new explosive not only established Alfred Nobel's lasting fame, but it also found such spectacular uses as in the blasting of the Alpine tunnel on the St. Gotthard rail line, the removal of underwater rocks at Hell Gate in New York City's East River, the clearing of the Danube River at the Iron Gate, and the cutting of the Corinth Canal in greece. Dynamite was also a factor in oil drilling in the Baku fields of Russia, an enterprise in which Nobel's two brothers were so active and became so wealthy that they were known as the Russian Rockefellers. Alfred was the largest single stockholder in his brothers' companies.

Although Nobel held patent right to dynamite and its later refinements in all the world's major countries, in the 1870s he was constantly harassed by competitors who stole his processes. In these years he refused to hire a secretary or a full-time lawyer, and he was forced to spend much time in patent litigation as his factories steadily increased production.

In the 1870s and 1880s, Nobel expanded his network of factories into the chief European countries, either besting his rivals or forming cartels with them to control prices and markets. Eventually, he established a worldwide web of corporations for the manufacture and sale of his explosives, which, in addition to an improved dynamite, by then included a blasting gelatin. The military uses of these substances began in the Franco-Prussian War of 1870–1871, but during his lifetime, the investments Nobel made in military inventions lost considerable amounts of money. The profits from his industrial ventures came from the use of dynamite in the construction of tunnels, canals, railways, and roads.

Describing the consequences to Nobel of the discovery of dynamite, Bergengren has written:

Not a day passed without his having to face vital problems: the financing and formation of companies; the procuring of trustworthy partners and assistants for managerial posts, and suitable foremen and skilled laborers for a manufacturing process that was extremely sensitive and contained very dangerous ingredients; the erection of new buildings on remote sites, with intricate security measures in accordance with the differing laws of each country. The inventor took part eagerly in the planning and starting of a new project, but he seldom lent his personal assistance to the detailed working of the various companies.

The biographer characterized Nobel's life in the ten years after the invention of dynamite as "restless and nerve-racking." After his move from Hamburg to Paris in 1873, he was sometimes able to escape to his private laboratories, one a part of his house. To help him there, he employed Georges D. Fehrenbach, a young French chemist, who remained with him for eighteen years.

Given a choice, Nobel would have preferred his laboratory to his business, but his companies always seemed to claim a priority as the trade in explosives increased and new factories were established to meet the demands. Indeed, at Nobel's death in 1896, some ninety-three factories were in operation producing 66,500 tons of explosives, including ammunition of all kinds as well as ballistite, a smokeless blasting powder that Nobel patented between 1887 and 1891. The new substance could be used as a substitute for black gunpowder and was relatively inexpensive to manufacture.

In marketing ballistite, Nobel sold his Italian patent to the government, an action that aroused the anger of the French. He was accused of stealing the idea for the substance from the French government's monopoly, and his laboratory was ransacked and shut down; his factory was also forbidden to make ballistite. Under these circumstances, in 1891, Nobel decided to close his Paris home and to leave France for a new residence in San Remo on the Italian Riviera. Apart from the uproar over ballistite, Nobel's last Paris years were not totally happy; his mother died in 1889, a year following the death of his older brother Ludvig. Moreover, his French business associate had involved his enterprises in dubious speculations in connection with an unsuccessful venture to build a Panama canal.

At his San Remo villa, which was set in an orange grove overlooking the Mediterranean, Nobel built a small chemical laboratory, where he worked as time permitted. Among other things, he experimented in the production of synthetic rubber and silk. However much he liked San Remo for its climate, Nobel had warm thoughts of his homeland, and in 1894 he bought the Bofors ironworks in Värmland, where he fitted out a nearby manor house for private quarters and built a new laboratory. He spent the last two summers of his life at the Värmland manor house. During the second summer, his brother Robert died, and Nobel himself began to feel unwell.

Examined by specialists in Paris, he was warned that he had angina pectoris, a lack of oxygen supply to the heart, and was advised to rest. He then returned to San Remo, where he worked on a play he hoped to complete and where he drew up a remarkable will in his own hand. Shortly after midnight on December 10, 1896, he suffered a cerebral hemorrhage and died. Except for Italian servants who could not understand him, Nobel was alone at his death, and his final words went unrecorded.

The origins of Nobel's will, with its provisions for awards in a number of fields of human endeavor, are imprecise. The final document is a revision of earlier testaments. Its bequests for science and literature awards, it is generally agreed, are extensions of Nobel's lifelong concern with those fields—physics, physiology, chemistry, and the elevation of the art of writing. Evidence suggests that the award for peace may well have been the fruition of the inventor's long-standing aversion to violence. Early in 1886, for example, he told a British acquaintance that he had "a more and more earnest wish to see a rose red peace sprout in this explosive world."

As an inventor with a fertile imagination and as a businessman with a robust eagerness to exploit the industrial and commercial aspects of his brainchildren, Alfred Nobel was typical of his times. Paradoxically, he was a reclusive and lonely person whose worldly success failed to bring him the consolations of life for which he so avidly yearned.

Nobel Prizes and Nobel Institutions

by Carl Gustaf Bernhard

Alfred Nobel died on December 10, 1896. In his remarkable will, written in Paris on November 27, 1895, Nobel stated:

> The whole of my remaining realizable estate shall be dealt with in the following way:
> The capital shall be invested by my executors in safe securities and shall consti-
> tute a fund, the interest on which shall be annually distributed in the form of
> prizes to those who, during the preceding year, shall have conferred the greatest
> benefit on mankind. The said interest shall be divided into five equal parts,
> which shall be apportioned as follows: one part to the person who shall have
> made the most important discovery or invention within the field of physics; one
> part to the person who shall have made the most important chemical discovery or
> improvement; one part to the person who shall have made the most important
> discovery within the domain of physiology or medicine; one part to the person
> who shall have produced in the field of literature the most outstanding work of
> an idealistic tendency; and one part to the person who shall have done the most
> or the best work for fraternity among nations, for the abolition or reduction of
> standing armies, and for the holding and promotion of peace congresses.
> The prizes for physics and chemistry shall be awarded by the {Royal} Swedish
> Academy of Sciences; that for physiological or medical works by the Karolinska
> Institute in Stockholm; that for literature by the {Swedish} Academy in Stock-
> holm; and that for champions of peace by a committee of five persons to be
> elected by the Norwegian Storting {Parliament}. It is my express wish that in
> awarding the prizes no consideration whatever shall be given to the nationality of
> the candidates, so that the most worthy shall receive the prize, whether he be a
> Scandinavian or not.

The invitation to assume the responsibility of selecting laureates was accepted by the awarding bodies designated in Nobel's will only after considerable discussion. Several members of these organizations were doubtful and, referring to the vague formulation of the will, claimed that it would be difficult
to implement. In spite of these reservations, in 1900 the Nobel Foundation was established and statutes
were worked out by a special committee on the basis of the will's stipulations.

The foundation, an independent, nongovernment organization has the responsibility of administering
the funds in a manner "destined to safeguard the financial basis for the prizes, and for the activities associated with the selection of prizewinners." The foundation also protects the common interests of the
prize-awarding institutions and represents the Nobel institutions externally. In this capacity the foundation arranges the annual Nobel Prize ceremonies on behalf of the awarding institutions. The Nobel
Foundation itself is not involved in proposing candidates, in the evaluation process, or in the final selections. These functions are all performed independently by the prize-awarding assemblies. Today, the
Nobel Foundation also administers the Nobel Symposia, which since 1966 have been supported mainly
through grants to the foundation from the Bank of Sweden's Tercentenary Foundation.

The statutes for the Nobel Foundation and the special regulations of the awarding institutions were
promulgated by the King in Council on June 29, 1900. The first Nobel Prizes were awarded on December 10, 1901. The political union between Norway and Sweden came to a peaceful end in 1905. As a
result, the current special regulations for the body awarding the peace prize, the Norwegian Nobel Committee, are dated April 10, 1905.

In 1968 the Bank of Sweden at its tercentenary made a donation for a prize in the economic sciences.
After some hesitation, the Royal Swedish Academy of Sciences accepted the role of prize-awarding
institution in this field, in accordance with the same rules and principles that apply to the original Nobel
Prizes. This prize, which was established in memory of Alfred Nobel, is also awarded on December 10,

following the presentation of the other Nobel Prizes. Officially known as the Prize in Economic Sciences in Memory of Alfred Nobel, it was awarded for the first time in 1969.

Today, the Nobel Prize—independent of the monetary award which at present exceeds 2 million Swedish kronor ($225,000)—is widely regarded as the highest recognition of intellect that can be bestowed on a man or woman. It is also one of the few prizes known by name to a great part of the non-scientific public, and probably the only prize about which almost every scientist knows. According to the statutes, the Nobel Prize cannot be given jointly to more than three persons. As a consequence, relatively few, however distinguished, can hope to receive the award.

The prestige of the Nobel Prizes depends on the serious work devoted to the selection of the prize-winners and on the effective mechanisms for this procedure, which were instituted from the very outset. It was felt desirable to obtain properly documented proposals from qualified experts in different countries, thereby also emphasizing the international character of the prizes.

For each prize there is a Nobel committee. The Royal Swedish Academy of Sciences appoints three committees, one each for physics, chemistry, and the economic sciences. The Karolinska Institute names a committee for physiology or medicine, and the Swedish Academy chooses a committee for literature. In addition, the Norwegian Parliament, the Storting, appoints a peace prize committee. The Nobel committees play a central role in the selection process. Each consists of five members but may also request temporary assistance from additional specialists in relevant fields.

Nominations of candidates for the prizes can be made only upon invitation, and these invitations are distributed in the fall of the year preceding the award. The recipients are invited to submit a written proposal stating the reasons for their choice. For each prize, more than 1,000 individuals in different parts of the world are invited to submit nominations. Invitations for the science prizes are sent out to active scholars at universities and research institutions. For the literature prize, submissions are invited from academic representatives in the fields of literature and languages as well as from members of distinguished academies and societies of the same character as the Swedish Academy. In order to obtain proposals for the peace prize, representatives from the fields of philosophy, history, and the legal and political sciences, as well as those active in various peace activities, are contacted. Some individuals always receive invitations to submit nominations; among them are previous Nobel laureates and members of the Royal Swedish Academy of Sciences, the Nobel Assembly of the Karolinska Institute, and the Swedish Academy, as well as permanent and active professors in the respective fields from all the Scandinavian countries. Invitations to propose names are confidential, as are the nominations.

Nominations must be received by February 1 of the award year. At that date, the work of the Nobel committees begins, and from then until September committee members and consultants evaluate the qualifications of the nominees. Committees meet several times, with proposals assigned to different committee members as well as to outside experts, all of whom attempt to determine the originality and significance of the nominee's contributions. Several committee members or outside experts may report on various aspects of a single proposal. Every year several thousand persons are involved in the preparatory work. After this work is completed, the committees submit their secret reports and recommendations to the respective prize-awarding bodies, which have the sole right to make the final decisions.

By September or the beginning of October, the Nobel committees are ready with their work. In physics, chemistry, and the economic sciences, they submit their reports to the respective "classes" of the Royal Swedish Academy of Sciences, each of which has about twenty-five members. The classes then send their recommendations to the academy for the final decision. The procedure for the prize in physiology or medicine is similar, except that the recommendation of the Nobel committee goes directly to the fifty-member Nobel Assembly of the Karolinska Institute. In deciding the literature prize, the eighteen members of the Swedish Academy make the decision on the basis of the proposal from the Nobel committee. The decision for the peace prize is made by the Norwegian Nobel Committee itself.

In October, final votes are cast in the various assemblies. The laureates are immediately notified of the decisions, which are then announced internationally at a press conference held in Stockholm and attended by representatives of the international news media. The messages contain the names of the laureates and a short statement describing the reasons for the awards. At this occasion, specialists in the various fields are also present to give a more comprehensive explanation of the winners' achievements and their significance.

Subsequently, the Nobel Foundation invites the laureates and their families to the Nobel ceremonies held in Stockholm and Oslo on December 10. In Stockholm the prize ceremony takes place in the Concert Hall and is attended by about 1,200 persons. The prizes in physics, chemistry, physiology or medicine, literature, and the economic sciences are presented by the King of Sweden following a short résumé of the laureates' achievements presented by representatives of the prize-awarding assemblies. The celebration continues at a foundation banquet in the Town Hall.

In Oslo the peace prize ceremony takes place in the Assembly Hall of the University of Oslo in the presence of the King of Norway and the royal family. The laureate receives the prize from the chairman of the Norwegian Nobel Committee. In connection with the ceremonies in Stockholm and Oslo, the laureates present their Nobel lectures, which are later published in the volume *Les Prix Nobel.*

Obviously, a considerable amount of work is devoted to the sifting process by which laureates are selected. In the sciences, the distribution of more than 1,000 invitations for each prize results in 200 to 250 nominations. Since the same scientists are often proposed by several nominators, the number of actual candidates is somewhat less. In literature the Swedish Academy makes the choice from 100 to 150 candidates. Generally, most of the strong candidates are proposed over several years, and very rarely is a laureate selected after having been proposed only once.

The Nobel selections have often been criticized in the international press, as has the secrecy of the selection procedure. As to the complaints about the secrecy, suffice it to say that the statutes mandate that the deliberations, opinions, and proposals of the Nobel committees in connection with the awarding of prizes may not be made public or otherwise revealed. They direct that no protest shall be laid against the award of an adjudicating body and that if conflicts of opinion have arisen, they shall not be recorded in the minutes or otherwise revealed.

As to the singularity of the prizes, it is certainly true that there are many more worthy candidates than prizes. The 1948 Swedish Nobel laureate in chemistry, Arne Tiselius, who served as chairman of the Nobel Foundation for several years, described the situation in the following way: "You cannot in practice apply the principle that the Nobel Prize should be given to the person who is best; you cannot define who is best. Therefore, you are left with the only alternative: to try to find a particularly worthy candidate."

Naturally, the handling of the prizes is based on the principles delineated in the will of Alfred Nobel. In physics, chemistry, and physiology or medicine, the will speaks of an important discovery, improvement, or invention within these fields. Thus, the science prizes are awarded not for the work of a lifetime, but for a specific achievement or a particular discovery. As an experimenter and inventor, Nobel knew very well what a discovery was. Concepts are extremely useful, but concepts change; what remains are the experimental facts—the discoveries. The contributions of some scientists may be of great importance in the development of their fields, but they may not fulfill the specific requirements stipulated by the Nobel Prize rules.

The performance of scientific work and the conditions under which scientists now labor are quite different from those in effect during Alfred Nobel's lifetime, a fact that complicates the selection of laureates. Today, teamwork is common and often results in significant discoveries. The prizes, however, are meant for individuals and not for large groups. This contemporary situation has resulted in a dilemma with which the prize-awarding juries have had to deal in their efforts to fulfill Nobel's intentions.

In his will, Nobel declares that "an idealistic tendency" should be an essential qualification for the prize in literature. This vague expression has caused endless arguments. In *Nobel, The Man and His Prizes* (1962), Anders Österling, a past secretary of the Swedish Academy, writes: "What he really meant by this term was probably works of a humanitarian and constructive character which, like scientific discoveries, could be regarded as of benefit to mankind." Today the Swedish Academy by and large refrains from trying to find guidance from this expression.

To appraise achievements in widely different fields with reference to the phrase "for the benefit of mankind" is, of course, extremely difficult. A glance at the lengthy list of Nobel Prize winners in all fields shows, however, that serious efforts have been made to pay respect to a great variety of claims. For instance, the science prizes have been given for discoveries in pure sciences as well as for advances in applied fields. Lars Gyllensten, a former secretary of the Swedish Academy, has noted, "One has to adopt some sort of pragmatic procedure and take into consideration the basic view in Alfred Nobel's will to promote science and poetry and to distribute prizes in an international perspective to the benefit of mankind, not to distribute empty status awards."

At an early point, it became clear that the stipulation that the prizes be awarded for literary or scientific achievements made during the preceding year could not be observed in practice while at the same time maintaining a high standard. To resolve this difficulty, the following rule was inserted in the regulations: "The provision in the will that the annual award of prizes shall refer to works during the preceding year shall be understood in the sense that the award shall be made for the most recent achievements and for older works only if their significance has not become apparent until recently." The discovery of penicillin, for instance, took place in 1928, but the prize was not given until 1945 when the drug's value had been established by practical use. Likewise, the importance of literary contributions may not be fully appreciated until they can be seen in the context of an entire body of work. Therefore, many laureates in literature have received their prizes late in their careers.

That the choice of laureates for the peace and literature prizes often arouses controversy is self-evident; that there are some unfortunate mistakes in the list of the science prizes must also be admitted. These circumstances reflect the difficulties that the prize juries encounter. It is, however, surprising that criticism is so relatively scarce in the extensive literature that has been written about the Nobel Prizes and the Nobel work.

Very often the Nobel Foundation is criticized for not awarding prizes in other fields. The reason is simply that it was Nobel's wish that only the five specific areas he designated be taken into account. The single exception is the Nobel Prize in Economic Sciences, also administered by the foundation. Nonetheless, contemporary juries are in fact acting within successively widening frameworks. In 1973, for instance, the medicine prize was given to three ethologists for their discoveries concerning organization and elicitation of individual and social behavior patterns, and in 1974 pioneering research in radio astrophysics was honored. The physics prize in 1978, given for the discovery of cosmic microwave background radiation, also provides an example of the increasingly liberal interpretation of the prize field.

For twenty-five years, while a professor of physiology at the Karolinska Institute, I served as a member and chairman of its Nobel committee. Subsequently, as president and later secretary-general of the Royal Swedish Academy of Sciences, I also had the pleasure of taking part in the Nobel work in physics, chemistry, and the economic sciences for ten years. During this thirty-five-year period, I saw firsthand the diligence with which the members of the science prize juries fulfilled their delicate mission and witnessed the painstaking work of the specialists in various fields when adjudicating the prize proposals.

While engaged in work relating to the Nobel Prizes, I was often asked by representatives of organizations around the world to discuss the Nobel selection process when some new international prize was going to be created. I usually gave three pieces of advice. First, define the topics carefully so that a proper assessment can be made. We know how extremely difficult it is to make a selection, even in a "hard science" like physics. Second, allow enough time for the selection process. Third, ask for sufficient funds to cover the costs of the selection process, one which may involve a great many specialists and consist of several steps. Actually, the magnitude of the costs of selecting the Nobel laureates and of organizing and conducting the prize ceremonies is more or less the same as that of the Nobel Prizes themselves.

The Nobel Prizes are unique and carry with them considerable prestige. It is frequently wondered why the prizes attract more attention than any other twentieth-century award. One reason may be that they were created at the right time and that they epitomize some of the principal historical transformations of the age. Alfred Nobel was a true internationalist, and from the very beginning, the international character of the prizes made an important impression on society. The strict rules of the selection process, which were implemented from the outset, have also been crucial in establishing the importance of the awards. As soon as the prizes are awarded in December, the task of selecting of the next year's Nobel laureates begin. This year-round activity, in which so many of the world's intellectuals are engaged, plays a decisive role in directing the interest of society to the importance of the work that is proceeding in the various fields covered by the prizes, for "the benefit of mankind."

NOBEL PRIZE WINNERS

1997–2001 Supplement

Peg Skorpinksi/Courtesy of the University of California Berkeley

Akerlof, George A.

(June 17, 1940–) Nobel Prize for Economics, 2001 (shared with A. Michael Spence and Joseph E. Stiglitz)

The economist George A. Akerlof was born on June 17, 1940 in New Haven, Connecticut. He attended Yale University in New Haven. Having grown up in the shadow of the Great Depression, he wanted to understand the root causes of poverty—an interest that drew him to the study of economics. "I've always been interested in why people are poor," he told a writer for the *Berkeley Campus News* (October 10, 2001, on-line). "What economics is about is trying to prevent poverty insofar as that is possible." Akerlof cited in particular his interest in the economic disparity between blacks and whites, which he feels is one of the most important issues in America, yet one that is insufficiently addressed by contemporary economic theory. He received his B.A. from Yale in 1962, and earned a Ph.D. in 1966 from the Massachusetts Institute of Technology, in Cambridge. After graduation he accepted an assistant professorship at the University of California at Berkeley. From 1967 to 1968 he served as a visiting professor at the Indian Statistical Institute, in Calcutta, India, and in 1969 he was a research associate at Harvard University, in Cambridge, Massachusetts. In 1970 he became an associate professor at Berkeley.

In "The Market for 'Lemons'," Akerlof's groundbreaking paper published in the *Quarterly Journal of Economics* (1970), he developed the notion of "information asymmetry." In the market for used cars, the potential buyer has less information than the seller about the quality of the car. The buyer, forced to make inferences about the car, will naturally be suspicious of its quality, and accordingly will only be willing to offer a low price—even if he or she would be willing to pay a higher price for a car that was in good condition. This results in adverse selection, where only the poor-quality cars come on the market, since the owners of cars that are in good condition will choose to keep their cars rather than sell them at such low prices. Under these circumstances, the quality of available products is lowered for everyone involved, and owners retain cars that they should have been able to sell. The asymmetrical nature of information prevents deals that would benefit both buyers and sellers.

In the same paper Akerlof discussed an example that was based on his studies of credit markets in India in the 1960s, where rural moneylenders charged interest rates that were twice as high as the rates in the cities. Akerlof explained that a middleman who borrows money in cities and lends it in rural areas—without knowledge of the borrowers' ability to repay—is induced to raise interest rates to cover the risks of lending to those who may default. Akerlof's analysis also applies to the health-care market, where individuals seeking insurance coverage know more about their health than insurance companies do. Insurance providers, accordingly, are compelled to raise rates to avoid the possible losses that would be incurred by insuring too many high-risk customers. By doing so, however, the companies may discourage the healthy—and therefore desirable—potential customers from purchasing their services.

Akerlof's focus on market imperfections presented a bold break from mainstream economic thought, which held that in unregulated markets the agreed-upon price must be the right price. The traditional view that competition and rational behavior lead to market "equilibrium," Akerlof argued, had presupposed that both buyers and sellers were fully informed. By incorporating the effects of informational inequalities in market transactions, it becomes possible to explain the existence of certain institutions that aim to correct the market. Used-car dealerships, for example, can be seen as attempting to bridge the informational gap by offering guarantees and establishing a positive reputation with consumers. Other institutions that the theory seems to explain include brand names, chain stores, franchises, and different types of contracts. Akerlof's fellow economics laureates, A. MICHAEL SPENCE and JOSEPH STIGLITZ, developed theories to account for the various ways institutions adapt to the information inequality. Spence introduced the idea of "signaling" to explain how participants in a market transaction use observable practices to convey the value or quality of their products. Spence looked at education, for example, as a signal to potential employers of productivity. Stiglitz investigated the "screening" processes adopted by insurance companies to gather information about their customers.

In 1977 Akerlof became a full professor at the University of California at Berkeley. In that same year he met his wife, Janet Yellen, in Washington D.C. Yellen was an economist for the Federal Reserve Board at the time, where Akerlof was a visiting researcher. They were married in July 1978. Yellen became the head of the Board of Governors of the Federal Reserve System in the mid-1990s and served as the chair of the Council of Economic Advisers from 1997 to 1999.

Akerlof recently collaborated with Rachel E. Kranton, a professor of economics at the University of Maryland in College Park, on a research project examining the effects of an individual's sense of self on economic outcomes. In such areas as gender discrimination, the economics of poverty, and the division of labor, Akerlof and Kranton argued that including factors of personal and social identity significantly alters the conclusions of traditional economic analysis. As a part of their work they examined how group identity among black children in inner-city schools affected employment prospects. They argued that some schools in poor neighborhoods have succeeded in improving student performance by altering conceptions of identity, and therefore expectations. They cited the Central Park East Secondary School, in the Harlem neighborhood of New York City, as an example. Mainstream economic theory, which maintains that training and education are the determining factors in a child's success, fails to acknowledge the role that identity plays in shaping students' success and job prospects.

Akerlof has become well known for his practice of incorporating the perspectives of social sciences other than economics in his work. In a paper titled "An Economic Theorist's Book of Tales" (1984), as quoted in the *Berkeley Campus News*, he explained that "economic theorists, like French chefs in regard to food, have developed stylized models whose ingredients are limited by some unwritten rules. Just as traditional French cooking does not use seaweed or raw fish, so neoclassical models do not make assumptions derived from psychology, anthropology, or sociology. I disagree with any rules that limit the nature of the ingredients in economic models." Henry Aaron, a senior fellow at the Brookings Institution, told a writer for the *Berkeley Campus News* that "more than any other person in economics, [Akerlof] has worked to show how the insight from sociology and psychology could broaden, enrich and increase the power of economics. He is, in my opinion, perhaps the most imaginative and creative applier of insights from other disciplines."

In a statement posted on the Nobel e-Museum Web site, the Nobel committee praised Akerlof's paper as "the single most important study in the literature on economics of information. It has the typical features of a truly seminal contribution—it addresses a simple but profound and universal idea, with numerous implications and widespread applications."

Akerlof has received many honors and awards. He is the recipient of a Guggenheim Fellowship and Fulbright Fellowship. He is a fellow of the Econometric Society, the American Academy of Arts and Sciences, and the Institute for Policy Reform. He is vice president of the American Economic Association and a senior adviser for the Brookings Panel on Economic Activity. He is the former vice president of the American Economic Association. Akerlof and his wife, who is now also an economics professor at Berkeley, live in Berkeley, California. Their son, Robert, is working toward a degree in math and economics at Yale University.

ABOUT: Denver Post October 17, 2001; New York Times October 11, 2001, October 14, 2001; Nobel e-Museum Web site.

© The Nobel Foundation

Alferov, Zhores I.

(March 15, 1930–) Nobel Prize for Physics, 2000 (with Jack St. Clair Kilby and Herbert Kroemer)

The physicist Zhores I. Alferov was born on March 15, 1930 in Vitebsk, Belorussia, in the former Soviet Union. He studied in Leningrad at the Department of Electronics of V.I. Ulyanov (Lenin) Electrotechnical Institute (now St. Petersburg State Electrotechni-

cal University) and received his degree in 1952. Later he earned two additional scientific degrees, both from the Ioffe Physico-Technical Institute: a candidate of sciences in technology in 1961 and a doctor of sciences in physics and mathematics in 1970.

Since 1953, Alferov has been a staff member of the Ioffe Institute, where he has held the following positions: junior researcher, from 1953 to 1964; senior researcher, from 1964 to 1967; head of the laboratory, from 1967 to 1987; and director of the institute, since 1987. The institute has a prestigious history as a preeminent center for physics. Founded in 1918 by Abram Ioffe, a student of Wilhelm Conrad Röntgen, who discovered the X-ray and won the first Nobel Prize for physics in 1901, the institute has been on the forefront of technological developments since its inception. One area in which the institute is particularly strong is semiconductor research; Abram Ioffe himself took up semiconductors as an area of study in the early 1930s.

During the Cold War, when the Soviet Union and the United States were competing for supremacy in all things, especially technological advancements, the Ioffe Institute and other scientific research organizations benefitted from strong governmental support. It was during this period that Alferov developed a semiconductor-based laser, the groundbreaking work for which he was awarded the Nobel Prize. Since 1962 he has worked in what was then the relatively new field of semiconductor heterostructures, and in 1963 he outlined the principles for using these heterostructures to create a new type of laser and applied for a Soviet patent. (Working independently, Kroemer applied for a U.S. patent that same year for the same concept.) Semiconductors are materials whose ability to conduct electricity lies between that of conductors and insulators. A semiconductor's band gap, an indicator of whether the semiconductor more resembles a conductor or an insulator, is the amount of energy needed to produce moving, charge-bearing particles—either negatively charged electrons, or "holes," which behave like positively charged particles but are actually spaces vacated by electrons as they move through the semiconductor. By the late 1950s the semiconductor silicon was becoming the material of choice for many electronic components, particularly transistors. It was Kroemer who discovered in 1953 that by combining layers of different semiconductors, the performance of silicon transistors could be greatly improved. These composite, or heterostructured semiconductors, are made of complementary semiconductors; a common combination is gallium arsenide and aluminum gallium arsenide. Heterostructed semiconductors are called such because they are made from several thin layers, which differ in thickness from a few atom layers to micrometers, of semiconductors with differing band gaps. Researchers select such layers so that their crystal structures fit together, thereby allowing charge-bearing particles to move almost freely from one layer to another.

It took a number of years to develop methods of building heterostructured semiconductors efficiently, an effort in which Alferov played a major role. He was the first to produce what is known as a lattice-adapted heterostructure that exhibited distinct borders between the semiconductor layers. This in turn led to the development by Alferov and his team of researchers of many types of components using heterostructures, including the injection laser, the device he patented in 1963. In the early 1960s, both Alferov and Kroemer realized that heterostructured semiconductors could be used to create lasers by arranging the materials in such a fashion that the moving electrons and holes become trapped together in a specific region of the heterostructure. As Charles Seife described the process in *Science* (October 20, 2000): "When an electron and a hole meet inside this trap, they recombine, releasing light. This light, in turn, incites more trapped electrons and holes to recombine. It's just like a traditional laser, but it can be made out of semiconductors." Conventional lasers, invented in 1960, were created using expensive, specially made crystals, and lasers based on heterostructures gradually made laser technology more accessible and opened up a number of important applications. They are used in the reading heads in compact disc players, bar-code readers, laser markers, and optical data storage, among other things. Light-emitting diodes based on heterostructures are found in car brake-lights, traffic lights, and other warning signals, and some researchers believe that they may one day replace electric bulbs. Perhaps the most significant application for heterostructured-semiconductor lasers evolved after 1970, when Alferov and

his team became among the first to develop lasers that were able to work continuously at room-temperature. This refinement enabled the practical development of fibre-optic communication technology, a vital component of the Internet.

In 1970 Alferov was one of the "trusted elite of young scientists," according to Quirin Schiermeier for *Nature* (November 23, 2000), who were given permission to visit the West. Alferov spent six months in the U.S. working at the laboratory of Nick Holonyak at the University of Illinois at Urbana-Champaign, where Alferov did important new work on the structure and properties of semiconductor lasers. In 1973 Alferov became the chairman of optoelectronics at St. Petersburg State Electrotechnical University and in 1988 he became dean of the faculty of physics and technology at the St. Petersburg Technical University.

Since the collapse of the Soviet Union in 1991, Alferov's Ioffe Institute, along with virtually all scientific research in the former nation, has suffered drastically from a lack of funds. Although in 1985 the Soviet Union's electronics industry was the world's third largest, following those of the U.S. and Japan, research and development in the U.S.S.R. were geared towards the military-industrial system, with little emphasis on consumer electronics. Once that system disappeared, so did the country's electronics industry, as well as research funds for the Ioffe Institute and other organizations like it. Foreign investment has kept the Ioffe Institute afloat, and its ability to attract such funding has been attributed to Alferov's international reputation for scientific excellence. Both private companies and foundations, some formed for the purpose of fostering international scientific collaboration, have contributed grants. The International Science and Technology Center (ISTC), for example, founded in 1992 as a joint venture between Russia, the United States, Japan, and the European Union, seeks to redirect money that had originally been allocated to weapons research into civilian projects. Another contributor, the International Science Foundation, funded by the Hungarian-born billionaire George Soros, gave $2 million in the form of 80 research grants to scientists at the Ioffe Institute between 1994 and 1996.

"Despite all our difficulties," Alferov remarked to Quirin Schiermeier, "the Ioffe institute is still home to some high quality research, particularly in plasma physics, astrophysics and semiconductor physics." Some of this research includes the development of nanotechnology—the engineering of electronic components on the scale of individual atoms. Another major area of research involves uncovering the physical properties of spherical plasmas, part of an effort to decrease the costs of fusion reactors. The institute's division of nanoheterostructures, closely linked with Alferov's own research, has contracts with companies in China, Germany, and South Korea; Alferov has lamented the lack of Russian microelectronics companies, which might otherwise be first in line to capitalize on his discoveries. In addition to its research facilities, the Ioffe has an educational center that takes talented secondary school students and helps to shape them into the next generation of researchers. Around a quarter of the students stay in the sciences, and many of the finest graduates become part of the institute's staff. In Russia, education and scientific research rarely overlap as they do in the U.S., where much research is carried out at universities. The Ioffe's educational center is a rare exception, and Alferov intends to use a large portion of his Nobel Prize money to support the center—an investment, as Alferov sees it, in the future of science in Russia. "We may have an abundance of problems," Alferov told Schiermeier, "but we certainly have no lack of scientific talents."

Shortly after receiving the call from Stockholm telling him that he had won the 2000 Nobel Prize for Physics, Alferov received a second call from Russian President Vladimir Putin offering congratulations. Some days after the announcement the two men had a confidential meeting, in which Putin, at Alferov's suggestion, agreed to set up an advisory council of science and technology experts, presumably to provide advice on how to improve Russia's scientific research and development sectors. In his *Nature* article, Schiermeier noted: "Although the full significance of this move remains unclear, Russian researchers are monitoring keenly Alferov's emerging status as Putin's unofficial science advisor." Alferov believes the Russian president is ready to put more emphasis on research, and indeed Putin has agreed to a 10 percent increase in funding in the hope that new research will help stimulate Russian industry. Alferov himself is a Communist member of the Rus-

sian state parliament, the Duma, and at his urging that body has allocated an additional $16 million in the 2001 budget to fund development in electronics particularly. Alferov has expressed confidence that Russian scientific research will experience a renaissance.

In addition to the Nobel Prize, Zhores I. Alferov has received many international awards for his work, including the Stuart Ballantine Medal from the Franklin Institute in the United States (1971); the Lenin Prize (1972); the Hewlett-Packard Europhysics Prize (1978); the State Prize from the Soviet Union (1984); the Ioffe Prize from the Russian Academy of Science (1996); and the Nicholas Holonyak, Jr. Award (2000). He has been a member of the Russian Academy of Sciences since 1979 and its vice president since 1989. He is the editor-in-chief of a Russian journal that is also published in English under the title *Technical Physics Letters*, and a member of the editorial board of a Russian journal whose title has been translated as "Science and Life." The author of 400 articles and 50 inventions in semiconductor technology, Alferov has also written four books. In his article for *Nature*, Schiermeier described Alferov as "engaging and charismatic, expansive in his gestures and quick to laugh," also noting, "it is clear that junior colleagues regard him with a respect that approaches awe."

ABOUT: Ioffe Institute Web site; Nature November 23, 2000; Nobel e-Museum Web site; Science October 20, 2000; Science News October 14, 2000.

Annan, Kofi

(AN-non, KO-fee)

(April 8, 1938–) Nobel Prize for Peace, 2001 (shared with the United Nations)

The diplomat Kofi Atta Anna was born in Kumasi, Ghana, on April 8, 1938, a member of an upper-class merchant family descended from tribal chiefs of the Fante group. His penchant for activism and leadership skills became apparent early on: friends have recalled a successful hunger strike that he organized at the Ghanaian boarding school he attended in the 1950s, during which he and

United Nations

Kofi Annan

fellow students demanded—and got—better food. After attending the University of Science and Technology at Kumasi, he enrolled at Macalester College, in St. Paul, Minnesota, where he completed his bachelor's degree in economics, in 1961. In the following year he continued his education, at the Institut des Hautes Études Internationales, in Geneva, Switzerland.

In 1962 Annan accepted a position as an administrative and budget officer at the World Health Organization (WHO), a branch of the U.N. with headquarters in Geneva. After serving in various other U.N. posts in Geneva, New York City, and Addis Ababa, the capital of Ethiopia, he was named Alfred P. Sloan fellow for the 1971–72 academic year at the Massachusetts Institute of Technology, in Cambridge, where he received a master's degree in management. Except for a two-year stint between 1974 and 1976, when he served as managing director of the Ghana Tourist Development Company, Annan has been on the U.N.'s staff since 1972.

Building his career primarily in a variety of behind-the-scenes, low-profile bureaucratic jobs, Annan has acquired unusually broad expertise in peacekeeping and refugee issues as well as in management, administration, budgeting, and finance. Considered an honest, straightforward manager and negotiator with a singular ability to remain cool and good-humored under fire, Annan

has, in four decades with the UNITED NATIONS, gained the respect of diplomats and national leaders alike. He is known for his kindness and politesse among people at the grassroots level as well as among high-ranking diplomats, and he is said to command unusual loyalty from lower-echelon U.N. staffers. Between 1976 and 1983 he worked in the personnel department at the Office of the U.N. High Commissioner for Refugees, eventually rising to deputy director of administration and head of personnel. He was then reassigned to the U.N. headquarters, in New York City, where he held an array of managerial positions, including director of budget in the Office of Financial Services (1984–87), assistant secretary-general in the Office of Human Resources Management, security coordinator for the U.N. (1987–90), and assistant secretary-general for program planning and controller of budget and finance (1990–92).

In 1992 Annan advanced to the U.N.'s high-profile peacekeeping division. Early in the post–Cold War period, when regional conflict and ethnic strife seemed the order of the day, he quickly distinguished himself, first as assistant secretary-general of peacekeeping operations and then, from March 1993 until his appointment as secretary-general, under-secretary-general of peacekeeping operations. In that last, highly sensitive position, Annan oversaw 17 military operations and a $3.5 billion budget, more than 15 times the size of the 1988 budget. Although he was noted for his smooth diplomacy regarding U.N. involvement in the civil wars that erupted in Somalia and Bosnia, Annan expressed clear frustration at governments—chief among them that of the U.S.—that were unwilling to throw military and financial support behind the Security Council's peacekeeping resolutions. "Peacekeeping is always cheaper than war," he said at a press conference in March 1994.

Annan drew notice as the special representative for the U.N. peacekeeping operations in the former Yugoslavia, where, between November 1995 and March 1996, he supervised the transfer of peacekeeping duties from U.N. to NATO-led forces. People with whom he worked in Yugoslavia applauded Annan for his negotiating skills, which he demonstrated in his frequent discussions with the U.N. ambassadors from the U.S., Great Britain, France, and Russia. As one American official commented to a reporter for *Newsweek* (December 23, 1996), "To come out of that, with all four [ambassadors] feeling that they had never been misled, is what's called diplomacy."

By the fall of 1996, it had become clear that the U.S., alone among the members of the Security Council, was firmly opposed to Boutros Boutros-Ghali's reelection as U.N. secretary-general, and the council, which makes that appointment, began considering other candidates—specifically, African diplomats, primarily because no African diplomats had yet served as secretary-general. Most countries came out in support of Annan, who enjoyed an international reservoir of good will and was frequently touted as the only candidate who could successfully extinguish the widespread resentment triggered by the U.S.'s refusal to consent to Boutros-Ghali's reappointment. The French government stated its preference for a leader from a francophone country, but in late December, when all three African nations on the Security Council—including Egypt—threw their support behind Annan, France withdrew its dissent.

Soon after his appointment, on December 17, 1996, Annan remarked, as quoted in *Newsweek* (December 23, 1996), "I have 185 masters," referring to the U.N.'s 185 member nations and thus indicating his keen appreciation of the U.N. as a truly international organization. (The number of member nations has since risen to 189.) His dedication to consensus-building became clear when he announced that a comprehensive U.N. reform package—upon which the U.S. Congress had predicated the payment of its massive debt to the organization—would not be announced until at least mid-summer 1997, after all U.N. members had been consulted. "A good leader must also be a good follower," he was quoted as saying by Elaine Sciolino in the *New York Times* (February 9, 1997). Earlier, an editorial in the *Chicago Tribune* (December 18, 1996) had expressed optimism about his chances of successfully instigating organizational reform because of his "insider's ability to read between the lines of the U.N. organization chart and [to see] . . . where the skeletons are buried—so they can be dug up and exposed." But others expressed doubt about whether a career U.N. civil servant like Annan could summon the political will to change the very bureaucracy that had nurtured his advancement.

In July 1997 Annan unveiled a plan for streamlining the U.N.'s bureaucracy, which at the time supported 50,000 employees in 30 agencies worldwide. His proposal included the consolidation and regrouping of 24 agencies that reported to the secretary-general into five divisions—peace and security, humanitarian affairs, economic and social welfare, development programs, and human rights—that would report to the secretary-general and also to a deputy secretary-general, with the creation of the latter position being part of the plan. (On January 12, 1998 Louise Frechette, Canada's deputy minister of national defense, was appointed to the post.) While some viewed this effort as an important step toward saving money, others contended that the plan "simply reshuffles the deck at a time when the number of cards needs to be reduced," as Minnesota senator Rod Grams, the Republican chairman of the Senate Foreign Relations Committee, expressed it. Despite such objections, in November 1997 the General Assembly approved the first package of proposed reforms, which were designed to save the U.N. $123 million. (Even after it was approved, the United States remained intransigent regarding its refusal to clear its debt. Failure to pay a specified percentage of the arrears by January 1, 2000 would have resulted in the loss of the United States' seat in the General Assembly. Finally, in November 1999, Congress passed budget legislation earmarking $819 million for repayment of the back dues, which by then totaled some $1 billion.)

Annan has expressed a strong commitment to economic development and the pursuit of social justice everywhere. "Intolerance, injustice, and oppression—and their consequences—respect no national frontiers," he declared in an address to the U.N. General Assembly shortly after his appointment as secretary-general, as quoted by the Council for a Livable World (January 10, 1997, on-line). He also said, "We now know more than ever that sustainable economic development is not merely a matter of projects and statistics. It is, above all, a matter of people—real people with basic needs: food, clothing, shelter, and medical care."

The year 1998 opened with the threat of a violent confrontation between Iraq and the United States over the issue of weapons inspections. Saddam Hussein, the president of Iraq, insisted that unless the U.N. lifted the economic sanctions that it had imposed in 1990, after Iraq's invasion of Kuwait, his country would continue to bar inspectors from sites (including what were labeled presidential palaces) where, it was believed, Iraq had stockpiled biological and chemical weapons, long-range ballistic missiles, and other weapons of mass destruction. The United States, meanwhile, had warned Hussein that the U.S. was prepared to unleash air strikes on Iraq if he did not cooperate with the inspectors; indeed, in anticipation of such an attack, the U.S. had deployed an armada of warships in the Persian Gulf. Determined to end the deadlock by means of diplomacy rather than force—"I kept asking, 'After the bombing, then what?'" he explained to Crossette—Annan met face-to-face with Hussein in Iraq. "I had to deal with him to avoid a tragedy and to save lives," Annan said during an interview for *Time* (March 9, 1998). "Once I got through to him and explained what was at stake, and what he could do for his nation and his people, and what he would face if he did not agree, he got focused. . . . When he said, 'I know you are a courageous man,' I realized he was probably warming to me, but otherwise I saw no sign. It was at that point that I moved into the critical issues. . . . [The Iraqis] are very keen to get rid of the sanctions. I made it very clear to him that the only way to do that is to cooperate with [the U.N. Special Commission, which was set up in 1991 to ensure the elimination of Iraq's weapons of mass destruction]."

The result was the so-called Memo of Understanding, dated February 22, 1998, whereby Iraq, by accepting all previous Security Council resolutions pertaining to the issue, agreed to "unconditional and unrestricted" inspections and the eradication of various weapons. The Security Council approved the pact on March 2; at the same time, the council raised from $4 billion to $7.4 billion the annual limit on Iraq's sales of oil, the money from which was to be used to buy food and medicine and pay for repairs of the country's crumbling infrastructure. In some quarters, Annan was regarded as a hero for securing the agreement; others expressed doubt that Iraq would abide by the agreement for long. The skeptics were right: On August 5, 1998 Hussein again halted inspections, claiming that Iraq had fulfilled its end of the deal and demanding that the sanctions be removed. Annan's renewed

efforts to resolve the issue came to naught, and on December 16, 1998—in what Annan described as a "sad day" for the world and himself—the U.S., with support from Great Britain, bombed targets in Iraq. But Saddam Hussein refused to budge, and no inspections of suspected Iraqi storage sites took place in 1999. "Yes, [the Iraqis] didn't live up to the undertaking," Annan acknowledged to Barbara Crossette. "But does that mean we should not try diplomacy? I know some people have accused me of using diplomacy. That's my job. That's what I'm paid for."

In March 1998 Annan visited the Middle East. In a speech to the Palestinian Legislative Council in Gaza City, he urged patience regarding the Arab-Israeli peace process and nonviolence. Later, addressing the Israeli Foreign Relations Council in West Jerusalem, he said that the U.N. had sometimes acted unfairly toward Israel. But he also accused Israel of purposely undermining the good will of its neighbors by establishing settlements in Palestinian areas and imposing hardships on Palestinians, and he called upon Israeli officials to soften their attitude toward Palestinians. Two months later he went to Africa, where he made stops in eight countries. In what he termed a "healing mission" to Rwanda, he appeared before the Rwandan Parliament. Following a vehement denunciation by Anastase Gasana, the country's foreign minister, of the U.N.'s actions in Rwanda in 1994, Annan—who had then been under-secretary-general for peacekeeping operations—acknowledged the inadequacy of the organization's response to the widespread massacre of Tutsi civilians by Hutu militants. His failure, in that speech, to apologize for the U.N.'s dismal performance or to assume part of the blame himself angered many Rwandan lawmakers, among them the nation's president, Pasteur Bizimungu, and deputy president, Paul Kagame, who refused to attend a reception held in Annan's honor.

At the opening session of the General Assembly in September 1998, Annan urged the organization to intervene in the growing conflict between Serb forces and ethnic Albanians in the Serbian province of Kosovo. That intervention started to materialize in June 1999, when the Security Council voted to send a NATO-led peacekeeping force of 50,000 troops into Kosovo and to assign temporary responsibility for administering the province to the U.N. The newly created U.N. Mission in Kosovo (UNMIK), headed by the French minister of health, Bernard Koucher (a co-founder of DOCTORS WITHOUT BORDERS), was given the formidable task of forming a 3,000-member multinational police force, setting up a judicial system, dealing with human-rights abuses, tackling the problems antici-pated with the return of hundreds of thou-sands of ethnic Albanian refugees, and re-building homes and infrastructure. The con-tinuing presence of the Kosovo Liberation Army (a guerrilla group composed of ethnic Albanians) and still-intense animosity be-tween Serbs and ethnic Albanians com-pounded the difficulties UNMIK faced. As of late November 1999, Steven Erlanger re-ported in the *New York Times* (November 22, 1999), intolerance and the widespread desire for revenge were thwarting progress toward the creation of a peaceful, multieth-nic, democratic, self-governing province.

In June 1998, in what Annan referred to, in an interview with Afsané Bassir Pour for *Le Monde* (on-line), as "a giant step that we have taken for future generations," the U.N. created the International Criminal Court, in Rome, to bring to justice "those who commit crimes against humanity." Describing what he termed the "completely unjust situation" that had existed "because the necessary in-ternational framework did not exist," he noted that someone who kills an individual would, "in all likelihood, be tried and pun-ished, but someone who kills a hundred thousand will not be brought to justice; that is unacceptable. We have seen that crimi-nals like the former chief of the Khmer Rouge [in Cambodia], Pol Pot, have never been punished." Other matters that required Annan's attention included reported mis-conduct of U.N. peacekeeping troops (who are citizens of various member nations). In August 1999 Annan issued a directive stipu-lating that all troops under U.N. command must follow international laws—prominent among them the Geneva Conventions—governing behavior of soldiers during war-time, with the aim of safeguarding civilians and prisoners of war. Signed to date by 188 nations (but not the United States), the Ge-neva Conventions prohibit the use of land mines, booby traps, and other weapons of indiscriminate destruction.

In April 2000 Annan issued what the U.N. referred to as a millennium report, entitled *We the Peoples: The Role of the United Na-tions in the 21st Century*. According to a U.N. press release, the report was "the most comprehensive presentation of the UN's mission in its 55-year history." In particular, it set forth an ambitious agenda that includ-ed reducing by 50 percent, by the year 2015, the number of people living in extreme pov-erty and lacking safe water; ensuring, also by 2015, that all children complete the primary grades and that females and males have equal access to education; decreasing by 25 percent HIV infection rates among people 15 through 24 years old within the next decade; improving the living conditions of some 100 million slum dwellers in the next 20 years; expanding the access of poor nations to the markets of industrialized countries by phasing out duties and quotas; instituting debt-forgiveness measures for poor coun-tries; taking steps to increase world security, "through firmer enforcement of internation-al humanitarian and human rights law" and programs to encourage disarmament; and ensuring the health of the planet for future generations. "We must put people at the centre of everything we do," Annan de-clared. "No calling is more noble, and no re-sponsibility greater, than that of enabling men, women and children, in cities and vil-lages around the world, to make their lives better. Only when that begins to happen will we know that globalization is indeed be-coming inclusive, allowing everyone to share its opportunities."

Annan faced many challenges in 2000. Peacekeeping missions in East Timor, Sierra Leone, Kosovo, and the Democratic Repub-lic of Congo, among others, severely strained the resources of the United Nations peacekeeping department, which, with ap-proximately 400 employees, is only half the size of the organization's public-information staff. In March 2000 Annan appointed an in-ternational panel to come up with ways in which peacekeeping missions could be han-dled more effectively. "Partly it is a question of being clearer about what [the missions] are trying to do. And partly it is a question of getting the nuts and bolts right," Annan explained, as quoted by Barbara Crossette in the *New York Times* (March 8, 2000). Backed up by the panel, Annan called for strengthening and reorganizing the peacekeeping department and enlarging the U.N. Security Council.

Annan also asked member states to respond more generously to the U.N.'s requests for help. His plea came on the heels of a United States offer of military aircraft to transport needed personnel from various nations to Sierra Leone during a crisis there in which 500 U.N. soldiers were taken hostage; the Pentagon's charter rates for the job were higher than those of commercial airlines or private charter companies. In another case, U.N. operations in Congo were jeopardized because of insufficient aid from the member states. "One country which had undertaken to provide four airfield crash-rescue units subsequently withdrew the offer and proposed only one unit instead," Annan declared in a report to the Security Council, according to Barbara Crossette in the *New York Times.* "Another, which was supposed to provide an infantry battalion, ha[d] none of the 20 armored personnel carriers required and lack[ed] significant amounts of other materiel, including generators, engineering equipment, and radio-equipped jeeps."

In late September 2000 violence broke out between Israelis and Palestinians, following a visit by the Israeli politician Ariel Sharon, the leader of the right-wing Likud Party, to a site in Israel considered holy by both Jews and Muslims (the Temple Mount, known to Arabs as Haram al-Sharif). In an effort to defuse the crisis, Annan flew to Paris to talk with the Israeli prime minister, Ehud Barak, the Palestinian leader, YASIR ARAFAT, and the U.S. secretary of state, Madeleine Albright. After Sharon became prime minister, relations between the Israelis and the Palestinians deteriorated even further and a vicious cycle of violence (suicide bombing attacks followed by Israeli military retaliation) brought the two groups to the brink of war. The violence in the region continued to intensify after the September 11, 2001 terrorist attacks on the United States, in which the Pentagon outside Washington, D.C. and the World Trade Center in New York City were attacked with hijacked commercial airliners by Muslim extremists bent on punishing the United States for its role in Middle East politics and its support of Israel.

In light of these bold terrorist attacks, Annan faced a new world, one in which the United Nations was needed to prevent all-out war from breaking out between the West and the Middle East, keep the United States from unilaterally attacking terrorists and

their host nations, and negotiate a cease-fire between the Israelis and Palestinians before the entire region was embroiled in the conflict. Since the September 11th attacks, Annan has traveled the world over to ease tensions as well as give support to the needy. One particular country that commanded the secretary-general's attention was Afghanistan, in which the Taliban regime had aided and supported the Al Qaeda terrorist network. When the United States and its antiterrorist coalition allies completed military actions in Afghanistan, the Taliban regime was overthrown and the Al Qaeda network was disrupted. These military campaigns, however, left the people of Afghanistan— already devastated by more than two decades of war—with few resources. Annan promised United Nations aid in the form of food, economic relief, and peacekeeping troops.

In October 2001 the Norwegian Nobel Committee announced that it had chosen Annan and the United Nations as the co-recipients of the Nobel Peace Prize "for their work for a better organized and more peaceful world." The committee further distinguished the secretary-general by noting: "In an organization that can hardly become more than its members permit, he has made clear that sovereignty can not be a shield behind which member states conceal their violations." Annan, upon hearing of the award proclaimed that it "is going to be a great encouragement for me, personally, and for all my colleagues around the world," as quoted on the *U.N. News Centre* Web site (October 12, 2001). Annan recommitted the United Nations in the 21st century to respecting the rights of every person on earth, regardless of religion or race. "This will require us to look beyond the framework of States, and beneath the surface of nations or communities," he remarked in his speech during the awards ceremony on December 10, 2001. "We must focus, as never before, on improving the conditions of the individual men and women who give the State or nation its richness and character."

Annan has a daughter, Ama, and a son, Kojo, from his first marriage, which ended in divorce. His second wife, Nane Lagergren, who is Swedish, has a daughter, Nina, from her previous marriage. Annan and Lagergren live in the official residence of the U.N. secretary-general, on the East Side of Manhattan, in New York City. A prominent lawyer in Sweden, Lagergren formerly served as a legal officer for the U.N. High Commissioner for Refugees; she is now an artist. (She is also the niece of the Swedish diplomat, Raoul Wallenberg, who saved 100,000 Hungarian Jews from Nazi death camps.)

Asked during a 1998 visit to the Commonwealth Club of California what he hoped his legacy to the U.N. would be, Annan replied, as reported on the club's Web site, "I think I will be very pleased if by the time I leave, the U.N. is considered as an organization that has renewed itself, and is responsive to the needs of the world, and it is seen as an organization that is doing what it was established to do. In other words, a United Nations that is focused, that is effective, and that is responsive. If by the time I leave, we are there, I will be very happy."

ABOUT: Commonwealth Club of California Web site; Ebony October 1998; Newsweek December 23, 1996; New York Times December 14, 1996, December 28, 1998, December 31, 1999; New York Times Magazine March 29, 1998; Nobel e-Museum Web site; Time March 9, 1998; (Toronto) Globe & Mail December 14, 1996; Washington Post December 14, 1996; United Nations Official Web site.

Courtesy of Rockefeller University

Blobel, Günter

(May 21, 1936–) Nobel Prize for Physiology or Medicine, 1999

The physician and researcher Günter Blobel was born on May 21, 1936, in Waltersdorf, Silesia, Germany, now part of Poland. His childhood was marked by World War II. "I saw the firebombing destruction of Dresden from very near," Blobel told Lawrence K. Altman for the *New York Times* (October 12, 1999), "only a few kilometers away; for an 8½-year-old, this was all very impressive. The bombing was so bright that you could read the newspaper by the red sky." Blobel's father, a veterinarian who owned one of the few working cars in Dresden, was able to shuttle his family through the rubble with it. During the final days of the war, one of Blobel's sisters was killed. When the war ended he and his six remaining siblings found themselves in the Soviet-occupied East German state of Saxony. Refusing to join the Communist Party, Blobel escaped to West Germany through Berlin in the early 1950s, shortly after graduated from high school.

In 1960 Blobel received his M.D. at the University of Tübingen, in West Germany. Over the next two years he interned at a small hospital where he "realized that treatment of disease was irrational and not based on profound knowledge," as he told Lawrence Altman. He decided to turn his attention to research, where he hoped he would make more of an impact in battling diseases. During this time, his brother Hans held a Fulbright-sponsored faculty post at the University of Wisconsin, in Madison. Hans, believing that medical training was insufficient for research, urged his brother to come to the university to study for his Ph.D. Blobel followed his brother's advice, studying under Dr. Van R. Potter and receiving his degree in oncology in 1967. Upon receiving his degree, Blobel joined the staff at Rockefeller University, in New York City, as a postdoctoral fellow in their cellular biology laboratory because he wanted to work with GEORGE E. PALADE, then a trailblazing cell biologist and later a 1974 Nobel laureate.

In 1969 Blobel became an assistant professor at Rockefeller University, and his early work there built on the principals he had learned from Palade's laboratory. Throughout the 1960s, researchers used the electron microscope to investigate the structure of a cell. They discovered that cells contain many different structures known as organelles, which carry out a number of different functions and are surrounded by a membrane. However, they did not know how the cell worked and were baffled by how large proteins were able to get through the tightly sealed cell membranes surrounding the organelles. They also had no idea how newly created proteins were able to find their correct location within the cell.

The first mystery Blobel confronted was how a newly created protein was targeted to a specialized intracellular membrane system called the endoplasmic reticulum. In 1971 he and David D. Sabatini proposed a "signal hypothesis," which argued that proteins coming out of the cell contained an intrinsic signal that brought them across and towards membranes. Four years later Blobel was able to describe the process: the signal consists of a peptide, or a sequence of amino acids in a particular order, that formed a main part of the protein, which then traveled the endoplasmic reticulum's membrane through a channel. During the next 20 years, Blobel and his fellow scientists proved that the signal hypothesis was correct. They also discovered that it was universal—operating in the same fashion for animal, plant, and yeast cells.

In 1980 Blobel began formulating general principles for the movement of these proteins, since he had been able to show that similar signals were used to transport proteins to other intracellular organelles. According to the October 11, 1999 press release from the Nobel Assembly at the Karolinska Institute: "Each protein carries in its structure the information needed to specify its proper location in the cell. Specific amino acid sequences (topogenic signals) determine whether a protein will pass through a membrane into a particular organelle, become integrated into the membrane, or be exported out of the cell."

Blobel discovered that each newly made protein had an organelle-specific address, or signal sequence, which was recognized by receptors on the surface of an organelle. He compared these signals to zip codes or address tags for luggage—something that enables the parcel to arrive at the correct destination. Similarly these signal sequences, made up of a chain of different amino acids, exhibit a short tail at one end of the protein that allows it to pass through the membrane and find its proper place in the cell.

The Nobel Assembly awarded the 1999 Nobel Prize in Physiology or Medicine for Blobel's series of discoveries during the past three decades. According to their press release: "Blobel's research has substantially increased our understanding of the molecular mechanisms governing [cell functions]. Furthermore, knowledge about the topogenic signals has increased our understanding of many medically important mechanisms. For example, our immune system uses topogenic signals, e.g. in the production of antibodies." Such an understanding of the workings of antibody cells could help to cure such illnesses as AIDS, cancer, and Alzheimer's disease. Scientists now know that a cell works because it is able to move proteins to their correct locations. While some proteins function as enzymes that start thousands of chemical reactions, other proteins are the very building blocks of the cell. Blobel's work in the discovery of signals has shown scientists that a variety of hereditary diseases occur because there are errors within these proteins that disrupt their functioning.

Blobel continues to work at Rockefeller University as a full professor and is currently researching the trafficking of signals between the cell's nucleus and cytoplasm. He believes that a better understanding of these functions is fundamental to understanding what goes wrong in cancerous cells. Blobel stated that he was donating most of the $960,000 in prize money to the Friends of Dresden, an independent American group that supports the restoration of Dresden's artistic and architectural works, much of which was destroyed or heavily damaged by American bombers during World War II.

Blobel is a contributor to professional journals and chapters of books on cell biology. Since 1986 he has been an investigator at the Howard Hughes Medical Institute. In addition to the Nobel Prize, he has won numerous awards for his work, including the U.S. Steel Award in Molecular Biology (1978), the 1982 Gairdner Foundation Award, the 1983 Warburg medal of the German Biochemical Society, the Richard Lounsbery

Award (1983), the Louisa Gross Horwitz Prize (1987), the 1989 Waterford Bio-Medical Science Award, the 1992 Max-Planck Forschungspreis, and the Albert Lasker Basic Medical Research Award (1993). With other researchers he has won the Ciba Drew Award in Biomedical Research (1995), The King Faisal International Prize for Science (1996), and the Mayor's Award for Excellence in Science and Technology (1997).

Günter Blobel, who became a U.S. citizen in 1980, lives in New York City and Fubine, Piemonte, Italy, with his wife Laura Maioglio, a restauranteur, whose profession, he has admitted, allowed him to indulge his demanding work habits while keeping peace at home. "Our schedules meshed because she worked late at the restaurant," he told Lawrence Altman, "and that gave me the opportunity to come home late from the lab."

ABOUT: New York Times (on-line) October 12, 1999; Nobel e-Museum Web site.

Courtesy of the University of California, Los Angeles

Boyer, Paul D.

(July 31, 1918–) Nobel Prize for Chemistry, 1997 (shared with John E. Walker and Jens C. Skou)

The biochemist Paul D. Boyer was born on July 31, 1918 in Provo, Utah, one of five children born to Dell Delos Boyer, an osteopathic physician, and Grace (Guymon) Boyer. In an autobiographical statement on the Nobel e-Museum Web site, Boyer attributed his desire to study biochemistry to his mother's death—when she was 45 and he just 15—from Addison's disease, a rare (and now treatable) hormonal disorder. Boyer attended public schools in Provo and credits much of his intellectual curiosity to having read from his father's set of *The Books of Knowledge* while a young student. He performed his undergraduate work at Brigham Young University, where he received his B.S. in 1939. He then enrolled at the University of Wisconsin, where he earned his Ph.D. in biochemistry in 1943. After graduation he worked on a military research project on blood proteins at Stanford University, in Stanford, California. In 1946 Boyer accepted a position as an assistant professor at the University of Minnesota, and by 1956 he was a full professor. In 1963 he became a professor of chemistry at the University of California at Los Angeles (UCLA), and in 1965 he became the founding director of the Molecular Biology Institute there, serving in that capacity until 1983.

All living cells are able to derive energy from their environments by using certain enzymes. In 1929 the German chemist Karl Lohmann discovered adenosine triphosphate (ATP), the "fuel" that powers many cell processes and exists in all living organisms. ATP captures the chemical energy released by the combustion of nutrients and then transfers that energy to drive the myriad processes that sustain life, including movement, breathing, and the actions of nerve cells.

The chemical structure of ATP was clarified nearly 20 years after its discovery through the work of the Scottish scientist AL-EXANDER TODD. Todd succeeded in chemically synthesizing ATP, and his efforts were rewarded with a Nobel Prize in 1957. FRITZ LIP-MANN, the 1953 Nobel Prize winner in Medicine or Physiology, recognized that ATP is the universal carrier of cell energy. Beginning in the 1940s, scientists began to discover how ATP is formed. In plants, ATP is created during photosynthesis. In animals, including humans, ATP is formed during a process known as cell respiration, which occurs in a cell's mitochondria—membrane-enclosed, irregular structures found outside the nucleus that contain the catalysts for using oxygen and making ATP. In 1960 the American scientist Efraim Racker isolated the enzyme ATP synthase from mitochondria. This enzyme was also found to exist in plants and bacteria. The following year the British biochemist PETER MITCHELL made what he called the "chemiosmotic hypothesis." He theorized that cell respiration leads to a difference in hydrogen ion concentration inside and outside of a mitochondrial inner membrane, and that a stream of hydrogen ions drives the formation of ATP. In essence, he proposed that the movement of hydrogen ions back through the mitochondrial membrane somehow causes the ATP synthase (which is found in the membrane) to create ATP. For his groundbreaking research, Mitchell received the 1978 Nobel Prize in Chemistry.

By the 1970s researchers had concluded that the ATP synthase essentially consists of three sets of proteins. The first resembles a wheel, and is affixed to the mitochondrial membrane. The second piece is a rod that projects out from the membrane to the center of the third piece, a cylindrical structure containing catalytic sites for making ATP. Further research demonstrated that ATP is created at three sites on the cylinder, and that the rod is essential for such catalysis. However, in spite of all these crucial findings, the underlying mechanism of ATP's formation remained obscure.

Boyer had begun to study the formation of ATP in the 1950s, focusing on how ATP synthase utilizes energy to create new ATP. In the 1970s he began to put the remaining pieces of the ATP puzzle together. He theorized that hydrogen ions cause the protein wheel to spin as they pass through the mitochondrial membrane back to the central region of the mitochondria. This process happens, according to Robert F. Service in *Science* (October 24, 1997), "much as rushing water turns a water wheel." Since the rod protein is attached to the wheel, it also rotates, causing the other portion of the rod to rotate within the cylinder. The cylinder itself is kept from rotating by another attachment from the membrane. The rod's rotation causes structural changes in the cylinder, so that the active sites within it bind the building blocks of ATP, induce them to form tightly bound ATP, and then release the ATP. Boyer obtained evidence that the three catalytic sites proceed in a compulsory sequence through these steps. That such participation and the rotational movement can cause key changes at catalytic sites was a new concept in the understanding of enzyme catalysis. Joseph Robinson, a professor of pharmacology at the State University of New York Health Science Center, told Robert Service that Boyer's model was "a startling new idea." Most researchers felt that energy would be used primarily to link the chemical building blocks together. Boyer recognized that the ATP synthase uses energy mostly for the release of ATP that is tightly bound when initially formed.

Boyer's model was substantiated in 1994 by the British biochemist JOHN WALKER. Through Walker's use of x-rays to create an atomic-scale map of the portion of the enzyme on which ATP is manufactured, researchers could deduce details of the enzyme's mechanism.

In 1997 Paul Boyer and John Walker shared half of that year's Nobel Prize in Chemistry for what the Nobel Foundation termed their "elucidation of the enzymatic mechanism underlying the synthesis of adenosine triphosphate (ATP)," as archived on the Nobel e-Museum Web site. The Danish scientist JENS C. SKOU was awarded the other half of the prize in recognition of his discovery of the ion-transporting enzyme known as sodium, potassium-ATpase. The chemist Steven M. Block told C. Wu for *Science News* (October 25, 1997) that Boyer's theory "was extremely controversial when it was first enunciated, and now we take it in stride." Boyer was, Block told Wu, "a voice in the wilderness for a long time about this." When asked whether or not his work had practical applications, Boyer responded: "Imagine trying to repair a TV if you didn't know how it worked. This tells how the machinery of the cell works," as quoted by William J. Broad in the *New York Times* (October 16, 1997).

Paul D. Boyer has been a professor emeritus in UCLA's Department of Chemistry and Biochemistry since 1990. He was made a member of the National Academy of Sciences in 1970. In addition to the Nobel

Prize, he has been awarded the Tolman Medal (1984) and the Rose Award from the American Society of Biochemistry and Molecular Biology (1989). He and his wife, the former Lyda Whicker, were married in 1939 and have three children and eight grandchildren. In a press release posted on the UCLA Web site, Boyer described winning the Nobel Prize as "the experience of a lifetime," adding that he feels like "one of the most fortunate people to have the opportunity to satisfy my own interest in how things work—I just happen to be lucky."

ABOUT: American Men and Women of Science, 1988–99; New York Times October 16, 1997; Nobel e-Museum Web site; Science October 24, 1997; Science News October 25, 1997; UCLA Web site; University of Oxford Chemistry Department Web site; Washington Post October 16, 1997.

Courtesy of Carlsson Research

Carlsson, Arvid

(January 25, 1923–) Nobel Prize for Physiology or Medicine, 2000 (shared with Paul Greengard and Eric Kandel)

The pharmacologist Arvid Per Emil Carlsson was born on January 25, 1923 in Uppsala, Sweden, the son of Gottfrid O.H. and Lizzie (Steffenburg) Carlsson. He enrolled at Sweden's University of Lund to study medicine and excelled in his classes, winning the university's Magnus Blix Prize in 1947. Carlsson received his M.D. in 1951 and decided to pursue a career in pharmacology, which assesses the effectiveness of drugs in treating specific diseases, disorders, and ailments. In 1951 he joined the University of Lund as a member of the faculty, and in 1956 he was promoted from assistant to associate professor. In 1959 he became a professor of pharmacology at Göteborg University.

Carlsson began his research on dopamine in the late 1950s, gradually sparking a major reassessment of how dopamine functions in the brain. Dopamine is one of the brain's neurotransmitters, chemical substances that stimulate neurons, or nerve cells, and thus allow impulses to pass from one cell to another. At the time of Carlsson's initial work, scientists and medical researchers believed that dopamine was simply a precursor to noradrenaline, another neurotransmitter, and was thus of little importance in its own right. Carlsson initially developed a highly sensitive method for measuring the presence of dopamine in the brain and found heavy concentrations in several regions, particularly the basal ganglia, the region responsible for controlling the human body's motor functions. By contrast, he did not find noradrenaline in these parts of the brain. Since dopamine was present in more areas and in greater quantities than originally believed, Carlsson theorized that it too must be a neurotransmitter.

To confirm his theory, Carlsson performed a series of experiments on mice by giving them reserpine, a naturally occurring substance that depletes the brain's stores of several neurotransmitters, including dopamine. After being given reserpine, the mice gradually lost control of their movements. Carlsson observed that the symptoms experienced by the mice were similar to those of patients suffering from Parkinson's disease, a neurological disorder that causes the gradual loss of motor functions. To see if the effects of reserpine could be reversed, Carlsson injected the mice with L-dopa, a dopamine precursor that is converted into dopamine by the brain. After receiving L-dopa, normal levels of dopamine in the brain were restored and the mice regained the ability to move. By contrast, he discovered that the mice did not regain motor control when given a precursor to serotonin, another neuro-transmitter. Carlsson established that dop-amine is central to the successful perfor-mance of motor functions.

On the basis of Carlsson's research and discoveries, other researchers were able to link Parkinson's disease to low levels of dopamine in the brain, especially in the ba-sal ganglia. The disease, which takes dec-ades to progress and can completely disable a person by causing symptoms such as trem-ors, rigidity, and a reduced ability to move spontaneously, is caused when the neurons that produce dopamine gradually degener-ate. Medical researchers adapted L-dopa into a drug that remains the best treatment for alleviating the debilitating symptoms of Parkinson's disease, thereby allowing pa-tients to lead a more normal life. In addition, other drugs that treat Parkinson's by restor-ing dopamine levels were eventually devel-oped. "Dopamine has turned out, of all the neurotransmitters, to be the most involved in common human illnesses, including Par-kinson's, manic-depressive illness and schizophrenia," Steven Hyman of the Na-tional Institute of Mental Health said in an interview with Thomas H. Maugh II, report-ing for the *Los Angeles Times* (October 10, 2000). "Parkinson's used to be a disease of which people would die a horrible death, of-ten by suffocation," Ralf Patterson, the chairman of the Nobel committee, told Maugh. Patterson added that the current ex-istence of millions of Parkinson's sufferers whose symptoms are controlled with L-dopa, is "almost a magical thing."

During the 1960s Carlsson shifted his fo-cus to the study of drugs such as chlorprom-azine that are used to treat schizophrenia, in an attempt to determine how they produce their therapeutic effects. He discovered that chlorpromazine and other antipsychotic drugs affect synaptic transmission by block-ing dopamine receptors on neurons. In the late 1960s, Carlsson and his research team developed zimelidine, a new type of antide-pressive medication that worked by inhibit-ing cells' uptake of the neurotransmitter se-rotonin. This research provided the founda-tion for the development of selective seroto-nin uptake inhibitors, an important new class of antidepressive drugs that includes Prozac, one of the most widely used treat-ments for depression. "The discoveries of Arvid Carlsson have had great importance for the treatment of depression, which is one

of our most common diseases," an October 9, 2000 press release published on the Nobel e-Museum Web Site stated.

Carlsson expressed surprise upon hearing that he been awarded the 2000 Nobel Prize for Physiology or Medicine, which he shares with PAUL GREENGARD of Rockefeller Universi-ty, in New York City, and ERIC KANDEL of Co-lumbia University, also in New York. In the award presentation speech on behalf of the Nobel Assembly at the Karolinska Institute in Sweden, assembly member Urban Unger-stedt said the trio were being honored for their contributions to the understanding of "signal transduction in the nervous system," as quoted from a transcript on the Nobel e-Museum Web site (October 9, 2000). Carls-son's research laid the foundation for future discoveries that revealed how Parkinson's disease, schizophrenia, and depression could be more effectively treated. "Carls-son's discovery has had a massive effect on the lives of hundreds of thousands of people with Parkinson's disease," Peter Jenner, a pharmacologist at King's College in London, told Joanna Marchant for *New Scientist* (Oc-tober 13, 2000). "It was absolutely funda-mental. He should have been given the No-bel Prize years ago."

Since Carlsson's retirement from teaching in 1989, he has remained active in research to develop new drugs to treat schizophrenia. In an interview with *Science* (August 19, 1994), he said that several newly identified receptor subtypes that receive dopamine in the brain, named D2, D3 and D4, could be the key to developing more effective drugs with fewer side effects for combating the ill-ness. In 1999 he joined the Scientific Advi-sory Board (SAB) of ACADIA Pharmaceuti-cals, which develops drugs to treat central nervous system disorders.

Arvid Carlsson has been honored with many prestigious awards and prizes, includ-ing the first annual James Parkinson Lecture and Award (1970); Pehr Dubb's Gold Medal from the Medical Society of Göteborg (1970); Anders Jahre's Medical Prize from the University of Oslo in Norway (1974); the Wolf Prize in Medicine (1979); the Gairdner Foundation Award (1982); the Paul Hoch Prize from the American Psychopathologi-cal Association in New York (1990); the Open Mind Award in Psychiatry from the Janssen Research Foundation, Paris; the Ja-pan Prize in Psychology and Psychiatry (1994); the Research Prize of the Lundbeck

Foundation in Roskilde, Denmark (1995); and the Antonio Feltrinelli International Award from the Accademia dei Lincei in Rome, Italy (1999). Carlsson noted that his wife will decide how his share of the Nobel Prize money will be spent, because "she is the one who makes such decisions," as quoted by Maugh.

Arvid Carlsson is the author of hundreds of articles and papers on dopamine and pharmacology. He has been married to Ulla-Lisa Maria Christoffersson since 1945. They reside in Göteborg and have five children: Bo, Lena, Hans, Maria, and Magnus.

ABOUT: Los Angeles Times October 10, 2000; New Scientist October 14, 2000; New York Times October 10, 2000; Nobel e-Museum Web site; PR Newswire (on-line) September 13, 1999; Science August 19, 1994.

Courtesy of Steven Chu

Chu, Steven

(February 28, 1948–) Nobel Prize for Physics, 1997 (shared with William D. Phillips and Claude Cohen-Tannoudji)

The physicist Steven Chu was born on February 28, 1948 in St. Louis, Missouri, to Ju Chin Chu and Ching Chen Li. Chu's father had come from China to the U.S. in 1943 to study chemical engineering at the Massa-

chusetts Institute of Technology (MIT); two years later Chu's mother joined him at MIT to study economics. With the power struggle between the Nationalists and the Communists raging in China, the Chus made the decision to remain in the U.S. after completing their education. After moving from MIT to Washington University, in St. Louis, Missouri, Chu's father accepted a position as a professor of electrical engineering at the Brooklyn Polytechnic Institute. The family settled in nearby Garden City, in Long Island, New York, where few Chinese families lived but the public high schools were excellent. Chu explained his parents' move in an autobiographical essay posted on the Nobel e-Museum Web site. "Education in my family was not merely emphasized, it was our raison d'être," he wrote. "Virtually all of our aunts and uncles had Ph.D.s in science or engineering, and it was taken for granted that the next generation of Chus were to follow the family tradition."

At first, Chu was what he described as the "academic black sheep" in the family; he was not particularly devoted to excelling in all of his high-school courses. This changed when he discovered physics, thanks to a particularly inspiring high-school physics teacher. He attended the University of Rochester, graduating in 1970 with bachelor's degrees in both physics and mathematics. He then pursued a Ph.D. in physics at the University of California at Berkeley, earning the degree in 1976. For the next two years, Chu remained at Berkeley as a postdoctoral fellow.

Chu joined the technical staff of Bell Labs, in Murray Hill, New Jersey, in 1978. In 1983 he moved to the AT&T Bell Labs in Holmdel, New Jersey, where he was appointed head of the quantum electronics research department. While at AT&T Bell Labs, Chu embarked on the research into atom manipulation that would earn him the 1997 Nobel Prize in Physics. Chu's work was built on research conducted in the 1970s, in which ions, or charged subatomic particles, were cooled through exposure to laser light and thus slowed down. Light is made up of a stream of particles called photons, which carry a specific momentum. When a photon collides with an atom, the photon's momentum may be transferred to that atom—if the photon has the right energy. In other words the light must have the right frequency, or color. The energy of a photon is proportional to the frequency of the light, which itself determines the color. For instance, red light is made up of photons having a lower energy than the photons in blue light.

The Doppler effect states that if an atom is moving toward a beam of light, the photons within that light must have a lower frequency than the atom if they are to be absorbed by the atom. If an atom is struck by photons that have the correct energy, the atom will then slow down and emit the photon it just absorbed. That atom can then immediately absorb a new photon from the oncoming stream of photons. After a series of absorptions and emissions, the speed of the atom diminishes greatly. Therefore, in order to properly slow down an atom, an intensive laser beam is needed.

In 1985 Chu first applied the laser-cooling technique to neutral (non-charged) atoms, which are much more difficult to control. Aiming six lasers at a single point in space, Chu created a region of slow-moving atoms, which he termed "optical molasses." This technique is explained on the Nobel e-Museum site: "In this configuration [of lasers] an atom, regardless of what direction it is moving, will encounter a friction force. In this way the velocity spread (and the temperature) will be reduced. The action of the laser light on the atoms is like that of a sticky medium, giving rise to the term optical molasses." Chu then introduced a gas made up of sodium atoms into the region. The velocity of the atoms was lowered as they collided with the photon particles that constitute the laser light. The greater the amount of photons with which the atoms were bombarded, the more they slowed down. Using this laser method, known as "Doppler cooling," Chu was able to chill the atoms to 240 millionths of a degree above absolute zero (negative 273 degrees Celsius). This temperature was termed the "Doppler limit." At room temperature, atoms travel at nearly a kilometer per second; Chu succeeded in bringing atom speed down to 30 centimeters per second.

While Chu succeeded in cooling the atoms, they still could not be properly studied because gravity caused them to drop out of the optical molasses in about a second. However, in 1986, Chu developed a device called a magneto-optical trap (MOT) to capture the chilled atoms. After slowing down the atoms by cooling them in laser light, the MOT then trapped them through the use of

magnetic fields and held them in place for further experimentation. This produced a glowing cloud about the size of a pea.

Chu shared the 1997 Nobel Prize in Physics with WILLIAM PHILLIPS and CLAUDE COHEN-TANNOUDJI, two physicist who built upon his work. The work of the three Nobel laureates has enabled scientists to study and manipulate atoms at a previously unattainable temperature. Trapping or slowing the atoms allows properties that are not apparent in a normal environment—where atoms move at high speed—to be revealed; as a result, subatomic technology is now being developed. Scientists have also been able to create a new state of matter, one that was originally postulated by ALBERT EINSTEIN in the 1920s. Called a Bose-Einstein condensate, this state of matter arises when a group of atoms is slowed to the point that they begin to act like a single entity, forming "a kind of super atom," according to a writer for the *Stanford Online Report* (October 15, 1997).

Among the applications of Chu's research is the creation of more precise atomic clocks for use in space navigation. His work might also prove useful in building high-precision devices for measuring gravitational pull. For the latter application, Chu has designed an "atomic fountain" in which atoms are fired out of a laser-driven device. The rate at which the atoms rise and fall provides a highly accurate measurement of the Earth's gravitational pull. This technique is now being used by oil companies to search for underground petroleum deposits. Atomic lasers are being constructed that have the ability to manufacture extremely small electronic components. "There's much more to come," Chu told James Glanz for *Science* (October 24, 1997). "Most of the applications, I didn't dream of in 1985."

In an interview with a reporter for the *American Scientist* (January–February 1998, on-line), Chu described his approach to science. "You want to try to put something that you learn in your own language, so that it's no longer something that's merely memorized but something you transfer from your head to your gut," he said. "It's only when you understand your science in this very obvious, intuitive way that you have a chance of thinking of something new."

In 1987 Chu left Bell Labs to become a professor of physics and applied physics at Stanford University, in Stanford, California. He became the Frances and Theodore Geballe Professor of Physics and Applied Physics at Stanford in 1990, and he continues to hold this post. Chu was also a lecturer at Harvard University, in Cambridge, Massachusetts, from 1987 to 1988, and a visiting professor at the College de France, in Paris, in 1990.

In addition to the Nobel Prize, Chu received the King Faisal Prize for science from the King Faisal Foundation in 1993. He is a fellow of the American Physics Society, the Optical Society of America, and the Americans Academy of Arts and Sciences. He married in 1980 and is the father of two children, Geoffrey and Michael.

ABOUT: American Men and Women of Science, 1998–99; American Scientist (online) January–February 1998; Nobel e-Museum Web site; Science October 24, 1998; Stanford Online Report October 15, 1997.

Courtesy of Collège de France

Cohen-Tannoudji, Claude

(April 1, 1933–) Nobel Prize for Physics, 1997 (shared with Steven Chu and William D. Phillips)

The physicist Claude Cohen-Tannoudji was born to Sarah Sebbah and Abraham Cohen-Tannoudji on April 1, 1933 in Constantine, Algeria, which was then a colony of France. Cohen-Tannoudji's family has roots in Spain, Tunisia, and Algeria. Then, in 1870, after Algeria became a French colony, the family was granted French citizenship along with other Algerian Jews. In an autobiographical essay posted on the Nobel e-Museum Web site, Cohen-Tannoudji credited his father for sharing with him what he regards as "the fundamental features of the Jewish tradition—studying, learning and sharing knowledge with others." He attended high school in Algeria and, in 1953, won admission to the prestigious École Normale Supérieure (ENS), a "grand école" in Paris. After hearing lectures by ALFRED KASTLER, the winner of the 1966 Nobel Prize in Physics for the development of optical methods for studying atoms, Cohen-Tannoudji focused his course of study on physics. In 1955 he spent a summer at Les Houches, a school in the French Alps, where he studied theoretical physics. In 1957 he passed the "agrégation," a competitive examination required in order to teach in high school in France. He then completed 28 months of mandatory military service, a tour of duty that was lengthened by the Algerian war.

In 1960 he began a dissertation program at the ENS under the supervision of Alfred Kastler and another physicist, Jean Brossel, with whom Kastler had developed his optical methods. He also began to work at the CNRS (the French National Center for Scientific Research), where he began his study of the optical pumping cycle, the topic that had led Kastler to a Nobel prize. He earned a Ph.D. in atomic and molecular physics in 1962.

After completing his studies Cohen-Tannoudji began teaching at the University of Paris. He lectured on quantum mechanics and co-wrote with Bernard Diu and Franck Laloë a textbook on the subject that is widely used by students and researchers. In 1973 he was elected to a position of professor at the Collège de France, in Paris. As a lecturer there, he was required to teach a different topic each year, an unusual rule that he credits with helping expand his knowledge. He is currently professor of atomic and molecular physics at the Collège de France, and an active member of the Laboratoire Kastler Brossel, a physics laboratory—named after his former mentors—run jointly by the ENS, CNRS, and the Université Pierre and MARIE CURIE, in Paris.

COHEN-TANNOUDJI

Cohen-Tannoudji has performed extensive research in the fields of atomic and molecular physics, focusing on the interactions between atoms and electromagnetic waves. He discovered that excitation by quasi-resonant light can produce small shifts in the energy levels of an atom, which can be interpreted in terms of "virtual" absorption and reemission of photons by the atom. His findings revealed that this "light shift," as he termed it, could be a significant obstacle to producing the highly accurate atomic clock scientists had hoped to create through the process of optical pumping. Optical pumping, a method of aligning atomic spins, is also used to produce population inversions between energy levels, a condition that is essential for lasers.

Cohen-Tannoudji's next significant breakthrough was his "dressed atom approach." This was a new way to describe the behavior of atoms in intense quasiresonant fields. Rather than view the atom and the photons that constitute the electromagnetic field as separate entities, he viewed them as a single system. This theory was applied to atoms in laser fields.

Throughout the 1970s and 1980s, Cohen-Tannoudji carried on his investigation of atom-photon interactions by trying to work out simple physical pictures for radiative corrections, such as the Lamb shift and the electron spin anomaly, which play an important role in Quantum Electrodynamics. By the mid-1980s, he had returned to his exploration of the behavior of atoms and laser light, first from a theoretical approach, and also through several experiments performed with a variety of collaborators. The problem facing scientists for years was that, at room temperature, atoms and molecules move in various directions with an average speed of 4,000 kilometers per hour. Thus it is difficult to study and observe atoms because they quickly disappear from the area in which they are being observed. There is also a Doppler broadening of the spectral lines due to the atomic velocity spread. Lowering the temperature of the atomic sample reduces average velocity and the velocity spread and is therefore a great challenge, because even at a temperature of -270 degrees Celsius the atoms still move at a speed of nearly 400 kilometers per hour. One needs to cool atoms to a few millionths of a degree above absolute zero to get interesting situations where atoms move at velocities on the order of a few centimeters or millimeters per second. This work on atom cooling ultimately led STEVEN CHU, Claude Cohen-Tannoudji and William Phillips to the Nobel Prize.

In 1985 the physicist Steven Chu, working at Bell Laboratories, was the first to design a method of cooling atoms based on the Doppler effect, a method that was suggested in 1975 by Theodor Hansch and ARTHUR SCHAWLOW. Using six laser beams (opposed in pairs at right angles to each other), Chu and his fellow researchers created an area known as "optical molasses," being the space where the six laser beams intersected. Chu then placed sodium atoms into the optical molasses. As the atoms were bombarded with the photons from the laser beam, they cooled or slowed down. This method of cooling atoms was later named Doppler cooling. The lowest temperature that could be reached through Doppler cooling was 240 microkelvin (or 240 millionths of a degree above absolute zero), which was termed the "Doppler limit."

After Chu's successful optical molasses experiment, in 1988, the physicist WILLIAM D. PHILLIPS discovered that temperatures as low as 40 microkelvin could be reached using slow atomic beams and optical molasses. In effect, Phillips had broken Chu's Doppler limit. At the time, Cohen-Tannoudji and Jean Dalibard had also been working out theories of new ways to cool atoms. In 1986, Cohen-Tannoudji revealed that, as he wrote in his essay, "a moving atom is running up potential hills more frequently than down. . . . In fact, this new scheme was the first high intensity version of what is called now 'Sisyphus cooling,' a denomination that we introduced [with Jean Dalibard] in 1986." (Sisyphus is a figure in Greek myth who is doomed to roll a heavy stone up a slope in the Underworld, only to find after reaching that the peak that the stone would roll down again and he would have to begin all over again.) This phenomenon explained how Phillips was able to achieve such a low temperature. An article posted on the Nobel e-Museum site elaborates: "The atoms move on a sinusoidally [shaped like a sine wave] modulated potential surface, which occurs through changes in their energy levels when they interact with light (light shift). When they travel 'uphill' they lose speed. As they reach the top of the 'hill' they are optically pumped to the bottom of a 'valley.' In this way the atoms will always travel 'uphill,' and thus their velocity will gradually be reduced."

In 1989 Cohen-Tannoudji, Phillips, and their collaborators teamed up to show that cesium atoms could be collected in an optical molasses to as low as two microkelvin. In later research, they showed that, if the proper laser settings are used, it is possible to trap the atoms in potential wells associated with a laser standing wave so that they will form groups at regular intervals in a structure known as "optical lattice." These atoms can also be cooled to a temperature far lower than the Doppler limit.

The next obstacle Cohen-Tannoudji and his team sought to overcome was that even the slowest atoms continually absorbed and emitted photons that communicate some recoil momentum to the atom. With these processes occurring, the atom still has a small momentum, and therefore the gas constituted by the atoms has a finite temperature. Cohen-Tannoudji and his colleague Alain Aspect set out to make the slowest atoms neglect all the photons in the optical molasses and enter what is known as a "dark" state where they no longer absorb light and consequently where they no longer undergo the random recoil due to the reemitted photons. From 1988 to 1995, Cohen-Tannoudji's team worked to covert the slowest atoms to a dark state; they were eventually able to show that the dark state cooling method functions in one, two, or three dimensions. They found that when they used six laser beams on the atoms, a state was reached in which the atoms were lowered to a temperature of 0.18 microkelvin—nearly 100 billion times colder than room temperature. With these conditions in place, helium atoms achieved speeds of only two centimeters per second.

In 1997 the Royal Swedish Academy of Sciences awarded Cohen-Tannoudji, Steven Chu, and William Phillips the Nobel Prize in Physics. In their citation, as posted on the Nobel e-Museum Web site, they stated that "the new methods of investigation that the Nobel laureates have developed have contributed greatly to increasing our knowledge of the interplay between radiation and matter."

The work of the three Nobel laureates has many possible applications. With the new control over the handling of atoms, the French scientists Christophe Salomon and André Clairon have constructed atomic clocks 100 times more precise than currently exists. The work on atom cooling also forms the basis for the 1995 discovery of the Bose-Einstein condensation, in which a macroscopic number of atoms coalesce in a single quantum state. The cooling processes may allow the creation of microscopic technology that works on a molecular—rather than a mechanical—level.

Cohen-Tannoudji is a member of the French Académie des Sciences and an associate member of the National Academy of Sciences, in the U.S., the Academia dei Lincei, in Italy, and the Pontifical Academy of Sciences, in Rome. In addition to the Nobel Prize, he was awarded the 1992 Lilienfield Prize from the American Physical Society and the 1996 CNRS Gold Medal.

Cohen-Tannoudji married Jacqueline Veyrat, a high school physics and chemistry teacher, in 1958. They had three children; one, Alain, died in 1993 after a long illness.

ABOUT: Chronicle of Higher Education October 24, 1997; CNN.com October 15, 1997; Nobel e-Museum Web site; San Francisco Examiner (on-line) October 16, 1997; Science October 24, 1997; Science News October 25, 1997.

Cornell, Eric A.

(December 19, 1961–) Nobel Prize for Physics, 2001 (shared with Carl E. Wieman and Wolfgang Ketterle)

The physicist Eric A. Cornell was born in Palo Alto, California, on December 19, 1961. He attended Stanford University, in Stanford, California, and graduated with honor and distinction in 1985. While an undergraduate, Cornell spent time teaching English in Taichung, Taiwan. From 1982 to 1985 he served as a research assistant at Stanford and, in 1985, he earned the Firestone Award for Excellence in Undergraduate Research. He completed doctoral work in physics at the Massachusetts Institute of Technology (MIT) as a National Science Foundation Graduate Fellow, earning his Ph.D. in 1990.

That same year Cornell joined the former Joint Institute for Laboratory Astrophysics (JILA), in Boulder, Colorado, a research and graduate program institute run by the Na-

© Geoffrey Wheeler

Eric A. Cornell

tional Institute of Standards and Technology (NIST) and the University of Colorado. (The Lab is now known simply as JILA.) He teamed up with CARL WIEMAN to work on a problem that had been eluding scientists for 70 years—creating a kind of matter known as the Bose-Einstein condensation (BEC). In 1924, an Indian physicist named Satyendra Nath Bose sent some calculations he had made about light particles to ALBERT EINSTEIN, who in turn expanded these calculations to a particular kind of atom. Einstein theorized that if a gas of such atoms were cooled to temperatures nearing absolute zero (the hypothetical temperature at which a substance would have no motion or heat: -459.67 degrees Fahrenheit or -273.15 degrees Celsius), all of the atoms would merge together in the lowest possible state of energy. This state is called condensation because of its similarity to the drops of liquid that form from a gas. The BEC would be a very particular kind of gas, made up of atoms in which almost all motion has stopped. In this nearly frozen state, the wavelengths of individual atoms would grow extremely large (though never becoming less than microscopic) and would overlap in order to form what has been described as a super-atom. Such a large atom would allow physicists to study the rules of quantum mechanics (the physics of particle matter) in much greater detail than ever before.

Creating a BEC had eluded scientists ever since its existence was first postulated by Einstein. Then, on June 5, 1995, after several years of intense research, Cornell and Wieman produced a condensate of about 2,000 rubidium atoms at 20 billionths of a degree above absolute zero—the lowest temperature ever achieved. Aided by a team of researchers, Cornell and Wieman used magnetic and laser traps to catch the ball of rubidium atoms as a condensate. The atoms were confined to the traps by intersecting laser beams that slowed and cooled them. The atoms were then further cooled by an evaporation procedure that used a magnetic trap that was strong enough to hold the coldest atoms but still allowed the warmer ones to escape. A problem arose with this method: when the coldest atoms moved to the point where the magnetic force of the trap fell to zero, the atoms' own magnetic forces allowed them to escape the field, thereby ruining the conditions needed to create the BEC. Cornell solved this dilemma by developing a method that plugged the leak by quickly rotating the magnetic field. As the field rotated, the leaky spot through which atoms escaped would race ahead of the coldest atoms, thus preventing their escape.

Independent of Cornell and Wieman, WOLF-GANG KETTERLE of MIT conducted similar experiments on condensates of sodium atoms. His condensates contained more atoms, and he was thus able to examine the BEC in great detail, make measurements, and observe specific properties of this new matter. He also produced a stream of small "BEC drops" that fell with the force of gravity and can be considered a type of laser beam that uses matter instead of light.

On October 9, 2001, the Royal Swedish Academy of Science awarded the Nobel Prize in Physics to Cornell, Wieman, and Ketterle "for the achievement of Bose-Einstein condensation in dilute gages of alkali atoms, and for early fundamental studies of the properties of the condensates," as noted on the Nobel e-Museum Web site. The academy said that the physicists' work forms a bridge between the everyday world and the invisible, microscopic world by enabling the study of quantum mechanics at the subatomic level. They also speculated that this work could prove valuable in the development of precision instruments and for the field of nanotechnology—in which materials are manipulated on a molecular scale to build microscopic devices, including cellular machines, molecular motors, medicines that target specific cells, and advanced microcomputers.

In addition to the Nobel Prize, Eric Cornell has won the Samuel Wesley Stratton Award from the National Institute of Science and Technology (1995), the Newcomb-Cleveland Prize from the American Association for the Advancement of Science (1995–96), the Fritz London Award in Low Temperature Physics from the International Union of Pure and Applied Physics (1996), the Department of Commerce Gold Medal (1996), the Presidential Early Career Award in Science and Engineering (1996), the I. I. RABI Prize in Atomic, Molecular and Optical Physics from the American Physical Society (1997), the Alan T. Waterman Award from the National Science Foundation (1997), the 1998 Lorentz Medal from the Royal Netherlands Academy of Arts and Sciences, and the Benjamin Franklin Medal in Physics from the Franklin Institute (2000). He is a fellow of the American Physical Society and a member of the National Academy of Sciences.

ABOUT: CNN.com October 9, 2001; Eric A. Cornell Web site; JILA Web site; New York Times July 14, 1995, September 12, 1995; Nobel e-Museum Web site; Scientific American March 1998; University of Colorado at Boulder Web site.

Doctors Without Borders

(Founded in 1971) Nobel Prize for Peace, 1999

Doctors Without Borders was founded on December 20, 1971 in Paris, France. The organization, which is officially known by its French name, Médecins Sans Frontières, was formed by a small group of doctors who had been involved in the 1968 student uprisings in France. They subsequently volunteered to work with the International Red Cross to provide humanitarian aid during the Biafran War in Nigeria. The doctors left Nigeria angered by what they regarded as the failure of humanitarian agencies to overcome obstacles in the delivery of emergency medical aid. They accused the Red Cross, among other agencies, of yielding to intimidation by local governments and breaking their responsibility as doctors to provide medical attention to those in need. In response they formed a group of their own that, according to a report in the *BBC News* (October 15, 1999, on-line), "declared itself the world's first non-governmental, non-military agency dedicated to providing emergency medical assistance." In 1972 the group sent out its first missions: one providing aid to flood victims in East Pakistan (now Bangladesh), the other helping earthquake survivors in Nicaragua.

According to the organization's charter, its volunteer members offer without discrimination assistance to anyone in need due to warfare or natural disasters; observe strict impartiality and maintain independence from all political powers; and understand the risks they take in their work and expect no compensation for themselves. Doctors Without Borders provides assistance only after carefully studying a situation. It first surveys the situation through a team already stationed in the area, then sends out an exploratory team to evaluate the population's medical needs. If the local medical aid is inadequate, the area is accessible, and their staff is guaranteed safe passage, the organization sends a relief mission. While Doctors Without Boarders prefers to work with local organizations or authorities, it will work without them if necessary.

The group was praised in the media for its rapid response to Hurricane Fifi in Honduras in 1974, particularly since it was their first long-term medical assistance program. Two years later war in Lebanon erupted, becoming the organization's first mission to assist casualties of combat. During the course of seven months, 56 doctors and nurses took turns in a Beirut hospital providing aid for Shi'ite civilians who had been attacked by Christian militia.

Prompted by the spread of war across Africa and the Middle East, Doctors Without Borders set up its first refugee programs in 1979. That year the former Soviet Union, seeking to secure a warm-water port, invaded Afghanistan. Heavy civilian casualties precipitated the involvement of Doctor Without Borders. The organization considers this their most difficult mission to date, because its teams of doctors had to work secretly with the Afghan resistance fighters to channel aid to the civilian population. A year later civil war broke out in Somalia and with it came drought, sending thousands of Somalis across the border to Kenya. They were interred at refugee camps in which Doctors Without Borders implemented its first nutritional program. In the same region, meanwhile, thousands of Ethiopians were dying in one of the worst famines ever recorded. By 1984 malnutrition had claimed more than 100,000 victims. Doctors Without Borders responded with food and medical assistance, but the group was expelled from Ethiopia in 1985 for claiming that the government had been forcing migration and diverting aid. In the late 1980s the organization shifted its attention to two countries savaged by earthquakes: El Salvador and Armenia. Then after the Berlin Wall fell in 1989, Doctors Without Borders went into the former Eastern bloc countries to help establish modern health programs.

In the largest emergency effort since its inception, Doctors Without Borders went into the Kurdish refugee camps in northern Iraq to provide medical and sanitary assistance during the Gulf War. The organization widened its operations to aid the Kurds in Iran, Jordan, and Turkey, as well. Later in 1991, as civil war broke out in Somalia, the group went into the city of Mogadishu and was the only international medical response team in that war-torn area. In 1992, when civil war engulfed the region that was once Yugoslavia, the group set up a medical-logistical base in the city of Sarajevo and provided medical aid to all sides of the conflict. The group also continued their work in Somalia that year as the war escalated, a drought developed, and thousands of people were displaced. As the natural and man-made horrors spilled over into South Sudan and Kenya, the group expanded its efforts in those countries.

Between 1993 and 1995 Doctors Without Borders sent volunteers to care for the victims of the civil war in Burundi and the genocide of the Tutsi people by the Hutus in Rwanda. In 1995 the group was forced to leave Zaire (now known as the Democratic Republic of the Congo) and Tanzania after claiming that refugee camps in both countries were controlled by Hutu leaders who had carried out the massacres of 500,000 people in Rwanda. The same year brought more challenges for the organization as the

war in the former Yugoslavia widened. When the city of Srebrenica fell, Doctors Without Borders was the only humanitarian relief organization to witness it. About the same time, the organization established a presence in and around Chechnya to aid refugees fleeing from the conflict that ensued when the province declared its independence from Russia.

Doctors Without Borders vaccinated more than 4.5 million people in Nigeria when an outbreak of meningitis developed in 1996. In the same year, the organization continued medical aid to war victims in Burundi and Sierra Leone and assisted Rwandan refugees returning to their homeland. In 1997 Doctors Without Borders discovered the remains of missing Rwandans in Tingi Tingi and later that year, in a display of their growing diplomatic role and influence, briefed the UNITED NATIONS Security Council on the situation in Zaire. Most recently the group has been involved in Kosovo, Serbia, where they have provided assistance to the massive Albanian refugee population there, and in East Timor, where they have also given aid to the Timorese people, who overwhelmingly voted for independence from Indonesia in August 1999 and have since been terrorized by pro-Indonesian militias.

According to Charles Trueheart of the *Washington Post* (October 16, 1999): "The organization symbolically came of age earlier this year when one of its founders, Bernard Kouchner, was appointed the top U.N. coordinator for Kosovo. The outsider status that once gave Doctors Without Borders a swashbuckling reputation had given way to the ultimate insider status, the job of managing the international community's massive peace and reconstruction effort in the Yugoslav province." Regardless of status the group has worked tirelessly to bring stories of suffering across the globe to the public's attention. They have seen their ranks grow to 2000 physicians and nurses who hail from 48 countries and work in more than 80 providing assistance. Since the organization is privately funded, it takes no political sides in any dispute, except when they are confronted with a human rights violation.

In recent years Doctors Without Borders has struggled to raise funds. Upon hearing the announcement of the $960,000 Nobel Peace Prize, officials for the organization declared that the money would probably be put directly into their budget. They have also struggled to attract volunteers. "Many doctors today are facing economical constraints," Dr. Marc Gastellu Etchegorry, the medical director of Doctors Without Borders, told Suzanne Daley for the *New York Times* (October 16, 1999). "Taking six months off when they have school bills to pay is hard. And, yes, some of them are thinking more about playing golf."

The *BBC News* report stated that Doctors Without Borders "has frequently demonstrated an ability to highlight crises, seek donations for emergency missions, and speak out in situations where it feels morally obliged to do so. This approach, arguably part of the long-held French tradition of human rights activism, has led it to frequently clash with governments, including the authorities at home." In its citation released on October 15, 1999 from Oslo, the Norwegian Nobel Committee proclaimed: "In critical situations, marked by violence and brutality, the humanitarian work of Doctors Without Borders enables the organization to create openings for contacts between the opposed parties. At the same time, each fearless and self-sacrificing helper shows each victim a human face, stands for respect for that person's dignity, and is a source of hope for peace and reconciliation."

ABOUT: BBC News October 15, 1999; New York Times (on-line) October 16, 1999; Nobel e-Museum Web site; Washington Post October 16, 1999.

© The Nobel Foundation

Fo, Dario

(March 24, 1926–) Nobel Prize for Literature, 1997

The writer Dario Fo was born on March 24, 1926 in San Giano, on the shores of Lake Maggiore in northern Italy. He is the oldest of the three children of Felice Fo, a railway station master and amateur actor, and Pina (Rota) Fo, who published *Il paese delle rane* (Land of Frogs, 1978), a memoir of life in the Lake Maggiore area between the wars. Fo's brother, Fulvio, is a theater administrator and his sister, Bianca Fo Garambois, is a writer. From a young age, Fo was fascinated by the tales told by fisherman and glassblowers in local bars. "I built up a collection of these stories from the time I was seven," Fo wrote in the introduction to his play, *Mistero Buffo* (1977). "I didn't just learn the content of their stories, but also their way of telling them. It's first and foremost a particular way of looking at and interpreting reality. The way these people used their eyes, classifying people in a flash into characters or chorus, into story-builders or story-repeaters . . . was [to become] my main weapon." Fo also experimented as a child with a puppet theater, for which he and his brother designed sets and invented plays.

A talented painter, Fo had decided by his teenage years to become an artist, but World War II interrupted his plans. In 1940 he moved to Milan to study painting at the Brera Art Academy. He was then conscripted into the army and defected, hiding in his parents' attic and aiding them in their work with the Italian Resistance. Fo's father, a committed Socialist, guided escaped British prisoners of war and Jews across the border into Switzerland, and his mother nursed wounded partisans. When the war ended, Fo returned to his art classes and also began studying architecture at the Polytechnic University, in Milan.

When not studying, Fo spent many hours hiding in theater balconies, surreptitiously observing the celebrated director Giorgio

Strehler conduct rehearsals. Increasingly disillusioned with the fine arts, he eventually left art school and devoted himself to stagecraft. In 1950 he joined a theater troupe run by Franco Parenti, a well-known radio comedian and actor. The troupe improvised sketches based on stock characters in the tradition of the comic form known as *commedia dell'arte*. In 1951 the Italian State Radio, RAI, invited Fo to perform on air; he developed his *Poer Nano* (Poor Little Thing) monologues based on a character he created, a sly fool who habitually turns historical and biblical incidents upside down, preferring, for example, Cain to the unbearably priggish Abel. After 18 broadcasts Fo's radio show was pulled off the air for its irreverence.

In 1953 Fo teamed up with Parenti and the comic actor Giustino Durano to form a trio called *I Dritti* (The Straight Men). Their first big show, *Il dito nell'occhio* (A Finger in the Eye), became a hit from its opening, in 1953 at Milan's Piccolo Teatro, and later on a national tour. (The production set the pattern for Fo's later collaborations: he had a hand in writing, designing, and directing, as well as performing in the play. For Fo, the acts of writing and performing proved complementary.) *I Dritti*'s next production, *I sani da legare* (Lock Up the Sane), was a pointed criticism of the repressive political climate of the era; the performers enacted skits about red-baiting in the U.S. and Italy, the suppression of dissent in the Soviet Union, and the continued presence of fascist sympathizers in the Italian government. Citing violations of Italy's stringent libel laws, government authorities insisted on editing the script and on having police present at every performance to ensure compliance. Fo and his colleagues were censored by Italian authorities throughout the 1950s and 1960s and continued to draw vocal criticism from the Catholic Church.

In June 1954 Fo married Franca Rame, a talented actress who came from a family of traveling players; Rame became Fo's lifelong collaborator. The couple soon founded a joint theater company, and Fo's reputation as a comic virtuoso grew. Like the best of clowns, Fo became known for his ability to draw characters with simple gestures and facial expressions, and for his unrivaled skill as a storyteller. As the director Carey Perloff told Elizabeth Farnsworth for the *Online News Hour* (October 9, 1997), Fo is "tapping

into pure theater, which is that you break what we in the theater call the fourth wall and you land sort of right in the emotional and sort of political lap of the audience. . . . He will wander through a crowd, talking to people, arguing with people, improvising."

In 1959 the Fo-Rame company mounted its first season at Milan's Teatro del Odeon. They produced *Gli arcangeli non giocano a flipper* (*Archangels Don't Play Pinball*), a manic farce about a good-natured simpleton who triumphs over government bureaucracy. Fo took on a number of roles, in one scene portraying both an absent-minded priest and a bandit, leaving the audience to wonder whether they were not, perhaps, the same personage. In spite of its pointed social satire, the play became an enormous success with the Odeon's middle-class audiences, securely establishing Fo and Rame as personalities in the public eye.

Following the election of Italy's first center-left government, the conservative hold over Italy's state television network began to weaken. As a result, Fo and Rame were invited to appear on *Canzonissima* (Really Big Song), a highly popular variety show. In a biographical sketch of Fo posted on the Nobel e-Museum Web site, the writer described the show's impact: "For the first time, television is used to portray the lives and difficulties of common people. . . . During broadcasts even taxi drivers stop working, and bars with televisions are smack full of people. [The televison network's] management starts to get nervous. Cuts are demanded in texts that have already been approved. All hell breaks loose over a sketch with a Mafia theme that tells the story of a murdered journalist. Malagodi, a senator from Italy's Liberal Party, reports the sketch to the Italian Parliament's oversight committee for television, on the grounds that 'the honour of the Sicilian people is insulted by the claim that there exists a criminal organization called the Mafia.'" Matters came to a head when Fo, reacting to a series of highly publicized factory accidents, mounted a sketch about a worker in a meat-processing factory whose obese aunt visits the plant, falls into one of the enormous meat grinders, and—because the grinder cannot be turned off lest it delay production—is made into 150 cans of chopped meat. In response to complaints from the canned-meat industry, *Canzonissima*'s producers cracked down on Fo's work;

eventually, Fo and Rame walked off the set. They were subsequently sued by the network for loss of funds, since no other actors would agree to replace Fo and Rame and the show foundered. For the next 15 years, the pair were banned from appearing on the state-run radio and television networks.

Embittered by that experience, Fo returned to the theater, only to run into trouble with ideologues from the political left and the right. In 1963 he premiered *Isabella, tre caravelle e un cacciabelle* (often translated as Isabella, Three Sailing Ships and a Con Man), a revisionist history about the life of Christopher Columbus, the court of Queen Isabella, and the persecution of Spain's Arabs and Jews. The play marks the beginning of Fo's efforts to challenge textbook histories; he hoped to "look at the present with the instruments of history and historical culture in order to judge it better." Following the 1967 Soviet invasion of Czechoslovakia, Fo withdrew permission for his plays to be performed there, and further refused Soviet authorities permission to make cuts to another of his plays scheduled to open in the Soviet Union. Thereafter, his work was effectively banned from the Soviet bloc.

Fo became increasingly drawn to the counterculture of the Middle Ages. In particular, he found inspiration in the medieval Italian tradition of the *giullari*, wandering players who entertained peasants with bawdy skits that ridiculed the ruling classes and religion. From the surviving descriptions of such skits, Fo derived material for what is widely regarded as his masterpiece *Mistero Buffo*. Meaning literally "comic mystery," *Mistero Buffo* is a ever-evolving monologue—performed by Fo—that includes apocryphal stories, little-known legends, and slightly reworked biblical tales. For the monologue, Fo invented a language called *grammelot*, part northern Italian dialect, part medieval pastiche. Since premiering the work in 1969, Fo has performed *Mistero Buffo* thousands of times in Italy and abroad. When a version of the piece was televised, in the late 1970s, the Vatican termed it "the most blasphemous show in the history of television."

Eventually, Fo and Rame became disgusted with what they described as the "bourgeois" theater and disbanded their troupe. In 1968, using the profits from their earlier successes, they founded a theater cooperative, *Nuova Scena* (New Scene), which per-

formed satires for working-class audiences in union halls, sports arenas, and town squares. In a climate of political fervor and protest, Fo's work found a ready audience. *Morte accidentale di un anarchio* (1970; *Accidental Death of an Anarchist*) became one of his most controversial and famous works. It is based on a series of scandals involving the Italian secret police and a group of Fascists, who attempted to discredit the Italian Communist Party by staging a number of "terrorist" bombings. The worst of these attacks was blamed on a group of anarchists, one of whom died after falling from a fourth-floor window of the Milan police station where he was being held for interrogation. A subsequent investigation proved that the man had, in fact, been thrown from the window by police officers. In Fo's play, the action revolves around the invasion of the Milan police headquarters by a character who is identified only as "Maniac." Maniac assumes a succession of disguises, including that of a judge, a scientist, and a bishop, in an attempt to trick the police into confessing their part in the anarchist's death. As the scandal played out, Fo continually revised his play to keep pace with new revelations.

Fo and Rame's political involvement deepened after the international success of *Morte accidentale*. They performed regularly throughout the 1970s, donating many of the funds to political groups and worker's unions. They also became involved in international causes, including the resistance to General Pinochet in Chile and support for Palestinian refugees. They were accused of supporting terrorism because of their involvement with a radical group dedicated to helping political prisoners, *Soccorso Rosso Militante* (Militant Red Aid). In 1973 Rame was kidnapped by a Fascist gang, brutally assaulted and raped, and later thrown out of a car onto the street; no one was ever arrested for this crime.

Both Fo and Rame were repeatedly denied visas to appear in the United States under the "ideological provision" of the 1952 McCarren-Walter Act, which barred noncitizens from the country on the basis of their advocacy of communism. The American Civil Liberties Union, the New York Bar Association, and the New York–based Dramatists Guild lobbied vigorously on their behalf, and visas were finally granted in 1984, just in time for the Broadway opening of *Accidental Death of an Anar-*

chist. On that occasion, Fo thanked U.S. President Ronald Reagan for all the publicity he earned by being barred from the country.

As Italy moved away from intense left-right political divisions, Fo's plays became less overtly political and more allegorical. *Non Si Paga! Non Si Paga!* (1974; *Can't Pay! Won't Pay!*) is a farce based on consumers' strikes in poor neighborhoods in southern Italy. Driven by their hunger, characters "liberate" food from grocery stores and otherwise turn the world on end: men get pregnant, women give birth to cabbages. The play's translator, Ron Jenkins, told Farnsworth that "[Fo's] talking about people who are hungry not only for food but hungry for dignity, hungry for justice." The play has become one of Fo's most frequently produced works abroad. During the 1976–77 season, the Italian television network RAI 2 welcomed Fo back to television—after a 15-year absence—with a 20-hour retrospective series of his work.

Storia di una tigre (1980; *The Tale of a Tiger*) is based on a story Fo heard in Shanghai; its moral is that if you want to be a "tiger," you must never expect others to solve your problems or place your trust in a party—the enemy of both reason and revolution. One of Fo's most unusual works of the 1980s is set during the English Renaissance. *Quasi per caso una donna: Elisabetta* (1984; *Elizabeth Almost by Chance a Woman*) opens in its English version with a tongue-in-cheek warning by the author that practically everything in the play is faked: "Sentences attributed to Shakespeare . . . allusions to historical facts. . . certain characters who appear on stage are downright forgeries. . . . Yet the body of the text is, I assure you, laden with authenticity." Franca Rame played a power-hungry and lovesick Queen Elizabeth I to Fo's Dame Glosslady, a transvestite and confidante to the Queen.

In 1996 Fo suffered a stroke that left him partially blind. He has nonetheless continued writing, performing, and teaching. In awarding him the 1997 Nobel Prize for Literature, the Swedish Academy praised Fo as someone "who emulates the jesters of the Middle Ages in scourging authority and upholding the dignity of the downtrodden." Although Fo had been nominated for the prize as early as 1975, many observers were surprised by the choice of such a controversial and political writer; indeed, the Vatican loudly proclaimed their disapproval of the choice. Fo joins EUGENE O'NEILL, LUIGI PIRANDELLO, and a handful of other playwrights who have won the literature award. During his acceptance speech, archived on the Nobel e-Museum Web site, Fo thanked the Swedish Academy for taking a chance on him. "Yours is an act of courage that borders on provocation," he told members of the Academy. "Sublime poets and writers who normally occupy the loftiest of spheres, and who rarely take interest in those who live and toil on humbler planes, are suddenly bowled over by some kind of whirlwind. These poets had already ascended to the Parnassian heights when you, through your insolence, sent them toppling to earth, where they fell face and belly down in the mire of normality."

Fo has written some 70 plays, and his works have been translated into more than 30 languages and performed all over the world. In addition to the Nobel Prize, he has won the Sonning Prize, in recognition of his contributions to the "advancement of European civilization," from the Sonning Foundation at the University of Copenhagen. Fo and Franca Rame have three grown children. Their son, Jacopo, runs an alternative arts school in Santa Cristina di Gubbio, where Fo and Rame occasionally teach theater.

SELECTED PLAYS: Gli arcangeli non giocano a flipper, 1959; Isabella, tre caravelle e un cacciabelle, 1963; Mistero Buffo, 1969; Morte accidentale di un anarchio, 1970; Non Si Paga! Non Si Paga!, 1974; Storia di una tigre, 1980; Quasi per caso una donna: Elisabetta, 1984.

PLAYS IN ENGLISH TRANSLATION: Can't Pay, Won't Pay, 1978; Accidental Death of an Anarchist, 1980; The Tale of a Tiger, 1984; Archangels Don't Play Pinball, 1987; Elizabeth: Almost by Chance a Woman, 1987; Mistero Buffo: Comic Mysteries, 1988.

ABOUT: World Authors 1980–1985, 1991; Miami Herald (on-line) October 10, 1997; Nobel e-Museum Web site; Online News Hour October 9, 1997.

Courtesy of Robert F. Furchgott

Furchgott, Robert

(June 4, 1916–) Nobel Prize for Physiology or Medicine, 1998 (shared with Ferid Murad and Louis Ignarro)

The medical researcher Robert Furchgott was born in Charleston, South Carolina, on June 4, 1916. He became interested in the sciences at an early age. In an autobiographical statement for the Nobel e-Museum, he wrote, "I first became enamored of 'natural history' when I attended nature study classes and field trips to nearby beaches, marshes and woods, sponsored by the Charleston Museum. I became an avid shell collector and bird watcher." At age 13 Furchgott moved to Orangeburg, South Carolina, where his father (who had been running Charleston's Furchgott department store until the onset of the Great Depression) opened a women's clothing store. Furchgott attended high school in Orangeburg and became even more committed to pursuing a career in science. In his statement, he recalled, "I knew that I would like to be a scientist. My parents were encouraging: they gave me chemistry sets and a small microscope as presents. I liked to read popular books about scientists. . . . My father subscribed to the Sunday *New York Times*, in which there was often a column on science that I found very exciting."

After attending the University of South Carolina for one year, Furchgott transferred to the University of North Carolina at Chapel Hill, where he majored in chemistry, earning his B.S. degree in 1937. That year he accepted a teaching assistant position at the Department of Physiological Chemistry of Northwest University Medical School, in Chicago, where he also pursued graduate study. Furchgott completed his doctoral thesis on the physical chemistry of the red blood cell membrane in June 1940, earning his Ph.D. degree in biochemistry—a science concerned with the chemistry of biological processes. Soon after, Furchgott began postdoctoral research at the Cornell University Medical College, in Ithaca, New York, where he worked in the laboratory of Dr. Ephraim Shorr, primarily studying tissue metabolism and circulatory shock. His first full paper was published in the journal of *Biological Chemistry* in 1943. That year Furchgott was also invited to teach in Cornell's Department of Physiology. (The branch of biology known as physiology deals with the physical and chemical functions of organs, tissues, and cells.) Though he was teaching physiology, Furchgott continued to spend a great deal of time in Shorr's lab, where he was introduced to the pharmacology of smooth muscle. (Smooth muscle is found in the walls of most of the hollow structures of the body. Its movement is generally involuntary.) Here, he used drugs and other agents to study the contraction of this type of muscle under aerobic and anaerobic conditions. Pharmacology—which is the science of drugs, including everything from their effects as poisons to their applications as remedies for disease—soon became one of Furchgott's main research interests. In 1949 he moved his young family to St. Louis after accepting a position as assistant professor in pharmacology at Washington University School of Medicine.

In his statement for the Nobel e-Museum Web site, Furchgott characterized his seven years at Washington University as fulfilling, largely because of the opportunity he was given to work with the world-renowned researcher Oliver Lowry, whose department Furchgott described as "a stimulating place for research." The experience proved challenging, for Furchgott had never taken a pharmacology class as a pupil and was now teaching the discipline to medical students. In the lab, Furchgott continued the work he had begun at Cornell, studying the function of intestinal smooth muscle in rabbits and researching the effects of certain drugs in the contraction and relaxation of blood vessels. He was promoted to associate professor in 1952. In 1955 Furchgott became interested in the effects of light on vessel relaxation, discovering that vascular smooth muscle will relax when exposed to near ultraviolet light, in a phenomenon called photorelaxation. He also spent many years researching the pharmacology of cardiac muscles, namely the effects of drugs on heart rate and rhythm. Of Furchgott's tenure at Washington University, his former colleague F. Edmund Hunter, Jr. told a reporter for the university's on-line faculty newspaper, *WUSTL Record*, "He was very active, very well liked by all of the faculty, and, his work was well recognized. He was a major contributor in opening up this entire field of understanding the response of smooth muscle tissue. He has devoted nearly a lifetime to it."

In 1956 Furchgott left Washington University to become chairman of a new Department of Pharmacology at the SUNY College of Medicine in the New York City borough of Brooklyn. (The college's name was later changed to SUNY Downstate Medical Center and more recently to SUNY Health Science Center at Brooklyn.) In Brooklyn, Furchgott continued his research on the photorelaxation of blood vessels, the factors influencing the contraction and relaxation of cardiac muscle, and the theories on peripheral adrenergic (relating to adrenaline) mechanisms, a subject that allowed him to explore the effects of such drugs as cocaine on the heart.

Approximately 23 years after Furchgott moved his work to SUNY, he shifted the focus of his research to another aspect of blood vessel relaxation, the theory of endothelium-dependent relaxation. (Endothelium is the layer of flattened cells that line blood vessels and other body parts.) In previous research, Furchgott had observed that certain drugs had contradictory effects on vessel relaxation, sometimes causing the blood vessels to contract and at other times to dilate. He theorized that the condition of the endothelial cells lining the inside of the blood vessel could be the cause for such varying results. In 1980 Furchgott performed an experiment using acetylcholine, a neurotransmitter, concluding that the endothelial cells must be intact for the vessel to dilate;

he also determined that the cells produced an unknown "signal" molecule, which, in turn, prompted the smooth muscle cells to relax. Furchgott named this unknown signal the endothelium-derived relaxing factor (EDRF). In the Nobel Prize citation posted on the Nobel e-Museum Web site Furchgott's work is called "an ingenious experiment," which led to a quest to identify the factor.

One scientist participating in this quest was Furchgott's fellow Nobel laureate, LOUIS IGNARRO. Independent of Furchgott, Ignarro performed a series of experiments that allowed him to conclude that EDRF was identical to a gas called nitric oxide (NO), a close chemical relative to the anesthetic nitrous oxide ("laughing gas"), which is also known as a common air pollutant that forms when nitrogen burns, as in a car's engine. Although the scientific community knew that bacteria was capable of producing NO, it had not concluded that the gas was important to the physiology of humans and animals. Ignarro and Furchgott, who had also proved in his lab that EDRF was NO, reported their combined findings at a Mayo Clinic conference in Rochester, Minnesota, in July 1986. According to the Nobel e-museum Web site, "[The conclusion] elicited an avalanche of research activities in many different laboratories around the world. This was the first discovery that a gas can act as a signal molecule in the organism. . . . It was particularly surprising since NO is totally different from any other known signal molecule and so unstable that it is converted to nitrate and nitrite within 10 seconds." The third Nobel laureate, FERID MURAD, had proved that the gas could regulate cellular functions.

Through this and other research conducted in the years since Furchgott's original experiment, scientists have concluded that NO is of key importance in the cardiovascular and nervous systems and as a weapon against infections, a regulator of blood pressure, and a "gatekeeper" of blood flow to different organs. Scientists are already applying this new understanding toward the creation of better and more effective drugs. For example, Ignarro's work on the importance of NO for penile erection led to the development of the anti-impotency drug Viagra. In addition, many drug companies—which now have a new perspective on how medicines such as nitroglycerine, which replenishes the body's stores of NO, work in treating cardiovascular disease—are developing stronger heart medications. Scientists have also found that inhibitors of NO can be used to treat shock and are studying how inhalation of the gas may stop the growth of cancerous tumors. As research in this field continues, scientists are learning more about when and how they may use NO more effectively in the body, as well as when its release can have dangerous effects.

Though Furchgott and Ignarro presented their research in 1986—precipitating the release of thousands of papers on NO by scientists around the world—they did not publish their own findings until 1998. On October 12, 1998 the Nobel Assembly awarded Furchgott, Ignarro, and Murad the Nobel Prize in Physiology or Medicine for their contributions to science.

In addition to being recognized with the Nobel Prize, Furchgott has been the recipient of numerous other honors and awards, including: the Goodman & Gilman Award (1984), the CIBA Award for Hypertension Research (1988), the Research Achievement Award from the American Heart Association (1990), the Bristol-Myers Squibb Award for achievement in cardiovascular research (1991), the Gairdner Foundation International Award (1991), the Roussel-Uclaf Prize for research in signal transduction (1993), the Wellcome Gold Medal from the British Pharmacological Society (1995), the ASPET (American Society for Pharmacology and Experimental Therapeutics) Award for experimental therapeutics (1996), the Gregory Pincus Award for research (1996), the Albert Lasker Basic Medical Research Award (1996), and the Lucian Award (1997). He has earned honorary doctorates from the Universities of Madrid (Spain), Lund (Sweden), Ghent (Belgium), and North Carolina. Despite all the recognition for his work, Furchgott wrote for the Nobel e-Museum, "In thinking back about what aspects of my research have given me the greatest pleasure, I would not place the honors and awards first." He cites instead the satisfaction of conducting successful experiments and "the anticipated pleasure of discussing the results with others doing research in the same area."

In 1982 Furchgott resigned from his role as chairman of SUNY's Department of Pharmacology, though he remained a professor until retiring from his teaching duties in 1989. Since 1989 he has been an adjunct professor in the Department of Molecular and Cellular Pharmacology of the University of Miami School of Medicine. Furchgott is currently SUNY Health Science Center's distinguished professor emeritus and continues his research within the department. He is also a member of the American Association for the Advancement of Science, the American Chemical Society, the American Society of Biochemistry, the American Society of Pharmacology and Experimental Therapeutics (for which he served as president in 1971–1972), the Harvey Society, and Sigma Xi.

Furchgott married his first wife, Lenore, in 1941, and had three daughters with her. After Lenore's death, in 1983, he married his current wife, Margaret. The couple resides in Hewlett, New York, and spends three and a half months each winter in Miami.

ABOUT: CNN.com 1998; New York Times October 13, 1998, July 2, 1991; Nobel e-Museum Web site; Science October 23, 1998.

Gao Xingjian

(January 4, 1940–) Nobel Prize for Literature, 2000

The writer and artist Gao Xingjian was born on January 4, 1940 in Ganzhou, China, located in the eastern province of Jiangxi. His father was a bank official, and his mother was an amateur actress who was a member of a YMCA theater troupe prior to the Communist Revolution. She also had a serious interest in Western literature. "Thanks to her," Gao told Alan Riding for the *New York Times* (November 21, 2000, on-line), "we had lots of books everywhere, translations of classics, Balzac, Zola, Steinbeck. That's why I began to read at a very early age." Gao was also a highly creative child. He told Riding, "I always had a dream of being a writer or actor or playwright. My mother and I would do little theater pieces at home. Sometimes my father was the only audience. I wrote my first novel when I was 10. It was an adventure story. At the same time, I painted. Early on, I was doing oils, water colors, calligraphy—all sorts of things." Educated in China's public school

Courtesy of the University of Sydney

Gao Xingjian

could not trust anyone, not even my family," Gao is quoted as saying in the *Detroit News* (October 13, 2000).

In 1979, after the Cultural Revolution had ended, Gao began to publish short stories, essays, and dramas in Chinese literary magazines and he was able to travel abroad, to France and Italy. In 1981 he published a collection of essays, which has been published in English as *Contemporary Technique and National Character in Fiction*, and which sparked a debate in China about modernism versus realism. In 1985 he published a narrative work, which can be translated as "A Pigeon Called Red Beak", and a collection of plays. Another book of nonfiction, which can be translated as "In Search of a Modern Form of Dramatic Representation", was published in 1987.

Several of Gao's plays were performed in China in the 1980s while he was a writer and director with the People's Art Theater in Beijing. There, according to Anthony Kuhn for the *Los Angeles Times* (October 16, 2000), "Gao was part of a group of directors who used bold visual imagery, lighting, sound, and acting techniques to introduce Chinese audiences to postmodern Western drama." Gao's plays were among the first to take inspiration from Western dramatic forms in order to create a new genre of contemporary Chinese theater. Horace Engdahl, the permanent secretary of the Swedish Academy, stated at a press conference in Stockholm that "Gao has been one of the most important writers in creating what didn't exist before: a spoken drama in China as distinct from music drama, dance, and the old traditions," as quoted in the *Los Angeles Times* (October 13, 2000). An October 12, 2000 press release published on the Nobel e-Museum Web site notes that Gao's plays are also influenced by such traditional and popular Chinese performing arts as masked drama, shadow plays, drumming, and opera. Through his plays and his involvement with the People's Art Theater, Gao was part of a burgeoning avant-garde arts movement in China that has continued following his departure and, due in part to a loosening of governmental restraints on art, flourished.

In 1982 Gao made his debut as a playwright with *Warning Signal*, the "first experimental play staged in Beijing in years," according to John-Thor Dahlburg for the *Los Angeles Times* (October 13, 2000). Deemed

system, he earned a degree in French in 1962 from the Department of Foreign Languages in Beijing. His second language afforded him further exposure to Western literature, in particular experimental dramas by such writers as Eugene Ionesco, SAMUEL BECKETT, Jean Genet, and the writings of theater theorist Antonin Artaud, all of whom he claims as key influences. As part of his studies, Gao translated the works of French surrealist poets, and he later translated French dramas into Chinese as well, including Ionesco's *The Bald Soprano*.

In the early 1960s, as part of the economic initiative known as the Great Leap Forward, Gao, like many others, was sent to a reeducation camp where he labored for six years as an agricultural worker. His mother drowned in an accident at one such camp. Gao wrote extensively during this period, although, due in part to warnings from friends, he did not attempt to publish his work. In 1966 Mao Zedong, the chairman of the Chinese Communist Party (CCP), launched the Cultural Revolution, his attempt to bring the Party back under his control and to eliminate elitist and capitalistic elements from society. During this tumultuous episode in Chinese history, Gao's own wife denounced him as a traitor to the Party, and Gao felt it necessary to burn a suitcase full of stories, plays, and essays that he thought might incriminate him. "In China, I a success within the avant-garde community, the play provoked a polemic from the government but was not banned. In 1983 Gao further established his reputation with a production of *Bus Stop*, perhaps his best-known play, which he'd written in 1981 but was considered too experimental to be performed at that time. Bearing similarities to Samuel Beckett's *Waiting for Godot*, *Bus Stop* implies that life itself is a form of waiting. The play begins with eight people waiting in line for a bus at a bus stop. Though their hopes that the bus will come are often aroused, they are repeatedly disappointed. One day they realize with shock that they have been waiting for the bus for years. Simultaneously, they discover that they are now only seven; a silent man left the group long ago, they now remember. A spotlight suddenly illuminates the man, behind the audience on a raised platform, and the people at the bus stop are filled with remorse. They, too, should have walked. As the play closes, each of the actors addresses a different section of the audience at once, ruminating over the time they have wasted. In a critical essay in *Modern Drama* (Fall 1998) comparing *Bus Stop* and *Waiting for Godot*, Harry H. Kuoshu noted that Beckett's play seems to view waiting as inherent to the human condition, while Gao's seems to ascribe it to the inhibiting presence of a repressive political climate. "*Bus Stop*, after all, is not as nihilist as *Waiting for Godot*," Kuoshu wrote. "It attributes existential absurdity more to the political result of totalitarian control than to an epistemological crisis." According to Dahlburg, a Chinese official denounced *Bus Stop* as "spiritual pollution," a term used to refer to undesirable Western influences, and called it "the most pernicious text written since the creation of the People's Republic [of China]." Rather than deliver a public self-criticism as was ordered by the Party, Gao embarked on a 10-month walking tour, tracing the course of the Yangzi River in southwestern China from its source all the way to the coast. This trip figured largely in *Soul Mountain*, which he had begun writing in 1982. "I said to myself, 'I have already subjected myself to self-censorship, and still I was attacked,'" Gao told Alan Riding. "So I started writing a novel just for myself without thinking of having it published."

In 1985 a production of a new play by Gao, *Wild Man*, was mounted at the People's Art Theater and provoked derision from the CCP. Around that time, according to Riding, the political climate had again shifted and Gao could no longer publish his work. In 1986 Gao's play *The Other Shore* was banned by the party, and none of his plays have been produced in China since. Following the reception of *The Other Shore*, Gao was blacklisted as a writer, but he was allowed out of the country as a painter. In 1987 he left China and about a year later established residence in Paris as a political refugee. After hundreds of pro-democracy demonstrators were killed in Beijing's Tiananmen Square in 1989, Gao formally withdrew from the CCP. Following the publication of his play *Fugitives*, which uses the Tiananmen Square incident as its backdrop, he was declared persona non grata in China, and all of his writings were banned by the government.

A number of Gao's works have been translated into English, including *Wild Man*, published in 1990, and *Fugitives*, published in 1993. In 1999 the Chinese University Press, in Hong Kong, published a collection of five of Gao's plays translated by Gilbert C. F. Fong, under the title *The Other Shore: Plays by Gao Xingjian*. Included in the volume are *The Other Shore*, *Between Life and Death*, *Dialogue and Rebuttal*, *Nocturnal Wanderer*, and *Weekend Quartet*. The description of the collection posted on the Chinese University Press Web site reads, "One finds poetry, comedy, as well as tragedy in the plays, which are graced by beautiful language and original imagery. Combining Zen philosophy and a modern world view, they serve to illuminate the gritty realities of life, death, sex, loneliness, and exile, all essential concerns in Gao's understanding of the existence of modern man."

Soul Mountain was first published in Taiwan in 1990. An English translation, by Mabel Lee, was published in 1999 in Australia, where it became a best-seller. The novel recounts a spiritual journey through remote regions of China and is told from a variety of perspectives. The narrator speaks in the first-, second-, and third-person, which is also characteristic of the characters in Gao's dramas. "The book is a tapestry of narratives with several protagonists who reflect each other and may represent aspects of one and the same ego," according to the Swedish

GAO

Academy press release. "With his unrestrained use of personal pronouns Gao creates lightning shifts of perspective and compels the reader to question all confidences. This approach derives from his dramas, which often require actors to assume a role and at the same time describe it from the outside. I, you, and he/she become names of fluctuating inner distances." During the course of the journey, the narrator encounters many strange people and phenomena. Shamanistic beliefs and customs still hold sway in these regions of China, and in the novel old myths seem to come to life. At one point, the head of a village encourages the narrator to visit a magical hunter named Grandpa Stone, who once wove enchantments but has been dead for many years and supposedly still lies in his hut impervious to decomposition. His magical rifle, which never misses its target, is said to still be hanging in the hut as well. The narrator's journey in *Soul Mountain* is also an escape from the confines of intellectualism and the literary life. The narrator, who like Gao is a writer, feels that his concepts of life have often kept him from experiencing life more directly. "In those contaminated surroundings I was taught that life was the source of literature," says the narrator, "that literature had to be faithful to life, faithful to real life. My mistake was that I had alienated myself from life and ended up turning my back on real life. However, real life is not the same as manifestations of life." The Swedish Academy cited *Soul Mountain* as "one of those singular literary creations that seem impossible to compare to anything but themselves."

When Gao received the phone call informing him that he'd won the Nobel Prize, "They announced it to me very simply and told me I had to prepare a 45-minute speech. I said that's very long," Gao told Reuters Television in French after receiving the award, as reported by Dahlburg. In China, the Academy's choice was roundly criticized. Some Chinese intellectuals argued that there were plenty of Chinese authors still living in the country and sanctioned by its government who were of greater stature than Gao. China's Foreign Ministry, according to Anthony Kuhn, said the decision "shows again the Nobel literature prize has been used for ulterior political motives, and it is not worth commenting on." Shu Yi, the head of China's National Museum of Mod-

ern Chinese Literature, in Beijing, had a more moderate reaction. "We should congratulate [Gao] for his award," Kuhn quoted Shu as saying. Shu continued, however, "The award is stimulating and provocative for China. It makes us feel awkward—we don't know whether to laugh or cry."

On December 7, 2000 Gao gave his Nobel lecture, focusing on the importance of keeping literature free from the constraints of politics, commercialism, and reductive literary theories. "What I want to say here is that literature can only be the voice of the individual and this has always been so," Gao said, as translated from the Chinese on the Nobel e-museum Web site. "Once literature is contrived as the hymn of the nation, the flag of the race, the mouthpiece of a political party or the voice of a class or group, it can be employed as a mighty and all- engulfing tool of propaganda. However, such literature loses what is inherent in literature, ceases to be literature, and becomes a substitute for power and profit." The most valuable aspect of literature, said Gao, is that it is a "spiritual communication" between the reader and an author. "During the years when Mao Zedong implemented total dictatorship . . . to write even in secret was to risk one's life. . . . It was only during this period when it was utterly impossible for literature that I came to comprehend why it was so essential: literature allows a person to preserve a human consciousness."

Soul Mountain was published to great acclaim in the United States in 2000. Gao's second novel, *One Man's Bible*, was published in English in 2001 or 2002. The latter is an autobiographical fiction based on Gao's experiences during the Cultural Revolution. Gao continues to live and work in the Paris suburb of Bagnolet. He was awarded the Chevalier de l'Ordre des Arts et des Lettres, the French government's equivalent of knighthood, in 1992.

SELECTED WORKS IN ENGLISH TRANSLATION: drama—Fugitives (in Chinese Writing and Exile), 1993; The Other Shore: Plays by Gao Xingjian, 1999; fiction—Soul Mountain, 1999; One's Man's Bible, 2002; nonfiction—Contemporary Technique and National Character in Fiction, 1981.

ABOUT: Denver Post October 13, 2000; Detroit News October 13, 2000; Los Angeles Times October 13, 2000, October 16, 2000; Modern Drama Fall 1998; New York Times (on-line) November 21, 2000, December 8, 2000; Nobel e-Museum Web site.

© The Nobel Foundation

Grass, Günter

(October 16, 1927–) Nobel Prize for Literature, 1999

The writer Günter Wilhelm Grass was born on October 16, 1927 in Langfuhr, a suburb of the Free City of Danzig, the Baltic seaport that is now the Polish city of Gdańsk and the setting of many of his works. He is of German ancestry on his father's side and is descended from Kashubians—a West Slavic people native to the region near the mouth of Poland's Vistula River—on his mother's. His father was a grocer who also served as a minor government official. At an early age, Grass demonstrated a talent for painting and drawing, with an affinity for the bizarre, and at 13 he wrote an unpublished novel about his Kashubian forebears for a literary competition sponsored by a school newspaper. Although his father took a dim view of the creative arts, Grass's mother, Helene, encouraged her son's imaginative spinning of tales and nicknamed him "Peer Gynt."

Reared "between the Holy Ghost and Hitler's photograph," as he recalled in one of his poems, Grass became a *Pimpf*, or Hitler "cub," at the age of 10, joined the Hitler Youth at 14, and was drafted to serve as a *Luftwaffe* auxiliary when he was 16. Wounded at Cottbus during the defense of Berlin in April 1945, he was sent to a hospital in Marienbad, Czechoslovakia, before spending time in a prisoner of war camp in Bavaria, where he was forced to view the newly liberated Dachau death camp as part of his de-Nazification process.

Released in the spring of 1946, Grass tried his hand as a black marketeer, worked as a farm laborer in the Rhineland, took a job in a potash mine near Hildesheim, and was briefly reunited with his parents. In 1947 he tried to resume his interrupted schooling at Göttingen, but when he found that history, as it was being taught by his professor, consisted mainly of a compendium of wars and battles, he walked out on his first lesson and never completed his education. In 1949, after spending two years as an apprentice stonemason and tombstone engraver in Düsseldorf, Grass entered the *Kunstakademie* in that city, where he studied painting with Otto Pantok and sculpture with Sepp Mages. In his free time he played the drums and the washboard with a jazz band and wrote poems and dramatic sketches. During 1951 and 1952 he traveled in Italy and France.

In 1953 Grass moved to Berlin, where he studied with the metal sculptor Karl Hartung at the *Akademie der Künste*. Meanwhile, encouraged by the poet Gottfried Benn, Grass continued his literary efforts. In 1955, some of Grass's poems, entered by his wife without his knowledge, won third prize in a contest sponsored by a Stuttgart radio station. As a result, he was invited to join Gruppe 47, a loosely organized association of German avant-garde writers. His work began to appear in literary journals, and in 1956 his first volume, *Die Vorzüge der Windhühner* ("Advantages of Moorhens"), an illustrated collection of surrealist and satiric prose and poetry, was published by the Hermann Luchterhand Verlag.

In the mid-1950s Grass tried to gain recognition as a playwright with a series of avant-garde dramas, some of which seemed to reflect the influence of SAMUEL BECKETT. They include *Hochwasser*; *Onkel, Onkel*; *Noch zehn Minuten bis Buffalo*; and *Die bosen Koche*, which in English translation appear in the volume *Four Plays* (1967) under the titles *Flood*; *Mister, Mister*; *Only Ten Minutes to Buffalo*; and *The Wicked Cooks*. The stage productions of his plays were not well received, however, and Grass has indicated that his dismay with what he saw as the lack of perceptiveness on the part of theatregoers and critics helped to persuade him to write his first novel.

Aided by a small stipend from Luchterhand Verlag, Grass went to Paris in 1956, where he lived with his family on a subsistence level while working on his 1959 novel *Die Blechtrommel* (translated as *The Tin Drum* in 1963), the first book in his so-called "Danzig Trilogy." Its protagonist, the mischievous dwarf Oskar Matzerath, was born in Grass's imagination one day at a party, when he saw a child crawl under a table and plunge into his own world of fantasy, oblivious of the reality of the adult world around him. The book is an incisive evocation of the Hitler era and its aftermath as seen through the eyes of Oskar, who deliberately stopped growing at the age of three as a protest against the infantilism of the time, but whose brain develops into that of a mature man who can accurately recall the past by beating on his toy drum.

In 1958 Grass returned to Berlin, where he received the annual Gruppe 47 prize for his reading from the manuscript of *The Tin Drum*. With its publication in December 1959 by Hermann Luchterhand Verlag, which published all of his subsequent novels, Grass was recognized as a literary figure of international importance. The book was eventually translated into more than 20 languages. Like most of Grass's later works, *The Tin Drum* was translated into English by Ralph Manheim; it was published in 1962 in Great Britain by Secker and Warburg, and in 1963 in the United States by Harcourt Brace Jovanovich.

In the words of Joseph Bauke, writing for the *Saturday Review* (August 10, 1963), "Günter Grass has to his credit the most vigorous novel in postwar German writing. . . . With it German literature rid itself of the provincialism to which it succumbed so infamously in the days of the Third Reich, and won back an international audience." Hugh McGovern, in his review in *America* (March 9, 1963), called *The Tin Drum* "one long, crazy, unalleviated nightmare" from which "there emerges an authentic feeling, a burning horror and rage at the loathsomeness of the human condition." And Fred Grunfeld wrote in the *Reporter* (March 14, 1963): "Grass harks back to that superb and, except for Kafka, still forgotten group of expressionist writers, who accounted for the flowering of German literature during the 1920's and early 1930's." A film version of *Die Blechtrommel*, directed by Volker Schlondorff and released by New World Pictures in 1979, received several honors in West Germany and shared the Golden Palm award at the film festival in Cannes. In the United States it earned an Oscar from the Academy of Motion Picture Arts and Sciences as the best foreign language film of 1980.

Grass's second novel, the 1961 *Katz und Maus* (translated as *Cat and Mouse* in 1963), is a somewhat less ambitious work than its predecessor. Its protagonist, Joachim Mahlke, is set apart from his fellows by his uncommonly large Adam's apple, which singles him out as a potential nonconformist, and despite his heroic accomplishments he fails to win acceptance from the conformist "cats" of society. R. K. Burns, commenting in the *Library Journal* (August 1963), called the book "a sample of the best of modern European writing," while D. J. Enright noted in his review in the *New Statesman* (August 23, 1963) that "there are moments of miraculous freshness and hallucinatory clarity." A film version of *Katz und Maus*, with script and direction by Hansjürgen Pohland, was released by Modern Art Film in 1967.

The 1963 novel *Hundejahre* (translated as *Dog Years* in 1965), the third volume in Grass's "Danzig trilogy," is the most ambitious and challenging in that series. Covering the years 1917 to 1957, the story traces the love-hate relationship of Eduard Amsel, a half-Jew and a maker of scarecrows, and Walter Matern, his erstwhile friend and protector who later joins a Nazi storm-trooper attack on him. After the war, filled with guilt and rage, Matern travels through Germany with Prinz, Hitler's German shepherd dog, taking his revenge on his former cohorts by infecting their wives and daughters with venereal disease.

In *Commentary* (May 1964) George Steiner noted that Grass's greatest success was that he was able "to make the Germans—as no writer did before—face up to their monstrous past." Richard Kluger, analyzing Grass's methodology, wrote in *Harper's* magazine (June 1965), "His method is to seize upon what is latently poisonous in the Germanic character, display it in its benignly sentimental state, then show it stomping off on a sadistic rampage until it is checked and returned to mindless normality, the seeds of renewed virulence lurking just below the surface."

From the evils of the past, Grass turned to the present with his 1969 *Örtlich betäubt* (translated in 1970 as *Local Anaesthetic*). It is an ode to the 1960s generation of German students, capsuled in the story of Eberhard Starusch, a 40-year-old bachelor history teacher in Berlin, who tells his tale from the dentist's chair. Starusch is an advocate of the "pedagogical principle," favoring an ideal society in which all are students, while his dentist champions a program of "universal prophylaxis" under which everybody is a patient. Central to the story is Starusch's effort to prevent his student, Scherbaum, from immolating his dachshund in front of the cake-consuming ladies at the famous Berlin cafe Kempinski's as a protest against the use of napalm in Vietnam. To Anatole Broyard, writing in the *New York Times Book Review* (March 29, 1970), Grass's *Local Anaesthetic* seemed to be "technically . . . the most convincing demonstration . . . that the novel is not only alive and well, but healthier than ever."

In his partly autobiographical, partly historical, and partly fictional 1972 work *Aus dem Tagebuch einer Schnecke*, published in 1973 as *From the Diary of a Snail*, Grass tried to explain the human condition, German history, and himself to his children. Beginning with a brief history of German socialism, which he wrote on the road while campaigning for eventual West German chancellor and Nobel laureate WILLY BRANDT in 1969, he flashed back to the dispersal of the Jewish community of Danzig in the 1930s to tell the story of Hermann Ott, a Gentile schoolmaster—nicknamed "Doubt" because of his Schopenhauerian leanings—in a private Jewish school in Danzig. Interspersed in the narrative is an attack on Hegel, who, according to Grass, "sentenced mankind to history." Asked by his child in the novel, "What's progress?" Grass answered that progress means "being a little quicker than the snail."

Grass's monumental 1977 novel *Butt*, published in 1978 as *The Flounder*, is based on the misogynistic Brothers Grimm fairy tale "The Fisherman and His Wife," in which a talking flounder, rescued by a fisherman, grants him all his wishes until the man's wife, Illsebill, demands that she become king, pope, and finally God. In Grass's version of the tale, the narrator, married to a nagging Illsebill, tells the history of mankind in nine chapters, paralleling his wife's pregnancy. Each chapter is dedicated to one of the great priestess-cooks of the past, from the matriarchal, three-breasted goddess of the Stone Age, Awa, to the present-day surrogate goddess, the "women's libber." Convinced that history, written and directed by man, has been nothing more than chaos, Grass allows the magic flounder to give modern woman a chance to change history and establish peace by destroying the patriarchy. But instead of accepting the newly captured flounder's help in destroying the patriarchy, the women put the flounder on trial for his past sins as counselor of the male sex.

Although the book, which took Grass five years to write, sold a record 150,000 copies in the first month following its publication in Germany, reviews of it were by no means universally favorable: women critics objected to what they saw as the book's antifeminist tenor. Many reviewers, however, regarded it as a major work. "A comic epic stuffed with maniacal research and ingenious analogies, *The Flounder* is by far the most audacious product of [Grass's] historical imagination," Morris Dickstein wrote for the *New York Times Book Review* (November 12, 1978). "What stands up as vividly authentic in *The Flounder* is its original conception, the use of culinary history and sexual history as a vehicle for history."

In the 1979 novel *Das Treffen in Telgte* (translated in 1981 as *The Meeting at Telgte*), Grass fantasized about a conference of writers in Telgte, Westphalia, toward the end of the Thirty Years' War in 1647. The book was written by Grass as a tribute to Hans Werner Richter, who in 1947 founded Gruppe 47, an association of leading authors whose mission was to review unpublished manuscripts of aspiring German writers and purge the German language of the pollutions it acquired in the Nazi era. In Grass's book, the Telgte conference is called by the poet Simon Dach, who summons his literary colleagues to resurrect the ravaged fatherland through the living force of German language and literature. The writers quickly slip from

GRASS

their sublime heights of spirituality, greedily gobbling plundered food in a time of hunger, straying in the hay with female companions, and disputing literary forms in heated debates. All the characters are historical figures who lived in Germany in the 17th century but never met at Telgte. Theodore Ziolkowski opined in the *New York Times Book Review* (May 17, 1981) that Grass had "chosen his historical analogy with brilliant precision."

Grass's *Kopfgeburten: oder, Die Deutschen sterben aus*, translated in 1982 as *Headbirths, or The Germans Are Dying Out*, which he wrote on his return from a trip to China in 1979, is, in the words of John Leonard in the *New York Times Book Review* (March 14, 1982), "part fiction, part travelogue, part screenplay, and part political pamphlet . . . a wise, sad, witty mess." Included in the book are Grass's eulogy to his dead friend, the writer Nicholas Born; a commentary on West Germany's forthcoming 1980 elections; and a proposal that the two Germanys switch their political systems once every decade, to give the East Germans "an opportunity to relax under capitalism, while the Federal Republic could drain off cholesterol under Communism." Commenting on the concern shown by some politicians about the declining German birthrate, Grass mused about the prospect of an increase in the German population to nearly a billion and an accompanying decrease in the Chinese population to a mere 80,000,000, and asked, "Could the world bear it?" In one of the subplots, the schoolteacher couple Harm and Dörte Peters, products of the 1960s generation, debate while on a tour of Asia whether or not to have a baby. Should they create life to save their race, while at the same time allowing it to suffer their era's ecological and spiritual pollution?

In 1986 Grass published *Die Rättin*, translated in 1987 as *The Rat*. The novel reintroduces several characters from some of Grass's previous novels, including *The Tin Drum*, *The Flounder*, and *Headbirths*. Bordering on science fiction, the novel is set in a future time in which humanity has been virtually destroyed. The narrator of the novel engages in a series of discussions with a female rat who argues that her species will inherit the earth. Grass's final work of the 1980s was *Show Your Tongue* (1989), a nonfiction work depicting the experiences of

Grass and his wife during the six months they spent living in India. The author described the inhuman conditions he witnessed, accompanied by his own original illustrations. The memoir was translated into English by John E. Woods.

The razing of the Berlin Wall in 1989 and the subsequent reunification of Germany held major ramifications for Grass, his political philosophies, and his work. One of his most famous statements was that Germany had lost the right to be a unified nation because of the Holocaust, which demonstrated that such a nation was a danger to the world. Grass's first book published after the reunification was *Two States—One Nation?*, a collection of speeches and debates published in 1990 and translated by Krishna R. Winston and Arthur S. Wensinger. In the collection, Grass argues against the reunification, explaining that East Germany has a national character of its own and so deserves a state of its own. Grass even goes so far as to declare that a reunified Germany is a threat to world peace.

Grass returned to fiction in 1992 with *Unkenrufe* published the same year as *The Call of the Toad*. The novel is set just before the fall of the Berlin Wall and tells the story of a widowed woman and man who fall in love in the midst of great political turmoil. Although it is on the surface a love story, the novel also contains a great deal of satire on post-unification politics. Jackie Wullschlager of the *Financial Times* (October 11, 1992) described *The Call of the Toad* as "a funny, wise, hugely enjoyable fantasy." The reviewer also compared Grass's fixation with Danzig and the Baltic Coast as backgrounds for his fiction to James Joyce's depictions of Dublin and ISAAC BASHEVIS SINGER's use of Poland as a common setting. *The Call of the Toad* was the last Grass book translated by Ralph Manheim, who passed away shortly before the novel was published.

The 1995 novel *Ein weites Feld*, published in English as *A Wide Field*, was Grass's second novel inspired by the fall of the Berlin Wall. Set immediately after the incident in November 1989, the novel was blasted by many of Germany's influential literary critics for what they saw as Grass's distortion of the truth regarding the reunification of East and West Germany. Grass characterized the unification as an act of colonial annexation. The author responded to much of the criticism by arguing that his critics were letting their politics get in the way of their literary judgements.

The Royal Swedish Academy cited Grass's masterwork *The Tin Drum* as one of the achievements which earned him the prize in 1999. The academy declared in their announcement, "It is not too audacious to assume that *The Tin Drum* will become one of the enduring literary works of the 20th century." The Nobel Academy also praised Grass's gift for "reviewing contemporary history by recalling the disavowed and the forgotten: the victims, losers, and lies that people wanted to forget because they had once believed in them." Grass is the third German to receive the Nobel Literature Prize, after THOMAS MANN in 1929 and Heinrich Böll in 1972. The author John Irving, who has called Grass "simply the most original and versatile writer alive," wrote of him in the *Saturday Review* (March 1982): "Against the authoritative landscape of history, he creates characters so wholly larger than life, yet vivid, that they confront the authority of history with a larger authority— Grass's imagination. He does not distort history; he out-imagines it."

Around the time his award was announced, Grass's latest work, *Mein Jahrhundert*, or *My Century*, was published. Virtually assuring Grass's place among the major voices of the 20th century, *My Century* is a compilation of 100 short fiction pieces—one for each year—told from the perspective of a variety of narrators, who range from the common to the extraordinary. While the book features a series of fictional dialogues between famed German authors Erich Maria Remarque and Ernest Jünger, who argue about the First World War, such ordinary folk as a schoolboy, a soldier, and a teacher are also given a significant voice.

The leading literary influences on Grass's works include the poet Guillaume Apollinaire; the dramatist Georg Büchner; the novelist Alfred Döblin, in whose name he has instituted an annual prize for the best German manuscript; Herman Melville, especially his *Moby Dick*; and the German Expressionists. Among his favorite contemporary writers are SAUL BELLOW, Norman Mailer, Slavomir Mrožek, Georg Tabori, and John Updike. Although he considered Bertolt Brecht a major inspiration, he condemned Brecht in his play *The Plebeians Rehearse the Uprising* (1965) for failing to speak out in behalf of the East German workers' strike in June 1953.

Other writings by Grass include the volumes of verse *Gleisdreieck* (1960), *Ausgefragt* (1967) and, in English translation, *Selected Poems* (1966), *Poems of Günter Grass* (1969), and *In the Egg and Other Poems* (1978). As Keith Miles wrote in the book *Günter Grass* (1975), Grass's poems "can evoke the lightheartedness and delicacy of a Paul Klee or the nightmarishness and abrasiveness of a Georg Heym. They can be playful celebrations of innocence or grim reflections of experience." Among Grass's collections of prose are *Dich singe ich, Demokratie* (1965), *"Uber das Selbstverstandliche* (1968; *Speak Out!*, 1969), *Dokumente zur politischen Wirkung* (1972), *Der Bürger und seine Stimme* (1974), *Denkzettel* (1978), and *Aufsätze zur Literatur* (1981).

Among the many honors that Grass has received are the Georg Büchner Preis (1965), the Theodor Heuss Preis (1968), the Berliner Fontane Preis (1969), the CARL VON OSSIETZKY medal (1977), and honorary doctorates from Harvard University and Kenyon College. In 1979 he and his fellow writers Heinrich Böll and Siegfried Lenz caused something of a stir when they refused to accept the Federal Republic's Distinguished Service Medal.

Grass was once a staunch supporter of West Germany's Social Democratic party, serving as Willy Brandt's chief campaign speech writer for over a decade and formally joining the party in 1982. "I am a Social Democrat because to my mind socialism is worthless without democracy," he once asserted, "and because an unsocial democracy is no democracy at all." In the 1960s Grass actively promoted the independent socialist newspaper *Spandauer Volksblatt*, and he later founded the literary magazine *L 80*. The Berlin building that houses its offices once served as a refuge for expatriate writers from East Germany, before reunification. After visiting Nicaragua in early 1983, Grass spoke out in defense of its Sandinist government, whose situation he found in some ways analogous to that of Poland's Solidarity movement.

The author has continued to argue against the unified German state. In an interview for the London *Observer Review* (October 22, 1995), he commented, "It has failed in the course it has taken. The Wall is gone but it has been replaced in a terrible way by a system of first- and second-class Germans . . . . We took this didactic, colonial attitude . . . which turned into an annexation.

That's what I'm criticizing. I wasn't against German unity." Conflict over the issue has caused Grass to drift from the Social Democratic party of which he was once a vocal proponent.

Grass usually writes standing up and walks some ten kilometers around his manuscript on a productive day. His novels undergo at least three scrutinizing drafts of reconstruction. The end product is crowned with the author's illustrations and artistically designed jackets. To ensure the best possible translations, Grass conducts seminars for his translators upon completion of a new novel.

Günter Grass was first married in 1954, to Anna Margareta Schwarz, a Swiss dancer, with whom he had four children: Laura, Bruno, and the twins Franz and Raoul. In 1979 he married Ute Grunert. Grass commutes between his home in Berlin and a 16th-century house in a village near Glückstadt, north of Hamburg, which he uses as a retreat. A lapsed Roman Catholic, Grass says that he does not believe in God but still believes in the Virgin Mary. In addition to conducting culinary experiments, drawing, sculpting, etching, sketching, and politicking, Grass enjoys collecting mushrooms, jetsam, and shells.

SELECTED WORKS: fiction—Die Blechtrommel, 1959; Katz und Maus, 1961; Hundejahre, 1963; Örtlich betäubt, 1969; Aus dem Tagebuch einer Schnecke, 1972; Butt, 1977; Das Treffen in Telgte, 1979; Die Rättin, 1986; Unkenrufe, 1992; Ein weites Feld, 1995; Mein Jahrhundert, 1999; nonfiction—Kopfgeburten: oder, Die Deutschen sterben aus, 1982.

SELECTED WORKS IN ENGLISH TRANSLATION: drama—Four Plays, 1967; fiction—The Tin Drum, 1963; Cat and Mouse, 1963; Dog Years, 1965; Local Anasthetic, 1970; From the Diary of a Snail, 1973; The Flounder, 1978; The Meeting at Telgte, 1981; The Rat, 1987; The Call of the Toad, 1992; A Wide Field, 1995; My Century, 1999; nonfiction—Headbirths; or, the Germans Are Dying Out, 1982; poetry—In the Egg and Other Poems, 1978.

ABOUT: Hollington, Michael. Günter Grass: The Writer in a Pluralist Society, 1980; Encyclopedia of World Literature in the 20th Century, 1982; Oxford Companion to German Literature, 1976; World Authors: 1950–70, 1975; New York Times (on-line) September 30, 1999, October 1, 1999; New York Times Book Review June 23, 1985, October 22, 1995; Nobel e-Museum Web site; Paris Review Summer 1991; Publishers Weekly June 16, 1989; New Republic, February 24, 1986; London Observer Review October 22, 1995; World Literature Today Winter 1986.

Dirk Wesphal/The Rockefeller University

Greengard, Paul

(December 11, 1925–) Nobel Prize for Physiology or Medicine, 2000 (shared with Eric Kandel and Arvid Carlsson)

The neuroscientist Paul Greengard was born on December 11, 1925 in New York City. His mother died while giving birth to him. At age 17, he enlisted in the U.S. Navy during World War II, helping to develop an early warning system to detect incoming enemy planes. After the war, Greengard enrolled at Hamilton College in Clinton, New York. He studied mathematics and theoretical physics, receiving his A.B. in 1948 after two years of study. Greengard sought financial support in order to attend graduate school, and in the process decided against a career in physics. In an interview with Ira Flatow, a talk-show host with National Public Radio's *Talk of the Nation/Science Friday* program (October 13, 2000), Greengard explained, "At the time the only source of support for physics was really the Atomic Energy Commission. This wasn't too many years after the atomic bombs were dropped in Japan, and I felt I didn't want to . . . contribute anything that might be misused."

Greengard found another area that would allow him to apply what he had studied, seeing an opportunity for a rewarding career in an emerging field called "medical physics." As he explained to Flatow, a "physicist's type of approach" was needed, for example, to study the electrical properties of nerve cells and use radioisotopes to track metabolism. In 1948 Greengard began his graduate studies at the University of Pennsylvania, in Philadelphia, which had one of the country's two biophysics departments at the time. Greengard studied under Detlev Bronk, who is widely credited with laying the foundations for the modern field of biophysics. When Bronk left the University of Pennsylvania a short time later to become the president of Johns Hopkins University in Baltimore, Maryland, Greengard followed him. For his doctoral thesis at Johns Hopkins, Greengard studied, in his words, the "chemical changes associated with degeneration and loss of function in nerve axons. It was an early effort to understand the relationship between nerve function and biochemistry," as quoted in a press release posted on the Rockefeller University Web site (October 9, 2000).

After receiving his doctorate in biophysics in 1953, Greengard won several fellowships that allowed him to pursue postdoctoral studies and research in the United Kingdom for the next few years. As a National Science Foundation (NSF) fellow in neurochemistry, he spent two years at the Institute of Psychiatry at the University of London. After receiving a fellowship from the Foundation for Infantile Paralysis, he continued his postdoctoral studies at the Molteno Institute at the University of Cambridge from 1954 to 1955. From 1955 to 1958, he was a Paraplegia Foundation fellow at England's National Institute for Medical Research. A press release on the Rockefeller University Web site (October 9, 2000) states that during his stay in the United Kingdom, "Greengard made important findings about the biochemical regulation of the physiological functioning of brain cells."

In 1958 Greengard returned to the United States and became a fellow at the National Institute for Neurological Diseases and Blindness, part of the National Institutes of Health in Bethesda, Maryland. In 1959 he became the director of the biochemistry department at Geigy Research Labs, in Ardsley, New York, where he developed several drugs to treat depresssion.

Greengard left Geigy in 1967 and became a visiting associate professor of pharmacology at the ALBERT EINSTEIN College of Medicine, in New York City, where he remained on the faculty until 1970. There, his research greatly improved scientists' knowledge of the mechanisms by which local anesthetics work. In 1967 he also obtained an appointment as a visiting professor at Vanderbilt University in Nashville, Tennessee, where he worked in the lab of EARL SUTHERLAND, a biochemist. At Vanderbilt, Sutherland had earlier identified cyclic AMP, a molecule in liver cells that delivers a hormonal message to other cells, instructing them either to store carbohydrate or release it into the bloodstream. Another biochemist, Edward Krebs, subsequently proved that cyclic AMP works by activating an enzyme, a catalytic protein called a protein kinase. For their contributions, Sutherland and Krebs were awarded the Nobel Prize in 1971 and 1992 respectively. In 1968 Greengard became a professor of pharmacology and psychiatry at the Yale University School of Medicine in New Haven, Connecticut. In 1983 he left Yale to teach at Rockefeller University in New York City and serve as the head of the university's Laboratory of Molecular and Cellular Neuroscience.

In the late 1960s, biochemists and researchers knew that chemicals such as dopamine, noradrenaline, and serotonin acted as neurotransmitters in the brain, carrying signals between neurons. However, the exact, step-by-step process of how neurons communicated with each other remained unclear. Impressed with the findings of Sutherland and Krebs, Greengard, while at Vanderbilt, theorized that neurons in the brain might communicate using a mechanism similar to that employed by liver cells. At Yale he began to search the brain for protein kinase, finding it in high concentrations, particularly at the synapses. "This finding made me feel very confident that whatever the kinase was doing in the brain, it wasn't just breaking down carbohydrate,"

Greengard said, as quoted in a press release on the Rockefeller University Web site (October 9, 2000). Upon further observation, Greengard identified the protein kinase in the brain as a key player in protein phosphorylation, a process that regulates protein activity by placing a phosphate molecule on a protein. Acting as a master molecule, protein kinase activates other proteins through this process of adding a phosphate, which causes a change in the target protein's shape.

Greengard and his colleagues observed other cells and found that phosphorylation took place in virtually every tissue in the human body, as well as in a broad range of animals and other organisms. The next step was to prove that protein phosphorylation was regulating nerve signals in the brain. To accomplish this, Greengard and ERIC KANDEL, a fellow neuroscientist, found a way to purify kinases and inject them into individual cells that were not receiving any neurotransmitters. They were then able to compare the kinases' effects on physiological activity with those of neurotransmitters. After being injected with the kinases, the cells changed shape, indicating that phosphorylation had occurred. Greengard and Kandel were then able to observe how, through a series of biochemical steps, a phosphorylated protein produces in target cells the physiological response characteristic of a neurotransmitter. In 1972 Greengard identified synapsin I, a phosphoprotein that regulates the release of neurotransmitters. During the early 1970s, he also identified a receptor for the neurotransmitter dopamine, the first neurotransmitter receptor to be characterized biochemically—in other words, according to the specific neurotransmitter from which it receives signals. When signals transmitted by dopamine go awry, they can cause a number of neurological and psychiatric disorders, including Parkinson's disease, schizophrenia, attention deficit hyperactivity disorder, and substance abuse. Greengard also identified a phosphoprotein, named DARPP-32, in the basal ganglia region of the brain. This region is responsible for controlling the body's movement and also helps determine a person's mood, alertness, and sensory perception. DARPP-32 plays a key role in the process by which dopamine produces its effects in the brain.

On the basis of his research and findings, Greengard created a model describing slow synaptic transmission, the physiological process by which neurotransmitters such as dopamine, serotonin, and noradrenaline affect changes in the function of target cells that may last from seconds to days. Slow synaptic transmission is involved in a number of basal functions in the nervous system, and is important in determining alertness and mood, for example. Slow synaptic transmission can also, in certain instances, regulate fast synaptic transmission, which controls speech, movement, and sensory perception. When a neurotransmitter such as dopamine stimulates a receptor in the cell membrane, it causes an elevation of cyclic AMP, a "second messenger," in the cell. In turn, cyclic AMP activates Protein Kinase A, which adds phosphate molecules to other proteins in the neuron. "These protein phosphorylations," according to a press release on the Nobel e-Museum Web site (October 9, 2000), "lead to changes of a number of proteins with different functions in the cell. When for instance proteins in ion channels in the cell membrane are influenced, the excitability of a nerve cell and its ability to send impulses along its branches changes," thus affecting its communication with other neurons.

Greengard and his research team eventually identified over 100 phosphoproteins that are found exclusively in the brain. At the time of their initial findings, Greengard and Kandel's research into phosphorylation wasn't taken seriously by most biochemists and neuroscientists, who were concerned only with the question of whether or not a neuron fired a signal to another neuron. "No one was terribly interested—it wasn't ready for prime time," Greengard said, as quoted by Nicholas Wade, a reporter for the *New York Times* (October 10, 2000). "People said, 'Poor Paul, I'm sure he'll find his way back onto the right path.'" Greengard was awarded the Nobel Prize in Physiology or Medicine in 2000. He shared the prize with ARVID CARLSSON, a pharmacologist at the University of Göteborg in Sweden, and Eric Kandel.

Greengard's findings have increased scientists' understanding of how certain drugs are able to produce their effects on the body. The effectiveness and, in other cases, the toxicity of several classes of common antipsychotic, hallucinogenic, and antidepressant drugs can now be explained in terms of specific neurochemical changes, including phosphorylation, that affect the transmission of nerve signals in the brain. In an interview posted on the Online News Hour Web site (October 11, 2000), Greengard explained that by "elucidating the biochemical steps by which the dopamine produces its effects in its target cells, it's been possible to learn more about" a number of neurological and psychiatric diseases and "develop new targets for pharmaceutical industries to develop drugs that hopefully will have a better therapeutic action and fewer side effects."

Over the past several decades, Paul Greengard's contributions to neuroscience have been recognized many times. He is the recipient of the University of Pittsburgh's Dickson Prize and Medal in Medicine (1977); the Ciba-Geigy Drew Award (1979); the New York Academy of Sciences Award in Biological and Medical Sciences (1980); the 3M Life Sciences Award of the Federation of American Societies for Experimental Biology (1987); the Bristol Myers Award for Distinguished Achievement in Neuroscience Research (1989); the Mental Health Research Achievement Award (1987); the National Academy of Sciences Award in the Neurosciences (1991); the American Philosophy Society's Karl Spencer Lashley Prize (1993); the Society for Neuroscience Ralph W. Gerard Prize in Neuroscience (1984); the Biochemical Society's Thudichum Medal (1996); the Charles A. Dana Award for Pioneering Achievements in Health (1997), which Greengard shared with Eric Kandel; the Metropolitan Life Foundation Award for Medical Research (1998); and the Ellison Medical Foundation Senior Scholar Award (1999), among many other awards. Greengard is a member of the National Academy of Sciences and its Institute of Medicine, and of the American Academy of Arts and Sciences. He is also a foreign member of the Royal Swedish Academy of Arts and Sciences, and a member of the Norwegian Academy of Arts and Letters.

Greengard donated his share of the Nobel Prize money to Rockefeller University in order to establish an annual award for women in biomedical research. The award is being created to honor the memory of his mother. He is the author of the book *Advances in Biochemical Psychopharmacology* (1969), as well as many articles and research papers published in medical and scientific journals. In addition to serving as Vincent Astor Professor and head of the Laboratory of Molecular and Cellular Neuroscience at Rocke-

feller, he is also the director of the Fisher Center for Research on Alzheimer's Disease. Paul Greengard is married to Ursula von Rydingsvard, a sculptor, and the couple, who have three children, lives in New York City. Of his research, Greengard said, "We worked on this for many years without competition, because people thought we were insane," as quoted from the Rockefeller University press release.

ABOUT: Los Angeles Times October 10, 2000; New York Times October 10, 2000, October 15, 2000; Nobel e-Museum Web site; On-line NewsHour; Rockefeller University Web site; Talk of the Nation/Science Friday (on-line) October 10, 2000.

Courtesy Fred Hutchinson Cancer Research Center

Hartwell, Leland H.

(October 30, 1939–) Nobel Prize for Physiology or Medicine, 2001 (shared with Paul Nurse and R. Timothy Hunt)

The medical researcher Leland H. Hartwell was born on October 30, 1939 in Los Angeles. "I came from a family that was very non-academic, so I didn't recognize at an early stage the clear interest that I had in science as a child," he told Shelly Esposito, a professor of molecular genetics and cell biology at the University of Chicago, during an

October 1998 interview transcribed for the Albert and Mary Lasker Foundation Web site. "Looking back, it's easy to see now. I always collected bugs and took things apart and spent time at the library trying to learn things about radios and astronomy and various stuff like that without noticing that my peers weren't spending their time the same way." Hartwell also occupied his free hours by working for his father, who made neon signs, and for a time became chiefly interested in electricity. Despite his wide-ranging natural curiosity about science-related subjects, Hartwell has acknowledged that upon entering high school, he had little direction and a less-than-impressive academic record. He became a member of a Los Angeles gang called the Sinbads, who sported black wool jackets emblazoned with an image of a dragon, and spent his nights drinking and cruising city streets.

By midway through his junior year in high school, however, Hartwell had lost interest in the gang and enrolled at Glendale Junior College after graduation. There, he took several science courses, receiving broad encouragement from his teachers. Meanwhile, a counselor at Glendale arranged for Hartwell to interview with a visiting professor from the California Institute of Technology (Cal Tech), in Pasadena; soon after, he was admitted to that prestigious school as a second-year student "only because the recruiter had to fill in the sophomore class which was depleted by the dropouts after freshman year," Hartwell was quoted as saying in a profile of him in the *American Society of Cell Biology (ASCB) Newsletter* (February 1999). At Cal Tech, Hartwell told Esposito, "I discovered a whole fabulous world of science that I really didn't even know existed." He added that the school "was just an unbelievable sort of fairy tale place for me. You were spending your time thinking about really interesting scientific issues, and the faculty there treated the undergraduates like they were colleagues rather than students. It just gave me a sense of involvement and the possibility of participating in science, sort of an invitation, I guess I would say, that I look back on and just cherish those years." He initially chose to study physics, but a class on DNA prompted him to join the ranks of the six biology majors in his graduating class. (Biology was an unpopular major because of students' belief that there were few available jobs in the field.) Cal Tech gave undergraduates the opportunity to do research that would have been delegated to graduate students at other institutions, and Hartwell worked in a number of professors' labs during the academic year and summers.

Upon completion of his B.S. degree, in 1961, Hartwell entered the Massachusetts Institute of Technology, in Cambridge, where he studied gene regulation under the microbiologist Boris Magasanik. "He would come by every afternoon and ask you how your experiments were going," Hartwell told Esposito, "so it sort of kept you at a feverish pace for having results every day, but he never told you what to do. . . . He made it very clear that you were plotting your own course. . . . I think it . . . really helped me develop that sense of: I was the master of my research, and I had to find my own way." After receiving his Ph.D., in 1964, Hartwell began postdoctoral work at the Salk Institute of Biological Studies, in La Jolla, California, where he studied cell division under RENATO DULBECCO, a leader in that area of research. The Salk Institute was just getting off the ground, and its facilities were, in Hartwell's words, "a series of trailers." Despite the lack of amenities, he enjoyed a period of concentrated learning there, during which he studied cell division in mammals and became interested in the timing of the steps in cell division and abnormal cell growth.

In 1965 Hartwell took a position as an assistant professor at the University of California at Irvine. By the end of his year at the Salk Institute, he had grown frustrated with the research methods available, because he felt they were inadequate for the study of physiologically complex organisms. During the several months before his lab equipment arrived in Irvine, he searched for an organism simpler than mammals that was nonetheless relatively genetically advanced. He settled on baker's yeast—Saccharymyces cerevisiae—a one-celled fungus, and became one of very few scientists using yeast cells to research cell division. At that time few people recognized that yeast, like the fruit fly and the mouse, is an excellent "model organism," in that in many respects its systems are analogous to those in humans. As a young scientist embarking on a career, Hartwell was therefore taking a big risk by studying yeast. He now considers this leap of the imagination—which enabled him to see "that a study of cell division, even though it was motivated by an interest in human cells and medical problems like cancer, needed to be explored in a much simpler system using genetics as a powerful tool," as he explained to Esposito—his most significant contribution to science. Since the late 1980s yeast has been a popular experimental subject in research involving genetics and basic cellular processes, among other fields.

In 1968 Hartwell became an associate professor at the University of Washington, largely because "it was the premier genetics department, and I had not received any formal genetic training," as he was quoted as saying in the *ASCB Newsletter* (February 1997). He set up a lab at the university, where, at any given time, he oversaw an average of eight researchers, supported mainly by a single grant (renewed periodically) from the National Institutes of Health. In 1969 Brian Reid, an undergraduate working in Hartwell's lab who later joined him as professor at the University of Washington, began taking photographs of his research subjects through a microscope. Reid's work involved genes whose mutations became apparent only at certain temperatures, and in his photomicrographs he captured images of cells at stages when they were unable to divide. This work gave Hartwell much new information about the cell-division cycle—the process by which one cell becomes two, thus enabling an organism to grow—and he and his co-workers spent the next five years studying cell-cycle mutants.

In a series of yeast experiments from 1970–1971, Hartwell attempted to identify genes that might control the cell-division cycle, helping it move efficiently through several phases that allow the cell to duplicate its genetic material and divide. By studying mutations in the genes and looking at the primary defect each caused, Hartwell succeeded in determining the function of more than 100 individual genes involved in regulating the cell cycle, including ones that guided protein synthesis and other cellular processes involved in cell division. He found that one of these genes, which he designated CDC28, played a significant role in controlling the first stage of each cell cycle; Hartwell named this gene "start." Although all the ramifications of his research would not become clear until decades later, his findings provided invaluable insights into cell division and spurred the emergence of

cell biology as an important specialty. Hartwell's first published work on yeast appeared in the *Journal of Bacteriology*, in 1967, and what is considered his groundbreaking article was published in the *Proceedings of the National Academy of Sciences*, in 1970. "For over 30 years, a majority of the key insights into the cell cycle have been made by him," Mark Groudine, who directs the basic sciences division at the Hutch, told Jim Kling for *Current Biology* (1997).

In 1974 Hartwell theorized that the cell cycles of yeast and human cells had specific similarities, and that the cells had "originated in a common past," as Susan Luce described for the *Seattle Times* (August 8, 1995). In 1987 Hartwell's idea was corroborated by the work of PAUL NURSE, who found that a particular human gene that performs a specific function in the cell-division cycle can perform that same function when placed in a yeast cell that lacks the gene normally responsible for that function. That human gene and the gene it replaced in the yeast cell are called homologues; they perform the same function in different species. Homologues from different species sometimes have almost identical DNA. Scientists theorized that where there was one pair of homologue genes—the one consisting of that particular human gene and that particular yeast gene—there might be many more, and this idea proved to be correct. Hartwell and other scientists have since identified human counterparts to some of the genes that Hartwell isolated in yeast, and it is believed that many of the genes he discovered are found in both plants and animals. Thus Hartwell's research on how genes control cell division in yeast became directly applicable to the understanding of cell division in humans, and that knowledge is shedding new light on many diseases, including cancer.

In 1983 Hartwell took a sabbatical to do research at Stanford University, in California, funded by a Guggenheim fellowship he was awarded that same year. He spent the following year, again on sabbatical, at the Fred Hutchinson Cancer Research Center. The Hutchinson Center, sometimes referred to as the Hutch, one of 35 comprehensive cancer research centers designated and funded by the National Cancer Institute, is one of the few such institutions that have strong faculties in four distinct research divisions: basic sciences, which involves research in cellular and molecular biology; clinical research, which involves observations of patients and includes the center's bone-marrow transplant program, the largest in the world; public-health sciences, which encompasses research in biostatistics, cancer prevention, and epidemiology; and human biology, in which techniques drawn from molecular biology, cellular biology, and genetics are used along with those of other disciplines to achieve a greater understanding of human biology and diseases. Hartwell had briefly done research on cancer biology early in his career, and he had always been interested in the implications his work on cell division held for the understanding of cancer.

At about the time of his sabbaticals, Hartwell and Ted Weinert, a postdoctoral fellow working in his lab, began identifying genes that ensured that events in the cell cycle happened according to plan. These genes, which they dubbed "checkpoints," made sure that each stage of cell division was complete before the next began. Checkpoint genes also recognize defects in cells, caused by, for example, radiation or exposure to chemicals, and will prompt pauses in the cell-division cycle that allow DNA-repair mechanisms to fix the defects before the cell divides. When the checkpoint genes themselves have mutations that cause them to malfunction, cancer may result. Thus, a greater understanding of the checkpoint genes may provide important clues for the treatment of the disease.

By the mid-1990s Hartwell believed that strides in molecular biology had created a potential for major advances in the study of many diseases. "The entire yeast genome has been sequenced," he stated for an article on the Fred Hutchinson Cancer Research Center Web site (April 4, 1996). "There are 7,000 genes in yeast and 70,000 genes in humans. We will know the identity of most of those genes by the end of the century. While it will still be a long time before we understand their functions, we are now in a position to look at the impact of genetic factors in disease." This conviction was among the many reasons behind Hartwell's decision, in 1996, to become senior scientific adviser at the Hutch. In that position, which was created specifically for him by the center's director, Robert Day, Hartwell led a project dubbed the Interdivisional Research and

Training Initiative, which was intended to promote interdisciplinary education, training, and research among the center's four divisions. According to Hartwell, while the need to increase such cooperation was widely recognized among the biomedical research community at large, no other institutions—medicals schools, universities, and cancer centers—were making comprehensive efforts to do so. "When we've really got it right, it will be natural for the students to look at the full dimensions of whatever they work on," Hartwell was quoted as saying on the center's Web site (April 4, 1996). "That is, they will think about the basic, the clinical, and epidemiological dimensions of their problem, and they will find it easy to talk to people in each discipline. The cross-cultural exchange will be easy for students. That clearly is not there now."

While reactions to the initiative among scientists at the Hutch ranged from approval to skepticism, many were impressed by Hartwell's interest in tackling such a problem. "It was refreshing to me that a senior person with a very substantial reputation as a basic biological scientist was willing to move his base to [the Hutch] and commit half his time to interdisciplinary research program development," Ross Prentice, the director of the center's public-health division, told Jim Kling. "As scientists we tend to have the knee-jerk reaction that whatever we don't know about can't be important, so it takes somebody with confidence to step out and endorse the groups and areas that they are not a part of." Hartwell's interest in stimulating collaboration stems from his belief that such interdisciplinary work, by helping scientists to see "the big picture," as Kling put it, will speed the discovery of effective cancer treatments. In 1997 Day retired from his post as the Hutchinson center's president and director and, in a vote of confidence in Hartwell's initiative, Hartwell was named Day's replacement. Although as head administrator of an institution with 2,300 employees Hartwell has less time to conduct his own research, he still maintains a lab at the Hutch. He has expressed wholehearted optimism about the future of cancer treatment.

On October 8, 2001 Hartwell was honored with the Nobel Prize in Physiology or Medicine "for his discoveries of a specific class of genes that control the cell cycle," according to a press release on the Nobel e-Museum Web site. Specifically, the Nobel Assembly cited Hartwell's breakthroughs in locating the "start" gene and developing the concept of checkpoint genes as his major contributions toward aiding better understanding of the cell cycle. Hartwell shared his Nobel Prize with Paul Nurse and R. TIMOTHY HUNT, two researchers at the Imperial Cancer Research Fund in London, England, for their separate discoveries of key regulators within the cell cycle. The work of these three scientists is already providing broad applications in many areas of biomedical research, particularly in cancer research and tumor diagnostics.

In addition to the Nobel Prize, Hartwell has been the recipient of numerous prestigious awards, including: the Eli Lilly Award in Microbiology and Immunology (1973); the National Institutes of Health Merit Award (1990), the General Motors Sloan Award (1991), the Hoffman La Roche Mattia Award (1991), the Gairdner Foundation International Award for Achievements in Science (1992), the Sloan-Kettering Cancer Center Katherine Berkan Judd Award (1994), the Genetics Society of America Medal (1994), the Albert Lasker Basic Medical Research Award (1998), the Susan G. Ko-

men Breast Cancer Foundation-Brinker International Award (1998), the American Cancer Society Medal of Honor (1999), the Leopold Griffuel Prize (2000), and the Massry Prize (2000). He is a member of several professional societies, including the American Academy of Arts and Sciences, the American Academy of Microbiology, the American Society of Microbiology, the American Society for Cell Biology, the American Association for Cancer Research, the Genetics Society of America, and the National Academy of Sciences.

Hartwell has made his home in Seattle for more than 30 years. His sons, Todd and Gregg, live near him in Washington State, while his daughter, Sherie, lives on the East Coast with her husband, a molecular biologist at the University of Connecticut. Hartwell's wife, Theresa Naujack, works as a photographer at the Hutchinson Center.

ABOUT: Albert and Mary Lasker Foundation Web site; American Society for Cell Biology Newsletter February 1999; Current Biology 1997; Fred Hutchinson Cancer Research Center Web site; Nobel e-Museum Web site; Quest Winter 1997; Seattle Times August 8, 1995.

Heckman, James

(April 19, 1944–) Nobel Prize for Economics, 2000 (shared with Daniel McFadden)

The economist James Heckman was born on April 19, 1944 in Chicago, Illinois. He attended Colorado College, in Colorado Springs, and earned a bachelor's degree in mathematics in 1965. In an interview with Bertil Holmlund at the Nobel Foundation (December 13, 2000), archived as an audio file on their e-Museum Web site, Heckman recalled that as an undergraduate, he enrolled in an economics course out of curiosity and was given a copy of PAUL SAMUELSON's classic text *Foundations of Economic Analysis* (1947), which is widely considered one of the most important books on mathematical economics, credited with helping to shape the field of modern economics. Hooked, Heckman went on to get his master's and Ph.D. in economics at Princeton

University, in Princeton, New Jersey, graduating in 1971. Heckman spent a few years as a research fellow at the National Bureau of Economic Research and then in 1973 accepted a teaching position in the economics department at the University of Chicago, where he has worked ever since. He is also the director of social program evaluation at the university's Harris School of Public Policy and a senior research fellow at American Bar Foundation, an independent institute that performs empirical research on law and legal institutions.

Whether it be a report from the World Economic Forum, in Davos, Switzerland; the latest pronouncement made by Federal Reserve Chairman Alan Greenspan; or stock quotes from Wall Street; news from the world of economics can seem quite remote from most people's daily lives. In this respect, the work of Heckman is unusual: he has devoted much of his career to studying the economics of individuals' everyday lives—how people live and labor, and how they are affected by public policies.

Courtesy of James J. Heckman

James Heckman

Heckman works in a specialized field that combines statistics and economics, called "econometrics." "The methods [he and fellow Nobel Laureate DANIEL MCFADDEN] have developed have solid foundations in economic theory, but have evolved in close interplay with applied research on social problems," a Royal Swedish Academy press release, published on the Nobel e-Museum Web site, explained. "Real-life data often isn't in the right form for answering important questions," Robert Michael, one of Heckman's colleagues at the University of Chicago, explained to Jerry Hirsch for the *Los Angeles Times* (October 12, 2000). "Jim's contribution has been in recognizing that, being dissatisfied with that and going out and finding statistical techniques and improved data, so that one can in fact address important topics and get the answers that are important." Heckman has studied the impact of civil rights legislation and affirmative action programs in the United States; of taxation on labor supply and human capital accumulation; of public and private job training on earnings and employment; and of unionism on labor markets in developing countries. Many observers have speculated that Heckman and Daniel McFadden's work on pressing social issues was a factor in their being named to the 2000 Nobel Prize in Economics. "Awarding the prize to the two economists highlights a shift in the academy's approach, following the award of the prize to India's AMARTYA SEN for his contributions to welfare economics two years ago," a *BBC News* (October 11, 2000, on-line) reporter wrote. "That shift has led to a greater recognition of the role of government in shaping economic life, both through its role in regulation and institution-building and through its investment in human capital through education." "Economics is a field where you're solving real problems," Heckman emphasized to Charles Seife in *Science* (October 20, 2000). "Being able to tackle real problems has always been an attraction for me."

Much of Heckman's research has been in examining labor patterns. He has evaluated job training programs, measured wage differences between men and women, and estimated how the duration of unemployment affects a person's chances of getting a job, among other things. "Heckman has improved our understanding of the labor market and salaries," Bertil Holmlund told a *PBS News* reporter (October 11, 2000, on-line), adding that he is "at the forefront of our understanding of the welfare system in the U.S." "With the help of Heckman's models, you can figure out what effects one year of education will have on wages and one can study the differences in wages between men and women given a certain education and age," Karl Gustav Joereskog, a member of the Royal Swedish Academy of Sciences, told a reporter for *BBC News*.

During the late 1980s and into the 1990s, Heckman conducted groundbreaking research on race and public policy under the auspices of the American Bar Foundation. In one study, Heckman and a group of researchers assessed the correlation between federal anti-discrimination policies and what is described on Heckman's Research Center Web site as "the dramatic improvement of black economic status in manufacturing that occurred in South Carolina in the mid-1960's." After analyzing data on wages and employment by race, sex, and industry, the researchers found that the federal programs had contributed significantly to the upward trend. A related study looked at the contribution of Title VII of the 1964 Civil Rights Act, which forbids discrimination in employment, to the economic advancement of African-Americans between 1960 and 1975. Heckman's group concluded that a variety of factors accounted for this phenomenon, including fewer African-Americans in the work force, and improvements in education. However, according to the 1991 study, archived on Heckman's Research Center Web site, "a considerable portion of black economic gains cannot be explained using traditional supply-side arguments." This, say the researchers, "suggests a large role for government intervention." The Princeton University demographer Burton Singer commented on the significance of this report. "Government legislation had a more profound impact than schools per se," Singer told Charles Seife, adding that activism in the African-American community had also been key. This surprising conclusion, Singer said, "had almost been ignored by the economic community."

In 1995 Heckman and two other researchers embarked on what they termed the "Cognitive Ability Project," conceived as a response to the furor created by Richard J. Herrnstein and Charles Murray's book *The Bell Curve: Intelligence and Structure in American Life*, published earlier that year. In *The Bell Curve*, Herrnstein and Murray characterize the U.S. economy as a meritocracy, in which differences in wages— including those between men and women's earnings, and between the earnings of blacks and other ethnic minorities in comparison with those of whites—can be explained by differences in cognitive ability. According to Ed Vytlacil's synopsis on Heckman's Research Center Web site, Vytlacil, Heckman, and others were interested in examining "the relationship between measured cognitive ability and wages in a more serious manner than was done by Herrnstein and Murray." Heckman and his colleagues found that although cognitive ability can be correlated with wages, this correlation doesn't explain the variance in wages over time. Instead, they showed that cognitive ability is unequally rewarded across race and gender. Their conclusions are published as part of *Intelligence, Genes and Success: Is it all in the Genes? Scientists Respond to The Bell Curve* (1997). During a University of Chicago press conference, a transcript of which is archived on the University Web site, the fellow economist and 1992 Nobel laureate GARY BECKER described Heckman as an "economist's economist": "Virtually all of Jim's work deals with important practical questions, but deals with it the way a scientist deals with questions and not the way an advocate deals with questions," he said.

Although Heckman and Daniel McFadden have never collaborated, they have been friends for 30 years and have exchanged ideas often. Heckman told a reporter for *PBS News* (on-line) that although McFadden was never his teacher in the classroom, he has learned a lot from him. Through his career, Heckman has adapted and extended McFadden's methods in addition to developing his own tools. In their award citation, the Royal Swedish Academy of Sciences in particular praised Heckman "for his development of theory and methods for analyzing selective samples." Data collected through a survey of shoppers in a mall cannot be considered truly random, or "unselective," for example, because only certain types of shoppers will agree to stop and fill out a survey—perhaps those who are interested in marketing, or those who have spare time. Prior to Heckman's work, economists had no reliable method of accounting and adjusting for the biases in research data created by this phenomenon of self-selection. As a reporter for Reuters phrased it in the *New York Times* (October 11, 2000, on-line), Heckman's work "made it possible to work with samples of data taking into account particular characteristics of people surveyed that may be unknown to the researcher." During the University of Chicago press conference for Heckman, Robert Michael provided a real-life example of this research quandary by way of the Job Training Partnership Act (JPTA), which provides job training for low-income workers. Michael pointed to a study in which the earnings of workers who had gone through the training program were compared with those of workers who had not. "Those that have taken the training are not a subset, a random set, of all unskilled workers," Michael said. "They may be more motivated. They may be more skilled. They may be more energetic. They may be luckier. They have selected themselves into those programs, so one can't infer from the difference in their earnings compared to those without the program whether the program generated the increase in their earnings. Mr. Heckman has [developed] the technique for adjusting for that kind of selectivity." Heckman's first contribution lay in recognizing the misleading nature of much statistical data; he then came up with statistical tools that allow researchers to compensate for the inherently selective nature of sample data.

Heckman was in the Brazilian city of Rio de Janeiro, where he had been working with young Latin American economists, when he learned that he and McFadden had won the prize. At a press conference held at the University of Chicago, Heckman said via speaker phone that he was "very honored" and that he felt a "sense of deep gratitude," adding that the prize came as a complete surprise. "All surprises aren't as happy as this one is."

Heckman is a fellow of the Econometric Society and an elected member of the American Academy of Arts and Sciences and the National Academy of Sciences. He is a founding member of the faculty of the University of Chicago's Irving B. Harris Graduate School of Public Policy Studies, and a Fellow of the American Statistical As-sociation. In addition to the Nobel Prize, which has only been awarded to economists since 1968, Heckman received the John Bates Clark Award of the American Economic Association in 1983.

James Heckman and his wife, Lynne, have two children, Alma and Jonathan. When asked by an *Associated Press* reporter (October 11, 2000, on-line) how he plans to spend his half of the nearly million-dollar prize, Heckman quipped, "I'm going to pay a lot of taxes."

ABOUT: BBC News (on-line) October 11, 2000; Chicago Tribune (on-line) October 11, 2000; Los Angeles Times October 12, 2000; Nobel e-Museum Web site; Science October 20, 2000; University of Chicago News Web site.

Courtesy of Polymers & Organic Solids/UC - Santa Barbara

Heeger, Alan J.

(January 22, 1936–) Nobel Prize in Chemistry, 2000 (shared with Hideki Shirakawa and Alan MacDiarmid)

The physicist Alan J. Heeger was born in Sioux City, Iowa, on January 22, 1936. In 1957 he received a B.S. with high distinction from the University of Nebraska in Lincoln. He earned his doctorate from the University of California at Berkeley in 1961. In 1962 he became an assistant professor of physics at the University of Pennsylvania, in Philadelphia, moving up to associate professor in 1964, and full professor in 1967, a post he held until 1982. From 1974 to 1981 he was the director of the Laboratory for Research on the Structure of Matter at Penn, as the university is often called, and in his final two years there he was acting vice-provost for research.

It was while at Penn in the early 1970s that Heeger first made the discoveries that led to his selection for the Nobel Prize. He and ALAN MACDIARMID, who was also a faculty member at Penn at that time, were conducting experiments with polymers, a type of molecule that forms long, repeating chains; most plastics are polymers, and the two scientists were studying the changes that occur as insulators are chemically transformed into metals. In particular, they were working with the inorganic (containing no carbon) polymer sulphur nitride in the form of a golden metallic-looking film. In Japan, HIDEKI SHIRAKAWA had been experimenting with new ways to synthesize the organic polymer polyacetylene. During one of these experiments, a thousand times too much catalyst was accidentally added to the solution, and to the researchers' surprise, a silvery, metallic-looking film was produced. When Shirakawa happened to meet MacDiarmid at a conference, during a coffee break, Shirakawa mentioned the result produced by the extra catalyst. MacDiarmid invited

Shirakawa to Penn, and Heeger joined them to do further research on polyacetylene. Soon they had found a way to oxidize (or remove electrons from) polyacetylene using iodine gas in a process known as doping. When one of the scientists in Heeger's research group measured the conductivity of the doped polyacetylene, a form called *trans*-polyacetylene, it was discovered that the conductivity had increased by a factor of 10 million. Heeger, MacDiarmid, Shirakawa, and other members of their research team soon shared their findings in the article "Synthesis of Electrically Conducting Organic Polymers: Halogen Derivatives of Polyacetylene," published in the *Journal of Chemical Society, Chemical Communications* (Summer 1977).

Essentially, doping is a way of making semiconducting plastics act more like metals, which have electrons that are able to move freely along chains of molecules, creating an electric current. (Semiconductors are materials that find use in electronic device applications.) A polyacetylene molecule consists of a long chain of carbon molecules bound by immobile "sigma" bonds and by the "pi" electrons that are delocalized along the polymer chain. Each carbon atom is also bound to a hydrogen atom. Polyacetylene is a semiconducting polymer with all of the "pi" electrons in filled bands; in order to allow electricity to flow along the polyacetylene chain, electrons either have to be taken away from (through oxidation) or added to (through reduction) the delocalized pi bonds, thereby providing charge carriers which are mobile. Heeger was awarded a patent on April 5, 1977 for his method of doping polymers.

Various other conductive polymers with different molecular structures were soon discovered, each with different potential uses. As demonstrated by the Heeger-MacDiarmid collaboration, polymers can also be used as semiconductors. The principle interest in both semiconductive and metallic polymers is in using them to create low-cost electronic components and integrated circuits, which are often made of silicon or other, similar materials. In theory, polymers could be inexpensively processed into integrated circuits by way of a technology similar to that used in inkjet printing. One application already developed for conductive polymers, specifically polythiophene derivatives, is as an anti-static treatment for photographic film, which can be ruined by static electricity. Integrated circuits made of polymers may also soon be used to mark supermarket products in such a way that people will be able to check out groceries without removing them from their carts. Doped polyaniline is used to reduce static in carpeting and as a coating to reduce electromagnetic radiation from computer screens. Another useful property of some semiconductive polymers is electroluminescence, which means that they can be stimulated to emit light. Products under active development utilizing polymer electroluminescence include energy-saving light sources, lasers, thin and flexible TV and computer screens, and mobile phone displays.

In 1982 Heeger left the University of Pennsylvania to become a professor of physics and director of the Institute for Polymers and Organic Solids at University of California at Santa Barbara (UCSB), positions he still holds. In 1987 he also became a professor of materials in UCSB's engineering department. In 1990 Heeger founded the UNIAX Corporation. He served as chairman from 1990 through 1999 and as president and CEO from 1990–1994, and again from 1994–1999. The company, which develops polymer-based light-emitting display products, was sold to DuPont in March 2000. Since 1999 Heeger has served on the Board of Directors and the Scientific Advisory Board of QTL Biosystems, a developer of medical diagnostics and biosensing technologies utilizing conductive polymers.

The decision to award Heeger and his colleagues the 2000 Nobel Prize in Chemistry stirred some controversy; however, it is largely recognized that the discovery of semiconducting and metallic polymers and the development of their potential uses owed much to Heeger and his collaborators' efforts. "Now the research has more emphasis on semiconducting polymers," Zhenan Bao, a chemist for Lucent Technologies, told Robert F. Service for *Science* (October 20, 2000). "But it's all based on [Heeger, MacDiarmid, and Shirakawa's] early concepts." When asked by J. Gorman for *Science News* (October 14, 2000) how he felt about winning the award, Heeger said, "You can't explain how you feel. I knew it was important work back in the 1970s . . . but it took help from colleagues all over the world to bring those early ideas to a reality that will make these materials important in technology and lead to real products."

One of the possible future directions of computing would involve further reducing the size of the integrated circuits that serve as the brains of computers, which would greatly increase processing speeds. Many scientists believe that the size of integrated circuits will eventually be reduced to that of individual molecules. According to the Swedish Academy press release, published on the Nobel e-museum Web site, "A computer corresponding to what we now carry around in our bags would suddenly fit inside a watch.". Conductive and semiconductive polymers would likely play an important role in such advancements. As Heeger said to Nicola Jones for *New Scientist* (October 21, 2000), "I think we're on the verge of a revolution in polymer electronics."

Heeger's work marked an important advancement in interdisciplinary science. Collaboration and cooperative research across disciplines have since become increasingly important strategies in furthering scientific endeavor. Heeger has continued to explore the precise mechanisms involved in the conductivity of plastics and promote the development of practical applications for his discoveries, through both his work in the academic sphere, primarily at the UUCSB, and his business ventures. He has published more than 660 scholarly papers.

Heeger's awards and honors include the Alfred P. Sloan Foundation Fellowship (1963–65); the John Simon Guggenheim Foundation Fellowship (1968–69); the American Physical Society Fellowship (1968); the Oliver E. Buckley Prize for Condensed Matter Physics (1983); the John Scott Award (1989); the Charles A. Stiefvater Lectureship Award from the University of Nebraska at Lincoln (1994); and the Balzan Prize for Science of New Materials (1995). He has received honorary doctorates from the University of Linkoping in Sweden, the Abo Akademi University in Finland, the University of Mons-Hainaut in Belgium, the University of Nebraska, the University of Massachusetts at Lowell, the Japan Advanced Institute of Science and Technology, and the South China University of Technology. He was elected to the National Academy of Science (USA) and, as a Foreign Member, to the Korean Academy of Science in 2001. Also in 2001, he received the UC Santa Barbara Medal and the President's Medal of the University of Pennsylvania for Distinguished Achievement. Heeger is married, has two children, and lives in Santa Barbara, California.

ABOUT: Nature February 4, 1999; New Scientist October 21, 2000; New York Times October 11, 2000; Nobel e-Museum Web site; PR Newswire October 16, 2000; Science October 20, 2000; Science News October 14, 2000.

© Getty Images

Hume, John

(January 18, 1937–) Nobel Prize for Peace, 1998 (shared with David Trimble)

The politician JOHN HUME was born into the political and religious turmoil of Northern Ireland on January 18, 1937, in the city of Londonderry. Hume learned from his father, Samuel, a shipyard riveter who could not find work after World War II, the economic and social disadvantages of being raised in the Catholic minority. (Hume's mother, Anne, supported the family by working in a shirt factory.) Hume never believed, however, in the violent overthrow of the Protestant majority, as advocated by the Irish Republican Army (IRA), a paramilitary group that sought to end British rule in Northern Ireland and reunify the province with the Republic of Ireland. In an interview with a writer for *Forbes* (August 14, 1995), Hume explained one of his father's major lessons: "One day my Dad and I went to a nationalist meeting and they were waving the flag," he said. "Everyone was getting emotional, me included. My father put his hand on my shoulder and said, 'Don't get involved in that, son.' 'Why not, Dad?' I said. [He replied,] 'You can't eat a flag.'"

In 1947 Hume won a scholarship from the British Labour Party. "My life was changed because I passed an exam," he told a reporter for *Commonweal* (November 20, 1998). He entered grammar school at St. Columba's College, a co-educational boarding school in Dublin, where he studied alongside SEAMUS HEANEY, a poet and playwright who would go on to win the 1996 Nobel Prize for Literature. He then attended the National College of St. Patrick, at Maynooth, in County Kildare, intending to study for the priesthood. Ultimately, however, he decided to abandon that pursuit. "It just wasn't for me," he told a reporter for the *New Statesman* (September 19, 1997). "I never talk about it."

After his time in Maynooth, Hume turned to teaching. For several years he taught French and history at St. Columba's College, his alma mater. During this time, Hume, who has also held positions as a research fellow at Dublin's Trinity College and as an associate fellow at Harvard University's Center for International Affairs, began to get involved in political activism.

Hume had been born less than a generation after the British government partitioned Ireland, in 1920. In that year the British Parliament passed the Government of Ireland Act, which split Ireland into two self-governing districts under the control of the British Empire: Northern Ireland (also known as Ulster), which was more industrial, overwhelmingly Protestant, and loyal to the British crown and the Irish Free State (now the Republic of Ireland), which was Catholic and considerably more agricultural. The British, reeling from the political and religious division in Ireland during World War I, felt such a separation would alleviate tensions. This, however, proved false. Tensions continued to grow after Ireland established its political independence within the British Commonwealth in 1937 and its total independence in 1948. During this time many Catholics, in search of better economic conditions, immigrated from the Republic

to the more industrial north, but found only economic and political discrimination waiting for them. Between the 1920s and 1960s, violent conflicts between Catholics and Protestants occasionally flared on both sides of the partition, as Catholics sought to establish stronger ties with the Republic, while Protestants remained loyal to the crown.

By 1964 such tensions were about to break out into full-scale civil war. John Hume, still at this time a teacher, was repelled by the terrorist tactics of the IRA. Wanting to take nonviolent social action he helped to establish a housing association to build homes for Catholics. Local government denied him permission, spurring Hume, albeit unwillingly, into politics. "They had divided the city into three wards," he recalled to a reporter for the *Chicago Tribune* (November 18, 1986). "Two were 60–40 Protestant–Catholic and the third was 100 percent Catholic. It had eight representatives [on the council] but the other two had 12, so you see how they worked it." The Catholic area was full, but no new homes were being built in the other wards, for fear of shifting the political balance. "Our objective was to house people," he told the *Chicago Tribune* reporter, "but [the government's refusal] led to great agitation and there was a protest march which I helped organize." Although the march was intended to be a peaceful demonstration, a riot ensued, and Hume was beaten and dragged through the street by British soldiers. In 1969, the same year he married fellow activist Patricia Hone, Hume left teaching to become a full-time political activist, initially focusing his work on his hometown of Londonderry. "I've always believed Derry is the heart of the Irish problem," he commented to a reporter for The *New York Times* (August 4, 1972). "With its Catholic majority and its Protestant government, it was the Achilles heel of the sectarian state in Northern Ireland." He won his first political seat that year, when he became a member of Northern Ireland's Parliament. (He remained a member until 1973.)

The civil unrest enveloping the province worsened, and the IRA began to suffer from factionalism, with some of the more radical elements resorting to increasing levels of violence. Hume distinguished himself during this period by denouncing the group publicly. He later told the *Chicago Tribune* reporter, "[The IRA] bomb factories and shout about unemployment. They shoot a teacher in a classroom . . . and lecture us about education. They kill, maim and injure and they carry out attacks in hospital precincts and then they tell us about protecting the Health Service. They rob post offices, leaving people without benefit payments and then they preach to us about defending the poor." His remarks made him a target of the IRA almost instantly. (In one of the more serious incidents in 1985 his home was firebombed with his wife and five children inside.)

In 1970 Hume helped establish a new political party, the Social Democratic and Labour Party (SDLP), which sought union with the Republic through only nonviolent means. During the early 1970s Northern Ireland's government began imprisoning IRA members and other militants, including members of the Ulster Defense Association, a violent Protestant group. These imprisonments merely intensified the hostilities on both sides. In March 1972 British prime minister Edward Heath, frustrated by the violence, suspended the government in Ulster and appointed a secretary of state to rule over the province temporarily. By June an assembly was formed, largely made up of the moderate pro-English Unionist party. By the end of the year, the Unionists had formed an alliance with the SDLP, now the major moderate Catholic group, and the secular Alliance Party. As a member of the SDLP, Hume was elected for membership in the Northern Ireland Assembly, in 1973. While a member of the organization, Hume fought for closer ties to the Republic, a move that was advocated by both the British and Irish prime ministers. Catholic and Protestant extremists alike denounced such an agreement. The IRA accused the SDLP of collaborating with the British government and the Protestants; Ulster Protestant extremists were unhappy with the prospects of sharing governmental duties with the Catholics. Hume attempted to mediate such disputes, even as violence raged, but he, as a Catholic and a pacifist, was condemned from all sides.

In 1974 hard-line Ulster Protestants won a majority of seats in the British House of Commons and pledged to overturn the province's constitution in order to destroy the alliance of Protestant and Catholic moderates and stop all cooperation between the groups. After a general strike in May 1974, the British government again took control of the province through the Northern Ireland

Act of 1974. During this volatile year, Hume worked as Minister of Commerce for Northern Ireland, aiding in the effort to stimulate Ulster's economy.

While bombings and other terrorist activities began spreading to London and Dublin, Hume and his fellow SDLP members continued to search for a peaceful resolution to the troubles in Northern Ireland. In 1975–76 Hume was a member of the Northern Ireland Constitutional Convention, which sought to establish a new government for the province, and by 1979 he was solidly entrenched as one of the notable political voices in Northern Ireland after being elected to the European Parliament and becoming the leader of the SDLP. (In 1983 Hume was also elected to the British Parliament, where he was the only voice for Ulster's Catholic minority in the House of Commons.)

In 1982 Hume became a member of the Northern Ireland Assembly, which was formed with the intention of strengthening the governmental autonomy of Northern Ireland. The assembly was dissolved in 1986 for what was considered a lack of progress. Hume, however, made some progress as one of the architects behind the 1985 Anglo-Irish Accord, which was intended to lay the foundation for discussions between the Republic of Ireland and Northern Ireland. In essence, the accord established that the Republic did not dispute British sovereignty over Northern Ireland in exchange for the crown's understanding that the Republic maintained interest in how the province was governed.

By 1990 it seemed to many observers that the troubles in Northern Ireland would never be resolved. Terrorist activity continued and British forces remained on alert in the province, their numbers often in excess of 20,000. Hume, in the midst of such upheaval, continued to press for peaceful solutions. He sought to bridge the gap between the nonviolent SDLP and the IRA, even though the British government refused to include the radical group in peace talks. In 1993 Hume publically reached out to Gerry Adams, the head of the IRA's political wing Sinn Féin. Many who knew Hume were shocked at the gesture, since he had often claimed that no peace could be secured as long as the IRA refused to lay down their weapons. The first meeting between the leader of the SDLP and the leader of Sinn Féin had taken place in 1972, after Hume had arranged a brief IRA cease-fire. That meeting led to talks with the Northern Ireland secretary William Whitelaw, but came to no real resolutions. In 1988 Adams and Hume again met over a period of several months. The earlier meetings were kept secret, for fear of the political uproar they might have caused, and initially the 1993 meetings were kept quiet as well. James F. Clarity in a November 4, 1993 article for the *New York Times* quoted Hume from an Ulster Television interview in which he laid out his reasons for meeting with Adams: "Given that the British Government has stated it cannot defeat the IRA and that the IRA has stated it cannot defeat the British Government, my simple Irish mind tells me the logic of that is that the only thing that'll solve the problem is dialogue."

Though Sinn Féin was excluded from the official peace talks with the British government, Hume and Adams worked through late 1993 on, according to Mary Pat Kelly for *Commonweal* (October 21, 1994), "a declaration of principles establishing a framework for relationships between the Catholic and Protestant communities in Northern Ireland and between Great Britain and Ireland, a framework that could lead to peace." Though many Protestant Unionists were outraged that Hume extended an olive branch to the IRA, other critics realized that Adams and many of his generation could be tiring of the struggle and hoping to secure a peace for their children. As a result of these talks Hume and Adams secured a 17-month cease-fire, which was destroyed after the IRA set off a series of bombs in London.

In 1995 DAVID TRIMBLE, a Protestant politician with a reputation as a hard-liner, was elected to the leadership of the Ulster Unionist Party. He surprised and angered many of his followers that year by supporting a number of initiatives that suggested that the Protestant majority share their power with the Catholics. Peace talks began in the summer of 1996 and Trimble managed to convince eight of the 10 Northern Irish parties that the only way to peace was through nonviolent means. The peace process was accelerated in May 1997 when Tony Blair became prime minister of Great Britain. Two months later the IRA declared another cease-fire, which brought the major parties together for another round of talks. Hume, Trimble, and Adams were given unprecedented access to Blair, who worked with them to secure a lasting piece. Their efforts were also bolstered by the support of American president Bill Clinton.

On April 10, 1998, Hume, Trimble, and Adams signed an agreement with the British and Irish governments that guaranteed self-rule for Northern Ireland, providing that the IRA lay down its arms. This accord, known as the Good Friday Agreement, contends that the province will be run by its 12-member Executive and its 108-member National Assembly. It further guaranteed the nearly 2 million people living in Northern Ireland a cessation of violence. (The agreement has since been difficult to implement because of a reluctance on the part of the IRA to disarm.)

In October 1998 the Nobel Committee in Oslo awarded Hume, along with David Trimble, the Nobel Prize for Peace. As archived on the Nobel e-Museum Web site, the committee called Hume "the clearest and most consistent of Northern Ireland's political leaders in his work for a peaceful solution."

Hume perhaps best outlined his reasons for his commitment to the peace process in his interview with Mary Pat Kelly: "I've always believed that the basic right of all is the right to existence, bread on your table and a roof over your head, and that it's an accident of birth: what you're born and where you're born. And that accident of birth, whether it's race, nationality, or creed, should never be the source of hatred or conflict."

John Hume and his wife, Pat, have two sons and three daughters. The family lives in Derry, Northern Ireland. On September 17, 2001 Hume announced that he was stepping down as the head of the SDLP because of deteriorating health. (He had collapsed at a conference in Austria in late 1999 and has been hospitalized numerous times since.) Hume remains a member of the British Parliament and the European Parliament.

ABOUT: Biography (on-line) December 14, 1998; CNN (on-line) December 12, 1998; Commonweal October 21, 1994; Economist April 17, 1993; New Statesman and Society October 1, 1993, January 7, 1994; New York Times October 6, 1993; New York Times (on-line) October 17, 1998; Nobel e-Museum Web site.

Courtesy of CANCER RESEARCH UK

Hunt, R. Timothy

*(February 19, 1943–) Nobel Prize for
Physiology or Medicine, 2001 (shared with
Paul Nurse and Leland Hartwell)*

The biochemist Richard Timothy Hunt
was born on February 19, 1943 in England.
He first attended Magdalen College, at Oxford University, and later earned his B.A. in
natural sciences from Clare College, at the
University of Cambridge. He received his
doctorate from Cambridge in 1968. He then
did postdoctoral work at the ALBERT EINSTEIN
College of Medicine, in the New York City
borough of the Bronx.

Hunt became a lecturer in biochemistry at
Cambridge in 1981. He spent his summers
teaching at the Marine Biological Laboratory, in Woods Hole, Massachusetts, where he
made the discovery that eventually earned
him the Nobel Prize. He joined the Imperial
Cancer Research Fund in 1990, continuing
his scientific research in the research organization's Cell Cycle Control Laboratory.

Cells are the basic unit of all living organisms; human beings are made up of billions
of cells, which reproduce at breathtakingly
fast rates, continually replacing dying cells.
The cell reproduction cycle begins with a
single cell enlarging. When the cell reaches
a certain size, its chromosomes are duplicat-
ed in a process known as DNA synthesis.
The two sets of chromosomes then separate,
and finally the cell divides into two identical cells. Any malfunction in the cell cycle
can result in the production of cancer cells.

During the summer of 1982, while working at the Marine Biological Laboratory,
Hunt detected a key protein molecule in the
eggs of sea urchins. He had been investigating why red blood cells stopped manufacturing proteins after maturity; marine organisms like sea urchins are uniquely suited to
the study of cell division because they have
transparent eggs and embryos. Hunt noticed
that the levels of a certain protein in the cell
increased as it was about to divide, and then
vanished abruptly right before cell division.
He named this new protein "cyclin" to describe this cycle of variation. Hunt concluded that cyclin is an important regulator of
the cycle cell. "I knew I had made a very important discovery right from that very first
day," he told Tim Radford for the London
Guardian (October 9, 2001). "But it was a
very long time before everything was
worked out, and it would be fair to say there
are an awful lot of other people—much better scientists than me—who have made seminal contributions."

Hunt's work built on the research of his
fellow Nobel laureate, LELAND HARTWELL, who
in the early 1970s isolated several genes involved in the cell division process. PAUL
NURSE, the third scientist to share the prize,
discovered a gene, now called cdc2, in the
mid-1970s. In an interview with Julia Karow
for *Scientific American* (June 26, 2000, on-
line), Nurse explained that the cdc2 gene en-
codes a certain kind of protein, known as a
cyclin-dependent kinase (CDK), which controls the cell's entry into and exit from mitosis. Cyclins attach themselves to CDK molecules, regulating their activity and triggering
changes. An October 8, 2001 press release
on the Nobel e-Museum Web site elaborated: "CDK and cyclin together drive the cell
from one cell phase to the next. The CDK-
molecules can be compared with an engine
and the cyclins with a gear box controlling
whether the engine will run in the idling
state or drive the cell forward in the cell cycle." Hunt later found cyclins in other species, including frogs and clams; other scientists have since found 10 different cyclins in
the human body. Hunt's discovery of cyclins also demonstrated periodic protein
degradation in the cell cycle—an important
control mechanism in cell reproduction.

Taken together, the discoveries of Hunt, Hartwell, and Nurse have increased the scientific community's understanding of how the cell cycle works and hold promise for the development of more effective treatments for cancer. Hunt's discoveries contribute to the understanding of how parts of chromosomes are lost or rearranged in cell division, resulting in defective and potentially cancerous cells. Already, increased levels of CDK molecules and cyclins have been detected in breast cancers and brain tumors, and clinical trials assessing the effectiveness of inhibitors of CDK molecules as a cancer therapy are underway. "Protein kinases, of which the cyclin-dependent family make up quite a large and varied clan, are a very obvious target for inhibitors," Hunt explained to Helen Frankish in *The Lancet* (October 13, 2001), "and a number of companies have compounds in the pipeline or in trial. But whether they will have therapeutic potential is difficult to say."

At first, Hunt could not believe that he won the 2001 Nobel Prize for a discovery he had made 19 years earlier; he accepted the news only after seeing his name on the Nobel Foundation's Web site. "Both mine and Paul's research has opened up a new chapter in cancer research," Hunt told a reporter for the *BBC News* (October 8, 2001, on-line), "and it's fantastic that this has been recognised in this way."

Hunt is the co-author of two books, *Molecular Biology of the Cell Problems* (1989) with John Wilson and *The Cell Cycle: An Introduction* (1993) with Andrew Murray.

Hunt's first marriage ended in divorce in 1974. He is now married to Mary Katherine Levinge Collins, a professor, and is the father of two daughters.

ABOUT: BBC News (on-line) October 8, 2001; London Daily Telegraph (on-line) October 10, 2001; Guardian October 9, 2001; Imperial Cancer Research Fund Web site; The Lancet October 13, 2001; Nobel e-Museum Web site; Scientific American (on-line) June 26, 2000.

Ignarro, Louis J.

(May 31, 1941–) Nobel Prize for Physiology or Medicine, 1998 (shared with Robert F. Furchgott and Ferid Murad)

The pharmacologist Louis Joseph Ignarro was born on May 31, 1941 in the New York City borough of Brooklyn. His father had been a ship builder in Naples before coming to America to work as a carpenter; his mother, a homemaker, had emigrated from Sicily as a child. Ignarro's brother, Angelo, was born in 1944, and the family of four lived near the ocean in the town of Long Beach, about 25 miles east of the city. "My greatest joy came when I was 8 years old," Ignarro recalled in an autobiographical essay posted on the Nobel e-Museum Web site. "To my surprise and delight, mother and father finally responded favorably to my relentless request to have a chemistry set and bought me one. I can recall vividly following every step of every experiment and becoming overjoyed at the success of each one." Ignarro's love of chemistry took him to Columbia University, in New York City, where he received his undergraduate pharmacy degree

UCLA/Dept. of Molecular and Medical Pharmacology

in 1962. Although Ignarro was loath to leave New York, where he was able to indulge his passion for the beach, playing stickball with his friends, and drag racing at a local speedway, the University of Minnesota was widely thought to have one of the best pharmacology programs in the country; he earned his Ph.D. in pharmacology there in 1966. Ignarro, who focused his study on the sympathetic nervous system, has called his graduate school time "three of the most intense years of my life in the laboratory." Upon receiving his doctorate, Ignarro became a postdoctoral fellow in the Laboratory of Chemical Pharmacology at the National Heart, Lung, and Blood Institute (part of the National Institutes of Health).

From 1968 to 1972 Ignarro worked as a research scientist for Geigy Pharmaceuticals, a multinational pharmaceutical and chemical company, where he was in charge of the biochemical and anti-inflammatory drug program. He left the private sector in 1972 to become an associate professor at the Tulane University School of Medicine, in New Orleans, Louisiana. In 1973 he received a number of honors for his research work at Tulane, including an award from the Pharmaceutical Manufacturers Association and the Smith, Kline and French Award, given by the pharmaceutical giant.

Ignarro's work at Tulane included studies on inflammation and arthritis, cyclic nucleotides, and human-cell function. In addition, he looked at hormonal control mechanisms, free radicals and enzyme activation, and the regulation of vascular and platelet function. At Tulane he also began examining nitric oxide metabolics, the research which would later garner him a Nobel Prize. He received a number of grants, including the 1973–74 Merck research grant from Tulane, the Arthritis Foundation Grant for 1974–75, and the National Institute of Arthritis, Metabolic and Digestive Disorders grant for 1974–1977. Ignarro became a full professor at Tulane in 1979.

In 1985 Ignarro left Tulane to join the staff of the department of pharmacology at the UCLA School of Medicine, in Los Angeles, California (where he currently remains as the Jerome J. Belzer Distinguished Professor of Pharmacology). The next year he concluded that a substance fellow researchers had named "endothelium-derived relaxing factor" (EDRF) was, in fact, nitric oxide at work in the body. (Endothelium is the layer of flattened cells that line blood vessels and other body parts.) Working independently of Ignarro, Dr. ROBERT FURCHGOTT, a New York pharmacologist, had concluded in 1980 that a drug called acetylcholine widened blood vessels only when the inner layer of the blood vessel was still intact, leading him to theorize that blood vessels widen because the endothelial cells produce a signal molecule, which he called EDRF, relaxes the smooth muscle cells. In 1986 Ignarro provided evidence that the signal molecule was the gas nitric oxide. This was the first discovery that a gas could act as a signal molecule in an organism. (Gas, which diffuses and dissipates quickly, was long thought to be too unstable to act as a signaling molecule.)

Ignarro and Furchgott, who had worked separately and jointly, put forth their theories at a July 1986 symposium at the Mayo Clinic in Rochester, Minnesota, and triggered widespread research in laboratories all over the world. While the scientific community knew that nitric oxide was produced by bacteria, it had not concluded that the gas was indispensable in the functioning of the human body. It was not until the work of Ignarro and Furchgott—along with FERID MURAD who proved that nitric oxide could regulate cellular functions—that scientists saw the vast potential benefits of the gas. Doctors have noted that nitric oxide is involved in the regulation of blood pressure and is helpful in treating coronary artery disease. (Ignarro has predicted that death from cardiovascular disease will decrease by 20 percent in the next decade.) The gas is given to some newborns with persistent pulmonary hypertension, and Ignarro himself has received dozens of thank you notes and photographs from grateful parents whose infants have benefitted from nitric oxide therapy. Ignarro discovered that nitric oxide is necessary for penile erection, a conclusion that led to the development of the anti-impotency drug Viagra. (After his findings were printed in the *New England Journal of Medicine*, in 1992, Ignarro was abashed to find himself being courted for an interview by the pornographic magazine *Hustler*. He turned down the request.) Scientists also found that they could use inhibitors of nitric oxide to treat shock, and that it may help halt the growth of malignant tumors. Researchers are currently investigating the benefits of nitric oxide on memory and the sense of smell. In the past decade, thousands of scientific papers have been written on the gas, and a journal entitled *Nitric Oxide* has been founded. Nitric oxide is, however, a chemical relative to the anesthetic nitrous oxide, which is known as "laughing gas." Nitrous oxide is also an air pollutant caused by the burning of nitrogen in gasoline. Scientists have pointed out that nitric oxide, like its less innocuous cousin, is potentially poisonous and that too much of it can cause blood vessels to overdilate or precipitate such conditions as arthritis and colitis.

In 1998 the Nobel Prize committee presented Ignarro, Furchgott, and Murad with the Nobel Prize for Physiology or Medicine "for their discoveries concerning nitric oxide as a signaling molecule in the cardiovascular system." (There was controversy surrounding the announcement of the prize; some members of the scientific community felt that the work of Chandra K. Mittal, who performed extensive nitric oxide research, was being ignored.) Ignarro was traveling in Europe at the time the prize winners were announced and received the news at the airport in Nice, France. "From tomorrow on

. . . my devotion to research will be redoubled," he told reporters, according to *ABC News Online* (October 12, 1998). In addition to his other honors, Louis J. Ignarro has received 10 Golden Apple Awards for his teaching at UCLA. Known for the humor and passion of his teaching style, Ignarro often arrives at his office at four in the morning to prepare for lectures. He is the author of the books *Nitric Oxide: Molecular Biology and Therapeutic Implications* (1995) and *Advances in Pharmacology* (1996). Ignarro has a daughter, Heather, from his first marriage. He is now married to Sharon Williams, a family physician at UCLA, who has volunteered her time treating refugees in Albania.

ABOUT: American Men and Women of Science, 1998–99; CNN.com October 12, 1998; New York Times October 13, 1998; Nobel e-Museum Web site; UCLA Web site; Washington Post October 13, 1998.

Kandel, Eric R.

(November 7, 1929–) Nobel Prize for Physiology or Medicine, 2000 (shared with Arvid Carlsson and Paul Greengard)

The neuroscientist Eric Richard Kandel was born in Vienna, Austria, on November 7, 1929. He emigrated with his family to the United States in 1939, shortly after the Nazi occupation of Austria. The family settled in New York City, where Eric attended Erasmus High School in Brooklyn. He majored in history and literature at Harvard University, in Cambridge, Massachusetts, where he earned his B.A. in 1952. During his undergraduate studies he became interested in psychoanalysis, which as he told Nicholas Wade for the *New York Times* (October 10, 2000, on-line), "everyone thought was the gateway to the mind."

Kandel's burgeoning interest in how the mind worked made him want to go to medical school, so he returned to New York and entered the New York University School of Medicine. Because he felt he should know something about how the brain functioned biologically, he took an elective period in neurophysiology that sparked his interest in the biology of memory. By the time he earned his M.D. in 1956, Kandel was considering a career in research. "I began to think

Courtesy of Eric Kandel

about problems in neurobiology that are relevant to psychiatry," he remarked in a article on memory by Stephen S. Hall in the *New York Times Magazine* (February 15, 1998). "And I thought: Learning and memory is going to be a tractable problem in my lifetime. You know, not tomorrow, but in 20 or 30 years."

Kandel spent the next year as a medical intern at Montefiore Hospital in New York City. In 1957 he joined the staff of the neurophysiology lab at the National Institute of Mental Health as a research associate studying mammalian brain neurophysiology, a position he would hold for the next three years. From 1960 to 1964 he was a resident in clinical psychiatry at Harvard Medical School. After completing his residency, he served as a staff psychiatrist at the Massachusetts Mental Health Center in Boston, a position he held until 1965 while continuing to do research and teach at Harvard.

Kandel's early research attempted to analyze the activities of nerve cells in the hippocampus—the part of the mammalian brain involved in forming certain types of memories. The mammalian, however, possess approximately 1 trillion neurons with 70 trillion synaptic connections—a single neuron may have as many as 10,000 synapses. He sought a simpler system in which to study learning and memory, basing his decision on the premise that, as Hall put it, "simple animals with exceedingly simple brains can reveal some universal biological truths about how memory works." Kandel found what he was looking for in an invertebrate, the potato-shaped, purplish mollusk Aplysia californica, which has a total of only 20,000 neurons, some of which are color-coded naturally, making it easier to study the slug's circuitry. To many of his colleagues, Kandel's selection of the sea slug came as something of a surprise; most neuroscientists choose to study mice, rats, cats, or primates. But his choice proved to be a beneficial one. Because the Aplysia californica has relatively few nerve cells and simpler behavior patterns in comparison with humans or other mammals, it was easier to link changes at the neural level to changes in the sea slug's behavior that indicated that new memories had been formed.

Learning and behavior are crucial to the study of memory. As Hall points out, "Whether it's remembering not to touch a hot stove after a single bad experience or how to play the piano after repeated practice, behavior changes with learning." Learning, in turn, requires the formation of memories. In order to study memory in the sea slug, Kandel found a protective behavior, the animal's retraction of its gill, and then, using techniques developed by psychologists for the study of learning and behavior, Kandel trained Aplysia to perform this behavior under certain circumstances: as soon as the sea slug was touched in a certain way, it would expect an electric shock, and instantly remember to retract its gill. Over the course of years, Kandel and his research team were then able to examine changes in the neurons that occurred as the animal learned its new behavior pattern. As Hall recounted in his article, Kandel "took a simple behavior, the animal's withdrawal of its gill, and . . . identified the key cells participating in the behavior, worked out the neural circuitry and demonstrated that individual synapses changed when the animal learned to associate an electric shock with a touch—in crude terms, it would flinch at the slightest touch, a behavior known as sensitization." In the Nobel committee's press release, published on the Nobel e-Museum Web site (October 9, 2000), it was noted that Kandel "found that certain types of stimuli resulted in an amplification of the protective reflex of the sea slug. This strengthening of the reflex could remain for days and weeks and was thus a form of learning. He could then show that learning was due to an amplification of the synapse that connects the sensory nerve cells to the nerve cells that activate the muscle groups that give rise to the protective reflex."

Early in his research, Kandel was perplexed to find that the sea slug's nerve cells were always wired in the same way, meaning that the connections between its neurons formed specific, unchanging circuits. He also observed that each circuit accounted for a simple behavior pattern. The process of learning was thought to require flexibility in this wiring, with changes in the circuits arising as an individual creature learned. In time, Kandel made a major discovery; as he told a reporter for the New York Times (October 10, 2000, on-line), "I realized that the strength of the connections was not specific and that this could be modified by learning." In other words, basic circuitry did not in fact change as learning occurred; instead, certain synaptic pathways became better defined.

During his studies of the Aplysia, Kandel was able to identify key differences in how short-term and long-term memories were formed. In training the sea slug to modify its gill-retracting behavior, one or two stimuli resulted in a form of short-term memory that lasted from minutes to hours; five or more repeated stimuli resulted in a form of long-term memory that lasted up to weeks. At the molecular level, Kandel found that short-term memory involved chemical changes that resulted in an increase in the release of neurotransmitters—chemicals that transmit an electrical impulse from one nerve cell across the synapse to another nerve cell. This in turn causes a strengthening, or amplification, of the sea slug's gill retraction. Long-term memory, Kandel discovered, is associated with increases in the levels of a specific messenger molecule and protein. These changes are registered in the nucleus of a nerve cell and trigger substantial changes in the proteins present in the synapse and in the growth of new synapses. As stated in the Nobel press release, "This may lead to changes in the form and function of the synapse. The efficacy of the synapse can then be increased and more transmitter released." New synaptic connections may also be formed in the development of long-term memories. These processes involve the synthesis of proteins, a finding with important implications. As other scientists discovered during the 1960s and 1970s, if an animal's ability to make new proteins is blocked, it cannot form long-term memories, although its short-term memory will be unaffected. As Hall wrote, "Since genes must be switched on to make new proteins, genes were therefore involved in long-term memory."

Kandel's first paper on his Aplysia experiments was published in 1963, while he was associated with Harvard Medical School. He continued this vein of research over the following decades, first at New York University, where he served as an associate professor in the department of physiology and psychiatry from 1965 to 1974, becoming a full professor in 1968. In 1974 he and members of his research group moved to Columbia University, where in addition to his duties as a professor of physiology and psychiatry, Kandel became the director of Columbia University's new Center for Neurobiology and Behavior. Since 1992 Kandel has served as a professor of biochemistry and molecular biophysics as well, and in 1983 he was named a university professor at Columbia. The following year he was made a senior investigator at the university's Howard Hughes Medical Institute, where he maintains a large and active research laboratory.

In the spring of 1990 Kandel's group identified a molecule that is believed to represent a key to all the changes that lead to the creation of permanent memories. At Columbia, Kandel and his team reduced their experiments to two nerve cells taken from Aplysia and maintained in a dish. In these cells they observed the molecular changes that occurred after one was exposed to the neurotransmitter serotonin. They found that a chain reaction took place; a series of molecules formed, and their signaling activities, known as the cyclic AMP pathway, engendered the formation of new synaptic connections between the two nerve cells. In further experiments, Kandel and his fellow researchers found that specific set of molecules in the chain corresponded with a specific stage of memory formation; blocking one molecule made it impossible for an animal to learn, while blocking another stopped it from developing short-term memories. During the chain reaction a key molecule, called CREB, would bind with a tiny bit of DNA inside the nerve cell's nucleus, activating dozens of other genes. Kandel's group was the first to demonstrate that by blocking CREB, none of the activities associated with forming long-term memories, including protein synthesis and the growth of new synapses, could take place. As Hall noted in the *New York Times Magazine*, "CREB was the gateway to all the changes that lead to a permanent memory." Throughout the 1990s Kandel's group applied many of the techniques he developed in his work with Aplysia to research on memory in mammals—in particular, mice—and was able to show that the same types of changes in the synapses that occur due to learning in invertebrates take place in vertebrates as well.

Kandel's work since the 1960s has profound implications: it is now known conclusively that both short- and long-term memories are "located in the synapses," as the Nobel press release put it; that learning produces changes in the strength of synapses; and that short-term memory involves the modification of synapses, while long-term memory involves the growth of new synapses and changes in the shape and function of preexisting ones. While scientists are as yet far from a complete understanding of memory in humans, this area of study has greatly benefitted from Kandel's research. In humans as well as in other animals, synapses are central to the formation of memories. Kandel's work has provided a crucial foundation for the study of "how complex memory images are stored in our nervous systems, and how it is possible to recreate the memory of earlier events," as quoted from the Nobel press release. His contributions to scientists' knowledge of the cellular and molecular changes involved in memory and learning may facilitate the development of new medicines and treatments for patients with dementia, Alzheimer's, and other memory-related illnesses. "We are who we are because of what we learn and what we remember, the traumatic experiences such as those that I experienced [as a child] in Vienna and the more horrible experiences that others had who had more difficult times than I did, permanently scarring their lives," Kandel told a reporter for the *Los Angeles Times* (October 10, 2000). "To understand what happens to the brain when that occurs, I think, is just a wonderful problem."

In October 2000, the Nobel Assembly at the Karolinska Institute announced that Kandel, along with PAUL GREENGARD and ARVID CARLSSON, had won the Nobel Prize in Physiology or Medicine "for their discoveries concerning signal transduction in the nervous system." All three "have made important contributions to understanding the long-term changes in the brain that underlie memory and mood," according to Nicholas Wade for the *New York Times* (October 10, 2000, on-line). In addition Kandel has received numerous other awards for his work, including the Lester N. Hofheimer Prize for Research (1977), the Lucy G. Moses Prize for Research in Basic Neurology (1977), the Karl Spencer Lashley Prize in Neurobiology (1981), the Lasker Prize in Basic Medical Science (1983), the Howard Crosby Warren Medal (1984), the 1988 National Medal of Science, the 1989 Distinguished Service Award of the American Psychiatric Association, the Warren Triennial Prize (1992), the 1993 Harvey Prize, the New York Academy of Medicine Award (1996), and the 1999 Wolf Prize in Biology and Medicine, awarded by the country of Israel, among others. He is a member of the National Academy of Science and the American Philosophical Society. Kandel has maintained an active interest in clinical psychiatry, and throughout his career has promoted dialogue and cooperation among various disciplines involved in the study of the brain.

Eric R. Kandel was married in 1956 to Denise Bystryn, also a professor at Columbia. The Kandels have two children, Paul and Minouche, and four grandchildren. He continues to serve as a senior investigator at the Hughes Medical Institute at Columbia, and is the leading author of an influential textbook on neuroscience.

ABOUT: BioScience May 1997; Columbia News (on-line); New York Times July 26, 1996, December 3, 1996, September 8, 1998; New York Times (on-line) October 10, 2000; New York Times Magazine February 15, 1998; Nobel e-Museum Web site; Science News October 14, 2000.

Courtesy of Wolfgang Ketterle

Ketterle, Wolfgang

(October 21, 1957–) Nobel Prize for Physics, 2001 (shared with Carl Wieman and Eric Cornell)

The physicist Wolfgang Ketterle was born in Heidelberg, Germany, on October 21, 1957. As a young man, he attended the University of Heidelberg, where he received his pre-diploma in physics in 1978. He then attended the Technical University of Munich, where he studied physics, writing his thesis on spin relaxation in disordered systems. Ketterle earned his diploma, equivalent to a master's degree, in 1982. While working on his Ph.D. at the Ludwig-Maximilians University of Munich, Ketterle became a research assistant at the Max-Planck Institute for Quantum Physics, where he researched spectroscopy of small molecules in neutralized ion beams; spectroscopy is a technique used to analyze molecules or other forms of matter through the colors of light they emit or through their response when exposed to variables of light frequency. In 1985 Ketterle became a staff scientist at the Max-Planck Institute. He earned his Ph.D. in physics from the University of Munich in 1986, after writing his experimental doctoral thesis on spectroscopy of helium hydride and triatomic hydrogen. In 1989 Ketterle became a research scientist at the University of Heidelberg's Department of Physical Chemistry, focusing on combustion diagnostics with lasers. Combustion is the chemical reaction of two or more substances with the release of heat and light, commonly called burning; using lasers, Ketterle explored various aspects of combustion, including the determination of velocity fields, temperature field measurements, and diagnostics in a Diesel engine.

In 1990 Ketterle continued his postdoctoral research at the Massachusetts Institute of Technology (MIT), in Cambridge, Massachusetts, where he was invited by Professor David E. Pritchard, a pioneer in atom trapping and atom optics, to join MIT's research team developing methods for cooling and trapping atoms.

In 1924 the Indian physicist Satyendra Nath Bose made important theoretical calculations about light particles, which ALBERT EINSTEIN expanded to a particular type of atom, predicting that if a gas of atoms was cooled to temperatures nearing absolute zero (-459.67 degrees Fahrenheit or -273.15 degrees Celsius)—the lowest theoretical temperature—the atoms would merge into a type of "super-atom" in the lowest state of energy, where all motion essentially stopped. Within this condensed state of matter, the waves of the individual atoms would overlap, causing them to exhibit identical physical properties, such as their distribution in position and velocity, and behave as a single entity. Scientists named this process of cooling and condensing atoms Bose-Einstein condensation (BEC), and it became the so-called "Holy Grail" of atomic physics during the last 20 years.

A team led by CARL WIEMAN and ERIC CORNELL at JILA, formerly the Joint Institute of Laboratory Astrophysics, in Boulder, Colorado, and an MIT team led by Ketterle were working toward BEC. At MIT, Ketterle helped develop innovative techniques for laser cooling that became crucial in the later experiments that allowed scientists to successfully observe BEC. After the atoms had been cooled with lasers they were held in place by magnetic forces, providing further opportunity for "evaporative cooling." Here, atoms with the highest energy leap out of the trap carrying more than their share of energy and leaving the remaining atoms colder—a process similar to cooling a cup of hot coffee, in which the most energetic water molecules leap out of the cup as steam. Both groups of scientists encountered difficulties in the evaporative cooling stage, observing that too many atoms often escaped the magnetic field, thereby preventing BEC. Wieman and Cornell solved the problem by constructing a magnetic force with revolving fields, which kept the leaky spot through which atoms could escape rotating ahead of the coldest atoms; Ketterle, on the other hand, beamed a tightly focused laser into the hole to create an "optical plug," which prevented the atoms from escaping the trap while they cooled to sufficiently low temperatures.

Though Wieman and Cornell's team of JILA researchers beat Ketterle in the race to BEC, MIT's team soon followed with their own creation of a sodium condensate. Of the extra time his team required, Ketterle told Graham P. Collins for *Physics Today* (March 1996), "The problem was probably vibrations, which caused heating of the atoms and loss of atoms." After Wieman and Cornell's success, on June 5, 1995, Ketterle's team made minor alterations to their experiment that ultimately led to the formation of BEC. Collins explained: "If the laser beam they used to plug the hole in their trap moved relative to the magnetic fields that form the walls of the trap, then the motion of the beam would 'stir' the atoms. To counteract this effect, the researchers eliminated a vacuum pump that was causing vibrations and shielded the laser beam from air turbulence. They also decided to cool the atoms as fast as possible, to minimize whatever heating remained, even though doing so could lead to a denser and hence a less-stable condensate." On September 30, 1995,

Ketterle and his team cooled a gas of 500,000 sodium atoms to a temperature near one-millionth of a degree Kelvin and observed the second incident of BEC, in what Constance Holden's headline for *Science* (November 3, 1995) called "A Bigger, Better Bose-Einstein Condensate." Indeed, while Wieman and Cornell's condensate merged about 2,000 rubidium atoms after five minutes of cooling, the condensate induced by Ketterle's group condensed a half million sodium atoms in less than 10 seconds, results that impressed even his competitors. "They have a very convincing signature," Cornell told Holden, "and lots more atoms. This is a big advantage because if BEC is going to live up to its advance press, we're going to need bigger samples of condensates." Ketterle told Collins that he intended to use these advantageous factors to advance his own research of BEC. "Now we want to study properties of the condensate, for example by plotting a property of the condensate versus temperature, number of atoms, and so on," he said. "This involves much more data taking and some studies would be almost impossible at a repetition rate of one shot every five minutes." Ultimately, the condensates produced by Wieman, Cornell, and Ketterle offered great potential for the enhanced study of quantum mechanics, providing macroscopic manifestations of wave mechanics on a scale of a fraction of a millimeter.

While working toward BEC, Ketterle became a member of MIT's Research Laboratory of Electronics and joined MIT's faculty in the department of physics, first as assistant professor of physics in 1993 and as full professor in 1997. Since 1998 he has been MIT's John D. MacArthur Professor of Physics. Ketterle also advanced the field of BEC through his creation of the first "atom laser," a device that Curt Suplee for the *Washington Post* (January 27, 1997) described as firing "a narrow beam of perfectly matched 'matter waves' just as a laser shoots out a stream of identical light rays." In a traditional laser, the synchronized condition that distinguishes ordinary light from a laser beam where all the photons occupy a single mode is known as "coherence." In Ketterle's lab, he achieved the first example of a coherent stream of atoms by creating a laser that dispensed multiple pulses of Bose-condensed droplets, each containing 100,000 to several million sodium atoms each. "It looks just like a dripping faucet," Ketterle told Elizabeth Thomas for an *MIT News* press release (January 27, 1997, on-line). To achieve this coherent laser, Ketterle developed a technique for extracting and controlling the stream of atoms from his condensate by opening a tiny leak in the magnetic trap containing the sodium atoms. As Ketterle explained to Gary Taubes for *Science* (January 31, 1997), the trap would only confine atoms whose spin axis—or the intrinsic angular momentum of the particles—was pointing upward; by simply flipping the spins, Ketterle said, "the restoring forces become expelling or repulsive forces," a task he achieved by adding another magnetic field to his trap through a tiny burst of radio waves, which would serve to tilt the atoms' spins in any direction. He told Taubes, "We varied the angle between 0 and 180 degrees, and at 0 degrees the magnetic mirror was still reflective, so nothing was coupled out; and at 180 degrees, everything was coupled out." (An output coupler is the device used to emit a laser's narrow beam.) Taubes described: "By controlling the angle, the researchers could then 'pulse out' portions of the condensate, the way a laser pulses out dollops of coherent light."

The task of producing this primitive atom laser was not complete until Ketterle could prove that he had, in fact, created coherent condensates with identical quantum-mechanical wave functions; this second phase of the experiment took Ketterle's research team several months to accomplish. "For photons, it's much easier to show coherence," he explained to Thomas. "Photons don't interact with each other, they are not affected by gravity, and they are not affected by molecules in the air." To prove coherence in the atoms, Ketterle created two condensates from their sample by beaming a laser through the magnetic trap and essentially splitting the condensate into two discernible halves. Then, to prove that these separate samples were behaving as individual waves, Ketterle turned off the magnetic trap, releasing the samples into the surrounding vacuum, where they expanded until they overlapped and interfered. At 3:00 a.m. on November 16, 1996, Ketterle's team observed just this type of interference pattern through alternating waves of bright and dark fringes in a standing wave that could be photographed. "The signal was almost too good to be true," Ketterle told Thomas, "We were hoping for some signature of coherence, but what we saw was text-book-like, high-contrast interference patterns. When our camera showed this pattern, we knew that we had realized the atom laser."

Ketterle and his team reported the two different aspects of their experiment in the January 27, 1997 issue of *Physical Review Letters* and the January 31, 1997 issue of *Science*; of the long-term applications for his work, Ketterle told Thomas, "Today, if you have a demanding job for light, you use an optical laser. In the future, if there is a demanding job for atoms, you may be able to use an atom laser." In addition, he told Malcolm Browne for the *New York Times* (January 27, 1997), "Next we'll try to build a laser with more atoms in the beam. We don't know what this will lead to, but you must remember that when the laser was invented in 1960, no one could predict all the uses it has today."

The following year, 1998, Ketterle made further observations that helped to advance understanding of BEC. While some critics contended that his stream of coherent atoms was not a true laser because it did not exhibit "stimulated emission"—or the amplification process through which each wave in a conventional laser triggers another wave, thus rapidly building the laser's powerful beam—Ketterle theorized that Bose-Einstein condensates formed through an analogous process. He observed that when his gas of cooled sodium atoms approached the temperature threshold for BEC formation, his condensates first did nothing before beginning to converge through a process that he dubbed "stimulated scattering." Here, he claimed, the atoms forming BEC rapidly triggered other atoms to jump into the condensate. Alexander Hellemans for *Science* (February 13, 1998) explained: "Atoms in the cooled gas want to join the condensate because it is in a low energy state, but they need to shed some excess energy to do so. They do this by colliding with another atom outside the BEC and dumping their excess energy and momentum onto it." Ketterle's observations helped convince at least some skeptics, including the physicist Keith Burnett of Oxford University: "I believe the term [laser] is appropriate," Burnett told Hellemans. That year, Ketterle also developed a technique for confining the condensate without using a magnetic trap but only using laser beams. Without the presence of a mag-

netic field, Ketterle told Hellemans, "we can study 'spin waves,' we can study spin dynamics . . . all of a sudden we have rich physics." In late 1999 Ketterle reported that his team had generated even further evidence of true atom amplification.

On October 9, 2001 the Royal Swedish Academy of Science awarded Ketterle, together with Wieman and Cornell, the Nobel Prize in Physics. Since being recognized with the prize, Ketterle has continued his research on BEC with the goal of exploring new aspects of this ultra-cold atomic matter; he is also focused on studying practical applications for BEC and atom lasers, using coherent atoms for precision measurements and atom optics. Ketterle's research is supported by the National Science Foundation, the Office of Naval Research, the Army Research Office, the National Aeronautics and Space Administration (NASA), and the David and Lucile Packard Foundation. In addition to the Nobel Prize, he has received numerous awards, including the Michael and Philip Platzman Award from MIT (1994), the I. I. RABI Prize of the American Physical Society (1997), the Gustav-Hertz Prize of the German Physical Society (1997), the *Discover* Magazine Award for Technological Innovation (1998), the Fritz London Prize in Low Temperature Physics (1999), the Dannie-Heineman Prize of the Academy of Sciences, in Göttingen, Germany (1999), and the Benjamin Franklin Medal in Physics (2000). He is a fellow of the American Physical Society and the American Academy of Arts and Sciences, and a member of the Germany Physical Society and the Optical Society of America. A German citizen, Ketterle has permanent residency status in the U.S. and lives in Brookline, Massachusetts. He has three children.

ABOUT: MIT News (on-line) January 27, 1997, October 9, 2001; New York Times January 27, 1997; Nobel e-Museum Web site; Science November 3, 1995, January 31, 1997, February 13, 1998; Washington Post January 27, 1997.

Courtesy of Texas Instruments

Kilby, Jack St. Clair

(November 8, 1923–) Nobel Prize for Physics, 2000 (shared with Zhores I. Alferov and Herbert Kroemer)

The inventor Jack St. Clair Kilby was born in Jefferson City, Missouri, on November 8, 1923, the son of Hubert St. Clair Kilby and the former Vina Freitag. Kilby's father was an electrical engineer who sparked his son's interest in electricity at an early age. In 1927 Hubert Kilby moved his family to Salina, Kansas, after becoming president of the Kansas Power Company. In 1935 the family moved again, this time to Great Bend, Kansas, when the company transferred its offices to that city. During summers, Kilby accompanied his father on visits to power plants throughout western Kansas, and helped him look for faulty equipment. In 1937 a major blizzard hit Kansas, and to stay in touch with distant power stations, Kilby's father began using a ham radio. Jack Kilby was fascinated and after studying intensely, became a fully licensed ham radio operator. He began building his own radios, and by the time he entered high school, he knew he wanted to become an electrical engineer.

Kilby had his heart set on attending the Massachusetts Institute of Technology (MIT), and took the school's entrance exam in June 1941. With a score of 500 needed to pass, he received a 497, and according to

several sources he never completely recovered from the disappointment. Kilby had not applied anywhere else, and had to scramble to gain admittance to the University of Illinois, his parents' alma mater. Several months after he started college, the U.S. entered World War II, and Kilby served in the United States Army as a corporal for two years, from 1943 to 1945. He worked in a radio repair shop on a base in northeastern India, placing and maintaining transmitters used to communicate with personnel in the field. Following the war he returned to the University of Illinois, where he received a bachelor's degree in electrical engineering in 1947. In 1950 he completed his master's degree in that field, this time studying at the University of Wisconsin.

In 1947 Kilby joined the Centralab division of Globe-Union Inc., in Milwaukee, Wisconsin, which specialized in developing parts for radios, televisions, and hearing aids. There he helped to design and develop ceramic-based, silk-screen circuits and worked in the field of miniaturization, seeking new ways to manufacture smaller and more efficient electrical parts. During this era, the electronics industry as a whole had made great strides, particularly in that they had effectively eliminated the need for vacuum tubes, which were large, awkward, and fragile devices. Vacuum tubes also generated a lot of heat and used a good deal of power. In 1947 Bell Laboratories had invented transistors, which gradually replaced vacuum tubes. In comparison to their predecessors, transistors were tiny, more durable, produced less heat, used less power, and generally lasted longer. With the onset of transistors, engineers began making more complex electronic circuits that could have hundreds or even thousands of components such as capacitors, transistors, diodes, and rectifiers. Unfortunately, engineers began to notice a problem when large numbers of components had to be connected by bits of wire in order to make circuits; because each component had to be hand soldered to the next, there was always a chance that the connection could come apart. The more complex the circuit, the greater the number of components and connections it needed, and the more likely something would go wrong with it. In addition, hand-soldering was an expensive and time-consuming endeavor. This problem—which effectively held back the entire electronics industry until Kilby made his breakthrough—became known in engineering circles as "the tyranny of numbers."

After paying Bell Laboratories a licensing fee, Centralab became one of the first firms to manufacture transistors. In 1952 the company sent Kilby to a 10-day transistor symposium at Bell Laboratories's headquarters in Murray Hill, New Jersey. When he returned to Centralab he began working to develop germanium transistors that could be used in hearing aids. Though germanium had been the initial choice of material for transistors, by 1958 engineers recognized that silicon, which was harder to work with but could withstand higher temperatures, was a better semiconductor. It was also more readily available than germanium, and thus less expensive. Kilby wanted to pursue research with silicon, but Centralab was hesitant to part with the germanium-based electronics they had been producing. Unsatisfied with the direction his company was taking, Kilby left Centralab in 1958 for Texas Instruments Incorporated.

Based in Dallas, Texas Instruments was a young, cutting-edge company that manufactured transistors, resistors, capacitors, and semiconductors for commercial and military use. They had also built the first transistor radio, in 1954, as well as the first silicon transistor, and the company had several contracts with the United States government for producing the latter. Kilby was hired to work on the miniaturization of electronic components. One idea for miniaturizing circuits had come from the United States Army Signal Corps, whose idea was to make all components a standardized size and shape, with built-in wiring. The various modules could be snapped together to make circuits, so as to do away with the need for soldering wire connections. Micro-Modules, as the circuits were dubbed, were the focus of a major development initiative at Texas Instruments around the time Kilby was hired.

Kilby wasn't very satisfied with the Micro-Module; he felt a horizontal structure would be more efficient than the vertically stacked architecture of the Micro-Module prototype, and thought it would be more cost-effective to use only silicon, whereas the Micro-Module used germanium as well. Moreover, the Micro-Module, as an article on the Texas Instruments Web site stated, "didn't address the basic problem of large quantities of components in elaborate circuits." Rather than join Texas Instruments's Micro-Module program immediately, Kilby began trying to develop a viable alternative, using tubular components instead of the flat wafers used in the Micro-Module. He designed a version of a device known as an IF (intermediate frequency) amplifier, which was commonly used in radios, trying to incorporate the tubular components. After Kilby spent several months pursuing this idea and making models, a cost-analysis led him to conclude that his design would still require too much hand-labor.

This conclusion was reached just as Texas Instruments shut down for a two-week, company-wide vacation. As a new employee, Kilby had no vacation time pending and went to the deserted laboratories, where he reflected on his options. He realized that if he couldn't come up with a good idea before everyone returned from vacation, he would be assigned to the Micro-Module project, which he felt was not a worthy solution to the problem of miniaturizing and connecting circuits. In a 1976 article entitled "Invention of the IC [integrated circuit]," as quoted on the Texas Instruments Web site, Kilby wrote: "In my discouraged mood, I began to feel that the only thing a semiconductor house could make in a cost-effective way was a semiconductor. Further thought led me to the conclusion that semiconductors were all that were really required—that resistors and capacitors [passive devices], in particular, could be made from the same material as active devices [transistors]. I also realized that, since all of the components could be made of a single material, they could also be made in situ interconnected to form a complete circuit." This notion, detailed in his lab notebook on July 24, 1958, would come to be known as the monolithic idea; if all circuit elements were made of the same material, everything, including the connections, could be included on the same chip, thus eliminating the need for wiring and increasing the potential number of components and the complexity of circuits. Kilby quickly sketched out a design and showed it to his boss, Willis Adcock, when Adcock returned from vacation. He was impressed but somewhat apprehensive about whether or not a circuit made completely from semiconductors could work. He asked Kilby to first make a working resistor and capacitor out of separate pieces of silicon. Kilby did so, and incorporated them into a circuit called a phase-shift oscillator, a device that oscillates signals at a given rate. This first unit, assembled and demonstrated on August 28, 1958, proved that circuits using elements made only from semiconductors were viable. Adcock then gave the go-ahead for Kilby to build a completely integrated circuit on a chip, as Kilby had originally envisioned. That device, another phase-shift oscillator, contained two circuits on a small germanium chip. (Germanium was used because its properties were still better known than those of silicon). It was demonstrated before several Texas Instruments executives, including former chairman Mark Shepard, on September 12, 1958. What the executives saw was a chip about a half-inch long with protruding wires, glued to a glass slide. Kilby hooked the chip to a battery and an oscilloscope. When the power was turned on, the circuit oscillated at about 1.3 megacycles, creating a green sine wave across the screen of the oscilloscope. The world's first microchip worked.

Kilby and Texas Instruments filed for a patent for their "miniaturized electronic circuit" in February 1959. In March of that year, Mark Shepard announced the concept at a press conference in New York, declaring: "I consider this to be the most significant development by Texas Instruments since we divulged the commercial availability of the silicon transistor," as quoted on the Texas Instruments Web site. The company began offering their integrated circuits at the Institute of Radio Engineers Show for $450 a piece. Although the U.S. Air Force was quick to show interest in the IC, the electronics industry in general remained skeptical for some time; the Texas Instruments Web site, quoting from Kilby's writings, noted that the IC "provided much of the entertainment at major technical meetings over the next few years [following its introduction]." This resistance was due mostly to engineers' disbelief that effective capacitors and resistors could be made out of silicon. There was also a preconception that integrated circuits would be difficult to manufacture.

Unbeknownst to Kilby and Texas Instruments, Robert Noyce of Fairchild Semiconductor had invented a device similar to Kilby's integrated circuit, but with a key improvement, and applied for a patent in July 1959. Kilby's main concern had been integrating the various components on one chip,

and in his rush to build a prototype, he had connected those components by hand with gold wire. Although he indicated in his patent application that hand-wiring would not be necessary in future versions of his chip, and had outlined other, more effective methods that could be used to interconnect the components, Noyce's patent application included a new chemical etching technique that simplified the manufacturing process and increased the chips' speed. The battle over the patent would last through much of the 1960s. In 1962 Texas Instruments filed a lawsuit against Noyce and Fairchild Semiconductor for patent interference. Two years later, Kilby and Texas Instruments received their patent for the miniaturized electronic circuits, though the case was not settled. Noyce also received his patent around the same time. A settlement was finally reached in 1969, when the United States Court of Customs and Patent Appeals ruled in favor of Noyce's invention. Texas Instruments and Fairchild had made a deal years earlier that enabled both companies to market the chip. Today, most historians credit Kilby for inventing and building the first working integrated circuit, and acknowledge Noyce for improving on the idea by solving the problem of interconnections. The two men, however, were not bitter towards each other; as Frederic Golden noted in *Time* (October 23, 2000): "The gentlemanly Kilby and the equally gentlemanly Noyce . . . were always content to call themselves coinventors." Noyce died in 1990, and many have commented that were he alive, it is very possible he would have shared the Nobel Prize with Kilby.

Kilby's integrated circuit was first put to use in military applications. Texas Instruments began building the first computer to use silicon chips for the United States Air Force in 1961. A year later the microchip replaced the transistor in the Minuteman Missile, with each missile using 2500 integrated circuits for guidance control. The IC's use in the missiles increased the device's credibility, and the electronics industry began to take its presence seriously. Kilby was promoted to manager of engineering in Texas Instruments's semiconductor networks department in 1960. By 1962 he was in charge of the entire semiconductor networks department, overseeing the development of microchips for the Minuteman.

During the mid-1960s, the management at Texas Instruments wanted a "demonstration project" that would help speed the use of integrated circuits in the commercial market. Patrick E. Haggerty, then chairman of Texas Instruments, suggested to Kilby that he design a calculator as powerful as the bulky desktop models of the era, but which, by virtue of the microchip, would be small enough to fit in a pocket. In September 1965 Kilby spoke with two of his associates at Texas Instruments, Jerry D. Merryman and James H. Van Tassel, about building such a calculator. They knew that a year earlier, a Japanese company had introduced a desktop calculator that used transistors, but it was much larger and more expensive than what they had envisioned, weighing in at 55 pounds and costing around $2,500.

Over the next two years, Kilby, Merryman, and Van Tassel developed their pocket-sized calculator based on integrated circuits; their "miniature calculator" could perform the four basic functions—addition, subtraction, multiplication, and division—and print results on a low-energy, thermal printer, invented by Kilby. Unveiled in 1967, the calculator ran on batteries, weighed 45 ounces, and measured about 4 1/4 inches, by 6 1/8 inches, by 1 3/4 inches. Texas Instruments filed for a patent later that year and received it on June 25, 1974. The Smithsonian Institute accepted Texas Instruments's donation of the prototype in December 1975.

The calculator proved that Kilby's microchips were viable in commercial, mass-market products. By the late 1980s, more than 100 million pocket calculators were being purchased annually worldwide, in what had become a $1 billion industry. Another popular application that could not have existed without the microchip, the digital watch, was introduced in 1971, and millions of those products continue to be sold. Microchips opened up other new avenues of technology that had formerly been impossible due to the bulkiness of the electronic equipment. The microchip was used in a variety of deep space probes and in the onboard computers on manned flights to the moon. By the mid-1970s the modern computer industry began to hit its full stride, developing machines that were continually smaller, faster, less expensive, and more durable, and gradually giving rise to the desktop computer. Without the microchip, computer technology might not yet be available to the average consumer.

In 1968 Kilby became an assistant vice president at Texas Instruments, and in 1970 he was named the director of engineering and technology for their components group. In November of the latter year, he took a leave of absence from Texas Instruments in order to pursue other interests, though he remains on staff as a part time consultant. Since that time he has been a self-employed inventor, and he holds more than 60 patents obtained over the course of his career. Between 1975 and 1984 he devoted much of his time to an innovative solar energy project in which the processes of collecting and storing the energy were combined. Although the system proved commercially feasible and Texas Instruments acquired the rights to the idea, it was never marketed because a drop in oil prices decreased consumer interest in solar power. Between 1978 and 1985 Kilby served as a distinguished professor of electrical engineering at Texas A & M University. Now semi-retired, he travels worldwide as a consultant for the electronics industry and the U.S. government. In 1998, in honor of the 40th anniversary of the invention of the microchip, Texas Instruments dedicated a research building in Kilby's honor.

In October 2000 the Nobel Committee awarded half of the Nobel Prize in Physics to Kilby, with the other half going jointly to ZHORES I. ALFEROV and HERBERT KROEMER for their contributions in the area of "semiconductor heterostructures used in high-speed- and opto-electronics." While many in the scientific community believe that a Nobel Prize for Kilby was long overdue, Kilby himself was much more modest about his accomplishments. "The integrated circuit didn't have much new physics in it," he said with a shrug to reporters at his front door, as quoted by Golden in *Time*. The Swedish Royal Academy, however, didn't see it that way: Kilby's invention has spawned an industry worth more than $230 billion worldwide and is the building block for nearly every electronic device on the planet. As quoted on the Texas Instruments Web site, a 1997 television program called Kilby, "one of the few people who can look around the globe and say to himself, 'I changed how the world functions.'"

In addition to the Nobel Prize, Jack Kilby has been the recipient of a variety of distinguished awards for his contributions to technology, including the National Medal of Science, presented in a ceremony at the White House in 1970. He has also received the Ballantine Medal from the Franklin Institute (1967), the Alumni Achievement Award from the University of Illinois (1974), and the 1982 Holley Medal from the American Society of Mechanical Engineers. He was inducted into the National Inventors Hall of Fame at the United States Patent Office in 1981, and is a fellow of the Institute of Electrical and Electronics Engineers (IEEE) and the National Academy of Engi-neering. He holds a number of honorary doctorates, including ones from the University of Miami (1982), the Rochester Institute of Technology (1986), the University of Illinois (1988), the University of Wisconsin (1990), and Yale University (1996).

On June 27, 1948, Jack St. Clair Kilby married Barbara Annegers; they have two daughters, Ann and Janet Lee.

ABOUT: Computer Pioneers, 1995; Larousse Dictionary of Scientists, 1994; Slater, Robert. Portraits in Silicon, 1987; Nobel e-Museum Web site; Science October 20, 2000; Texas Instruments Web site; Time October 23, 2000.

© The Nobel Foundation

Kim Dae Jung

(kim die zhun)

(January 6, 1924–) Nobel Prize for Peace, 2000

The politician Kim Dae Jung was born on January 6, 1924 on the island of Hayi-do off South Korea's southwestern Cholla province, the second of seven children born to a middle-class farmer and his wife. In 1943 Kim graduated from a commercial high school in the port city of Mokpo in Cholla, and he later studied economics at Kyung Hee University in Seoul. When he entered the freight-shipping business, Kim demonstrated such acumen that he headed his own company within a few years, as the relatively wealthy owner of nine small freighters; at the same time, he published a daily provincial newspaper, the *Mokpo Daily News*. Although Kim joined a hybrid Korean nationalist organization in 1946, he soon repudiated its Communist elements by quitting the group.

When Communist North Korean forces invaded South Korea in 1950, setting off the Korean War, Kim was arrested in Mokpo by the occupying forces as a "reactionary capitalist" and barely escaped execution by a firing squad. After the conflict's resolution in 1953, North and South Korea were divided as allies of the Soviet Union and of the United States, respectively, and Kim embarked on his political career, running unsuccessfully three times, beginning in 1954, as a representative in the party opposing President Syngman Rhee. In the brief and unstable period of democracy that followed Rhee's forced resignation in 1960, he served as official spokesman for Prime Minister Chang Myon and went on to win an assembly seat in a by-election that year. But Kim's tenure had barely begun when a military coup led by Major General Park Chung Hee overthrew the government and dissolved the legislature in May 1961. Along with many other political figures, Kim was arrested and briefly imprisoned by the junta. The electoral process was restored in 1963, and Kim, determined to "agitate for democracy," won a landslide victory as assembly representative from the Mokpo district. He won reelection in 1967, a mandate that, in his opinion, indicated a general discontent with Park's autocratic policies.

Exploiting his advantageous position, which was further strengthened by two more successful reelections, Kim roundly opposed Park's rightist political agenda for South Korea. The surprise choice over older opposition figures, he then emerged as the favored candidate for the New Democratic party in the campaign for the presidential election slated for 1971. Addressing huge crowds throughout the country, he advocated liberal reforms that, unlike Park's policies, acknowledged the thaw in the Cold War: a softened diplomacy with North Korea and the USSR; gradual disbandment of the South's two-million–member home militia; and a "hands-off" agreement by the United States, Soviet Union, China, and Japan with regard to Korea. On the domestic front, Kim called for economic policies that would benefit all Koreans, not just an elite. He accused Park's government of excessive corruption and charged Park himself with blatantly seeking to crush democratic institutions in order to "prolong his regime in the name of anti-communism and national security." Although Kim lost to Park in the April 1971 election, amid charges of government fraud, the 46 percent of the vote he drew testified to his popularity and marked him as a formidable challenge to the establishment.

After his defeat Kim continued to press for more democratic processes in South Korea, though his voice was muffled by the government-sanctioned ban against mentioning his name that had been imposed upon the newspapers. That year he was injured in an automobile accident, which was later acknowledged to be an assassination attempt staged by the South Korean Central Intelligence Agency (KCIA). Despite the harassment and surveillance that he endured during that trying period, Kim managed to cultivate ties with the international Korean community. In San Francisco, for example, he established a chapter of the National Congress for the Restoration of Democracy and Promotion of the Unification of Korea, known as the Han Min Tong, with the stated aim of opposing Park's "dictatorial regime." In October 1972, while Kim was away on a trip to Japan, his worst fears were realized by Park's imposition of martial law, suspen-

sion of the constitution, and roundup of opposition critics under what was called the Yushin, or "revitalization," system.

Refusing to return to Korea lest he be silenced there, Kim mounted a vigorous protest against the repressive developments in his native land, and he sought American diplomatic intervention for the restoration of parliamentary democracy. But in August 1973 his activity was cut short. While attending a conference in Tokyo to establish a Han Min Tong chapter there, Kim was abducted from his hotel by suspected operatives of the KCIA. Gagged and tied with weights, he was taken back to Korea by boat. Just as he was about to be thrown overboard, a helicopter fired signal flares and deterred his captors from killing him. After five days, Kim was delivered to his home in Seoul, where he was placed under arrest. It was widely believed that only the international outcry that followed his disappearance had spared his life, and relations between South Korea and Japan, which argued that its sovereignty had been violated, were strained for a considerable time afterward. (Kim believes that the signal flares came through the intervention of the American CIA, though no such connection has been proven.)

A Japanese diplomatic initiative brought about Kim's release from house arrest after two months. Because, as he put it, South Korea offered "no freedom of the press, no freedom of assembly, no freedom of political activity," Kim hoped to continue his organizational work abroad, possibly in the United States. Although the government promised no discriminatory delay in acting on his passport application, some eight months later Kim was still languishing in Seoul under sporadic surveillance. There he was charged with minor election-law violations dating back to 1967 and 1971, along with a miscellany of other indictments for criticizing the administration. The verdict in that case, given in December 1975, sentenced him to a year's confinement and fined him $100.

By South Korean standards of the time, Kim had received only a mild rebuke. If anything, President Park's grip on the country, which he vowed not to relax any time soon, had intensified in the mid-1970s. Although his restrictions on basic freedoms had somewhat eased following a visit from President Gerald R. Ford in late 1974, a new "emergency" decree in 1975 proscribed all political actions that could remotely be construed as being anti-government in nature. Denouncing that measure as "a method to suppress the people's will," Kim decried the official pretext that national security required the curtailment of political and religious expression, and he called for "moral support and sympathy" for his stance from the United States, which still had some 40,000 troops based in South Korean territory.

In early 1976 Kim joined a dozen distinguished Koreans, among them religious leaders, university professors, and a former president, in signing a statement urging Park's resignation, restoration of the parliamentary system, and an independent judiciary. Arrests swiftly followed the letter's public reading, which took place on the March 1st anniversary of the Koreans' uprising against their Japanese overlords in 1919, at Myongdong Roman Catholic Cathedral in Seoul. The subsequent trial provoked clashes between police and the dissidents' supporters, some of whom placed tape over their mouths in the form of a cross to signify the "crucifixion" of democracy. Incarcerated while the case dragged on, with no opportunity for bail, that August the ailing Kim was hit with an eight-year prison term for advocating the overthrow of the government. He served about 33 months of his sentence, during which he was allowed one ten-minute visit each week from his wife.

In the same month that Kim was released from prison, in December 1978, under a suspended sentence because of ill health, the New Democratic party (NDP), tamed but still existing under the Park regime, outpolled the ruling Democratic Republican party in the general election. That victory, though in name only, emboldened Kim Young Sam, the NDP leader, to mount more vocal criticisms of Park than he had attempted for some years, and in so doing, he inspired a popular reawakening as well. Although Kim Dae Jung no longer held an official NDP position, he gave behind-the-scenes support, despite his restricted status under house arrest, to Kim Young Sam's "determination to fight . . . to restore democracy." He welcomed President Jimmy Carter's visit to South Korea in 1979, calling him "a man of faith" who had spelled out a clear human-rights policy, but warned in an interview for *Sojourners* magazine (October 1979) that Carter's praise of South Korea's "economic miracle" "implied that economic development should come first, sacrificing every-

thing else, including human freedoms and workers' rights." "You cannot break a person's body, mind, and spirit and then tell him he's free to exercise his rights," he continued. " . . . The spirit, the determination, the moral fabric of the nation is steadily declining under the present system. People are saying, 'What's the use?'"

On October 26, 1979 President Park was assassinated by the chief of the KCIA, Kim Jae Kyu, and Choi Kyu Hah, a career diplomat, was installed as acting president by the martial law commanders, who seemed ready to end Park's authoritarian system. Taking advantage of the hiatus as an opportunity for reform, Kim Dae Jung lifted his moratorium on political activity by releasing a statement, a week after the assassination, that called for direct election of the president and the national assembly "according to the will of the people." He also asked the United States to "assure the neutrality of the [South Korean] military" during the transition. When he was released from confinement the following month, under a general amnesty that freed some 70 other dissidents at the same time, Kim voiced his fears of political and social chaos if the restoration of democracy were delayed. At the same time he made clear that he hoped to run for president. To bring the political life of South Korea back to normal, he advocated the early lifting of martial law, amendment of the constitution, and appointment of a cabinet representing the diverse political parties, dissidents, journalists, and scholars who had previously been silenced.

When his civil rights were restored in March 1980 along with those of several hundred other activists, Kim began to criticize the NDP and the passivity, vacillation, and personal ambition of its leader, Kim Young Sam. He apparently took preliminary steps to form his own opposition party, and his stance, which was later termed "political suicide" by one observer, led army leaders to accuse him of having a communist background and of holding radical views. But he refuted the charges, which originated from the cadre surrounding Lieutenant General Chun Doo Hwan, the strongest figure in the new junta, by declaring: "I am a moderate, a pragmatist. I am a Christian and have made Christianity the standard for all my actions. Above all, I believe in nonviolence. At the same time, I never compromised. . . . I am not a socialist."

Impatient for the vaguely promised reforms, thousands of student demonstrators took to the streets of Seoul and other cities in early May. On May 16 Kim was arrested, following the release of a military report charging him with sedition in the form of "mass agitation," sympathies with North Korea, Marxist connections, and incitement of student leaders. The next day rebels successfully overran Kwangju, capital city of the Cholla province, in a fierce uprising that was quelled over the next few weeks, with some 1,000 Koreans reportedly killed. When Kim was hauled into military court in July to be tried for sedition by four generals, responsibility for that revolt was added to his indictments, along with accusations of communism that largely stemmed from his involvement with the Han Min Tong, which in 1978 had been declared "anti-state" on claims that it was funded by North Korean sources. An official campaign to discredit him inundated the Korean press. "Kim has the erroneous image of a patriot, a democrat, an anti-Communist, a hero and a martyr," one writer fumed. "Kim's positive image abroad is a mask behind which hides a dedicated, ruthless, methodical, and lifelong revolutionary idealist."

Kim later reported that he underwent 60 days of continuous questioning under threats of torture before his trial, which was joined to that of 23 of his supporters, including one of his sons and a younger brother. Faced with a prosecution that failed to call witnesses, and saddled with "gagged" and court-appointed lawyers, he denied every major charge, arguing that he "sought to gain power through elections" and had "never advocated the use of violence for political purposes." (No independent source has ever confirmed claims of the Han Min Tong's Communist backing.) Many demands for leniency, along with assertions that the charges were "farfetched," came from the United States, including a personal letter from President Jimmy Carter to Lieutenant General Chun, while Japanese diplomats also applied pressure for a fair and rational handling of the case. But in September 1980 Kim was sentenced to death by hanging for sedition, despite his conciliatory summing up in which he admitted that he had not reported American and Japanese currency that he held, conceded that he had held meetings without permission, and accepted "some moral responsibility for the demonstrations."

Chun Doo Hwan, who became president following Choi Kyu Hah's resignation, commuted Kim's sentence to 20 years' imprisonment in early 1981, just before leaving for Washington, D.C., as the first head of state to be received by President Ronald Reagan. Then, in December 1982, Kim was released from prison, for official reasons of "humanitarianism and the desire to promote national unity"—and with the proviso that he leave South Korea. Ostensibly to receive medical treatment for arthritis, Kim arrived in Washington, D.C., with his wife and two of his sons that month. Although grateful for his American reception, he lamented what he considered to be official United States support for "dictatorial regimes in the name of anti-Communism, security, and economic rehabilitation." During his American exile, Kim helped to create the Korean Institute for Human Rights in Arlington, Virginia, and accepted a fellowship at the Center for International Affairs at Harvard University. He tried to visit President Reagan during his stay, but without any success.

Dissatisfied with his efforts to sway events in South Korea from a point as remote from Seoul as Washington, D.C., in the fall of 1984 Kim announced his plan to return there, even though the Chun regime made clear its view that "political and social instability" would ensue. After consulting Seoul authorities, members of the State Department tried to persuade him to delay his trip until after the national assembly elections, slated for February 1985, offering Chun's guarantee not to arrest him again if he did so. But, encouraged by the eager anticipation of his arrival among opposition groups, who had formed the New Korea Democratic Party (NKDP) in early 1985, Kim rejected the compromise proposal.

With memories still fresh in their minds of Benigno Aquino Jr.'s fatal shooting when he returned from exile to the Philippines in 1983, some 20 American human-rights activists concerned about official reaction to Kim joined his flight on February 8, 1985, along with a number of reporters. When they disembarked at Seoul airport, which had been made off-limits to thousands of Kim's supporters, security guards apparently forced Kim and his wife out of the grip of their companions—among them Robert E. White, the former ambassador to El Salvador, and Patricia Derian, an assistant secretary of state for human rights in the Carter administration—who said they had been kicked and punched and Kim had been knocked down in the scuffle. Making headlines around the world, the incident was either downplayed as mere "manhandling" or inflated into a "beating," and Richard L. Wilbur, the United States ambassador to South Korea, registered an official complaint requesting an inquiry. Kim was then confined to his home in Seoul.

By capturing an electoral majority in South Korea's largest cities and winning nearly 30 percent of the vote nationwide, the NKDP emerged as a strong, legitimate contender in the national assembly elections that were held four days after Kim's return. The party had openly campaigned for constitutional reforms, including direct presidential elections, and Kim's presence in South Korea was widely credited with inspiring the voters' trust in that platform. Perhaps most surprising was the official response to the NKDP groundswell: a spokesman for Chun's ruling Democratic Justice Party, which retained the assembly majority, acknowledged the balloting as "a demand for change in our attitude . . . [and for] gradual democracy and more liberalization."

Even Kim expressed much optimism, which was borne out the following month when he and Kim Young Sam were among the last names removed from a political blacklist in recognition of the "new political climate . . . born of a harmonizing blend of freedom and order." Because he was still barred from joining or organizing a political party, Kim restricted his activity to cochairing, with Kim Young Sam, the Council for the Promotion of Democracy, which worked as a support group for the NKDP. In April 1985 several opposition parties, reportedly shepherded by Kim, merged under the NKDP banner, arousing hopes that a genuine democratic dialogue was finally underway in South Korea.

Yet those prospects appeared less certain by the fall of 1985. Kim, informed that he must "repent" in order to regain his full rights and threatened with reinstatement of his suspended 20 year sentence, had to bear surveillance and periodic confinement, and a new series of campus arrests and dismissals of activists was started. "I am much afraid of the possibility of polarization, with the military dictatorship on one side and radical elements on the other," Kim ex-

plained, as quoted in the *New York Times* (October 1, 1985). "In that case, we moderate democrats will lose our base."

After the South Korean government lifted Kim Dae Jung's ban on holding political office, he and Kim Young Sam ran as opposition candidates for president in 1987, the first direct election in 16 years. Many who followed South Korean politics viewed Kim Dae Jung as the more progressive candidate and believed he was less likely to win the presidency because, they suspected, the military would never let him assume office. Kim Young Sam, though a pro-democracy candidate, voiced a more moderate approach and therefore was less feared by the military. The two Kims battled each other fiercely during the campaign and as a result split the pro-democracy votes, allowing Roh Taw Woo, President Chun Doo Hwan's handpicked successor, to assume the presidency in 1988. Kim Dae Jung was reappointed to the National Assembly in April 1988 on the national constituency ticket of the Party for Peace and Democracy.

Relations between the two Kims were further strained in 1990 when Kim Young Sam merged his opposition political party with President Roh's ruling party, which enabled Kim Young Sam to run for president as the ruling party candidate in the 1992 election. Kim Dae Jung, outraged by what he saw as a great shift in his former partner's politics, ran for the presidency as an opposition candidate. Kim Young Sam won the 1992 election and began to make a series of reforms intended to fortify democracy in South Korea. He repeatedly stated that he wanted to "right the wrongs of history," starting with punishing those involved in the May 1980 massacre of pro-democracy protestors in Kwangju. In 1995 former presidents Chun and Roh were arrested and imprisoned for their roles in the suppression of fundamental democratic and human rights.

After the 1992 election Kim Dae Jung announced he was leaving politics, and he did—for 31 months. In 1995 he formed a new political party, the National Congress for New Politics, in part as a response to growing corruption in President Kim Young Sam's government as well as the faltering South Korean economy. Kim Dae Jung ran for president again in 1997, attempting to hammer home his accusation that President Kim's party was merely an extension of the Roh regime, despite the name change. (In

1996 President Kim had changed the ruling party's name to the New Korea Party.) In a typical stump speech, as quoted in the *Los Angeles Times* (January 24, 1996), Kim Dae Jung demanded: "What is the New Korea Party? If you look at the party registration . . . , the first president of that party is Chun Doo Hwan, the second president is Roh Tae Woo and the third president is Kim Young Sam. How can he separate from the past if he inherits the name of the party, the assets of the party and the people of the party? Merely changing the name does not change the party."

In the 1997 election, Kim Dae Jung claimed that his sole intention was to force Kim Young Sam to respect opposition parties, as he had when he was a member of one. However, the issue that sold South Koreans on electing a new president was the downward spiraling economy, which had led to growing unemployment, escalating food prices, and daily bankruptcies. The instability of the economy led President Kim Young Sam to accept a $57-billion loan from the International Monetary Fund in order to keep his government solvent. In a three-way election, in which the candidates included Kim Dae Jung, Lee Hoi Chang, and Rhee In Je, Kim won the presidency on a minority of the popular vote. Despite his lack of a strong mandate, his election was seen worldwide as a significant step towards stabilizing South Korea's democracy and economy. Nisid Hajari, writing for *Time* (December 29, 1997–January 5, 1998) proclaimed Kim's election to be "an epochal choice for Korea, ushering in a promise of political transformation after a half-century of authoritarian orthodoxy and one-party rule."

Kim Dae Jung took several bold actions before he was sworn in as president in February 1998. He met with outgoing President Kim and arranged for the release of former Presidents Chun and Roh, who accepted Kim Dae Jung's invitation to sit on the viewing stand during his inauguration. Long a champion of labor unions and small businesses, he met with the executives of Korea's largest conglomerates, called chaebols, and discussed corporate restructuring that would lead to freer trade. (The chaebols have controlled most of the industry in the country since the Korean War, with the top 30 of them responsible for 80 percent of South Korea's gross national product.) Since becoming president he has sought to open South Korea to foreign markets, lower trade barriers, and stimulate foreign investment. In his inaugural address he promised that his government would "actively pursue reconciliation and cooperation" with North Korea and would work to improve relations between the North and the United States and Japan.

Kim's approval ratings soared following his election, and supported by the vast majority of the Korean people, he has been able to accomplish many of his goals since becoming president. By July 1999, a year and a half after he took office, the South Korean economy was showing signs of rebound, having benefitted greatly from economic discipline and foreign investment streaming in from American companies such as Hewlett-Packard. He has had more difficulty in dismantling the chaebols, though he has extracted promises from their executives to halve the number of companies controlled by the conglomerates and to raise money to bolster their financial health.

In foreign affairs, Kim has continued to maintain good relations with the United States and has brought his country remarkably closer to Japan, Korea's ancient rival in the region. There is a long history of mutual resentment between Japan and Korea, dating back to arguments about whether Japan was originally populated by people from Korea, as most experts believe, or vise-versa. This hostility was exacerbated when the Japanese military, during its 36-year occupation of Korea before and during World War II, attempted to destroy the Korean language, made Koreans take Japanese names, and forced many Korean women into prostitution. In 1999, President Kim was able to do what no other Korean president had managed to achieve—namely, he obtained a written apology from the Japanese government for its vicious colonization of Korea. As of 2001 these two countries, bonded by a common threat in North Korea as well as mutual free market systems, are rapidly deepening their ties as they plan to jointly host the 2002 World Cup international soccer tournament.

Kim Dae Jung's greatest accomplishment thus far as South Korean president has been his "sunshine policy" towards Communist North Korea. Kim described the philosophy behind the policy to Alvin Toffler for the *New Perspectives Quarterly* (Winter 1998): "The idea comes from the old fable in which the wind and the sun compete to make a man take off his jacket. The cold, blowing wind only makes him bundle up tighter; the warm sunshine compels him to take the jacket off by his own volition. If you let the sun shine in instead of closing them off, North Korea will change." Through this policy, as well as humanitarian aid to the famine-scourged North, Kim has sought to bring about an end to the 50-year-old formal state of war that has existed between the two Koreas. In 1998 Kim's government began the first formal talks in four years with the government of Chairman Kim Jong Il, North Korea's Communist leader. Kim Dae Jung also lifted restrictions on business deals between the North and South; promoted South Korean tourism of the North; sought to ease the American embargo on North Korean goods; and has stepped up efforts to reunite family members separated since the Korean War on opposite sides of the two countries' hostile and heavily armed border.

In June 2000 Kim Dae Jung made history when he traveled to North Korea to meet with his counterpart, for the first in what it is hoped will be a series of summits that will ultimately pave the way for the reunification of North and South Korea. President Kim was warmly received by Chairman Kim Jong Il, whom he found receptive to the idea of better relations between their two countries. The emphasis of these talks was on initial reconciliation, rather than instant reunification. As Kim Dae Jung stated in his Nobel Lecture, the specifics of his policy regarding the North are as follows: "First, we will never accept unification through communization; second, nor would we attempt to achieve unification by absorbing the North; and third, South and North Korea should seek peaceful coexistence and cooperation. Unification, I believe, can wait until such a time when both sides feel comfortable enough in becoming one again, no matter how long it takes." During the summit, the two leaders agreed that they should develop a "loose form of federation," in which their countries would have closer economic ties that would allow them to be "one people, two systems, two independent governments," as a prelude to future reunification. In addition, they agreed to the continued presence of American troops as a stabilizing force along the 38th parallel, which separates the two countries. They also agreed that the demilitarized zone surrounding

their border should not be a complete blockade; rather, there should be more travel between the North and South, particularly to allow families separated since the Korean War to reunite. Since the summit many such families have been brought together, and the Korean people, for the first time in 50 years, competed in the Olympics under the same flag.

Kim Dae Jung, who stands five-feet-six-inches tall, walks with a slight limp and sometimes uses a cane due to injuries sustained during the 1971 KCIA-sponsored automobile accident that nearly took his life. He has two sons by his marriage to his first wife, who died in 1959, and one son by Lee Hee Ho, a former YWCA administrator in South Korea, whom he married in 1962. Kim is a devout Roman Catholic, and by his own accounts, he often called upon his faith to help him through the darkest periods in his life. He is also an expert calligrapher, and an avid reader in three languages—Korean, Japanese, and English. The last of these Kim learned from an American Peace Corps volunteer and by teaching himself, using a Korean-English dictionary to help him read Korea's English-language daily newspaper, the *Korea Times*. "He loves to study, and that's very important to understanding Kim Dae Jung. That's what makes him young," Kim Min Seok, a Korean National Assembly Member, told Nicolas D. Kristof for the *New York Times* (February 23, 1998). When Kristof asked Kim Dae Jung who his heros are, one of Kim's responses was Abraham Lincoln. "What I respect most about Lincoln is his spirit of forgiveness," Kim told the reporter, going on to quote Lincoln's second inaugural address: "With malice toward none, with charity for all."

On October 13, 2000, the Norwegian Nobel Committee announced its decision to award the Nobel Peace Prize to Kim Dae Jung "for his work for democracy and human rights in South Korea and in East Asia in general, and for peace and reconciliation with North Korea in particular." Acknowledging that the struggle for peace is an open-ended quest, Kim declared in his Nobel lecture: "I humbly pledge to you, as the great heroes of history have taught us, as ALFRED NOBEL would expect of us, I shall give the rest of my life to human rights and peace in my country and the world, and to the reconciliation and cooperation of my people. I ask for your encouragement and the abiding support of all who are committed to advancing democracy and peace around the world."

ABOUT: Christian Science Monitor July 9, 1979; Los Angeles Times January 24, 1996; The Nation March 30, 1998, July 10, 2000; New Perspectives Quarterly Winter 1998; New York Times March 29, 1971, September 17, 1980, February 9, 1985, February 23, 1998, March 30, 1998, December 2, 1998, February 25, 1999, April 25, 1999, July 3, 1999, July 20, 1999, September 20, 1999; New York Times Magazine December 23, 1984; Nobel e-Museum Web site; Sojourners October 1979; Time December 29, 1997–January 5, 1998; Time (on-line) June 26, 2000, January 17, 2001; Wall Street Journal July 3, 1999; Washington Post August 25, 1973, August 26, 1973, December 18, 1997, December 21, 1997; U.S. News and World Report p39 March 9, 1998.

© The Nobel Foundation

Knowles, William S.

(June 1, 1917–) Nobel Prize for Chemistry, 2001 (shared with K. Barry Sharpless and Ryoji Noyouri)

The chemist William Standish Knowles was born on June 1, 1917 in Taunton, Massachusetts. He studied chemistry at Harvard University, in Cambridge, Massachusetts, receiving his B.A. in 1939. He received a Ph.D. in steroid chemistry from Columbia University, in New York City, in 1942. Upon graduation he accepted a position at Monsanto, a chemical company located in St. Louis, Missouri. In 1951 he studied the total synthesis of steroids while working in the laboratory of the Harvard chemistry professor and Nobel laureate Robert B. Woodward—an opportunity made possible through a postdoctoral fellowship sponsored by Monsanto. Knowles later referred to the experience as "a turning point in my career," as quoted by Stu Borman in *Chemical & Engineering News* (November 5, 2001). Under Woodward he was exposed to a type of synthesis that was much more complex than the industrial-process development projects he had worked on at Monsanto. Up to that point, Knowles had specialized in exploratory process development on organic chemicals and intermediates. His experience with Woodward led him to focus on the total synthesis of steroids.

In the late 1960s Knowles served as the head of a three-man team that included Monsanto organic chemists Billy D. Vineyard and M. Jerry Sabacky. Knowles and his co-workers were hoping to find a catalyst that could produce individual enantiomers of chiral compounds. The term "chiral" refers to molecules that are mirror images of each other. Human hands can be described as chiral—the right hand is a mirror image of the left. The individual molecules of a chiral pair are called enantiomers. Most molecules have chiral opposites; however, the enantiomers of a chiral pair can have very different properties. In some cases, one of the enantiomers may have harmful effects. In the early 1960s, thalidomide, a morning-sickness drug, was prescribed to pregnant women. The drug contained a 50-50 combination of both enantiomers. One of the enantiomers successfully eased morning sickness. The other, as was discovered only later, tended to cause fetal abnormalities. The reason for this is that in the cells of the human body, frequently only one form of a chiral pair is found. This is the case in all of the body's naturally occurring amino acids (the molecular building blocks that compose proteins), as well as in the carbohydrates and nucleic acids such as DNA and RNA. Pharmaceutical companies, accordingly, were very interested in devising methods to produce drugs that were "pure enantiomers"—drugs that contained only the desired enantiomer, and not its mirror opposite. The process of producing more of one enantiomer than the other was called "asymmetric synthesis"—and it was this goal that Knowles and his team sedulously pursued.

The breakthrough came in 1968 when Knowles discovered that rhodium—a hard, white, ductile metal—when combined with a chiral phosphine, could be used as a chiral catalyst in a hydrogenation reaction (hydrogenation is the process in which hydrogen is added to organic molecules). Knowles and his co-workers initially obtained only a modest success, producing a 15 percent excess of one enantiomer. Although of little practical use, the results showed that catalytic asymmetric hydrogenation was possible. Encouraged, Knowles pursued an industrial synthesis of the amino acid L-DOPA, which is used in the treatment of Parkinson's disease. Knowles and his team succeeded in producing rhodium catalysts that produced enantiomeric excesses of up to 95 percent. The rhodium catalyst was very expensive, but was so efficient in producing large quantities of L-DOPA that Monsanto was able to capitalize on the discovery. Knowles's achievement thus became the "Monsanto Process," the first commercialized catalytic asymmetric synthesis, which has been in operation since 1974.

In 1981 Monsanto presented Knowles, Vineyard, and Sabacky with the Charles A. Thomas and Carroll A. Hochwalt Award, along with the sum of $25,000, in honor of their work. Dr. Howard A. Schneiderman, Monsanto's senior vice president of research and development at the time, said that "this achievement capped a century-long effort by organic chemists to control in a practical way the introduction of asymmetry in a molecule." Knowles's research was later used in the production of antibiotics, anti-inflammatory drugs, and heart medicines.

RYOJI NOYORI, a scientist from Nagoya University, in Japan, further developed Knowles's work, producing catalysts that are used in the creation of fine chemicals and other pharmaceutical products. K. BARRY SHARPLESS, a scientist from the Scripps Research Institute, in La Jolla, California, developed similar chiral catalysts for use in oxidation reactions. His work has led to, among other things, the development of drugs for reducing blood pressure. On Octo-

ber 10, 2001 the Royal Swedish Academy of Sciences announced that the three would share that year's Nobel Prize in Chemistry. Upon the announcement of the award Knowles's colleagues expressed their approval of the Nobel committee's decision to honor his work. "Knowles's monumental contributions cannot be overstated," the chemistry professor emeritus Jack Halpern of the University of Chicago said, as quoted by Stu Borman in *Chemical & Engineering News* (November 5, 2001). "The recognition and praise, albeit belated, are richly deserved and highly gratifying." Eric N. Jacobsen, a chemistry professor at Harvard University, explained to Borman that the decision may have been a surprise to some, "partly because [Knowles] worked in industry and partly because the work that he did is now 30 years old. So a lot of people just aren't aware of it. But when I was a postdoc with [K. Barry] Sharpless, I asked him what was the event or who was the person who gave him the inspiration and the confidence to work in the field of asymmetric catalysis. He didn't even think for a second. He immediately said, 'It was Knowles.'"

Knowles retired from Monsanto in 1986. He currently lives in St. Louis, Missouri.

ABOUT: BBC News (on-line) October 10, 2001; Chemical & Engineering News November 5, 2001; Nature (on-line) October 11, 2001; Nobel e-Museum Web site.

Kohn, Walter

(March 9, 1923–) Nobel Prize for Chemistry, 1998 (shared with John A. Pople)

The physicist WALTER KOHN was born on March 9, 1923 in Vienna, Austria, into a middle-class Jewish family. His father operated a business that commissioned and sold high-quality art postcards; his mother was an educated woman who sent her son to a high school in Vienna that offered a classical education in Latin and Greek. When the Nazis annexed Austria, in 1938, Kohn was expelled from this school. The next year he was admitted to a Jewish high school, where Dr. Emil Nohel, a physics teacher, and Dr. Victor Sabbath, a mathematics teacher,

© The Nobel Foundation

Walter Kohn

sparked his interest in science. "While outside the school walls arbitrary acts of persecution and brutality took place," Kohn recalled in an autobiographical essay posted on the Nobel e-Museum Web site, "on the inside these two inspired teachers conveyed to us their own deep understanding and love of their subjects."

In 1939, at age 16, Kohn qualified for passage on *Kindertransport*, a transport program that brought Jewish children from Nazi-occupied countries to Great Britain. Kohn's parents, Salomon and Gittel Kohn, remained in Austria and were killed by the Nazis. Kohn and his older sister lived for two years with an English family in Sussex. In May 1940, with Hitler sweeping through Western Europe, Kohn was sent to a British internment camp as a male "enemy alien"— someone in possession of a passport from a country that was then part of Germany. In July of that year he was shipped to Canada, to internment camps in Quebec and New Brunswick. Thanks to a camp education program, he was able to continue his scientific studies. In July 1942 Kohn was released and taken in by a Toronto family, who helped support his study of mathematics and physics at the University of Toronto. In 1944 he joined the Canadian Army, and the next year he completed a wartime degree in mathematics and physics. In 1945 he was discharged from service and earned a master's degree in applied mathematics at the University of Toronto.

Kohn then won a Lehman fellowship to enter a doctoral program in theoretical physics at Harvard University, in Cambridge, Massachusetts. He earned his Ph.D. in 1948 and stayed at Harvard for two years as a researcher and teacher.

In 1950 Kohn became an assistant professor in the physics department at Carnegie Institute of Technology (now Carnegie-Mellon University), in Pittsburgh, Pennsylvania. After teaching for only one semester, he took a leave of absence to pursue a National Research Council fellowship in Copenhagen. He returned to the Carnegie Institute in 1952 and taught there until 1960, eventually becoming a full professor. (He became a naturalized American citizen in 1957.) He also worked as a consultant to the Westinghouse Research Laboratories (1953–1957) and Bell Telephone Laboratories (1953–1966).

Kohn became a professor of physics at the University of California at San Diego in 1960. In 1963 he went to Paris on a Guggenheim fellowship as a visiting professor at the École Normale Supérieure, where he met the American physicist Pierre Hohenberg. The pair began work on a theory that eventually unlocked the secrets of quantum mechanics by suggesting an alternative to the wave equation suggested by the Austrian physicist and 1933 Nobel laureate Erwin Schrödinger. Schrödinger's equation described the movement of an electron in an atom as a wave. According to a writer for *Physics Today* (December 1998), Schrödinger's equation is "straightforward enough to write down, but nearly impossible to solve exactly." In other words, it is easy to figure out how electrons behave around atomic nuclei of small bits of matter like a hydrogen atom, but it is quite another thing to use this equation with molecules of 10 or more atoms.

Kohn returned to the University of California in San Diego and continued to work on this problem. In 1964 he developed the density-functional theory, a simple method of mapping the spatial distribution—or density—of electrons. In essence, Kohn proved that density can be used in place of the wave function. Using density as a point of reference, he developed a "density map" from which chemists can uncover the shape, stability, and reactivity of a given molecule's system. Kohn's two research papers, the first written with Hohenberg and the second with a graduate student named Lu J. Sham, gave scientists a new way to look at quantum mechanics. Kohn proved that it is not necessary to consider the motion of every single electron; rather, it is possible to make computations based on the average number of electrons found in a given point in space.

In work done with the postdoctoral student Norton Lang, Kohn expanded his density-functional theory in the early 1970s. He applied his theory to surfaces as well as to the development of time-dependent density functional analysis. Today, the theory is used by researchers and chemists to study large molecules or chains of molecules. According to the *Science News* (October 17, 1998) writer C. Wu, density-functional theory is "one of the main theoretical tools of chemists." A *Science* (October 23, 1998) writer noted: "Observers say that at least half of all research papers incorporating computational chemistry now use density-functional theory."

In 1979 Kohn left San Diego to become the first director of the National Science Foundation's Institute of Theoretical Physics, at the University of California in Santa Barbara (UCSB). At the end of his five-year term, he became a professor of physics at the Institute; in 1991 he became an emeritus and research professor at UCSB.

Walter Kohn and John Pople shared the 1998 Nobel Prize for Chemistry for what the Nobel Committee termed their "pioneering contributions in developing methods that can be used for theoretical studies of the properties of molecules and the chemical processes in which they are involved." Building on Kohn's theoretical groundwork, Pople developed in 1970 the first computational system for modeling the shape of molecules and predicting the outcome of chemical reactions; Pople's computer program, GAUSSIAN, opened quantum chemistry to the general scientific community.

In addition to the Nobel Prize, Walter Kohn has received a number of awards for his work, including the 1960 Oliver Buckley Prize for solid state physics, the 1977 Davisson-Germer Prize for surface physics, the 1988 National Medal of Science, the 1991 Feenberg Medal for many-body physics, and the 1998 NIELS BOHR/UNITED NATIONS Educational, Scientific and Cultural Organization (UNESCO) Gold Medal. He has also received special recognition for his work from the Royal Society of London and the International Academy of Quantum Molecular Physics.

Kohn's first wife was Lois Kohn. With his second wife, Mara, he has three daughters and three grandchildren. "A person, like myself, who . . . loses a lot of really close relatives somehow through accident or whatever, they automatically have a sense of carrying the lost relatives on his shoulders," Kohn is quoted as saying in UCSB's student newspaper, the *Daily Nexus* (January 17, 2001, on-line). "I feel like I'm doing this work not only on my own behalf but on the behalf of people who didn't make it."

ABOUT: Economist October 17, 1998; New York Times October 14, 1998; Nobel e-Museum Web site; Physics Today December 1998; Science October 23, 1998; Science News October 17, 1998; University of California at Santa Barbara Web site.

Courtesy of Herbert Kroemer

Kroemer, Herbert

(August 25, 1928–) Nobel Prize for Physics, 2000 (shared with Zhores Alferov and Jack St. Clair Kilby)

The physicist Herbert Kroemer was born in Weimar, Germany, on August 25, 1928. He earned a doctorate from the University of Gottingen in Gottingen, Germany, in 1952, writing his dissertation on the flow of electrons in the transistor, a new invention at that time that became the building block of modern computers. After earning his doctorate, Kroemer worked at a laboratory in Germany, and in 1954 he was hired by Radio Corporation of America (RCA), in Princeton, New Jersey.

One of the main contributions to information technology for which Kroemer received the Nobel came in 1957, when he figured out a way to drastically improve the performance of transistors and articulated his idea in a paper entitled "Quasi-Electric and Quasi-Magnetic Fields in Non-Uniform semiconductors," published in the *RCA Review* (1957, vol. 18). At the time, transistors were made from a single layer of a semiconducting material, usually germanium. However, there were inherent obstacles to the efficiency of current flow in the traditional transistor. As electrons flowed through the semiconductor in one direction, so-called "holes"—spaces left in the "sea" of electrons that behave as if they carry a positive charge—flowed in the opposite direction, reducing the amplification of the current, and thus the transistor's power. Kroemer proposed the idea of building a transistor from two layers of semiconductors, called a heterostructure, in such a way that the counter-flow of holes was reduced or eliminated. The first layer might be gallium arsenide, for example, and the second aluminum gallium arsenide. (The original idea was germanium-silicon, but this proved extremely difficult to implement, and is entering heterostructure technology only now.) These complementary semiconductors, Kroemer realized, can be arranged in such a way that either the electrons or the holes, but not both, can flow from one layer to another. In this manner, "You prevent holes from flowing in the reverse directions—they run into a potential barrier," Jim Merz, a physicist at Notre Dame University, told Charles Siefe for *Science* (October 20, 2000). "This was Kroemer's idea; he realized that it had huge implications." It was several decades before the technology required to easily build heterostructured transistors caught up with Kroemer's theory. Eventually heterostructures were used to create high-speed transistors and the low-noise, high-frequency amplifiers used in satellite communications and cell phones.

Kroemer left RCA in 1957 to be a group leader for the German Philips Lab, where he stayed until 1959. He then took a position as a senior scientist at Varian Associates, in Palo Alto, California, where he would remain until 1966. In 1962 the first semiconductor lasers had been demonstrated, but they would operate only at low temperatures and in short pulses. One year later, Kroemer devised a new principle for using heterostructured semiconductors to make lasers. Nearly simultaneously, Zhores Alferov made a similar discovery in the Soviet Union. Lasers fire when electrons in a crystal or other material are stimulated into high energy states and then drop back down to lower energy states nearly simultaneously, emitting a high-energy pulse of light. Kroemer showed that the layers of a heterostructured semiconductor could be configured to direct electrons and holes into a trap from which they cannot flow out. When the electrons and holes are forced to interact inside this trap, it causes the electrons to annihilate each other and emit light, just as in a traditional laser. Kroemer published his findings in "A Proposed Class of Heterojunction Injection Lasers" in *Proceedings of the IEEE* (1963, vol. 51) and filed for a U.S. patent just one week after Alferov applied for a Soviet patent. These new lasers provided the basis for fibre-optic communications, the heads used to read compact discs, and optical data storage. Without the lasers invented by Kroemer and Alferov, these technologies would not exist. Barcode readers are another widely used application. A related technology, heterostructure-based light-emitting diodes (LEDs), are used in brake lights on cars, traffic lights, and other types of warning signals, and may in time replace conventional electric lights. Many scientists expect that, in all applications for which colored light is required, heterostructure LEDs will replace tungsten filament light bulbs before the year 2010, a development that may eventually extend to white light. However, whereas Alferov proceeded to explore and refine his discovery, Kroemer found no support for his invention at Varian Associates. "I was told that the new device could not possibly have any practical applications," Kroemer explained to Richard Fitzgerald for *Physics Today* (December 2000).

In 1966 Kroemer went to work in the New Phenomena section of the Semiconductor Research and Development team at Fairchild Semiconductor. He left Fairchild in 1968 to become a professor of electrical engineering at the University of Colorado at Boulder, where he stayed until 1976. That year Kroemer convinced members of the Electrical and Computer Engineering department at the University of California at Santa Barbara to hire him and expand the department's involvement in semiconductor research, particularly heterostructure research. Thanks to Kroemer's incentive, the university soon became the leader in that field, and Kroemer picked up the thread of his earlier work by focusing on the new area of molecular beam epitaxy, a method for creating heterostructured semiconductors. This sophisticated procedure, greatly furthered by Kroemer's research, is a way of depositing one layer of semiconductor onto another of different chemical composition while maintaining a high degree of purity.

More recently, Kroemer has expanded his research in molecular beam epitaxy by experimenting with untried combinations of semiconductors that might be used to create new heterostructures well-suited to specific applications. This research includes working with superconductor-semiconductor hybrid structures, and devising ways to produce a type of ultra-high-frequency oscillator, known as a Bloch oscillator, which—if successful—would generate signals in the terahertz regime. In 1980 Kroemer gave an address called "Heterostructures for Everything," a statement that has proved true. As Fitzgerald remarked in *Physics Today* (December 2000), "Heterostructures have emerged as the basic building block of semiconductor devices."

Kroemer has received honorary doctorates from the Technical University of Aachen in Germany (1985) and the University of Lund in Sweden (1998). His awards include the J. J. Ebers Award from the Institute of Electrical and Electronics Engineers (IEEE) in 1973; the Jack A. Morton Award from the IEEE in 1986; the Senior Research Award from the American Society for Engineering Education (ASEE) in 1982; the Heinrich Welker Medal of the International symposium on GaAs and Related Compounds in 1982; the Alexander von Humboldt Research Award in 1994; and membership in the National Academy of Engineering begin-

ning in 1997. Kroemer continues to teach at the University of California at Santa Barbara. He married in 1950 and has five children.

ABOUT: Chemical and Engineering News October 16, 2000; New Scientist October 21, 2000; Nobel e-Museum Web site; Physics Today December 2000; Science October 2000; Science News October 14, 2000; Washington Post October 11, 2000.

Courtesy of Stanford University

Laughlin, Robert B.

(November 1, 1950–) Nobel Prize for Physics, 1998 (shared with Daniel C. Tsui and Horst L. Störmer)

The physicist Robert B. Laughlin was born on November 1, 1950 in Visalia, California, the eldest of four children. His father, an attorney, and his mother, a schoolteacher, created a home environment that encouraged thought, debate, and imagination, as Laughlin recalled in an autobiographical essay posted on the Nobel e-Museum Web site. "At dinnertime one of my parents, usually my father, would lead a discussion about some controversial matter, such as racial integration of schools, whether John Lennon should have compared himself with Jesus Christ, support of Israel, or the morality of the Vietnam war, and all of us were expected to air and defend our views on these things, even if we did not want to. Over the course of time this gave us a deep respect for ideas, both our own and those of others, and an understanding that conflict through debate is a powerful means of revealing truth." Laughlin described himself as "an extremely reclusive and introverted boy," not fond of the French or piano lessons his parents arranged for him, but fascinated by electronic appliances and chemistry sets. The beauty of the San Joaquin Valley and nearby Sequoia Park fostered in Laughlin a deep appreciation for the natural world that, he wrote in his essay, "motivates my scientific thinking to this day." Laughlin has also credited his father with instilling his interest in mathematics. As he described in his essay, "[My father] knew very little mathematics himself but was always reading about it and encouraging everybody else to do the same. He even mounted blackboards in the hall so that a person could write down a brilliant idea if he happened to be passing by." In order to understand the electron motion in the vacuum tubes he had been experimenting on, Laughlin taught himself calculus in high school.

In 1968 Laughlin enrolled at the University of California at Berkeley, studying to be an electrical engineer. He found particular inspiration in the physics department, describing it in his essay as having "a palpable sense of history going back to [Werner] Heisenberg, [Wolfgang] Pauli, and Einstein."

During Laughlin's last year of school, President Nixon canceled the program of student deferments, which had kept many college students out of the Vietnam War, and Laughlin was drafted into the army. "I remember vividly the day it was announced and the coldness I felt as the full implications slowly became clear," he recalled in his essay. "It was common knowledge that theoretical physicists do their best work before age 27, sometimes even earlier. I could not possibly meet this deadline now." As the stress of his impending service began to affect his schoolwork, Laughlin failed a laboratory course and ultimately graduated from Berkeley with only a B.A. in mathematics rather than the degrees in mathematics and physics that he had hoped to earn.

In the army Laughlin trained as a Pershing missile specialist and served most of his tour in southern Germany. He returned to the U.S. in 1974, enrolling in a graduate program at the Massachusetts Institute of Technology (MIT). He studied with the research team of Professor John Joannopoulos, learning from him both the basics of solid state physics and the principles of organizing and executing an experimental program. From 1976 to 1978 Laughlin was an IBM Fellow at MIT. He earned his Ph.D. in 1979.

Laughlin obtained a research position at Bell Laboratories, in Murray Hill, New Jersey, joining the theoretical physics group that included his fellow Nobel laureates, Daniel Tsui and Horst Störmer. Tsui and Störmer introduced Laughlin to their research into the two-dimensional electron gas formed through the "Hall effect." This collaboration prompted Laughlin to begin the work that eventually led to his Nobel Prize.

The Hall effect is an electronic phenomenon that was discovered in 1879 by the American physicist Edwin H. Hall, then a 24-year-old college student. Hall conducted an experiment in which he placed a thin gold plate in a magnetic field at right angles to its surface; when he applied the magnetic force, an electric current accumulated on one side of the strip, deflecting in a stream that was perpendicular both to the plate and the magnetic field. Hall observed that this voltage drop, which became known as the Hall effect, was directly proportional to the force of the magnetic field. Hall's contribution has allowed physicists to determine the charge carriers in conductors and semiconductors, facilitating the study of quantum physics. Nevertheless, the cause of the effect remained unexplained for many years, in part because experiments were conducted at room temperature with only a moderate magnetic field. By the late 1970s, however, members of the scientific community were experimenting with the parameters of the Hall effect by using extremely low temperatures, near absolute zero, and strong magnetic fields. In 1980 a German physicist named KLAUS VON KLITZING applied a strong magnet to high-quality silicon and observed that the electrons exhibited a voltage drop that changed in steps—or "quanta"—that were proportional to integer values. For this reason, the effect was named the "integer quantum Hall effect." Von Klitzing's discovery garnered him the Nobel Prize for Physics in 1985.

Just two years after von Klitzing's experiment, Tsui and Störmer, still working at Bell Labs, made a discovery of their own. In preparing their experiment, they used extremely thin layers of arsenic and gallium to, in effect, "sandwich" the electrons so that they could only move along a two-dimensional surface. They placed their device in an ultrapowerful magnet at the Francis Bitter National Magnet Laboratory of MIT and brought its temperature close to absolute zero. While Tsui and Störmer expected the integer quantum Hall effect to occur in regular steps, they were surprised to discover that the magnetic field increased not only in regular steps, but also in thirds, or fractions, of a step. This discovery was named the "fractional quantum Hall effect."

Although Laughlin had left Bell Labs in 1981 for a research position at the Lawrence Livermore National Laboratory, in Livermore, California, he closely followed the results of Tsui and Störmer's experiment. Laughlin worked with Livermore researchers to explore the mathematics of hot plasmas and other aspects of condensed matter physics, which, he believed, could help him explain the fractional quantum Hall effect. "I was around researchers who understood fluids," he told Arnie Heller for a 1998 press release posted on the Livermore Laboratory Web site. "I realized that the fractional quantum Hall ground state had to be a new kind of fluid. There was no other easy way to explain why the experimental findings were so accurate. You had one-third charge 'things' in there. It's a great case of truth being stranger than fiction." Though Laughlin had some initial ideas about the fractional quantum Hall effect, he did not immediately come up with his Nobel Prize–winning theory. In fact, as Laughlin told Malcolm W. Browne for the *New York Times* (October 14, 1998), his first explanation was completely wrong; then, about one year after the discovery, he hit upon the theoretical explanation. "It took about a day," he told Browne. "Science is like that. You spend a long time in the desert, and then the truth suddenly dawns." Laughlin published his theory of fractional quantum Hall effect in *Physical Review Letters*, arguing that extremely low temperatures and a high magnetic field prompt electrons to condense into a quantum fluid; if an electron is then added by an outside force, a number of "quasi-particles" materialize, each exhibiting a fractional electronic charge. Laughlin's theory thus contradicted previous subatomic theory, which states that all electrons share

the same charge. Laughlin was also the first to develop a wave function, a simple formula that has subsequently been used to explain the fractionally charged steps that scientists have observed in the Hall effect.

Practical applications for the fractional quantum Hall effect such as the development of advanced computers or power-generating devices may still be years away, and physicists are still absorbing the significance of the groundbreaking discovery. The Royal Swedish Academy of Sciences noted that the contributions of Laughlin, Tsui, and Störmer have "led to *yet another breakthrough in our understanding of quantum physics* and to the development of new theoretical concepts of significance in many branches of modern physics."

In 1985 Laughlin became an associate professor in the Physics Department of Stanford University, in Stanford, California; he became a full professor in 1989. In 1992 he was named the Robert M. and Anne Bass Professor of Physics, earning a joint appointment in Stanford's Applied Physics Department the following year. His most recent work focuses on developing theories about the biological, chemical, and physical properties of the most basic matter of living systems. Laughlin leads this research for the Institute for Complex Adaptive Matter, an independent unit of the Los Alamos National Laboratory and the University of California at Berkeley.

In addition to the Nobel Prize, Laughlin has been honored with the E. O. Lawrence Award for physics from the Lawrence Livermore National Laboratory (1985), the Oliver E. Buckley Prize from the American Physical Society (1986), and the Franklin Medal from Philadelphia's Franklin Institute (1997). Laughlin is a fellow of the American Academy of Arts and Sciences and the American Association for the Advancement of Science, and a member of the National Academy of Sciences. He has also been an Eastman Kodak Lecturer and a Van Vleck Lecturer at the University of Rochester.

Laughlin married Anita Rhona Perry in 1979. The couple have two boys, Nathaniel and Todd.

ABOUT: MIT News (on-line) October 14, 1998; New York Times October 14, 1998, April 24, 2001; Nobel e-Museum Web site; Science October 1998; Washington Post October 14, 1998.

Courtesy of Dept. of Chemistry/University of Pennsylvania

MacDiarmid, Alan G.

(April 14, 1927–) Nobel Prize for Chemistry, 2000 (shared with Hideki Shirakawa and Alan J. Heeger)

The chemist Alan G. MacDiarmid was born in Masterton, New Zealand, on April 14, 1927. As a boy, MacDiarmid repeatedly borrowed from the local library *The Boy Chemist*, a chemistry text for children, and gradually performed all the experiments outlined in it, purchasing the necessary chemicals with the money he earned delivering milk. In 1948 he received his bachelor's degree in science from the University of New Zealand, going on to get his master's degree in 1950. After being turned down for fellowships to study in England, he was granted a Fulbright Fellowship and attended the University of Wisconsin in Madison, where he earned a Ph.D. in radiochemistry in 1953. He then received a fellowship from the New Zealand Shell oil company to attend the University of Cambridge, in England, from which he received a second Ph.D. in 1955. That year he worked for several months as a lecturer at the University of St. Andrews, in Scotland, while his wife, an American whom he married in 1954, stayed in Wisconsin. Then, partly because his wife couldn't tolerate the cold in the Midwest, he applied to the University of Pennsylvania, in Philadelphia, and they hired him sight unseen as an instructor. MacDiarmid steadily climbed the ranks and has remained there ever since. He has held the title of Blanchard Professor of Chemistry at the school since 1988.

As MacDiarmid told J. Gorman for *Science News* (October 14, 2000), his initial research with plastics was "done purely from the point of view of curiosity." In 1973 he began experimenting with polymers, a type of molecule that forms long, repeating chains; most plastics are made up of polymers. In particular, MacDiarmid was working with the inorganic (containing no carbon) polymer sulphur nitride, which during his experiments had created a metallic-looking film on the inside of the reaction vessel. In Japan, Shirakawa had been experimenting with new ways to synthesize the organic (containing carbon) polymer polyacetylene. During one of these experiments, a thousand times too much catalyst was accidentally added to the solution, and to the researchers' surprise, a metallic-looking film was produced. After MacDiarmid mentioned his finding at a conference in Tokyo, Shirakawa related his own discovery to MacDiarmid during a coffee break. Intrigued, MacDiarmid invited Shirakawa to the University of Pennsylvania, and Heeger joined them to do further research on polyacetylene. Soon, with the help of a grant from the Office of Naval Research, they had found a way to oxidize (or remove electrons from) polyacetylene using iodine gas in a process known as doping. When one of Heeger's students measured the conductivity of the oxidized polyacetylene, called trans-polyacetylene, it was discovered to have increased by a factor of 10 million. MacDiarmid, Heeger, Shirakawa, and other members of their research team soon shared their findings in the article "Synthesis of Electrically Conducting Organic Polymers: Halogen Derivatives of Polyacetylene" published in the *Journal of Chemical Society, Chemical Communications* (Summer 1977).

Essentially, doping is a way of making plastics act more like metals, which have free-floating electrons that can readily be made to flow along a chain of molecules, producing a current of electricity. A polyacetylene molecule consists of a long chain of carbon molecules bound by immobile "sigma" bonds. Each carbon atom is also bound to a hydrogen atom by a more flexible "pi" bond. In order to allow electricity to flow along the polyacetylene chain, electrons either have to be taken away from (through oxidation) or added to (through reduction) the pi bonds, which effectively destabilizes the bonds and permits electron flow. MacDiarmid explained the process of oxidizing polymers to Margaret Warner for *Online NewsHour* (October 10, 2000): "In a regular polymer, the electrons are bound very, very tightly to the polymer backbone so that when you apply an electric voltage . . . the electrons have very great difficulty in moving. . . . However, when you so called dope it . . . the iodine then pulls some of the electrons out of the polymer, and the remaining electrons then have much greater freedom of movement. For example, if you have a million people say packed into a city square, then it's very difficult for one person to move from one side of the square to the other. However, if you remove a whole lot of people from the square, then a person can then very much more easily move from one side to the other."

"Before Shirakawa, MacDiarmid, and Heeger made their seminal discovery . . . the idea that a plastic could conduct electricity as well as a metal would have seemed ludicrous," a writer for *Chemical and Engineering News* (October 16, 2000, on-line) phrased it. Such was the impact of their work, however, that as a University of Rochester chemistry professor told the *New York Times* (October 11, 2000, on-line), "It's spawned a small industry. There are many thousands of us working in this general area now." Following their initial finding, various other types of conductive plastics were soon discovered, each with different potential uses. Polymers, as other scientists later found, can also be used as semiconductors, materials that conduct electricity better than insulators, but not as well as conductors. One of the principle interests in both semiconductive and conductive polymers is in using them as a low-cost alternative to transistors and integrated circuits, which are often made of silicon and other similar materials. As MacDiarmid related to Sandy Smith for the *Pennsylvania Current* (October 26, 2000, on-line), "Philips, the electronics company in the Netherlands, has beautiful little plastic chips about the size of a 50-cent piece. Flexible, you can bend them . . . and these they will be producing for about one cent each. They will never replace durable silicon-chip technology . . . but if you just

want to have something which will be used once, which will have a life of, say, 20 days or 20 weeks or 20 months, and where cost is the important thing, then this is fascinating." While the electronic response of conductive polymers is similar to metals, they retain the structural aspects of plastics; namely, they are flexible, lightweight, and can be produced easily and inexpensively. In theory, polymers could be processed into integrated circuits by way of a technology similar to that used in ink-jet printing.

One application already developed for conductive polymers, specifically polythioprene derivatives, is as an anti-static treatment for photographic film, which can be ruined by static charges. Polythioprene derivatives may soon be used to mark supermarket products in such a way that people will be able to check out groceries without removing them from their carts. Conductive polymer technology is also being used to produce lightweight, rechargeable plastic batteries. Doped polyaniline, on which MacDiarmid has conducted extensive research, is used to reduce static in carpeting and as a coating to reduce electromagnetic radiation from computer screens. Another useful property of some semiconductive polymers is electroluminescence, which means that they can be stimulated to emit light, primarily in the form of light-emitting diodes, or LEDs. Related applications under development include energy-saving light bulbs, thin and flexible TV and computer screens, and car dashboard and mobile phone displays that light up while using little energy.

Though MacDiarmid and his collaborators' 1977 discovery marked an enormous breakthrough, they still had a long way to go in making conductive polymers of practical use. Doped polyacetylene by itself is sensitive to humidity and unstable when exposed to air. The task that lay ahead for MacDiarmid and other scientists—and which still lies ahead in many applications—was to find ways to make conductive polymers stable and easy to process. In 1986 MacDiarmid made an important stride when he issued a paper on his discovery of a new way to dope analine, transforming it into a pure form of polyaniline, which would become increasingly important in technological applications for conductive polymers. "Since Alan's seminal paper on the doping of polyaniline in 1986," one of MacDiarmid's colleagues told Ron Dagani for *Chemical and*

Engineering News (January 18, 1999), "1,500 papers and patents have appeared on this conducting polymer alone!"

MacDiarmid continued to focus on polyaniline throughout the 1980s and 90s, developing ways to increase its conductivity while retaining the mechanical properties of a plastic. He also succeeded in showing conclusively for the first time that the shape of polymer molecules directly affects their conductivity. For example, polyaniline, which has a structure, or conformation resembling a spiral, can be increased in conductivity 1,000-fold by loosening its coils, rather like stretching out a slinky. In the 1990s MacDiarmid also figured out a way to improve the performance of LEDs by adding a layer of polyaniline.

When MacDiarmid was awarded the Nobel Prize in Chemistry, he missed the phone call from the Royal Swedish Academy of Sciences and heard the news first from a friend who called and said he had learned on the Internet that MacDiarmid had received the award. "I thought it must be a hoax," MacDiarmid told Robert F. Service for *Science* (October 20, 2000). "But then I immediately got calls from reporters in France and Germany and thought maybe this is real." MacDiarmid viewed his winning of the award as more than just a personal a victory. "I feel that this award is really an extremely big boost for interdisciplinary science," he told Gorman, referring to the collaborations between physicists, materials scientists, and chemists necessary to the study of conductive polymers.

In addition to the Nobel Prize, MacDiarmid has received a series of awards from the American Chemical Society, including the Philadelphia Section Award (1967); the Frederic Stanley Kipping Award (1970); the Marshall Award (1982); and the Doolittle Award (1982). He was also awarded the Royal Society of Chemistry Centenary Medal and Lectureship (1983); the Chemical Pioneer Award from the American Institute of Chemists (1984); the "Top 100" Innovation Award from *Science Digest* (1985); the John Scott Award from the City of Philadelphia (1989); the Francis J. Clamer Award from the Franklin Institute (1993); and the Chemistry of Materials Award from the American Chemical Society (1999). In 1990 he received an honorary doctorate from Linkoping University, in Sweden. MacDiarmid lives in Philadelphia and has four children.

ABOUT: Chemical and Engineering News April 13, 1998, January 18, 1999, October 16, 2000; New Scientist October 21, 2000; New York Times (on-line) October 11, 2000; Nobel e-Museum Web site; Pennsylvania Current (on-line) October 26, 2000; Science October 20, 2000; Science News October 14, 2000.

Courtesy of University of California, Berkeley

McFadden, Daniel

(July 29, 1937–) Nobel Prize for Economics, 2000 (shared with James Heckman)

The economist Daniel L. McFadden was born on July 29, 1937 and grew up on a small farm in Raleigh, North Carolina. His father was a banker and his mother was a schoolteacher. An only child born during the Great Depression, McFadden has said that reading was his family's favorite activity. At age 16 he left for the University of Minnesota, graduating in 1957 with a degree in physics. After that, as he told Bertil Holmlund in an interview at the Nobel Foundation (December 13, 2000), archived as an audio file on their e-Museum Web site, McFadden gradually migrated to economics. Interested in the factors that influence people's life choices, he enrolled in an interdisciplinary program in behavioral science at the University of Minnesota, earning a Ph.D. with a focus on eco-

Nobel Prize Winners 87

nomics in 1962. In 1963 he took a job as an assistant professor of economics at the University of California, Berkeley. The following year McFadden was working with a graduate student who was collecting data on how California policymakers had chosen one freeway route over another. McFadden helped the student develop an analytical technique to examine this question, and in this way began the work on "discrete choice" that would shape his career. McFadden left Berkeley in 1977 to spend a year as a research professor at Yale University, and then accepted a position at the Massachusetts Institute of Technology. In 1990 he was wooed back to UC Berkeley, where he became the E. Morris Cox Chair in economics and founder and director of the university's econometrics laboratory.

"Econometrics" is a kind of applied economics; its practitioners apply statistical methods to the study of economic data. McFadden works on the "micro" level of econometrics, or microeconometrics, looking at economic questions in terms of individuals, households, or businesses, rather than on the "macro" level, in which whole systems and overall levels of income and output are studied. The Econometrics Laboratory at Berkeley is a center for empirical research, instruction, and hands-on learning in the field. McFadden argued for the creation of the Laboratory as a condition of his return to the university.

If psychologists attempt to probe an individual's "inner" life—how people learn, why they behave in certain ways—then one might say that economists tend to look at the "outer" life—what individuals do, where they live, and what they buy. McFadden's work on "discrete choice" allowed economists to quantify the many trade-offs individuals consider when making such decisions. "Before McFadden did his work, economists were concerned with buying amounts—how many oranges a consumer buys, et cetera," Northwestern University economist Charles Manski told Charles Seife for *Science* (October 20, 2000). "But many important choices are discrete: Do you go to college or not? Do you buy an auto or not?" Economists were good at predicting, for example, how consumers behave when prices of goods and services change, but they had no tools for predicting the results of decisions that involve choosing from a limited set of alternatives, even though such decisions greatly affect economic data.

In the early 1970s McFadden received a National Science Foundation grant to analyze a high-speed subway line, the Bay Area Rapid Transit system (BART), that was being planned in the San Francisco Bay area. "We used the data that was in place before BART was built to try and predict what [prospective passengers] would do after it was built," McFadden told Jerry Hirsch in the *Los Angeles Times* (October 12, 2000). McFadden began by applying the basic economic theory of self-interest, which holds that individuals and groups generally seek to get as much as possible of what is important to them, to statistical data about the behavior of commuters. McFadden broke down a complex phenomenon—whether or not individuals will use public transportation—into separate questions, realizing that commuters would make this decision based on many factors, including speed, cost, and the relative ease or difficulty of the trip. If commuters had to choose between cars, buses, and subways, for example, McFadden would identify a set of values for each. "If you think of an auto as a bundle of characteristics—values for travel time, cost, and comfort—and a bus as a different bundle, you can compare them," Charles Manski told Seife. Driving offers comfort but is more expensive than, say, taking a bus, which is cheaper but less convenient. In Seife's words, McFadden figured out a way to compare "apples and oranges," or cars, buses, and subways. McFadden next measured the probability of each outcome: a commuter might have a 20 percent chance of taking a car to work, a 40 percent chance of taking a bus, and a 40 percent chance of taking a subway, for example. By quantifying the trade-offs people make as they pursue their self-interest, McFadden helped BART officials decide how much to charge and how often to run trains in order to persuade people to use them. His predictions about commuter behavior in San Francisco have proved accurate over time; as Karl-Gustav Joereskog told Kim Gamel for *Science News* (October 11, 2000, on-line), "The train stations are in the right places. There are sufficient parking spaces for vehicles, and people perceive the prices to be right."

Recently, McFadden and a UC Berkeley colleague, Kenneth Train, studied what it would take to persuade commuters to drive alternative fuel vehicles, a question of some concern to policymakers in California, where there are high levels of car-related air pollution. Their research revealed that consumer concerns about refueling, the limited power of the vehicles, and their high cost would limit their viability in California—conclusions borne out by the low sales of electric cars in the state.

In another case, McFadden measured the economic cost of the disastrous oil spill caused by the *Exxon Valdez* tanker off the coast of Alaska in 1989. McFadden gauged how the oil spill affected tourists' decisions about whether or not to visit the state, thus helping to impart a dollar figure to the environmental damage. For the past 15 years he has studied the economics of health, in particular looking at housing and care-taking for the elderly and connections between health and wealth. According to Zuckerman, one of McFadden's conclusions is that greater wealth doesn't seem to increase life expectancy, though it does decrease the likelihood of depression.

At 2:30 in the morning on October 11, 2000, Daniel McFadden was awakened by a call from Nobel Foundation officials, who warned him that they were about to announce that he, along with JAMES HECKMAN, had won the Bank of Sweden Prize in Economic Sciences in Memory of ALFRED NOBEL. More commonly known as the Nobel Prize in Economics, the award is considered the most prestigious in that field and draws worldwide attention to its recipients. McFadden, who has devoted his life to predicting outcomes, was stunned. "The economics community is just a few thousand," he told an Associated Press reporter in an article published on *Yahoo! News* (October 11, 2000, on-line). "I guess one always figures you have a one in a thousand chance." McFadden's colleagues in the economics community were also surprised, not because they thought he was unworthy, but because the Nobel committee has not typically rewarded the kind of highly technical research that McFadden and Heckman perform. In their announcement of the prize, quoted on the Nobel Foundation e-Museum Web site, the Swedish Academy stressed that McFadden and Heckman's work combines the theoretical and the practical, and has valuable social applications: "The methods they have developed have solid foundations in economic theory, but have evolved in close interplay with applied research on social problems." The Academy singled out McFadden's "development of theory and methods for analyzing discrete choice," a technique for determining how individuals or groups will behave when faced with a limited number of alternatives.

McFadden's techniques have practical applications in many fields and have been adopted by marketers, sociologists, political scientists, and policy makers. UC Berkeley Chancellor Robert Berdahl praised McFadden's work on evaluating social issues, telling Becky Bartindale and Lisa Fernandez in the *San Jose Mercury News* (October 12, 2000) that McFadden puts economics "squarely in the service of society." Paul Rudd, a former graduate student under McFadden, described him to Bartindale and Fernandez as an unusual figure in that he cares passionately for both theory and practice, ideas and actions. "He fits the image of a Renaissance man in economics better than anyone I can think of," Rudd said.

Although McFadden and Heckman have never worked together, they have been friends for 30 years and have exchanged ideas often. According to Dale Jorgenson, a Harvard University economist cited by Jerry Hirsch, "Theirs is a very natural pairing. Heckman's work builds directly on what McFadden has done."

McFadden is an elected member of the American Academy of Arts and Sciences and the National Academy of Sciences. In addition to the Nobel Prize, he has been awarded the John Bates Clark Medal of the American Economics Association and the Frisch Medal of the Econometric Society. In May 2000 he was awarded the Erwin Plein Nemmers Prize in Economics from Northwestern University, one of the highest honors in his field.

McFadden is married to Beverlee Tito Simboli McFadden; the couple has a grown daughter and two grown sons. McFadden plans to use his half of the $915,000 Nobel award to help support his Napa Valley farm. The farm, where the McFaddens spend weekends tending their cows, ducks, and chickens and raising figs, olives, and grapes, has been a refuge for McFadden throughout his hectic career. "I can go to work in the vineyard and think about my problems more effectively than sitting at my desk," he told Bartindale and Fernandez.

ABOUT: Los Angeles Times October 12, 2000; Nobel e-Museum Web site; San Jose Mercury News October 12, 2000; Science October 20, 2000; SFGate (on-line) October 12, 2000.

Courtesy of Harvard University

Merton, Robert C.

(July 31, 1944–) Nobel Prize for Economics, 1997 (shared with Myron S. Scholes)

The economist Robert C. Merton was born to Robert K. and Suzanne (Carhart) Merton on July 31, 1944 in New York City. He grew up in a small New York suburb, Hastings-on-Hudson. (Robert K. Merton was a celebrated professor of sociology at Columbia University from 1941 until his retirement in 1979. In 1994 he won the National Medal of Science for his work on the sociology of science; he was the first sociologist to win this honor. He is also well known for his study of deviance and the notion of the self-fulfilling prophecy.) As a child Merton built hot-rod cars, which he raced on drag strips in upstate New York and Long Island. Hoping to be an automobile engineer—which would combine his love of cars and his mathematics skills—he spent two summers working for the Ford Company while in college.

Merton attended Columbia University's School of Engineering, graduating in 1966 with a B.S. in engineering mathematics. He then enrolled in a Ph.D. program in applied mathematics at the California Institute of Technology (Cal Tech), in Pasadena, but left after one year to pursue economics. "I felt that working in economics could 'really matter' and that potentially one could affect millions of people," Merton recalled in an autobiographical essay posted on the Nobel e-Museum Web site.

Merton was accepted in an economics Ph.D. program at the Massachusetts Institute of Technology (MIT), in Cambridge. He had been introduced to the stock market by his father, and had bought his first share of stock at age 10. At MIT, Merton discovered that what he called his "after/before hours" interest in the stock market could become part of his academic research. He became a research assistant to the prominent MIT economist PAUL SAMUELSON, who was also interested in developing mathematical models for the stock market.

Merton earned his Ph.D. in 1970 and then became an assistant professor of finance at MIT's Sloan School of Management, where he embarked on his work on options pricing. An option is a special type of investment that allows the investor to purchase stocks or bonds at a fixed price in the future. Options and other derivatives (named after the fact that their value is derived from the assets to which they are attached) allow investors to protect themselves from potential losses and help to ensure profits. Because they are not stocks, options have long been difficult to valuate.

At the same time that Merton began his work, the MIT professor MYRON SCHOLES met the mathematician Fischer Black, and the two men pooled their efforts to develop a formula for pricing options. Black and Scholes published their findings in 1973, crediting Merton for his assistance. Merton published his own findings in the *Bell Journal of Economics and Management Sciences* in 1973.

Merton's work was an extension of what became known as the Black-Scholes formula. What Black and Scholes had envisioned as a formula to price derivatives became, with Merton's insights, a model that could be applied to many other areas of finance, including home mortgages and student loans. Before 1973, the options market was impeded by the inherent difficulty of determining the value of an option. Derivatives were given value through risk premiums, which depended largely on the amount of risk an investor was willing to take. The Black-Scholes formula takes into account such factors as the price of the option, its time to expiration, the value of the stock, the stock's volatility, and interest rates; in doing so, it makes the derivatives market less risky and therefore more attractive to investors.

Merton contributed ideas about how options should be priced under conditions of continuous trading. Such ideas extended the insights of the Black-Scholes formula to other types of transactions, enabling a broad range of potential uses. Using the formula, investments in equipment can be designed to allow for greater or lesser flexibility. If it is relatively easy to end production at a silver mine if the price of silver is low, for example, then that flexibility can be viewed as an option. Farmers also use derivatives to help guard against drops in crop prices.

The insights of Merton, Scholes, and Black have resulted in more accurate options pricing and an overall increase in the derivatives market. "If you ask what idea in the last 50 or 60 years coming from economic research has had the biggest impact on the world," the Princeton University economics professor Avainash Dixit is quoted as saying on the International Association of Financial Engineers Web site, "this is it. It's changed the way the financial markets . . . allocate risks among different types of investors."

Merton became a full professor at MIT in 1974; in 1980 he was named the J. C. Penney professor of management at the Sloan School of Management. In 1988 he joined the faculty of the Harvard Business School, in Cambridge, Massachusetts, as a professor of business administration. He has also been a research associate at the National Bureau of Economic Research since 1979.

In awarding Scholes and Merton the 1997 Nobel Prize in Economics, the Royal Swedish Academy of Sciences noted that their "pioneering formula . . . [and] methodology has paved the way for economic valuations in many areas. It has also generated new types of financial instruments and facilitated more efficient risk management in society." When Merton first joined the academic world, finance was not a big part of economics. Referring to Merton's efforts to bring re-

spect and prominence to the study of finance, Paul Samuelson said that "Bob Merton is the Isaac Newton of his field," as quoted by Peter Passell for the New York Times (October 15, 1997).

Federal Board Chairman Alan Greenspan told Clay Chandler for the Washington Post (October 15, 1997) that the spread of derivatives has made world financial markets more efficient, but he also warned that "the new technologies, and the financial instruments and techniques they have made possible, have strengthened interdependencies between markets and market participants, both within and across national boundaries." Though they are now easier to valuate, derivatives can still be an extremely risk-prone investment. Derivatives played a role in the bankruptcy of Orange County, California, and the downfall of Barings, a British investment bank.

In 1994 Scholes and Merton co-founded Long-Term Capital Management (LTCM), in Greenwich, Connecticut, a hedge-fund company that uses the Black-Scholes formula to make investment decisions. By the end of 1997, the firm had generated more than $1 billion in revenues. Then, in 1998, a global economic downturn nearly caused the bankruptcy of LTCM. The Federal Reserve organized a bailout of the company, but many have since called for greater regulations of the derivatives market and questioned the company's risk-management techniques.

In addition to the Nobel Prize, Merton has won the Leo Melamed Prize from the University of Chicago School of Business (1983); the Roger Murray Prize from the Institute for Quantitative Research in Finance (1985; 1986); the Distinguished Scholar Award from the Eastern Finance Association (1989); the FORCE Award for Financial Innovation from the Duke University Fuqua School of Business (1993); and the title of Financial Engineer of the Year by the International Association of Financial Engineers (1993).

Merton married the television actress and model June Rose in 1966. The couple had three children and separated in 1996.

ABOUT: Harvard Business School Web site; International Association of Financial Engineers Web site; New York Times October 15, 1997; Nobel e-Museum Web site; Time.com October 14, 1997.

© The Nobel Foundation

Mundell, Robert

(October 24, 1932–) Nobel Prize for Economics, 1999

The economist Robert Alexander Mundell was born October 24, 1932 in Kingston, Ontario, Canada, the son of William C. and Lila (Knifton) Mundell. He grew up on a small farm in Latimer, Ontario, and in 1946 moved with his family to Maple Ridge, British Columbia, Canada. In his final year of high school, he became interested in economics. He attended the University of British Columbia, in Vancouver, where he majored in economics and Slavonic studies and attained his B.A. in 1953. He pursued postgraduate studies at the University of Washington, in Seattle, and the London School of Economics, before receiving a Ph.D. from the Massachusetts Institute of Technology (MIT) in 1956. His dissertation focused on international capital movements. He continued his postdoctoral studies at the University of Chicago until 1957.

Mundell took his first teaching position as an instructor of economics in 1957 at the University of British Columbia. The following year he took a position as acting assistant professor of economics at Stanford University in California. After a year at Stanford, Mundell traveled to Italy, where he was a visiting professor of economics at the School for Advanced International Studies,

a part of the Johns Hopkins University Center, in Bologna.

Once Mundell came to the International Monetary Fund (IMF) in 1961, he began to focus on the specific areas of economic studies for which he would later become known. While working as a senior economist in the IMF's research department, he developed an analysis of monetary and fiscal policy in open economies, otherwise known as "stabilization policy." A pioneering article published by Mundell in 1963 stressed the importance of foreign trade and championed the notion of an open economy. It also addressed the issue of currency exchange rates, with Mundell arguing in favor of the floating exchange rate, in which the rate is determined by the market with little interference from the central bank.

Mundell's work on stabilization policy in open economies, which was illustrated in his articles published during this period, was similar to research being conducted simultaneously but independently by Marcus Fleming, the head of the IMF research department. Although Mundell's contribution to the body of research is predominant, their work regarding stabilization policy became known as the Mundell-Fleming Model. His years with the IMF brought Mundell into contact with the Kennedy administration, which was interested in revitalizing the American economy. His theories had an impact on the administration's economic policy, making Mundell one of the most influential young economists in the country.

After leaving the IMF in 1963, Mundell returned to his role as visiting professor of economics, first at McGill University, in Montreal, Quebec, Canada, from 1963 to 1964, and then at the Brookings Institution, in Washington, D.C., from 1964 to 1965. He then joined the faculty of the University of Chicago as a Ford Foundation visiting professor of economics in 1965. After a year he became a full professor at the University of Chicago. At the time the University of Chicago was known as a leader in creative economic research, and Mundell was recognized as one of its intellectual leaders until his departure in 1971. After leaving the University of Chicago, Mundell spent two years as a professor of economics and chairman of the economics department at the University of Waterloo in Ontario, Canada. In 1974 he joined the economics faculty of New York City's Columbia University, where he has continued to teach ever since.

In addition to his duties at Columbia, Mundell served as director of a graduate economics training program at the University of the Eastern Republic of Uruguay, in Montevideo, between 1979 and 1984. "I wanted to learn what students in other parts of the world were learning," Mundell told Kate Bohner for *Forbes* (December 16, 1996), discussing his time in Uruguay. During his five years there, Mundell preached his views on international currency and his supply-side theory, which is based on the belief that lower tax rates encourage production, increase supply, stimulate savings and investment, slow inflation, and promote business growth. Many of the top financial bureaucrats in Uruguay today were pupils of Mundell during these years.

Mundell embarked on another international mission when he traveled to China in 1995 to help organize a conference on how to control Chinese inflation without threatening the nation's economic growth. "I could see the effect on the [Chinese] students, on the professors," Mundell told Kate Bohner; "it was as if a whole new world was opening up for them. I realized then that providing this kind of intellectual stimulation and getting discourse started would be the only way to teach young economists and keep them in China." With help from the Chinese government and investments from major corporations, he helped establish the Beijing School of Advanced Economics, where he intended to teach his supply-side economic philosophy to students raised under a Communist government.

Another major contribution to economic theory by Robert Mundell is the Mundell-Tobin Effect, which explains how anticipated inflation can have real economic effect by coaxing investors to lower their cash balances in favor of increased real capital formation. Mundell has also contributed to international trade theory, illustrating how commodity prices among countries tend to be equalized by the international mobility of labor and capital.

Today, Mundell's theories of monetary and fiscal policy directed toward the stabilization of the economy dominate the study of monetary and fiscal policies in open economies. Generations of researchers have been inspired by his work, and continue his research. Much of the teaching of macroeconomics in contemporary classrooms is heavily influenced by Mundell's work. He has been credited with originating the concept behind the euro, the unified currency now in use among many European nations. His "supply-side" theories contributed to the economic philosophy employed during the 1980s by President Ronald Reagan, which became known as "Reaganomics." It has often been said that Mundell has become the most influential economic theorist since John Maynard Keynes, whose theories have dominated the study of economics for the majority of the 20th century. For his body of work, Mundell was awarded the 1999 Nobel Prize in economics.

Robert Mundell has been a consultant to numerous organizations over the years, including the U.S. Treasury Department (1969–1974) and the government of Panama (1970–1973). He has published several books on the subject of economy, including *The International Monetary System— Conflict and Reform* (1965), *Man and Economics* (1968), *International Economics* (1968), *Monetary Theory—Interest, Inflation, and Growth in the World Economy* (1971). He was a Guggenheim fellow from 1970–1971 and won the Jacques Rueff Prize in 1983.

ABOUT: Forbes December 16, 1996; Fortune May 11, 1987; Toronto Globe & Mail Report on Business Magazine March 1986; Maclean's May 27, 1985; New York Times January 12, 1986; Nobel e-Museum Web site.

Murad, Ferid

(September 14, 1936–) Nobel Prize for Physiology or Medicine, 1998 (shared with Robert F. Furchgott and Louis J. Ignarro)

The pharmacologist and physician Ferid Murad was born on September 14, 1936 in Whiting, Indiana. His father, Jabir Murat Ejupi, arrived to Ellis Island in 1913 from Albania. (The immigration officer abbreviated his name to John Murad.) Murad's mother, Henrietta Josephine Bowman, ran away from her Illinois home at age 17 to marry the 39-year-old Albanian immigrant, and the couple settled in Indiana and opened a restaurant. Murad and his two younger brothers were raised in an apartment behind the restaurant. "The restaurant business had a

Courtesy of The University of Texas Medical School

Ferid Murad

profound effect on my future and that of my two brothers," Murad wrote in an autobiographical essay posted on the Nobel e-Museum Web site. "When we were able to stand on a stool to reach the sink we washed dishes and later when we could see over the counter, we waited tables and managed the cash register." Though his father had only one year of formal education, he had learned to speak seven languages before his death; Murad's mother had attended grade school for several years, but dropped out to help her mother raise her young siblings. Observing how hard his parents had to work at the family business, Murad decided at an early age to go to college and become a doctor. In fact, Murad wrote in an eighth-grade homework assignment that he wanted to become a physician, teacher, and pharmacist. "Today I do just that," Murad wrote, "as I am a board certified physician and internist doing both basic and clinical research with considerable teaching in medicine, pharmacology and clinical pharmacology."

Murad won a scholarship to attend De-Pauw University, in Greencastle, Indiana, earning a B.A. in 1958 in a pre-medical course. He enrolled the same year in a combined medical and pharmacology program that had recently been created at Western Reserve University (now Case Western Reserve University), in Cleveland, Ohio. After seven years, Murad received an M.D. from the School of Medicine and a Ph.D. from the Department of Pharmacology. While a student, Murad first became interested in intercellular communication—the area of research that would eventually lead to his winning a share of the 1998 Nobel Prize for Physiology or Medicine.

Murad completed his medical internship and residency at Massachusetts General Hospital, in Boston, from 1965 to 1967. He then became a clinical associate at the National Institutes of Health National Heart and Lung Institute. In 1969 he was placed on the Institute's senior staff.

In 1970 Murad became an associate professor of pharmacology and internal medicine at the University of Virginia School of Medicine, in Charlottesville. He was named director of the University's Clinical Research Center in 1971. Two years later he also became director of the Department of Internal Medicine's division of clinical pharmacology. In 1975, after five years as an associate, Murad was granted a full professorship, teaching internal medicine and pharmacology.

At the University of Virginia in the late 1970s, Murad first began studying "secondary messengers." Scientists knew then that hormones initiate communication among cells. Hormones give instructions to chemicals—the secondary messengers—which in turn instigate chemical reactions in the body that result in such important activities as fighting off infection, activating nerve cells, or regulating blood pressure. The secondary messenger chemicals are found just inside a cell's outer membrane, and wait for a signal from outside to pass on the message to the interior of cell.

Murad focused on the secondary messenger known as cyclic guanosine monophosphate, or cyclic GMP. He wanted to know how this chemical is formed by hormones, and how it works in the body. His research began rather crudely, comprised of what some of his trainees described as "dumping experiments" in which muscle tissue was exposed to various hormones to see which would cause cyclic GMP to be formed in the tissues' cells. After discovering that the tissue had to be intact in order for hormones to initiate cyclic GMP formation, Murad had the tissues treated with nitrogen-bearing substances. Surprisingly, some of these substances caused the chemical to be formed, whether or not the tissue was intact. Murad further discovered that the nitrogen-bearing substances caused the muscle tissue to relax.

Murad's next step was to expose the tissue to nitroglycerin to see if that, too, caused GMP formation. For more than a century, nitroglycerin has been used as a medication for disorders of the heart, since nitroglycerin is able to regulate blood flow by relaxing and dilating the blood vessels. Scientists had never understood the biochemical reason nitroglycerin worked this way, however. (Coincidentally, nitroglycerin is also an important ingredient in dynamite, which was invented by ALFRED NOBEL, creator of the Nobel Prize.) Murad proved that nitroglycerin releases nitric oxide gas, which in turn forms the cyclic GMP that causes the muscles of the blood vessels to relax.

Scientists had known that bacteria in the body produce nitric oxide, which is chemically related to nitrous oxide, an air pollutant created when gasoline is combusted in automobiles. But the presence of nitric oxide was thought to be insignificant to animals and humans. At the point when Murad proved that nitric oxide caused cyclic GMP formation, he knew that he was on to something significant. "Now we had a family of nitrogen-carrying compounds—some complicated, some simple—that promoted cyclic GMP production and smooth-muscle relaxation in both intact and broken-up tissue," he recalled to Jim Atkinson for *Texas Monthly* (December 1999). "We reasoned that the compounds were being reduced to some common intermediate, and we guessed that it was nitric oxide."

Murad had not only explained how nitroglycerin worked, he had also proved that a gas, however inherently unstable, can play a significant role in bodily functions. In the *Washington Post* (October 13, 1998), Rick Weiss explained that gases behave differently than hormones, which attach themselves to specific molecular sites to do their work. "Gases . . . can diffuse through cell membranes, trigger biochemical reactions and then dissipate within seconds—almost before they can be detected in the laboratory," he wrote. Thus, it was a controversial idea that a gas be responsible for such important bodily functions. Murad proved that nitric oxide could act as a secondary messenger within an individual cell or between different cells, causing many different cellular functions. "What does this suggest when a compound this simple plays such an important role," he asked Weiss. "To me it suggests that nitric oxide is one of the most primitive elements of cellular signaling, that it goes way back into evolution."

Murad's research was supplemented by work done by his two fellow Nobel laureates, the pharmacologists ROBERT FURCHGOTT and Louis Ignarro. In 1980 Furchgott discovered that the cells lining blood vessels secrete some natural substance—an unknown signal molecule—that makes them expand; he called this molecule the endothelium-derived relaxing factor (EDRF). (Endothelium is the layer of flattened cells that line blood vessels and other body parts.) Working with Furchgott and also on his own, Ignarro concluded, in 1986, that EDRF was, in fact, nitric oxide. There was now concrete experimental evidence to support Murad's work.

These discoveries led to the development of many new drugs and treatments; in fact, some have hailed nitric oxide as the most important medical discovery since penicillin. Most famously, the research into nitric oxide's function has led to the creation of the anti-impotency drug Viagra. By modulating blood flow, Viagra can help men with sexual dysfunctions to more easily achieve an erection. Nitric oxide has also proven valuable as a treatment for heart and pulmonary disease. It has proven particularly effective in helping premature infants born with underdeveloped lungs. Research is currently underway to explore the potential for nitric oxide to stop the growth of cancerous tumors. "It's taken some 20 years to see this all evolve," Murad told Michael Graczyk of the *Associated Press* (October 13, 1998). "I think what's had to happen is to see some clinical utility of this information. Designing drugs and attacking some diseases is often what it takes."

In 1998 the Nobel Prize was awarded jointly to Robert F. Furchgott, LOUIS J. IGNARRO, and Ferid Murad for their combined research proving that nitric oxide is a signaling molecule. News of the award sparked some controversy. The Nobel Committee is prohibited from selecting more than three winners for each prize, and factions within the scientific communities have claimed that essential nitric oxide researchers were neglected.

The Nobel Prize revived a discussion that first arose in 1996, when Murad and Furchgott were awarded the Albert Lasker Medical Research Award for their independent work toward understanding the function of nitric oxide as a messenger between cells. At that time, some members of the scientific community protested that Salvador Moncada, a pharmacologist who had conducted key experiments with nitric oxide in the 1980s, deserved to be recognized alongside Murad and Furchgott. In a separate controversy, some claimed that team members who did research into nitric oxide in the 1970s should have been recognized by the Nobel committee as well.

Murad left the University of Virginia in 1981 and went to California to join the faculty of Stanford University as a professor of medicine and pharmacology. He also returned to medical practice, becoming chief of medicine at the Palo Alto Veterans Administration Medical Center. From 1986 to 1988 he served as acting chairman of medicine at Stanford. In 1988 he became an adjunct professor of pharmacology at Northwestern University's Medical School, in Chicago, Illinois.

In 1990 Murad left academia to become a vice president of pharmaceutical research and development at Abbott Laboratories, in Abbot Park, Illinois. In 1993 he founded a biotechnology company, Molecular Geriatrics Corporation; as president and chief executive officer, Murad hoped to create an intensive research program. After some of the promised funding fell through, Murad left private research. In 1997 he accepted a position as chairman of the Department of Integrative Biology, Pharmacology and Physiology at the Health Science Center of the University of Texas. Murad discussed his love for his work in a press release from the University of Texas. "There aren't many professions where you can get excited about coming to work everyday," he commented. "I still wake up at night and jot down ideas." He also stressed the importance of grounding theoretical research in clinical practice. "Working with patients provides a different perspective," he said. "It connects basic science and helps raise the visibility of institutions with Congress. . . . Physician scientists have one foot in basic science and one in clinical science."

Murad currently resides in Houston, Texas, with his wife of 40 years, the former Carol Ann Leopold. The Murads have five children and seven grandchildren.

ABOUT: CNN.com October 1998; Lasker Foundation Web site; New York Times September 26, 1996, October 13, 1998; Nobel e-Museum Web site; Texas Monthly December 1999; Washington Post October 13, 1998.

© The Nobel Foundation

Naipaul, V. S.

(August 17, 1932–) Nobel Prize for Literature, 2001

The writer Vidiadhar Surajprasad Naipaul—known as Vidia to his friends—was born in Caguanas, Trinidad, on August 17, 1932, the grandson of a Brahmin from Uttar Pradesh, India, who came to the island as an indentured worker. Naipaul's father, Seepersad Naipaul, worked at odd jobs before becoming a reporter for the *Trinidad Guardian*, and he wrote short stories about Trinidadian Indians that his son helped publish posthumously as *The Adventures of Gurudeva* (1976). From his father he acquired, as he says, "a way of looking, an example of labour, a knowledge of the literary process"; from his mother he inherited "tenacity, toughness, and self-reliance." In

Trinidad, Naipaul's family—consisting of five sisters and a brother, Shiva, who is also a novelist—formed part of a minority Indian society from which he felt estranged. Although in later life Naipaul retained some rigid traits of Brahmin fastidiousness, even as a child he was an unbeliever amidst a devout Hindu culture, as well as an intellectual alien in the agitated disorder of modern Trinidad. He recalls in his travel book of the Caribbean, *The Middle Passage* (1962), that as a schoolboy at the Queen's Royal College, Port of Spain, he fled to books for fantasies of escape, and he resolved to emigrate: "When I was in the fourth form I wrote a vow on the endpaper of my Kennedy's Revised Latin Primer to leave within five years. I left after six; and for many years afterwards in England, falling asleep in bedsitters with the electric fire on, I had been awakened by the nightmare that I was back in tropical

In 1950, at age 17, Naipaul left the West Indies on a scholarship to University College, Oxford, in England. He studied English literature, but was disappointed with the quality of his education. After graduating, determined to maintain his freedom through self-employment, Naipaul went to London and began writing fiction. He also did freelance radio broadcasting, which led to his editing a literary program for two years for the BBC's Colonial Service. In 1955 he married an Englishwoman, Patricia Ann Hale. In about 1957 he started writing essays for periodicals and reviewing books, principally for the *New Statesman*, and that same year he held his only full-time position—grinding out public relations copy for a company manufacturing concrete—for 10 weeks. "I was a very accomplished hack," he recalls of his post-Oxford years, when London became still another pocket of isolation: "I was confined to a smaller world than I had ever known. I became my flat, my desk, my name."

Somewhat reluctantly Naipaul used the West Indies as material for his first four novels. As Alex Hamilton later viewed these beginnings in the London *Guardian* (October 4, 1971), Naipaul "hadn't realized that when you're born in the New World, you carry it with you forever. . . . The Caribbean was all he had to write about when he started." His first novel, *The Mystic Masseur* (1957), was greeted by reviewers as a genial comedy of manners about Indians in Trinidad. Its hero, Ganesh Ramsummair, is a Hindu

huckster who, by dint of consummate self-esteem and a flair for self-creation, rises from obscurity as a bumbling schoolmaster and a fumbling masseur to become a respected mystic guru healer, a best-selling author, and a representative to the U.N., glorying in his Anglicized name and a decoration from the Queen. The novel represented the first stage of Naipaul's detailed panorama of life on the islands, and Ganesh was the first in his series of humble characters struggling for self-definition in an alien society.

The Suffrage of Elvira (1958) and *Miguel Street* (1959) followed rapidly in much the same vein, the first about an imaginary Caribbean society undergoing farcical spasms of rudimentary democracy during its second general election, and the second, narrated from the viewpoint of a small boy, about the inhabitants of a tiny slum in Port of Spain, a beguiling kind of Catfish Row. Reviewing *The Suffrage of Elvira* in the *Spectator* (May 2, 1958), Kingsley Amis found Naipaul's depiction of island antics "subdued and kind . . . conducted throughout with the utmost stylistic quietude." Reviewers generally reveled in Naipaul's racy dialogue, his parade of zany characters, and what Whitney Balliett in the *New Yorker* (August 27, 1960) termed his "effortless sense of irony."

Naipaul won the John Llewelyn Rhys Memorial Prize for *The Mystic Masseur* and the Somerset Maugham Award for *Miguel Street*, but widespread acceptance and a decent living from his fiction proved slow in coming. He summed up his situation in "London," an essay in the *Times Literary Supplement* (August 15, 1958): "I have written three books in five years and made £ 300 out of them. The Americans do not want me because I am too British. The public here do not want me because I am too foreign." His next novel, *A House for Mr. Biswas*, helped remedy that neglect. Many consider it to be Naipaul's richest novel to date; it has been his most popular. Meanwhile, he weathered attacks by some who found his incisively comic treatment of the Caribbean area distorted and demeaning. The West Indian novelist George Lamming declared in *The Pleasures of Exile* (1960) that Naipaul's novels were "castrated satire," and charged their author with being "ashamed of his cultural background." In his defense Naipaul pleaded the normal liberties of the satirist. As he told Mel Gussow of the *New York Times* (December 26, 1976), in the late 1950s a damaging myth was fostered: "That I'm a reactionary, totally out of sympathy with progressive movements, that I'm hardhearted and cruel—none of which is true. . . . Because you are not left-wing, they automatically say that you're right-wing."

The publication of *A House for Mr. Biswas*, which forced his critics to reconsider their judgement of Naipaul's sympathies, marked the end of his period of apprenticeship. Focusing again on an ordinary man, Naipaul follows Mohun Biswas, a Trinidadian Indian, from birth to death as he tries to find self-realization in a culture without coherence, traditions, or values. Mr. Biswas' goal is to own a house, "one's portion of earth," a sign of emancipation from his quasi-slavery, and from ruthless domination by his wife's family, the Tulsis. A dry, sometimes contemptible man, Mr. Biswas is nevertheless admirable in his drive for independence. As a journalist in later life, in a home irretrievably mortgaged, he is finally freed from both a decaying Indian culture and an insular colonial society mimicking the empty ways of the great world. "A major performance," Morris Gilbert wrote of *A House for Mr. Biswas* in the *New York Times* (June 24, 1962), "a story told with virtually filial tenderness and understanding."

In September 1960 Naipaul returned to the West Indies under a travel scholarship from the government of Trinidad and Tobago, whose premier, Dr. Eric Williams, suggested the writing of *The Middle Passage*, which consists of "impressions of five societies in the Indies and South America." Ronald Bryden in the *Spectator* (August 3, 1962) pointed out that Naipaul's "ruthless and painful" journey to his roots ends with the inescapable conclusion that "the West Indies are Hell"; and Walter Allen in the *New Statesman* (August 3, 1962) found Naipaul's observations of "the contradictions and the tragic absurdities, the whole inheritance of cruelty and chaos" equally depressing.

Even more devastating were Naipaul's reactions to India, where he traveled in 1962, and which became the subject of *An Area of Darkness* (1964). "He was overwhelmed," said Alan Pryce-Jones in the *New York Herald Tribune* (April 20, 1965), "by the smells, the dirt, the crowds, the poverty, the helpless incompetence of officialdom." Naipaul's thin-skinned aversion to his immediate experiences caused some critics to contend that he had missed "the soul and music of India," but most praised his originality, accuracy, and honesty. In any event, Naipaul's return to the land of his ancestors was traumatic: India, he wrote, "has broken my life in two." In 1966 Naipaul resumed his travels, this time through Italy, Egypt, and Africa, where for a time he was a visiting lecturer in the English Department of Uganda's Makerere University. In his next book about the West Indies he took on the corruption of a utopian New World myth, *The Loss of Eldorado: A History* (1969), an imaginative historical narrative of Spanish, French, and British colonization from Columbus to the 19th century.

With *Mr. Stone and the Knights Companion* (1963), which won the Hawthornden Prize, Naipaul made his first fictional break with the West Indies. Peopled entirely by Britishers, the novel portrays the habit-ridden domesticity of London suburbanites while telling the story of an aging minor functionary of the Excal Company, who, beset by thoughts of death, tries to expand his horizons through marriage and the promotion of an honorific order, the Knights Companions, for Excal's pensioners. Most critics found the work fragmentary. More solid in substance, and more complex in structure, *The Mimic Men* (1967) takes the form of memoirs composed in London by Ralph Singh, a deposed Indian politician who at age 40 is trying to introduce order into his haphazard, pointless life on the imaginary Caribbean island of Isabella. Again, Naipaul's man is lost in a synthetic world offering only the most sordid, imitative opportunities. The novel, which won the W. H. Smith Award, verges on despair, despite its spurts of comedy.

A Flag on the Island (1967), Naipaul's first short-story collection, includes writing from 1950 to the early 1960s. Naipaul's true mastery of short fiction came with *In a Free State*—two stories and a novella that make up "an extraordinarily penetrating book and a disturbing one," according to Alfred Kazin in the *New York Review of Books* (December 30, 1971). Winner of the prestigious Booker Prize, the collection deals with people on journeys away from their roots: an Indian servant transplanted to Washington, D.C.; two West Indian brothers in London; and, in the title novella, a British man and woman in Africa. Besides expanding Naipaul's fictive geography, the stories stress the ominous mindlessness of human destructiveness. Francis Wyndham, in an article for the *New Statesman* (September 19, 1975), noted that Naipaul, in his writings of the period, "has been steadily working toward a vision of the modern world at the same time uncompromisingly bleak and refreshingly honest. In the process his style has become increasingly concentrated and allusive. . . . The structure is elaborate. . . . The matter resounds like a cry of pain."

That cry reaches a crescendo in Naipaul's *Guerrillas* (1975). Set in an unnamed republic, the novel ends with the brutal murder of a woman—an episode that Naipaul had used earlier in an article about a real event in Trinidad. Creating the decaying, chaotic island atmosphere with his customary accuracy, Naipaul builds up to the riots that erupt when police shoot a gang member, tracing their impact on his three main characters: Peter Roche, a white South African activist; his British mistress, Jane; and Jimmy Ahmed, a Chinese-black revolutionary overwhelmed by messianic daydreams. Clashes within that "menage made in hell," as one critic called it, end with Jane's death, as pointless as the general outbreak of violence, which is ultimately quelled by troops protecting American mining interests. Although quietly received in England, *Guerrillas* gained Naipaul an American audience, where many reviewers appreciated its Conradian themes, as well as the meaningful extensions of West Indian material into the present-day politics of the Third World.

India: A Wounded Civilization (1977) is a collection of essays that are as much about the nihilistic legacy left by Mahatma Gandhi as they are about the crumbling India of Indira Gandhi. Many reviewers found his critique of post-Nehru India too condemning, but some saw his stance as justified. "Naipaul is angry," Shernaz Mollinger wrote for *Library Journal* (July 1977). "In the face of his bleak thesis, his anger seems the only possible honorable attitude—one certainly more moral and far healthier than either the Western observer's usual ironic detachment or the Indian's customary placid acceptance of the continuing human horror that constitutes his country."

Naipaul followed *India* with another controversial work, *A Bend in the River* (1979). Set in an unnamed country in Central Africa, the novel focuses on Salim, an East African of East Indian descent, as he witnesses a bloody contest for power that re-

sembles events in the Congo in the 1960s and the brutal reign of Joseph D. Mobutu. Sousa Jamba, writing for the *New Statesman* (December 18, 1998), called it "one of the most perceptive novels about the disintegration of post-colonial Africa."

After a steady flow of fiction—at the rate of approximately one book every two years—eight years passed before Naipaul took up the genre again. In *The Enigma of Arrival* (1987), considered by some to be one of his masterpieces, Naipaul leaves the cultural detritus of the Third World behind to focus on the collapse of the colonial ruling culture through the portrayal of the decline of a landed English proprietor and his estate. The book's English setting also allowed Naipaul to explore concerns of a more personal nature, notably his artistic development. Thomas D'Evelyn, writing in *Christian Science Monitor* (April 15, 1987), commented that "as an account of the writer's romance with his cottage and the garden, it's principally a writer's confession of faith in the ordering and regenerative powers of his own 'walled garden,' his writing. . . . Difficult but never obscure, elaborate but finally as simple as flame, this book shines with the author's singular and passionate honesty."

In 1989, at the age of 58, Naipaul returned to India to retrace the journey he had made 30 years earlier, when he wrote *An Area of Darkness*. This time he encountered an India suffering from ethnic conflicts and religious violence, and he set about interviewing representatives of nearly every major dissident group in India. He compiled the results in a collection of essays, *India: A Million Mutinies Now* (1990). Elisabeth Bumiller, writing for the *Washington Post* (February 10, 1991), noted that the new book was "as full of optimism and sympathy as his earlier works were of disappointment and venom. Warm, human, rich with a cacophony of Indian voices, *India: A Million Mutinies Now* is about the passions and tragedies of a nation caught between the rush of modernity and the power of tradition." As a young man, Naipaul has said, he did not understand the caste system, regarding it as "a kind of racial division," as quoted by Mel Gussow in the *New York Times* (January 30, 1991); nor did he perceive the seeds of revolt, which he now began to understand as being triggered by religious, sectarian, and regional values. Naipaul writes that upon his return to India he found "a central will, a central intellect, a national idea," as quoted by Gussow. Although the book, like some of Naipaul's other work, is classified as travel writing, Naipaul has said that he finds the label somewhat misleading. "One is not looking at the sights. One is exploring the people. I love landscape, but a place is its people," he told Gussow.

The highly acclaimed *A Way in the World* (1994) is a partially autobiographical book about Naipaul's native Trinidad. Composed of nine narratives that are connected thematically, the book incorporates memoir, historical scholarship, and imaginative fiction. According to Paula Burnett in the *New Statesman* (May 13, 1994), Naipaul's tale "celebrates Caribbean pluralism, showing the cultural particularity and distresses of native Americans, Africans, Chinese and Indians at the hands of empire. . . . The book pinpoints human failures, but also celebrates survival by adaptation and hybridity. This is a mellower Naipaul, still at times alienating in his judgements, but much more tolerant after having come to terms with his own anguish."

For *Beyond Belief: Islamic Excursions Among the Converted Peoples* (1998), Naipaul traveled through the Islamic lands of Iran, Malaysia, Indonesia, and Pakistan. (He had made the same journey nearly two decades earlier, recording his experiences in *Among the Believers: An Islamic Journey*, which was published in 1981). Caryl Phillips, writing in the *New Republic* (May 29, 2000), contended that "since the publication of [*A Way in the World*], sadly, Naipaul appears to have rediscovered his antipathy towards people and ideas that are not in tune with his own. *Beyond Belief* . . . [is] a book in which Naipaul seems incapable of restraining his loathing for the Islamic world and its people. . . . Like so many of Naipaul's travel narratives, *Beyond Belief* is a serious book that is undermined by the author's inability to hold his own prejudices in check."

Naipaul's most recent novel, *Half a Life* (2001), follows Willie Somerset Chandran as he attempts to piece together an identity in the face of personal hardships and world events. The story begins with Willie's childhood in India during the 1930s, and a glimpse of his parents' ruinous marriage (Willie's father sought to defy tradition and married a woman of a lower caste). Willie gets a scholarship to a college in London,

England; once there he falls in with the bohemian scene in the London neighborhood of Notting Hill, where he fumbles his way through sexual mishaps, works on his writing, and eventually succeeds in publishing a book. He marries a woman named Ana, whom he meets after she writes him a fan letter. Willie goes with Ana to her parents' estate in a Portugese colony in Africa, where he remains for 18 years. He watches the fledgling nation fall into ruin after the colonial government is overthrown by Marxist-Leninist insurgents. Reviews of the book were largely positive. "Despite his railings against 'half-formed societies,' you discover in Naipaul repeated tributes to small beginnings and small triumphs," Amitava Kumar wrote in *The Nation* (November 26, 2001). "You get a record of the hurt of human failure. . . . [*Half a Life*] is a classic account about heartbreaking achievement and the daily, tragicomic routine of unacknowledged lives."

Naipaul was awarded the Nobel Prize for Literature in October 2001, "for having united perceptive narrative and incorruptible scrutiny in works that compel us to see the presence of suppressed histories," according to the press release of the Swedish Academy, archived on the Nobel e-Museum Web site. Naipaul told Mel Gussow in an interview for the *New York Times* (November 15, 2001) that on October 11, the night before the prize was announced, he had endured a restless sleep: "I was awakened by the most enormous melancholy. . . . [It] had to do with an intellectual fatigue because I thought of all the work I had done. It was as though I felt the labor of writing all those books. It seemed to be an absurdly long journey, and I felt very, very tired and was wondering how I would be able to go on." Then he received a call from the president of the Swedish Academy informing him of the prize, at which he became teary-eyed. "I felt less weary," he said. Naipaul has been on the short list of Nobel candidates for over two decades. (The last British author to win the prize was WILLIAM GOLDING, in 1983.) Naipaul has received numerous awards for his work, including the T. S. ELIOT Award for creative writing in 1986 and the British Literature Award in 1993. He received honorary doctorates from Columbia University, in New York City, and the Universities of Cambridge, London, and Oxford, in England. In 1990 he was knighted by Queen Elizabeth II. He lives in London, England.

SELECTED WORKS: fiction—The Mystic Masseur, 1957; Miguel Street, 1959; A House for Mr. Biswas, 1961; Mr. Stone and the Knights Companion, 1963; The Mimic Men, 1967; The Loss of Eldorado: A History, 1969; In a Free State, 1971; Guerillas, 1975; A Bend in the River, 1979; The Enigma of Arrival, 1987; A Way in the World, 1994; Half a Life, 2001; nonfiction—The Middle Passage: Impressions of Five Societies: British, French and Dutch in the West Indies and South America, 1962; An Area of Darkness, 1964; India: A Wounded Civilization, 1977; Among the Believers: An Islamic Journey, 1981; India: A Million Mutinies Now, 1990; Beyond Belief:

ABOUT: Hamner, Robert. V. S. Naipaul, 1973; Atlantic Monthly November 2001; Commentary August 1994; Guardian October 4, 1971; The Nation November 26, 2001; New Leader September/October 2001; New Republic June 13, 1994, July 13, 1998, May 29, 2000; New Statesman December 4, 1998, December 18, 1998; New Yorker May 23, 1994; New York Times October 17, 1971, December 26, 1976, January 30, 1991, November 15, 2001; New York Times Book Review September 27, 1998, January 16, 2000; Nobel e-Museum Web site; Publishers Weekly June 6, 1994; Washington Post December 26, 1971, February 10, 1991.

Courtesy of Nagoya University

Noyori, Ryoji

(September 3, 1938–) Nobel Prize for Chemistry, 2001 (shared with William S. Knowles and K. Barry Sharpless)

The chemist Ryoji Noyori was born in Kobe, Japan, on September 3, 1938. He attended Kyoto University, earning his B.S. degree in 1961 and his master's degree in 1963. While pursuing his doctorate, he became a research associate in the university's Department of Industrial Chemistry, where

he worked with chiral molecules. The term "chiral" refers to the pattern of many natural molecules that appear in two mirror forms, or enantiomers—similar to the way our hands mirror each other. Typically, one of these images acts as the dominant molecule and fits in the human cell "like a glove"; this is the case in all of the body's naturally occurring amino acids, peptides, enzymes and other proteins, as well as carbohydrates and nucleic acids such as DNA and RNA. In the case of pharmaceutical products, however, it can be dangerous for a drug to contain certain chiral molecules because the less-dominant enantiomer may have harmful effects on the body, as was the case in the drug thalidomide, which was used in the 1960s to treat nausea in pregnant women: While the drug's dominant enantiomer eased the nausea that accompanies early stages of pregnancy, its mirror image caused limb deformities in thousands of infants worldwide.

In 1966 Noyori developed the first asymmetric transition-metal catalyst. (Despite the fact that his catalyst produced less than 10 percent excess of the dominant enantiomer, Noyori's publication of a general principle for synthesizing chiral compounds helped fuel chemists' research toward developing the "pure enantiomers" with 100 percent excess that exist today.)

After earning his Ph.D. in 1967, Noyori became an associate professor in the department of chemistry at Nagoya University in 1968, where he was later promoted to professor in 1972. In addition, he spent the year of 1969–1970 conducting postdoctoral research with Elias J. Corey at Harvard University. He later served as director of the Chemical Instrument Center at Nagoya University from 1979–1991.

Following Noyori's modest success producing asymmetric synthesis, drug companies continued to pursue inexpensive methods for producing large quantities of pure enantiomers of chiral compounds. In 1968 Noyori's fellow Nobel laureate, WILLIAM S. KNOWLES, then a senior chemist at the Monsanto Company, made another breakthrough discovery. The Royal Swedish Academy of Sciences explained: "He discovered that it was possible to use a transition metal to produce a chiral catalyst that could transfer chirality to a non-chiral substrate and get a chiral product. The reaction was a hydrogenation in which the hydrogen atoms in H2 are added to the carbons in a double bond. A single catalyst molecule can produce millions of molecules of the desired enantiomer." By adding the hydrogen atoms to the carbon molecule, Knowles caused the molecule to twist outward, thereby creating only one mirror form determined by the direction of the turn. He then applied this technique to the creation of the Parkinson's drug L-dopa, with his reaction producing 97.5 percent L-dopa and only 2.5 percent of its toxic mirror form D-dopa, thereby allowing Monsanto to produce the drug safely and commercially.

In 1980 Noyori expanded upon Knowles's work with hydrogenation catalysts, announcing his success synthesizing both enantiomers of the diphosphine ligand BINAP, which in complexes with rhodium produced certain amino acids with enantiomeric excess of up to 100 percent. Further, Noyori explored ways to find more general catalysts with broader, and therefore less expensive, applications. In one example, he exchanged rhodium for another metal-based catalyst, ruthenium, Ru(II), using Ru-BINAP complexes that can hydrogenate many types of molecules with other functional groups to create reactions with high enantiomeric excess and high yields. By developing catalysts that offered wider applications and could be amplified for industrial use, Noyori helped enhance the synthesis of fine chemicals, pharmaceutical products, and advanced material; his catalysts, for example, have proven useful in the industrial synthesis of the antibacterial levofloxacin

and the anti-inflammatory drug naproxen. (K. BARRY SHARPLESS, meanwhile, contributed to the field by developing chiral catalysts for use in oxidation reactions.)

In later research Noyori studied the effects of "asymmetric amplification," as it was termed by Nobuki Oguni in 1988, an effect within certain metal- and non-metal-catalyzed reactions that exhibit a nonlinear departure between the amount of enantiomeric excess and the extent of the chiral's asymmetric induction. He continues to research and develop techniques for enhancing the purity and precision of chiral catalysts for hydrogenation, outlining his research on the Web site for the R. Noyori Network as follows: "The efficiency of the chemical method using man-made molecular catalysts rivals or, in certain cases, even exceeds that of natural enzymatic reactions. Thanks to the diverse catalytic activities of metallic species, coupled with the virtually unlimited permutability of the chiral organic ancillaries, the possibilities and the opportunities that asymmetric catalysis affords are enormous. We will pursue, on the basis of a new chemical concept, further powerful asymmetric catalyses that are fast, selective, and productive. The modern synthetic methods obviously require high cost-performance as well as environmental consciousness. Realization of perfect chemical reactions with 100 percent yield and 100 percent selectivity will be our ultimate goal."

Throughout the 1990s while conducting and publishing his research on catalytic asymmetric synthesis, Noyori served as director of the ERATO Molecular Catalysis Project of the Research Development Corporation of Japan from 1991–1996 and as science advisor for Japan's Ministry of Education for Science and Culture from 1992–1996. In 1993 he added to his duties a professorship at the Institute of Fundamental Research of Organic Chemistry at Kyushu University, where he served until 1996. Since 1996, he has also been a member of the Scientific Council of Ministry of Education for Science, Sports, and Culture, and a committee chairman for the Japan Society for the Promotion of Science. From 1997–1999, he served as dean of Nagoya University's Graduate School of Science, becoming director of the university's Research Center for Materials Science in 2000. In 1994 Noyori published the book *Asymmetric Cataly-*

sis in Organic Synthesis based on a series of lectures he gave at Cornell University in 1990. While the book's emphasis was primarily on Noyori's own research, critics generally praised the overall work as a resource outlining the basic principles and synthetic significance of asymmetric catalysis, covering developments in the field through 1992.

In addition to the Nobel Prize, Noyori has received numerous awards, including: the Chemical Society of Japan Award (1985), the Naito Foundation Research Prize (1988), the Toray Science & Technology Prize (1990), the John Gamble Kirkwood Award from the American Chemical Society and Yale University (1991), the Asahi Prize (1992), the Tetrahedron Prize for Creativity in Organic Chemistry from Pergamon Press in the U.K. (1993), the Keimei Life Science Prize (1994), the Japan Academy Prize (1995), the Arthur C. Cope Scholar Award from the American Chemical Society (1996 and 1997), the Bonn Chemistry Award from the University of Bonn and Pinguin Foundation (1996), the Chirality Medal from the International Symposium on Chiral Discrimination (1997), the George Kenner Award from the University of Liverpool (1997), the King Faisal International Prize for Science (1999), the Cliff S. Hamilton Award from the University of Nebraska at Lincoln (1999), the order of Culture from the Emperor Akihito (2000), the Wolf Prize in Chemistry (2001), and the Roger Adams Award from the American Chemical Society (2001). He is a member of the Chemical Society of Japan, the Pharmaceutical Society of Japan, the American Chemical Society, the Royal Society of Chemistry, the American Association for the Advancement of Science, and the Society of Synthetic Organic Chemistry in Japan, for which he served as vice president from 1994–1996 and president from 1997–1999. Throughout his career, Noyori has published more than 400 original papers, reviews, chapters, commentaries, and monographs and currently holds 145 patents.

Noyori married Hiroko Oshima on December 9, 1972; they have two sons, Eiji and Koji.

ABOUT: Chemical & Engineering News January 27, 1997, March 31, 1997; Chemtech June 1992; New York Times October 11, 2001; Nobel e-Museum Web site; R. Noyori Network Web site.

Courtesy of CANCER RESEARCH UK

Nurse, Paul

(January 25, 1949–) Nobel Prize for Physiology or Medicine, 2001 (shared with R. Timothy Hunt and Leland Hartwell)

The medical researcher Paul Nurse was born on January 25, 1949. His interest in science and scientific research began as a child. "I remember seeing Sputnik 2 when I was in London," he told Julia Karow in an interview for *Scientific American* (June 26, 2000, on-line). "As a young child, eight or nine years old, I read about it in the newspaper and went out in our garden and saw Sputnik 2 fly over, I think in 1957 or 1958, and this was truly amazing. And then when I was a little older I became interested in natural history, and I watched birds, and I collected beetles, and was interested in plants and so on. So my main entrée into biology was through natural history. I think that is quite common."

As he grew older, Nurse became interested in molecular and cellular biology, in part because this course of study enabled him to make controlled experiments in a laboratory—something he couldn't do in studying the vastness of nature. "I became interested in the cell cycle because it's a very simple example of development," Nurse wrote in an autobiographical sketch on the Lasker Living Library Web site. "Also as the most basic form of reproduction, a characteristic of all living things, I felt that its study would reveal something very important generally about what is life." After attending the Harrow County Grammar School from 1960 to 1966, he enrolled at the University of Birmingham, where he earned a B.S. in biological sciences in 1970 and was awarded the John Humphreys Memorial Prize in Botany. In 1973 he earned his Ph.D. from the University of East Anglia in cell biology and biochemistry.

Nurse served as a research fellow at the University of Bern's Institute of Microbiology, in Switzerland, before completing his postdoctoral work at the University of Edinburgh's Department of Zoology. At Edinburgh, Nurse was advised by Professor Murdoch Mitchson who, as he told Julia Karow, "gave me great freedom as a young investigator and allowed me to work in my own way. I owe him a great debt for that. He encouraged me, he spoke to me, but he really made no attempt to control me, a very good situation." At Edinburgh, Nurse began his research into the process of DNA replication and cell division in the cell cycle, building on the work of LELAND HARTWELL.

In 1970 Hartwell began to study budding yeast—a very simple organism, and thus a good subject for study. He eventually isolated over 100 genes that are involved in the cell cycle. In the mid-1970s, Nurse built on Hartwell's work with his own study of yeast. He isolated a gene, cdc2, that proved to be integral to controlling the cell cycle. When the cdc2 gene was activated in experiments, Nurse noticed that cells began to divide more quickly than normal. He concluded that cdc2 had to be an important regulator of the entire cell-division process. Nurse then proved that cdc2 contained the genetic instructions for a protein called a cyclin-dependent kinase (CDK), which is crucial to cell division. "It turned out that this particular one controls when the DNA is copied, which is necessary in every cell cycle, and also when the DNA is separated during the process of mitosis," Nurse told Karow. "So it controls the two major processes found in every cell cycle."

In 1980 Nurse left the University of Edinburgh for the University of Sussex, where he served as a senior research fellow for the next four years. In 1984 he joined the staff of the London-based Imperial Cancer Research Fund (ICRF), the largest cancer research organization in Britain, where he became head of the Cell Cycle Control Laboratory. Around this time, Nurse realized that, as he told Karow, "people were not that desperately interested in yeast." He began to look for the human gene that functioned similarly to the yeast gene cdc2. In 1987 he isolated CDK1—the key gene in the regulation of the human cell cycle. It was a laborious process, helped along by an unorthodox method devised by a researcher in Nurse's lab named Melanie Lee. Lee took a set of human genes and put them on yeast cells that had been treated in such a way that the yeast would take up the DNA of the human cells. Lee then put the human DNA on yeast cells that had defective cdc2 genes, and thus couldn't grow. The theory was that, if there was an equivalent human gene to cdc2, it would be taken up by the yeast cell and the cell would begin division. The method worked, and they were able to isolate the human gene that plays a key role in cell division. "What this showed is that in fact, you could substitute the yeast gene with the human gene, even though these two organisms had diverged hugely in evolutionary terms, maybe 1,000 million years ago," Nurse told Karow," and that the human gene could work perfectly well in yeast. That obviously implied that the way in which the cell cycle was controlled is basically the same in all living things, from yeast to human cells."

In the early 1980s, another ICRF researcher, R. TIMOTHY HUNT, discovered proteins known as cyclins that work to regulate the action of the CDK proteins. A Nobel e-Museum Web site press release elaborated: "The CDK-molecules can be compared with an engine and the cyclins with a gear box controlling whether the engine will run in the idling state or drive the cell forward in the cell cycle."

In awarding the Nobel Prize to Hartwell, Hunt, and Nurse, the Nobel committee recognized that the scientists' discoveries contribute to our understanding of how chromosomal defects arise in cancer cells. "All cancers cells have something wrong with the cycle," Dr. Klas Wiman, a member of the awards committee, told the Associated Press reporter Kim Gamel, as printed on CBS News.com (October 8, 2001). "These discoveries have laid the foundation for understanding how the cell cycle affects cancer." Research into new therapies based on their discoveries has already begun.

Nurse's work has earned him many awards, including the 1992 Gairdner Foundation International Award, the 1993 Royal Society Wellcome Medal, the 1997 General Motors Cancer Research Foundation Alfred P. Sloan Jr. Prize & Medal, and the 1998 Albert Lasker Award.

Nurse has been director-general of the ICRF since 1996. He was knighted in 1999. He is married and has two daughters. In addition to his scientific pursuits, he is also a licenced pilot and particularly enjoys flying glider planes.

ABOUT: Albert & Mary Lasker Foundation Web site; CBS News.com October 8, 2001; Ecologist July/August 1998; Nobel e-Museum Web site; Scientific American (on-line) June 26, 2000; New York Times September 20, 1998.

© Robert Rathe/Courtesy of National Institute of Standards and Technology

Phillips, William D.

(November 5, 1948–) Nobel Prize for Physics, 1997 (shared with Steven Chu and Claude Cohen-Tannoudji)

The physicist William Daniel Phillips was born in Wilkes-Barre, Pennsylvania, on November 5, 1948 to William Cornelius Phillips and Mary Catherine (Savine) Phillips. His parents were the first in their families to attend college, and both became so-cial workers in what Phillips described in an autobiographical essay posted on the Nobel e-Museum Web site as "the hard coal country of Pennsylvania." As a boy Phillips played with erector sets and ad-hoc chemistry sets. When his family moved to Camp Hill, Pennsylvania, he was placed in an accelerated program for advanced seventh-graders. "During this time," he recalled in his essay, "I had a laboratory in the basement of our family home. Ignorant and heedless of the dangers of asbestos, electricity, and ultraviolet light, I spent many hours experimenting with fire, explosives, rockets and carbon arcs." Over one summer in high school, he worked in a laboratory at the University of Delaware, where a graduate student told him, as he recalled in his essay: "An experimental physicist is someone who gets paid for working at his hobby." He graduated as valedictorian of Camp Hill High School in 1966.

Phillips attended Juniata College, in Huntingdon, Pennsylvania. While there, he enjoyed a French literature class, which later proved useful when he collaborated with the French physicist and fellow Nobel laureate, CLAUDE COHEN-TANNOUDJI. He earned a B.S. in physics in 1970, and then enrolled in graduate school at the Massachusetts Institute of Technology (MIT), in Cambridge. He completed his Ph.D. in physics in 1976 and then stayed at MIT for a two-year postdoctoral fellowship.

In 1978 Phillips became a professional physicist at the National Institute of Standards and Technology (NIST), in Gaithersburg, Maryland, where he has worked since. (NIST is a federal agency that develops measurements and standards for such technology as automated teller machines and semiconductors.) Phillips began in the Electricity Division, developing precision electrical measurements. In this way, he began to study methods of laser-cooling atoms. Specifically, he was trying to improve the atomic clock—a highly precise timepiece operated by an electrical oscillator and regulated by the natural vibrational frequency of atoms. Seeking to control the atoms as efficiently as possible, he worked to slow them down so that they could be studied. This meant that they had to be made extremely cold, since atoms at room temperature move in different directions at approximately 4000 kilometers per hour.

In the early 1980s Phillips developed a device to slow atoms using atomic beams. Called a Zeeman slower, the device was essentially a coil that projected a varying magnetic field. Along the coil's axis, laser beams were fired in direct opposition to the atoms. As the photon particles that constitute the laser beam collided with the atoms, the movement of the atoms was reduced and their temperature lowered. After the atoms were hit with the laser, they were trapped by the magnetic field. In 1985, using the Zeeman slower, Phillips slowed and captured sodium atoms. However, the trap created by the magnetic field was relatively weak, and the atoms had to be extremely cold if they were to remain inside of it.

Philips worked independently from STEVEN CHU and Claude Cohen-Tannoudji, but the three men shared their findings in scientific journals. To further cool the atoms, Phillips made use of a process known as Doppler cooling, which had been developed by Chu. Doppler cooling involved bombarding atoms with extremely powerful lasers. The intense barrage of photons slows the atoms down, cooling them to a temperature of 240 microkelvins—240 millionths above absolute zero or -273 degrees Celsius. This temperature was termed the "Doppler limit." Because the experiment was conducted in a vacuum, the density was kept at a point at which the gaseous body of atoms did not condense into liquid or solidify, which would have brought the atoms too close together to be studied.

In 1988 Phillips discovered that Chu's proposed Doppler limit could in fact be broken. Studying neutral atoms, Phillips developed a new system of measuring the temperature of the cloud in which the atoms floated. His analysis showed the atoms to be at a temperature of approximately 40 microkelvins, nearly six times lower than Chu's Doppler limit. Both Chu and Cohen-Tannoudji confirmed Phillips's finding, and it became clear that Phillips had made the next step forward in the quest to cool and slow atoms. Working together, in 1989, Phillips and Cohen-Tannoudji demonstrated that trapped atoms organize into regular groupings, termed an "optical lattice," when the correct laser setting is used.

Phillips's research enabled the improved atomic clock to be completed by 1990. The technology used in the clock may soon be implemented for space navigation and satellite positioning systems. The work may also contribute to an emerging area of study known as atom optics. Using the research of Phillips, Chu, and Cohen-Tannoudji, attempts are being made to channel beams of atoms to create pictures with greater sharpness than photographs, which use beams of light. Phillips also envisions using light to focus an atom laser, which could create extremely small electronic circuitry components.

"Winning an award like this is a very odd thing," Phillips told Joretta Purdue for the *United Methodist News Service* (November 19, 1997, on-line). "People think that somehow you have wisdom that goes beyond what you got the award for—which, or course, is not true." In public statements, Phillips credited his research team at NIST for their invaluable contributions.

In addition to his two decades of work at NIST, Phillips has been a visiting professor of atomic physics in Paris, at the École Normale Supérieure (1989–1990) and at the Collège de France (1997). He won the Outstanding Young Scientist Award from the Maryland Academy of Science (1982) and both the Silver Medal (1982) and Gold Medal (1993) from the U.S. Department of Commerce. He has also received the ALBERT A. MICHELSON Medal from the Franklin Institute (1995), among other honors. He is a member of the Physics Society, the Optical Society of America, and the American Academy of Arts and Sciences. In 1996 he became a fellow of the NIST.

Phillips is also highly active in the United Methodist Church as an adult Sunday school teacher and a member of the gospel choir. He married Jane Van Wynen in 1970; the couple lives in Gaithersburg, Maryland, with their two daughters, Catherine and Christine.

ABOUT: NIST Web site; Nobel e-Museum Web site; United Methodist News Service (on-line) November 19, 1997.

Courtesy of Evanston Photographics Studios, Inc.

Pople, John A.

*(October 31, 1925–) Nobel Prize for
Chemistry, 1998 (shared with Walter Kohn)*

The chemist John Anthony Pople was
born on October 31, 1925 in the British town
of Burnham-on-Sea, on the west coast of
England. His father, Herbert Keith Pople,
owned a men's clothing store and also sold
clothes door-to-door in far-flung villages
and farms. His mother, the former Mary
Frances Jones, was a private tutor and librar-
ian. As a boy of 10, Pople was sent to Bristol
Grammar School, in the city of Bristol nearly
30 miles from his home. "I persuaded my
parents to allow me to commute daily—two
miles by bicycle, twenty-five miles by train
and one mile on foot," he recalled in an autobiographical essay posted on the Nobel e-
Museum Web site. "I continued to do this
during the early part of the war, a challenging experience during the many air attacks
on Bristol. Often, we had to wend our way
past burning buildings and around unex-
ploded bombs on the way to school in the
morning. . . . In spite of all these difficulties, the school staff coped well and I received a superb education." Pople became
very interested in mathematics, setting himself complicated problems to solve and being coached by the school's mathematics
and physics teachers.

Pople enrolled as a scholarship student at
Trinity College, Cambridge University, in
1943, one of a small group of science and
mathematics students excused from war-
time service as part of a program to promote
military research in science-related projects.
With the war over in 1945, and many ex-
servicemen in need of university places, he
was asked to leave Cambridge after completing his mathematics degree. He worked at
the Bristol Aeroplane Company until 1947,
when he was readmitted to Cambridge, now
determined to apply his mathematical skills
to a scientific career.

Pople found postwar Cambridge to be a
very stimulating place. "There was a general
air of excitement as . . . people turned their
attention to new scientific challenges," he
recalled in his essay. He added that, while
many young people were drawn to the dy-
namic field of physics, he became interested
in the "less crowded" field of chemistry,
particularly in the theory of liquids. In 1948
Pople began working as a research assistant
to Sir John Lennard-Jones, a Cambridge
chemist also working in this area. In 1950 he
earned a master's degree in mathematics,
and the following year he earned a mathematics Ph.D. He remained at Trinity College
as a research fellow; in 1954, he became a
lecturer on the mathematics faculty.

Pople left Cambridge in 1958 to become
the director of the Basic Physics Division of
the National Physics Laboratory, in Teddington, England. The Teddington Laboratory had been the site of many important
breakthroughs during World War II and continued to be on the cutting edge of scientific
research. However, Pople found that administrative duties distracted him from his scientific pursuits. From 1961 to 1962 Pople
took leave from the Laboratory to serve as a
visiting professor of chemistry at the Carnegie Institute of Technology, in Pittsburgh,
Pennsylvania. In 1964 he returned to Pittsburgh as a professor of chemical physics at
Carnegie Tech. (In 1967 Carnegie Tech
merged with the Mellon Institute to become
Carnegie-Mellon University.) Pople remained on the faculty there until 1993, first
as a professor of chemical physics and then,
after 1974, as a professor of natural sciences.

At Pittsburgh, Pople set out to create
mathematical models for studying chemical
activity. Ever since the development of
quantum theory at the beginning of the 20th
century, which provided a mathematical

framework for describing the activities of subatomic particles, scientists had theoretically understood how electrons and atomic nuclei behave. However, on a practical level, it had proven difficult to calculate the complex mathematical equations that would describe such activities. The emergence of high-speed computers during the 1960s made such calculations possible. "By 1964," Pople recalled in his autobiographical essay, "it was clear that the development of an efficient computer code was one of the major tasks facing a practical theoretician and I learned the trade with enthusiasm."

Pople's fellow Nobel laureate, the physicist WALTER KOHN, laid out the theoretical groundwork for such calculations. In 1964 Kohn demonstrated that it was not necessary to calculate the movements of each individual electron; instead, calculations could be made based on the density of the electrons by figuring the average number of electrons at a given point. This method, which became known as the density-functional theory, greatly simplified the study of large molecules, and is currently used in many areas of chemistry.

Pople built on Kohn's work to become a trailblazer in the field of quantum chemistry, which applied quantum mechanics to the molecular system. (Quantum mechanics is the branch of physics that seeks to predict the behavior of atoms, subatomic particles, and molecules.) Experimenting with early computers, Pople began to develop approaches to studying the electronic structure of molecules. He refined a computational method that would work best with the widest variety of calculations. Pople was "almost always about five years ahead of everyone else in seeing what was possible with digital computing," the chemist Christopher J. Cramer is quoted as saying in *Science News* (October 17, 1998). "The vision he had was just spectacular."

The culmination of Pople's work was the computer program GAUSSIAN, completed in 1970. By creating a program based on the laws of quantum mechanics, Pople enabled chemists to study the behavior and makeup of molecules and chemical reactions with a precision never before known. After receiving input containing the properties of a particular particle or reaction, the GAUSSIAN program can predict the course a chemical reaction will take and the properties of the particles that will result.

In 1986 Pople accepted a second faculty position, at Northwestern University, in Evanston, Illinois. In 1993 he retired from the faculty of Carnegie-Mellon, though he continues to teach at Northwestern.

In 1998 John Pople and Walter Kohn were jointly awarded the Nobel Prize in Chemistry; according to the official press release, the Nobel Committee recognized Pople and Kohn for their "pioneering contributions in developing methods that can be used for theoretical studies of the properties of molecules and the chemical processes in which they are involved."

Among the current applications of the GAUSSIAN program are the intricate study of biological enzymes, the analysis of interstellar dust clouds, and the monitoring of the effects of pollution in the Earth's atmosphere. GAUSSIAN is also used by pharmaceutical companies to design drugs. A commercial version of GAUSSIAN is now marketed and sold by the Pittsburgh company Gaussian, Inc. "In the real world," according to a writer for the *Economist* (October 17, 1998), "[the program] could eventually mean that most chemical experiments are conducted inside the silicon of chips instead of the glassware of laboratories."

Pople has also been awarded the 1958 Marlow Medal from the Faraday Society, the 1970 IRVING LANGMUIR Award from the American Chemistry Society, the 1971 Harrison Howe Award, the 1972 Gilbert Newton Lewis Award, the 1975 Pittsburgh Award, the 1976 Morley Award, the 1977 Pauling Award, the 1981 Senior Scientist Award from the Alexander von Humboldt Foundation, the 1981 G. Willard Wheland Award from the University of Chicago, the 1982 Evans Award from Ohio State University, the 1992 Wolf Prize from Israel's Wolf Foundation, the 1994 Kirkwood Medal from the American Chemistry Society, and the J. O. Hirschfelder Prize in Theoretical Chemistry from the University of Wisconsin's Theoretical Chemistry Institute. In 1990 he was awarded an honorary doctorate from the University of Toronto.

Pople married Joy Bowers in 1952. The couple have four children, Hilary Jane, Adrian John, Mark Stephen, and Andrew Keith, as well as 11 grandchildren.

ABOUT: New York Times October 14, 1998; Nobel e-Museum Web site; Northwestern Observer (on-line) October

22, 1998; Science News October 17, 1998; Scientific American (on-line) October 19, 1998; Washington Post October 14, 1998.

Courtesy of The University of California San Francisco

Prusiner, Stanley

(May 28, 1942–) Nobel Prize for Physiology or Medicine, 1997

The neurologist and biochemist Stanley Ben Prusiner was born on May 28, 1942 in Des Moines, Iowa, to Lawrence Albert Prusiner and his wife, Miriam. In his youth he lived in both Des Moines and Cincinnati, Ohio. His intensive study of Latin at Walnut Hills High School, in Cincinnati, "was to help me immensely later in the writing of scientific papers," he wrote for an autobiographical sketch posted on the Nobel e-museum Web site. He attended the University of Pennsylvania, where he enjoyed what he described as the "extraordinary" intellectual environment and the opportunity to talk to internationally renowned scholars. During the summer of 1963, which followed his junior year, he began a research project on hypothermia with Sidney Wolfson; the project fascinated him, and he continued working on it as a senior. He earned an A.B. degree with honors from the University of Pennsylvania in 1964 and then enrolled at medical school at the same institution. As a second-year med student, he did research

on brown adipose tissue in hamsters. Thanks to that experience, he spent much of his fourth year of medical school in Stockholm, Sweden, studying brown fat cells with Olov Lindberg at the Wenner-Gren Institute. He earned his M.D. degree in 1968. During the next two years he interned at the University of California at San Francisco (UCSF). He then spent three years at the National Institutes of Health (NIH), where, as an employee of the U.S. Public Health Service, he studied the enzyme glutaminase in *E. coli.* "My three years at the NIH were critical in my scientific education," he recalled in his autobiographical sketch. "I learned an immense amount about the research process."

In 1972, soon after Prusiner began what proved to be an abbreviated residency in neurology at UCSF, a female patient of his died from a mysterious disorder called Cruetzfeldt-Jakob disease (CJD). That event inspired him to begin researching CJD. Upon completing his residency, in 1974, he decided to continue his work as a professional researcher of CJD instead of going into private practice, as he had originally planned. He began teaching at UCSF as an assistant professor in 1974 and became an associate professor in 1980.

In 1982 Prusiner made public his heretical belief that CJD is caused by rogue proteins, or "prions" (pronounced PREE-ahns), and not by a virus, as many scientists thought. The belief of the virus supporters was based primarily on the observation that victims of CJD were generally not young; but where or when the virus had infected its victims remained unknown, so scientists labeled it a "slow virus." They assumed that it attacked the nervous system after incubating in the body for 40, 50, or even 60 years, without causing any rise in a victim's white-blood-cell count. Researchers had not succeeded in isolating the virus and were therefore unable to find a way of killing it.

Several years before Prusiner had begun to study CJD, researchers had linked the disease to two other neurological disorders: scrapie and kuru. Scrapie afflicts sheep; its symptoms include irritability, severe itching (which leads the animals to rub, or scrape, against solid surfaces), and ataxia (loss of muscle control), the last of which often becomes so severe that the sheep become immobilized and eventually die. Kuru, at one time the leading cause of death among the Fore Highlanders of Papua, New Guinea, was believed to be transmitted when, in a ritualistic act of cannibalism, a tribesperson ate the brain of a deceased victim of the disease.

Nearly two decades before Prusiner had embarked on his CJD research, the virologist D. CARLETON GAJDUSEK had begun investigating the agents responsible for scrapie and kuru. The prime suspects included viruses. A typical virus consists of either DNA or RNA (deoxyribonucleic acid and ribonucleic acid, respectively) coated with protein. The virus propagates itself by inserting its genetic material into the cell of a host, an event that transforms the host cell into a virus factory. Gajdusek's research on scrapie included investigating various treatments known to destroy the nucleic acids that were believed to be the basis of the scrapie virus. The disease remained unaffected by his treatments, however. (Gajdusek won the Nobel Prize in Physiology or Medicine in 1976 for his work with what the Nobel Committee referred to as "unique infectious agents.")

Meanwhile, in the mid-1970s Prusiner was setting up his own laboratory to discover what causes scrapie—"a wonderful problem for a chemist," in his words. He told Gary Taubes for *Discover* (December 1986) that in his view, scientists who until then had "tried to unravel the chemistry of [scrapie] hadn't taken a very careful approach." He was initially unable to acquire funding from the NIH, which funded Gajdusek and others. To increase his chances of receiving NIH support, Prusiner took a course on virology and recruited some highly regarded researchers to his team, among them William Hadlow, an American who had studied scrapie in England, and Carl Eklund, a Swedish scientist. His strategy worked; he got the funding he needed and then aggressively set out to find the agent responsible for scrapie. "I was rash and naive enough to say, 'Let's treat it as a black box, as a macromolecule,'" he told Gina Kolata for the *New York Times* (October 4, 1994). "'Let's purify it and see what it is.'" The tactic that Prusiner and his co-workers came up with was to try to derive a pure sample of the scrapie-causing agent by infecting a number of mice with pieces, or fractions, of brain tissue extracted from mice that had died of the disease, observing which mouse had evidently received the deadliest fraction, then subdividing that mouse's brain into fractions and

using those bits of brain matter to infect the next batch of mice, and so on. With each passage of the virus, the scientists hoped to increase the purity of the virus. The process was costly and time-consuming, and after a few years, the NIH decided to stop funding Prusiner's team.

Gary Taubes described what follows as "a classic story of triumph through adversity." Prusiner came up with a much more efficient way of obtaining a pure sample, and "over the next two or three years," he said, "we did more experiments on the biochemistry of scrapie than everyone else in the history of scrapie combined." By 1981 Prusiner was claiming that his samples of the scrapie-causing agent were 99 percent pure. With these samples, he used "at least five different techniques to show that a protein was necessary for infectivity," as he told Taubes. "Then we used five different techniques to look for a nucleic acid. We couldn't find any," a result that strongly suggested that the scrapie-causing agent was not a virus. "So we introduced the term prion. That's when the modern era of all this began."

"Prion" is an abbreviation for "protinaceous infectious particle." The simple act of giving his infectious agent that name had a tremendous impact on Prusiner's career and the study of scrapie, kuru, and CJD, grouped together as spongiform encephalopathies. Prusiner immediately drew criticism from many in the scientific community who deemed his conclusion—that a protein, and not a virus, caused these diseases—to be irresponsible and hasty. The basic concept of an infectious protein had been discussed for at least 15 years, but there was no proof that it existed. Prusiner's critics did not accept his results as proof, either. He may have named it, but he had not been able to isolate it. But if prions did exist as self-replicating proteins, then Prusiner was on to something truly exciting—nothing less than a new form of life.

Whether by intent or by accident, in February 1982, two months before the publication of his paper about prions in *Science*, Prusiner suddenly became a celebrity scientist. An article by David Perlman on the front page of the *San Francisco Chronicle* (February 19, 1982) called Prusiner's prion "a newly detected class of life." A *New York Times* article appeared two days later reporting the same possibility. "That kind of thing did more than anything I could ever do," Prusiner told Taubes, commenting about the media's reaction to his work. "The prion became a household word among biologists immediately. They didn't even have to read *Science*."

And whether by intent or by accident, Prusiner's statements about the prion paid off in another way, in that his lab began to receive more funding. By the end of 1982, Prusiner believed he had obtained a sample so pure that it essentially consisted of a single protein, which he labeled PrP, for "prion protein." A year later Prusiner's team made a key link between the "prion diseases" (as CJD, scrapie, and kuru were beginning to be known) and Alzheimer's disease. The connection had been theorized for years, but there had been no evidence of it until Prusiner noticed a similarity between aggregations of "prion rods" and amyloid plaques, which are present in the brains of people afflicted with Alzheimer's disease.

Prusiner's next breakthrough came in 1984, when his group identified 15 amino acids at the end of the prion protein. Soon afterward laboratories in Switzerland and the United States found that there was a gene for producing PrP not only in scrapie-infected hamsters and mice, but also in healthy animals. "One interpretation of such findings was that we had made a terrible mistake," Prusiner wrote for *Scientific American* (January 1995). However, he and a colleague, Ronald A. Barry, were able to differentiate two kinds of prion proteins: the harmless "cellular prion protein," or PrPC, which occurs naturally, and the lethal "scrapie prion protein," or PrPSc.

Prusiner's team had hoped to clone the scrapie prion protein in their lab from the gene they had discovered, but after more than a year of trying, they admitted defeat. They found that they could produce only the harmless "cellular prion protein" version. However, Prusiner again looked into the lore of prion diseases and found that in some cases the diseases appeared to be inherited. In 1988 Prusiner and Karen Hsiao, a reseracher in his lab, obtained clones of a PrP gene from a sufferer of the CJD-related illness Gerstmann-Straussler-Scheinker disease (GSS) whose family medical history included other cases of the disease. When Prusiner and Hsiao compared the cloned gene with normal PrP genes, they found a mutation that had caused just one amino acid to be different in the proteins produced by the cloned gene. They passed the information on to researchers in New York and London, who soon confirmed the mutation in other families with the disease. Again Prusiner's results were at odds with scientific dogma: he appeared to have found a disease that could be both hereditary and transmissible.

As the 1990s began, Prusiner and his colleagues were still investigating PrPC and PrPSc. "Many details remain to be worked out, but one aspect appears quite clear: the main difference between normal PrP and scrapie PrP is conformation," Prusiner wrote in *Scientific American*. "Evidently, the scrapie protein propagates itself by contacting normal PrP molecules and somehow causing them to unfold and flip from their usual conformation to the scrapie shape. This change initiates a cascade in which newly converted molecules change the shape of other normal PrP molecules, and so on." Prusiner has further speculated that the spread of the disease from molecule to molecule might resemble a gradual crystallization.

Despite the hostility directed toward him as a result of his hypothesis, Prusiner persevered with his research, and over the years he has produced a wealth of evidence pointing to the existence of prions. What he has learned is even more interesting, in some respects, than the idea that there might be such things as infectious self-replicating proteins. His data seem to show that the prion is the product of a mutant gene, and that it causes disease by bending and otherwise altering the shape of normal versions of the same protein; once reconfigured, the now-abnormal proteins go on to twist and bend still more healthy proteins into prions. Although there are many in the scientific community who believe, and have always believed, that Prusiner is simply wrong, more and more researchers are joining the prion camp. "Even if the final proof is debatable, some of the most outstanding minds today think this is as solid as it can get," Jordan U. Gutterman, of the M. D. Anderson Cancer Center in Houston, told Gina Kolata for the *New York Times* (October 4, 1994). Among those who view the existence of prions with skepticism, many acknowledge that the data Prusiner has collected on the behavior of spongiform encephalopathies would still be of use even if a virus were discovered to be the cause of those diseases.

For his research on prions, Prusiner was honored with a Gairdner Foundation Award in 1993, and in 1994 he received the Basic Research Award from the Albert and Mary Lasker Foundation. He won the Wolf Prize for medicine in 1996. He has won many other awards as well for his scientific achievements. For a long time experts regarded him as a prime candidate for a Nobel Prize. He had only to show the Nobel judges unquestionable evidence that prions alone can cause disease. The obvious way to obtain such proof would be to induce a prion disease in cells by injecting them with cloned prions, something he has yet to do.

In March 1996 a nationwide panic erupted in Great Britain when the British health secretary, Stephen Dorrell, announced that 10 young people had contracted a new strain of CJD, and that there was reason to believe that these cases had been caused by the consumption of beef from cows infected with bovine spongiform encephalopathy (BSE), a fatal brain disease more commonly known as "mad cow disease." The ensuing hysteria focused renewed attention on Prusiner's work.

In January 1997 Dominique Dormont published a paper in *Science* that appeared to be the strongest evidence against the prion in years. Dormont ran experiments with lab mice similar to Prusiner's but concluded that prions are not always present in the brain tissue of the deceased mice. Despite this challenge, the Nobel Committee awarded Prusiner the 1997 Nobel Prize in Physiology or Medicine. "There are still people who don't believe that a protein can cause these diseases," Lars Edstrom, a committee member, told Lawrence Altman for the *New York Times* (October 6, 1997), "but we believe it." Edstrom's choice of words is fitting, as the prion controversy is likely to remain a matter of faith until Prusiner finds the ironclad proof that has so far eluded him. Predictably, critics of the prion hypothesis expressed disappointment at the Nobel Committee's decision. For his part, Prusiner, who was only the sixth person in 40 years to win the award without any co-winners, has tried to remain diplomatic. In recognition of his inability to conclusively prove the existence of a disease-causing protein, Prusiner told Altman, "No prize, not even a Nobel Prize, can make something true that is not true."

Prusiner and others are only beginning to understand the most basic aspects of prions and the prion diseases. Even if they seem close to proving the existence of prions, they have not yet begun work on finding any treatments for prion-caused diseases. They hope that their research will be of use in learning about potentially related diseases such as Alzheimer's disease, multiple sclerosis, amytrophic lateral sclerosis (Lou Gehrig's disease), and Parkinson's disease.

In a conversation with Michael Waldholz for the *Wall Street Journal* (March 25, 1996), Allen D. Roses, a neurologist at Duke University, called Prusiner "a towering figure in American neurology. . . . He took a very tough position, worked at it and solved it, often in the face of hostile attacks. The guy's brilliant, and he's courageous." In his autobiographical sketch for the Nobel Web site, Prusiner wrote, "The most rewarding aspect of my work has been the numerous wonderful friends that I have made during an extensive series of collaborative studies."

Stanley Prusiner is a professor of virology at the University of California at Berkeley, where he directs the Institute for Neurodegenerative Diseases. He is also a professor of biochemistry and neurology at UCSF. His publications include more than 250 articles in professional journals and eight books that he edited or co-edited, among them *Prions: Novel Infectious Pathogens Causing Scrapie and Creutzfeldt-Jakob Disease* (1987) and *Prion Biology and Diseases* (1999). He and his wife, the former Sandra Lee Turk, were married in 1970. The couple have two daughters, Helen and Leah.

ABOUT: Mendelsohn, Everett and Brian S. Baigrie, eds. Life Sciences in the Twentieth Century, 2001; Discover April 1983, December 1986, April 1991; New York Times October 4, 1994, October 7, 1997; New Yorker December 1, 1997; Nobel e-Museum Web site; Science December 20, 1996, October 10, 1997; Scientific American January 1995, January 1998; University of California, San Francisco Web site; Wall Street Journal March 25, 1996.

© The Nobel Foundation

Saramago, José

(sah-rah-MAH-goh, zhoh-SAY)

(November 16, 1922–) Nobel Prize for Literature, 1998

The writer José Saramago was born in the village of Azinhaga, in the central, Ribatejo section of Portugal, on November 16, 1922 to José de Sousa and Maria de Piedade, poor, landless peasants. "Saramago," the name of a wild plant whose leaves were eaten by the poor in those times, was the villagers' nickname for his father's family; when the writer was born, the village registrar put "Saramago," perhaps by mistake, after the boy's first name—where it remained. Saramago's older brother Francisco died of bronchopneumonia when José was two. (Saramago has called Francisco a "co-author" of his novel *Todos os nomes*, as the strange but true story of Francisco's never having been officially registered as dead was an inspiration for the plot and many of the ideas explored in the book.) Saramago's father had served in World War I as an artillery soldier in France. He left farm work and moved his family to Lisbon in 1924, finding work in the capital as a policeman. When Saramago was 14, the family moved into their own house for the first time. Saramago did well in school, but his parents could not afford to send him for very long, and so he had to learn a trade. He studied mechanics at a technical school for five years and subsequently worked for two years as a mechanic in a car-repair shop in Lisbon. The school had also offered a literature course, and Saramago has said that to this day he can remember poetry he read in the Portuguese anthology from which the course was taught. The course opened the door for him into the world of literature. He began going to a public library in Lisbon in the evenings after work, and there his taste for reading matured.

Saramago worked in the Social Welfare Service in Lisbon as an administrative civil servant. He published his first book, a novel, in 1947. He had titled it "The Widow," a name that was changed to *The Land of Sin*. He wrote a second novel, "The Skylight," which remains unpublished, then began a third; feeling that he had nothing important to say, however, he abandoned the project and, without regrets, disappeared from the Portuguese literary scene for almost 20 years. Saramago has stated that his long period of silence was not caused by the repressive regime of António de Oliveira Salazar in Portugal, as some have suggested; rather, he has insisted that it was simply a matter of having had nothing of interest to write.

Saramago reappeared with the publication of *Os poemas possiveis* (Possible Poems) in 1966. In the late 1950s, meanwhile, he had found work as the production manager of the Lisbon publishing company Estúdios Cor. Through that job, he made friends with some of the more important Portuguese writers of the time. To earn extra money Saramago began translating the work of Jean Cassou, Maupassant, Baudelaire, and, from the French, Tolstoy, among others; he enjoyed translating and continued the work into the 1980s. He also worked as a literary critic during 1967 and 1968. Saramago left Estúdios Cor in 1971 and spent the next two years at the newspaper *Diário de Lisboa*, where he served as an editor and the manager of a cultural supplement. In 1974 he published a collection of essays, editorials, and articles he had written for the *Diário de Lisboa*, under the title *Os opiniões que o D.L. teve* (The Opinions the DL Had). The collection captures the political and social state of Portugal at the end of Salazar's dictatorship. The following year Saramago became the deputy director of the morning paper *Diário de Notícias*. In 1975, in the aftermath of an anti-Communist coup, which set back the revolution that had helped topple the Sala-

SARAMAGO

zar dictatorship in 1974, Saramago, a member of the Portuguese Communist Party since 1969, was fired from his post. Again he collected his newspaper writings, this time from *Diário de Notícias*, and published them under the title *Os apontamentos* (Notes). *Deste mundo e do outro* (1971, From This World and the Other) and *A bagagem do viajante* (1973, The Traveller's Baggage) are additional collections of Saramago's newspaper articles. Critics consider these books important for understanding the writer's later work. In 1970 another book of Saramago's poems, *Provavelmente Alegria* (Probably Joy), was published, and in 1975 he published the long poem *O ano de 1993* (The Year of 1993).

For various reasons, Saramago found himself unemployed in the mid-1970s. Regarding his thoughts at that time in his life, Saramago wrote, in a short autobiography for the Nobel e-Museum Web site, "I decided to devote myself to literature: it was about time to find out what I was worth as a writer." In 1976 he went to the country village of Lavre for a few weeks to write and study, and he has credited that time of quiet observation with leading to his 1980 novel *Levantado do Chao* (Risen from the Ground, sometimes translated as Raised from the Ground)—which won the City of Lisbon Prize—and with helping to develop the narrative style he would employ in his future novels. *Levantado do Chao* is the saga of three generations of a poor Portuguese farming family; it was inspired by memories of Saramago's own parents and grandparents. Also during this period, in addition to *Manual de pintura e caligrafia* (translated as *Manual of Painting and Calligraphy* in 1994), a novel that focuses on the idea of the development of an artist, and *Objecto quase* (Quasi Object), a 1978 collection of short stories, Saramago wrote the 1979 play *A noite* (The Night). Other plays in Saramago's oeuvre are *Que farei com este livro?* (What Shall I Do with This Book?), *A segunda vida de Francisco de Assis*, (The Second Life of Francis of Assisi, and *In nomine dei*, which was inspired by the history of a 16th-century religious war in Munster, Germany, and from which Saramago would create the opera libretto *Divara* (1993).

For Saramago the 1980s were devoted mainly to the writing of novels. *Baltasar and Blimunda* (1982) proved to be Saramago's first big success, bringing the writer, than 60

years old, international acclaim. The story intertwines an account of the building of the convent of Mafra, outside Lisbon, and an anachronistic fantasy involving the two eponymous lovers as they try to flee the Inquisition in a flying machine. In the book, Saramago juxtaposed the privilege and power of the royal court and the hard lives of the laborers and other common people. Irving Howe, as quoted by Alan Riding in the *New York Times* (October 9, 1998), wrote in a review of *Baltasar and Blimunda* for the *New York Times Book Review*, "Mr. Saramago is constantly present as a voice of European skepticism, a connoisseur of ironies. I think I hear in his prose echoes of Enlightenment sensibility, caustic and shrewd." A press release on the official Nobel e-Museum Web site (October 8, 1998) stated, "[*Baltasar and Blimunda*] is a rich, multifaceted and polysemous text that at the same time has a historical, a social and an individual perspective. The insight and wealth of imagination to which it gives expression is characteristic of Saramago's works as a whole." Saramago adapted the novel for the libretto of the opera *Blimunda*, with music by the Italian composer Azio Corghi (who collaborated with Saramago on the opera *Divara* as well). *Blimunda* was first performed at Milan's La Scala in 1990.

Saramago followed with *O ano da morte de Ricardo Reis* (*The Year of the Death of Ricardo Reis*, 1984), which takes the form of a dialogue between the great Portuguese poet Fernando Pessoa, who died in 1935, and Pessoa's fictional alter ego, Ricardo Reis. The impossible meeting between the two leads to the discussion of profound questions. Riding quoted Herbert Mitgang as writing in the *New York Times* that the book is "a rare, old-fashioned novel—at once lyrical, symbolic and meditative." The fantastic event at the heart of *Jangada de pedra* (1986), translated as *The Stone Raft* in 1994—the Iberian peninsula's breaking off from the rest of the European landmass—allows Saramago to explore notions of Portugal's sometimes tense relationship with the rest of Europe and its place in the world. *História de cerco de Lisboa* (1989), translated as *The History of the Siege of Lisbon* in 1996, tells the story of proofreader Raimundo Silva, who, while proofing the scholarly text of a history of the siege of Lisbon in 1147, mischievously replaces one use of the word "yes" in the text with the word "not."

This act of tampering has ramifications that include Raimundo's finding love. In a commentary on the book for the Webster University Web site, Bob Corbett wrote, "Perhaps the central puzzle that gets raised in the novel is the question of how much historical truth can we have to begin with?" Saramago told Katherine Vaz for an article that appeared for the *Bomb* magazine Web site, "In fiction, the narrative is obviously about individuals, but to do that effectively, to convey the personal situation of one, two, or three people, the author must understand that everything is set in the context of history. We are 'subjected,' the subjects of history. One can't forget what is behind us and what exists now in a world that is fragmented, chaotic, corrupted, and always moving toward the unknown."

The Portuguese government at first vetoed the nomination of Saramago's 1991 novel *Evangelho segundo Jesus Cristo*, translated as *The Gospel According to Jesus Christ* in 1994, for the European Union's Ariosto Literary Prize, on the grounds that the book was offensive to Catholics. In the book Saramago retold many of the Gospel stories from an ironic point of view, imagined new prophesies, depicted God as something of a villain, and had Jesus enter into sexual relations with Mary Magdalene. As quoted in *Contemporary Authors*, John Butt described the book in the *Times Literary Supplement* as "an idiosyncratic, satirical, bitter and frequently comical account of Jesus' life." Some were offended by the book, including representatives of the Vatican, who issued statements of protest. Because of the Portuguese government's opposition to the book, which it later retracted, Saramago decided to leave Portugal with his wife, Pilar del Rio, moving to Lanzarote in the Canary Islands. Since 1993 Saramago has kept a dairy, and over the years he has published several volumes of it under the title *Cadernos de Lanzarote* (*Diaries of Lanzarote*).

In the 1995 novel *Ensaio sobre a cegueira*, translated in 1995 as *Blindness*, Saramago used the affliction of the title—which in the book sweeps an entire city—as an allegory for the horrors of human society in the 20th century. In an article that appears on the CNN Web site, Saramago is quoted as saying, "This blindness isn't a real blindness, it's a blindness of rationality. We're rational beings but we don't behave rationally."

The 1997 novel *Todos os nomes*, published as *All the Names* in 1999, tells the story of a civil-service clerk who goes on an obsessive hunt for a mysterious woman after coming across her birth certificate. The story explores themes of identity, loneliness, and human relationships. While some readers and reviewers found *All the Names* to be a compelling fable on a par with Saramago's previous books, others found it to be one of the writer's minor works.

In October 1998 the Nobel committee announced that Saramago, whose work is often compared to that of the literary giants Gabriel García Márquez and Franz Kafka, was the winner of that year's prize for literature. In awarding the prize, the committee praised him as a writer "who with parables sustained by imagination, compassion and irony continually enables us once again to apprehend an illusory reality," as posted on the Nobel e-museum Web site.

Saramago did not rest on his laurels after winning the award. He next published *Conto da ilha descohecida* (*The Tale of the Unknown Island*, 1999), a short, simple tale of a brave man who petitions a corrupt king for a boat in which to search for an undiscovered island; his 1985 travelogue *Viagem a Portugal*, which grew out of a cross-country trip through his homeland in 1979, was translated and published in English in 2001.

Saramago's distinctive prose style is characterized by long, unpunctuated passages, in which the narrative and the characters' dialogue, set down without quotation marks, are intermingled. Regarding his approach to writing a novel, Saramago said to Katherine Vaz, "Sometimes I say that writing a novel is the same as constructing a chair: a person must be able to sit in it, to be balanced on it. If I can produce a great chair, even better. But above all I have to make sure that it has four stable feet."

In addition to the Nobel Prize, Saramago has won three prestigious literary awards from Italy: the Grinzane Cavour Prize, the Mondello Prize, and the Flaiano. In 1995 he also won the Luís de Camoes Prize, named for the great 16th-century Portuguese poet. Saramago was awarded honorary degrees from the University of Turin, Italy, and the University of Sevilla, Spain, in 1991. Saramago married Ilda Reis, his first wife, in 1944. Their only child, Violante, was born in 1947; the couple divorced in 1970. After the divorce Saramago began a relationship with the Portuguese writer Isabel da Nóbrega, which lasted until 1986. He then met the Spanish journalist Pilar del Rio, whom he married in 1988.

The tall, thin, bespectacled Saramago told Katherine Vaz, "Writing is my job. It's the work I do, what I build. I don't believe in inspiration. I don't even know what that is. What I know is that I have to decide to sit down at my desk, and inspiration isn't going to push me there. The first condition for writing is sitting—then writing."

SELECTED WORKS: poetry collections—Os poemas possiveis, 1966; nonfiction—Os opiniões que o D.L. teve, 1974; short-story collections—Objecto quase, 1978; novels—Manual de pintura e caligrafia, 1976; Baltasar and Blimunda, 1982; O ano da morte de Ricardo Reis, 1984; Ensaio sobre a cegueira, 1995; Todos os Nomes, 1999

SELECTED WORKS IN ENGLISH TRANSLATION: Baltasar and Blimunda, 1988; Blindness, 1997; The Gospel According to Jesus Christ, 1994; The Stone Raft, 1995.

ABOUT: Bomb magazine Web site; Grand Street Winter 1999; Literature Awards Web site; New York Times October 9, 1998; Nobel e-Museum Web site; Paris Review Winter 1998; World Press Review January 1999.

Courtesy Stanford University School of Business

Scholes, Myron S.

(July 1, 1941–) Nobel Prize for Economics, 1997 (shared with Robert C. Merton)

The economist Myron S. Scholes was born on July 1, 1941 in the northern Ontario mining town of Timmins, in Canada. His father was a dentist and his mother co-founded and ran a chain of small department stores until the birth of her sons, David and Myron. When Scholes was 10, the family moved to Hamilton, Ontario. Scholes's mother died of cancer when he was 16, and Scholes himself soon developed scar tissue on his corneas that greatly impaired his eyesight. "I learned to think abstractly and to conceptualize the solution to problems," he recalled in an autobiographical essay posted on the Nobel e-Museum Web site. "Out of necessity, I became a good listener—a quality appreciated by subsequent associates and students." (When he was 26, Scholes underwent a cornea transplant that improved his vision.)

Scholes became interested in business and finance at a young age, serving as treasurer for clubs, investing in the stock market through accounts set up by his parents, and working with his businessmen uncles. He attended McMaster University, in Hamilton, majoring in economics. He earned his undergraduate degree in 1962, and then enrolled in graduate school at the University of Chicago. There, as he recalled in his essay, he fell in love with economic research. "I absorbed how my professors created and addressed their own research. This was empowering. They enjoyed the process." Scholes decided to enter the Ph.D. program in economics, putting aside his original plan to earn a master's degree and then go into business. In particular, Scholes became interested in the emerging field of financial economics.

After earning his Ph.D., in 1969, Scholes became an assistant professor at the Massachusetts Institute of Technology (MIT) Sloan School of Management. The economist ROBERT MERTON also joined the Sloan School and collaborated frequently with

Scholes. Through Scholes's work as a consultant for the Wells Fargo Bank, he met Fischer Black, a mathematician who worked for the consulting firm of Arthur D. Little. Scholes, Merton, and Black were all interested in creating pricing models for derivatives.

Derivatives are not stocks, but financial instruments that derive value from their connections to stocks. They are, essentially, bets on the future performance of a stock. A stock option is a kind of derivative, a contract that gives the owner the right to buy or sell a stock at a specified price in the future. It has always been difficult to assess the value of derivatives. In 1900 the French mathematician Louis Bachelier devised a method of setting a price on derivatives; the formula he came up with, however, proved flawed and incomplete. In consultation with Merton, Scholes and Black set out to find a formula to valuate derivatives and thus make them less risky and unattractive to investors.

By 1970 Scholes and Black had devised a mathematical formula that takes into account factors that affect an option's value, including the price of the option, its time to expiration, the value of the stock, the stock's volatility, and interest rates. Their formula, which became known as the Black-Scholes formula, was further developed by Robert Merton. In particular, Merton contributed ideas about how options should be priced under conditions of continuous trading. Such ideas extended the insights of the Black-Scholes formula to other types of transactions, enabling a broad range of potential uses.

Black and Scholes had difficulty attracting interest in the formula, mainly because corporate finance was then a small field within economics. In 1973 their formula was finally published in the *Journal of Political Economy*. (Merton published his findings independently in a 1973 issue of the *Bell Journal of Economics and Management Sciences*.) It did not take long before financiers were utilizing the formula; by the end of the year, Texas Instruments had come out with a calculator that could perform the Black-Scholes calculation. Today, the formula is used by options traders, investment bankers, financial mangers, and others trying to deal with complicated investment decisions.

The formula is widely credited with enabling the rapid growth of the derivatives market of the 1990s. Writing for *Time.com* (October 14, 1997), Frank Pellegrini praised Merton and Scholes for "crafting a reliable pricing method and standardizing, as it were, the currency of the game." He noted that derivatives—a $14-trillion market in 1997—can still be a very risky investment. "If you own a volatile stock, purchasing options on it can provide you with a hedge against a downturn or reserve you a great seat for an upturn. . . . Buying options without the stock to back it up, however, is speculative gambling, pure and simple, and the derivatives thruway is littered with some very fat corpses."

Most in the financial world continue to praise the work of Scholes, Black, and Merton. William Brodsky, chairman of the Chicago Board Options Exchange, told Peter Passell for the *New York Times* (October 15, 1997) that "This Nobel not only recognizes Merton and Scholes's accomplishments, it underscores the importance of options in the world of finance."

Fischer Black died in 1995 from lung cancer, but the Nobel committee cited his vital contributions when awarding the 1997 Nobel Prize in Economics to Myron Scholes and Robert Merton. According to the Nobel Committee, the work of Scholes, Merton, and Black "has paved the way for economic valuations in many areas. It has also generated new types of financial instruments and facilitated more efficient risk management in society," as quoted on the Nobel e-Museum Web site. Scholes has said that he plans to give part of his prize money to fund the MIT chair that was established to honor Black.

After serving as a visiting professor at the University of Chicago during the 1973–74 academic year, Scholes accepted a position at Chicago's Graduate School of Business. (Fischer Black had already moved there in 1972). Scholes then served on the faculty of Stanford University's Graduate School of Business, in Stanford, California, from 1983 to 1996. During this time he was also a professor of law at Stanford's Law School and a senior research fellow at the Hoover Institution. He is now a professor emeritus at Stanford. In 1994 Scholes and Merton co-founded the Long-Term Capital Management (LTCM) company of Greenwich, Connecticut. The firm utilizes the Black-Scholes formula to make investment decisions; by the end of 1997, the firm had generated more than $1 billion in revenues. Then, in 1998, a global economic downturn nearly bankrupted LTCM, causing many to question the efficacy of their risk-management strategies. The Federal Reserve organized a bailout of the company, but many in the financial world have since called for greater regulations of the derivatives market.

Scholes has two grown daughters, Sara and Anne, and resides in Greenwich, Connecticut.

ABOUT: Maclean's October 27, 1997; New York Times October 15, 1997, October 27, 1997; Nobel e-Museum Web site; Online News Hour October 14, 1997; Stanford University Web site; Time.com October 14, 1997.

Kris Snibbe

Sen, Amartya Kumar

(November 3, 1933–) Nobel Prize for Economics, 1998

The economist Amartya Kumar Sen was born on November 3, 1933 in Santiniketan, north of Calcutta, India, on the campus of Visva-Bharati College, where his maternal grandmother had taught Sanskrit and ancient and medieval Indian culture and where his mother had attended school. In an autobiographical profile posted on the Nobel e-Museum Web site, Sen wrote that he "was born in a University campus and seemed to have lived all my life in one campus or another." His father, Ashutosh Sen, taught chemistry at Dhaka University, in Dhaka, which was then part of India and is now the capital of Bangladesh. Sen grew up in Dhaka and spent three years, from ages three to six, living in Mandalay, Burma, where his father was a visiting professor. He attended St. Gregory's School, in Dhaka, then enrolled at Visva-Bharati, which had been founded by the Indian playwright, poet, and 1913 Nobel laureate in literature, RABINDRANATH TAGORE. (Tagore was a family friend of the Sens; Sen's mother, Amita, appeared as a dancer in many of his dramas, and Tagore suggested the name "Amartya," which in the Bengali language means "immortal.") "The emphasis [at Tagore's school] was on fostering curiosity rather than competitive excellence," Sen recalled in his essay. "The curriculum there did not neglect India's cultural, analytical and scientific heritage, but was very involved also with the rest of the world. . . . I loved that breadth, and also the fact that in interpreting Indian civilization itself, its cultural diversity was much emphasized. . . . Tagore and his school constantly resisted the narrowly communal identities of Hindus or Muslims or others." While studying at Visva-Bharati, Sen helped to run evening schools for illiterate children from neighboring villages.

In 1951 Sen moved to Calcutta to study at Presidency College, earning a B.A. in economics in 1953. He then moved to Cambridge, England, to study at Cambridge's Trinity College. In two years he completed another, accelerated bachelor's degree, this time in pure economics, and then embarked on a Ph.D. program in economics. After writing up the results of his first year of research, on social choices involving technology, he took a leave of absence and returned to Calcutta, where he served as chair of the economics department at Jadavpur University, from 1956 to 1958. (He was then in his early twenties.) On the strength of his doctoral research, he won a fellowship from Trinity College to study anything he liked for four years. He chose the field of philosophy, studying logic, ethics, and epistemology, among other topics. Meanwhile, he was awarded both his M.A. and Ph.D. degrees from Cambridge in 1959.

In an interview with David Barsamian for *The Progressive* (August 2001), Sen recalled a incident during his childhood that made a great impression upon him, and shaped the course of his career. When Sen was 10 years old, playing alone in his family's garden, a Muslim man arrived at the garden gate, bleeding profusely from a knife wound. The man had entered Sen's Hindu neighborhood to take a job that he had been offered, in spite of the fact that it was a time when, as Sen put it, "in Hindu areas Muslims were getting butchered and in Muslim areas Hindus were getting butchered." The Muslim man, who eventually bled to death, confessed to Sen that his wife had warned him not to go, but that he had no choice. "Because of the lack of freedom in his life, he had to take every opportunity that came his way, even at great personal risk, if he was to be a good father and feed his children. He took the risk and lost his life," Sen told Barsamian. "That made me realize that lack of economic freedom could be a very major reason for loss of liberty, in this case, liberty of life. The fact that different kinds of freedom interrelate has become a central notion for me."

In 1963 Sen left Cambridge to become a professor of economics at the Delhi School of Economics and the University of Delhi. There, he researched social choice theory—a mathematically oriented field of economics that analyzes individual values and collective choices; Sen brought issues of fairness and justice into this technical field. His research built on the work of the 1972 Nobel laureate in economics, KENNETH ARROW, who unearthed fundamental problems in majority-rule elections. Arrow demonstrated that, because voters may vote strategically, rather than simply voting for their preferred choice, elections and other collective-choice situations may produce results that are not desired by any one majority. He further showed that—in some situations—for each candidate in an election, it is possible to find another candidate whom the majority prefers. Arrow's "impossibility theorem" concluded that there were no existing tools to satisfactorily aggregate individual preferences (such as values or votes) into a collective decision. In his influential work, *Collective Choice and Social Welfare* (1970), Sen applied social choice theory to real-world examples, proposing ways to analyze social choice that do not run into the problems that

Arrow had highlighted. In defending individual rights, Sen argued that, just as no one person should be able to impose his or her choices on the group, the group decision-making process should be able to respect the individual preferences of at least some individuals in at least some respects. Sen further pointed out the inherent problems of analyzing how individuals choose among different alternatives. In an excerpt from *Prospect* (July 2000) published in the *Wilson Quarterly* (Summer 2001), the economist Meghnad Desai paraphrased one of Sen's examples. When a person chooses to buy fish rather than meat, Desai explained, he may not do so simply because he prefers fish: he may be acting on a whim, or out of sympathy with a meat boycott begun by striking meatpackers. "Sen showed that we must take into account notions of sympathy or commitment in order to understand voting behavior, paying for public goods . . . and so on," Desai explained, as quoted in the *Wilson Quarterly*. In *World Watch* (January/February 1999), Payal Sampat commented on the significance of such revelations. Traditionally, economists had assumed that individuals act solely on the basis of self-interest, which in turn fuels markets and, ultimately, healthy economies. Sen pointed out that such factors as ethical or social values also play a role in social choice. "In Japan, for instance," Sampat wrote, "duty, family, and collective interest drive individual behavior far more profoundly than self-interest does." Sampat concluded, "Sen's work pushes economists and policymakers to respond to human needs that markets usually ignore."

In 1971 Sen returned to London to become a professor of economics at the London School of Economics. In 1977 he became a professor of economics at Oxford University and a fellow of Oxford's Nuffield College. In 1980 he was made Drummond Professor of Political Economy at Oxford and a fellow of the university's All Souls' College. During these years, his research focused on the study of welfare and poverty—longstanding interests that grew out of his childhood experiences in India. Sen wondered why, during the Bengal famine of 1943, none of the families he knew had suffered. "Ninety to 95 percent of Bengalis' lives went on absolutely normally," he recalled to Barsamian, "while three million died." After studying the famine, Sen made the surprising conclusion that it was not caused by a shortage of food, but rather by the loss of wages of a small group of primarily rural workers. With World War II inflating prices, the wage earners were hit particularly hard. Sen told an interviewer for *Challenge* (January/February 2000) that "you cannot begin to understand famines in terms of aggregate phenomena such as the total food supply. You have to go into the question of how people acquire food and what I call entitlement, how they establish their ownership or entitlement over food," which is dependent on market mechanisms. Sen also discovered that "there had never been a famine in a democratic country, whether rich or poor," lending further support to his theory that famines are not natural phenomena. Indeed, at the time of the Bengal famine, India was part of the British Empire, which did little to help its hungry subjects. Because a democratic government has to concern itself with reelection, it is more likely to act to avert famine situations. Sen explored the links between economic needs and political freedom in his influential treatise, *Poverty and Famines* (1981).

Sen moved to Harvard University in 1987, becoming the Lamont University Professor of Economics and an adjunct professor at the Harvard Center for Population and Development Studies. Together with the Pakistani economist Mahbub ul Haq, Sen developed tools for measuring poverty that provided alternatives to the commonly used "poverty line"—a level of income, defined differently by different governments, below which one is classified as poor. Sen argued that more than just income should be taken into account when evaluating societies; such factors as life expectancy, educational attainment, and income inequality are also important indicators of social development. Influenced by Sen's work, the UNITED NATIONS designed a Human Development Index (HDI) that uses average income, educational attainment, and life expectancy to rank countries in its annual Human Development Report. Speaking of the revelations provided by comparing the HDIs of various societies, Sen told the *Challenge* interviewer that "there are no model countries in the world. In each region you look at, you find that there are different types of failures. The American economy is successful in some respects, indeed in many respects. And yet there are . . . many millions of people without medical insurance." He noted that African-American men, for example, have less chance of reaching advanced age than do Chinese or Sri Lankan men, despite the fact that those countries have lower average incomes than does America.

Sen was awarded the 1998 Nobel Prize in Economics for his many contributions to welfare economics. In a press release posted on the Nobel e-Museum Web site, the Royal Swedish Academy of Sciences cited his research into social choice theory, welfare distributions, and poverty. "By analyzing the available information about different individuals' welfare when collection decisions are made," the Academy wrote, "he has improved the theoretical foundation for comparing different distributions of society's welfare and defined new, more satisfactory, indexes of poverty."

Sen is an unusual figure in that he has operated both as an academic theoretician and an advocate for the poor. In a tribute to Sen for *Time* (October 26, 1998), Jeffrey Sachs wrote that "Amartya Sen . . . has helped give voice to the world's poor. . . . In a lifetime of careful scholarship, Sen has repeatedly returned to a basic theme: even impoverished societies can improve the well-being of their least advantaged members. . . . In a world in which 1.5 billion people subsist on less than $1 a day, this Nobel Prize can be not just a celebration of a wonderful scholar but also a clarion call to attend to the urgent needs and hopes of the world's poor."

Sen is now a professor emeritus of Harvard University, having returned to London in 1998 to accept a post as master of Trinity College, Cambridge. In his most recent book, *Development as Freedom* (1999), Sen attempts to synthesize competing theories of how development should be pursued in poorer countries.

Sen's first wife was Nabaneeta Dev, with whom he has two grown children, Antara and Nandana. Sen and Dev divorced in the early 1970s, and Sen married Eva Colorni. Sen and Colorni had two children, Indrani and Kabir. Colorni died of cancer in 1985.

ABOUT: Challenge January/February 2000, March/April 1999; Nobel e-Museum Web site; The Progressive August 2001; Time October 26, 1998; Wilson Quarterly Summer 2001; World Watch January/February 1999.

Jason S. Bardi/TSRL © The Scripps Research Institute

Sharpless, K. Barry

(April 28, 1941–) Nobel Prize for Chemistry, 2001 (shared with William S. Knowles and Ryoji Noyouri)

The chemist K. Barry Sharpless was born in Philadelphia, Pennsylvania, on April 28, 1941. His father was a physician, and his mother hailed from a family of Norwegian immigrants who had opened a fishery on the New Jersey Shore. Sharpless spent many weekends and holidays at the shore, and when he was a teen, he worked as a first mate on his cousin's boat. In an interview with Cath O'Driscoll for the November 2001 issue of *Chemistry in Britain*, a publication of the Royal Society of Chemistry, he recalled those days as "probably the happiest time of my life, working dawn to dusk on the fishing boats, because it's a very natural thing to exercise and your brain feels good." Sharpless even considered a career on a commercial fishing boat, but it dawned on him that the study of science could provide as much excitement as time on the open sea. "I suddenly realized that there was this whole great adventure where you could discover stuff that had never been done before," he told O'Driscoll.

Sharpless received a bachelor of arts degree in 1963 from Dartmouth College, in Hanover, New Hampshire, and in 1968 earned his doctorate in chemistry from Stan-

ford University, in Stanford, California. As an undergraduate he became fascinated with chiral molecules—molecules that exist in mirror forms, in the same way human hands are mirror images of one another. (The term chiral derives from the Greek word *cheir*, which means hand.)

If you place your right hand palm down, then place your left hand, palm down, on top of it, your thumbs will not overlap—they will be on opposite sides. The mirror-image molecules, known as enantiomers, share the same atomic weight, the same boiling and melting points, and the same infrared spectrum, yet because of their chirality (or "handedness"), the atoms in the enantiomers will never overlap. Amino acids, peptides, enzymes, and other proteins—as well as DNA and RNA—are all examples of chiral molecules; without the correct chirality, they would not act as the basic units of life.

Pharmaceutical companies have long recognized the importance of this phenomenon. Because a drug must exactly match the molecules it should bind with in the cells, it is necessary for the drug to have the correct chirality. In certain cases the mirror-image form may even be harmful. The drug thalidomide, which was marketed in the 1960s to pregnant women, is a good example of this. One of the enantiomers of thalidomide helped against nausea, while the other could cause fetal damage; mothers who used the drug sometimes gave birth to babies with deformed limbs. In another example, one enantiomer of the drug ethambutol is used to combat tuberculosis, while the other can cause blindness.

For the drug companies, finding a cheap method for producing large quantities of pure enantiomers or for separating the mixtures of enantiomers in a chiral compound was essential. Researchers sought to develop catalyst molecules that could produce only one of the two mirror-image forms of molecules. The catalysts (which were themselves chiral) were needed to speed up the chemical reactions while not being consumed themselves; the right catalyst molecule could produce millions of the necessary molecules. In 1968 Sharpless's fellow Nobel Prize winner, WILLIAM S. KNOWLES, succeeded in showing that catalytic asymmetric synthesis—or the creation of molecules with an excess amount of one enantiomer—was feasible. By using a transition metal as a catalyst, he was able to produce a hydrogenation reaction and create a synthesis of the amino acid L-DOPA, which proved to be a valuable medicine in the treatment of Parkinson's disease.

In 1970, after a year of postgraduate work at Stanford and another at Harvard University, in Cambridge, Massachusetts, Sharpless joined the chemistry department at the Massachusetts Institute of Technology (MIT) as an assistant professor. He left MIT, as a full professor, in 1977 to teach at Stanford. During Sharpless's time at Stanford he made a major breakthrough in the synthesis of chiral molecules. Since the early 1970s he had been working to develop chiral catalysts for another type of chemical reaction—asymmetric epoxidation. In 1980 he developed a practical method for the catalytic asymmetric conversion of allylic alcohols to chiral epoxides. (Epoxides are tremendously helpful "middleman" products for many types of synthesis and open up a host of other practical catalysts with commercial viability.) Using the transition metal titanium, he created a bounty of molecules with only one type of enantiomer. Sharpless's asymmetric epoxidation (AE) method is considered by many scientists to be the most significant advancement in synthesis in the past 20 years. It has proven exceptionally useful in the academic research fields of molecular biology and medicine. The method has already been applied to produce beta-blockers, which are used in various heart medicines, and has also been used in various sweetening agents and insecticides.

From approximately 1980 to 1987, Sharpless continued to perfect the asymmetric reaction to make it as catalytic as possible. In a 1995 interview with Bruce V. Bigelow for Science Watch (on-line), he noted: "This transformation, epoxidation, is so useful. It's something that organic chemists love. They take an olefin and they make an epoxide. The epoxide is then a key intermediate for making something else. If you can do this transformation, you can make wonderful things. It's central to organic chemistry." In 1987 he developed the asymmetric dihydroxylation (AD) process, which used osmium as a catalyst; in 1995 he developed a new reaction, asymmetric amniohydroxylation (AA). "What we've done so far is find three big reactions—the AE in 1980, the AD in 1987, and now the AA in 1995," Sharpless explained to Bigelow. "It's my own variation on the seven-year itch. Our pattern is to spend a few years developing applications—to kind of kick-start a new reaction by showing the world what it can do."

After leaving Stanford, in 1980, Sharpless returned to MIT, where he served as a member of the faculty until 1990. He then became a professor of chemistry at the Scripps Research Institute, in La Jolla, California, a position he currently holds.

On October 10, 2001, the Royal Swedish Academy of Sciences announced that K. Barry Sharpless, along with William S. Knowles and RYOJI NOYORI, had won the Nobel Prize in Chemistry for their development of catalytic asymmetric synthesis. Sharpless told J. Gorman for Science News (October 20, 2001) that he was glad that his 90-year-old father could see that all the science books he had bought him had paid off. "We all thought nature had a monopoly [on the development of chiral molecules]," he added. "But it turns out to be a whole lot easier than we thought."

In addition to the Nobel Prize, Sharpless has won many other awards for his contributions to chemistry, including the Allan Day Award from the Philadelphia Organic Chemists Club (1985), the Dr. Paul Janssen Prize from Belgium (1986), the Chemical Pioneer Award from the American Institute of Chemists (1988), the Scheele Medal from the Swedish Academy of Pharma Sciences (1991), the Centenary Lectureship Medal from the Royal Society of Chemistry (1993), the Cliff Hamilton Award from the University of Nebraska (1995), the King Faisal Prize for Science from Saudi Arabia (1995), the Rylander Award from the Organic Reactions Catalysis Society (2000), the Chemical Sciences Award from the National Academy of Sciences (2000), the Chiralty Medal from the Italian Chemical Society (2000), the Rhone Poulenc Medal from the Royal Society of Chemistry (2000), and the Benjamin Franklin Medal from the Franklin Institute (2001), among others.

K. Barry Sharpless married Jan Dueser on April 28, 1965; they have three children: Hannah, William, and Isaac.

ABOUT: American Men and Women of Science 1998–99; Chembytes (on-line) November 2001; Nobel e-Museum Web site; Science News October 20, 2001; Science Watch (on-line); Scripps Research Institute Web site.

© The Nobel Foundation

Shirakawa, Hideki

(1936–) Nobel Prize for Chemistry, 2000 (shared with Alan MacDiarmid and Alan Heeger)

The chemist Hideki Shirakawa was born in Tokyo, Japan, in 1936. He attended Takayama Daini Junior High School in the Gifu Prefecture, where he expressed an early interest in plastics. Just prior to his graduation, in 1952, he penned a composition in which he wrote about his hopes for the future, as quoted in the *Mainichi Daily News* (October 12, 2000, on-line): "Now plastic wrappers are available. When I wrap a hot bento box with the wrapper, it goes slack and then becomes useless because it is too susceptible to heat. I wonder how much people will be pleased if cheap plastic (products) without those defects are available." Shirakawa received his Ph.D. from the Tokyo Institute of Technology in 1966 and that year became an associate professor at the Institute of Materials Science at the University of Tsukuba, in Tsukuba City, Japan. He was promoted to full professor in 1982 and remained affiliated with the university until his retirement not long before receiving the Nobel Prize.

In the early 1970s Shirakawa began experimenting with new ways to synthesize the organic (containing carbon) polymer polyacetylene. Polymers are a type of molecule that forms long, repeating chains; most plastics are made up of polymers. During one of Shirakawa's experiments, a thousand times too much catalyst was accidentally added to the solution, and to the surprise of Shirakawa and his fellow researchers, a metallic-looking film was produced on the inside of the reaction vessel. "Intuitively, I knew the film would have valuable properties," Shirakawa told Charles Bickers for the *Far Eastern Economic Review* (November 2, 2000). Independently, Heeger and MacDiarmid, who were both then working at the University of Pennsylvania, in Philadelphia, had been conducting experiments with the inorganic (containing no carbon) polymer sulphur nitride, which also created a metallic-looking film under certain conditions. After MacDiarmid mentioned the sulfur nitride film at a conference in Tokyo, Shirakawa told him about the silvery polyacetylene film during a coffee break. Mac-Diarmid invited Shirakawa to the University of Pennsylvania, where Heeger joined them to do further research on polyacetylene. Soon, with the help of a grant from the Office of Naval Research, they had found a way to oxidize (or remove electrons from) polyacetylene using iodine gas in a process known as doping. When one of Heeger's students measured the conductivity of the oxidized polyacetylene, called trans-polyacetylene, it was discovered that the conductivity had increased by a factor of 10 million. Shirakawa, Heeger, MacDiarmid, and other members of their research team soon shared their findings in the article "Synthesis of Electrically Conducting Organic Polymers: Halogen Derivatives of Polyacetylene" published in the *Journal of Chemical Society, Chemical Communications* (Summer 1977).

Essentially, doping is a way of making plastics act more like metals, which have free-floating electrons that can readily be made to flow along a chain of molecules, producing a current of electricity. A polyacetylene molecule consists of a long chain of carbon molecules bound by immobile "sigma" bonds. Each carbon atom is also bound to a hydrogen atom by more flexible "pi" bonds. In order to allow electricity to flow along the polyacetylene chain, electrons either have to be taken away from (through oxidation) or added to (through reduction) the pi bonds, which effectively destabilizes the bonds and permits electron flow.

Various other types of conductive plastics were soon discovered, each with different potential uses. Polymers, as other scientists later discovered, can also be used as semi-conductors, materials that conduct electricity better than insulators, but not as well as conductors. One of the principle interests in both conductive and semiconductive polymers is in using them as a low-cost alternative to transistors and integrated circuits, which are often made of silicon and other similar materials. In theory, polymers could be inexpensively processed into integrated circuits by way of a technology similar to that used in ink-jet printing. Although plastic integrated circuits are not as durable as silicon ones and thus may never replace them in computer chips, for example, these plastic circuits may give rise to a new generation of inexpensive electronic devices. One application already developed for conductive polymers, specifically polythioprene derivatives, as an anti-static treatment for photographic film, which can be ruined by static charges. Polythioprene derivatives may also soon be used to mark supermarket products in such a way that people will be able to check out groceries without removing them from their carts. Doped polyaniline is used to reduce static in carpeting and as a coating to reduce electromagnetic radiation from computer screens. Conductive polymers are currently used to make light-weight, rechargeable batteries. Another useful property of some semiconductive polymers is electroluminescence, which means that they can be stimulated to emit light. Related applications under development include energy-saving light bulbs, thin and flexible TV and computer screens, and mobile phone displays that light up while using little energy.

After his initial discovery in the 1970s, Shirakawa continued to work indefatigably with conductive polymers, despite the fact that the response to his findings within the scientific community was not immediately overwhelming. As Katsumi Yoshino, a colleague of Shirakawa's, said of him to a reporter for *Japan Today* (on-line), "Unlike other researchers, he has been focusing on poly-acetylene nonstop, never losing his concentration. Scientists often jump at the popular or attractive fields. His insights and intuition, which are important for a scientist, are outstanding." Upon receiving the Nobel Prize, Shirakawa took the opportunity to express some controversial misgivings about the state of science in Japan, particularly his annoyance with what he sees as a pervasive conservativeness and lack of creativity. "There's a saying in Japan which goes something like: The fence pole that stands above the rest will get hammered back into place. If you stand out, you will be pushed down," he told Bickers. "The difference in succeeding from one country to the next," he added, "is the quality of facilities and how much money you have—but also how much you encourage freedom and creativity."

Now in his retirement, Shirakawa lives in suburban Yokohama, Japan.

ABOUT: Far Eastern Economic Review November 2, 2000; Japan Today (on-line); Mainichi Daily News (on-line) October 12, 2000; New Scientist October 21, 2000; Nobel e-Museum Web site; Science October 20, 2000; Science News October 14, 2000.

Skou, Jens C.

(October 8, 1918–) Nobel Prize for Chemistry, 1997 (shared with John E. Walker and Paul D. Boyer)

The medical researcher Jens Christian Skou was born on October 8, 1918 in Lemvig, Denmark, the eldest of four children born to Magnus Martinus Skou and Ane Margrethe Skou. Skou's father was a wealthy timber and coal merchant; he died from pneumonia when Skou was 12 years old. At age 15 Skou was sent to a boarding high school; he graduated in 1937. After a summer of uncertainty, he settled on a career in medicine and enrolled at the University of Copenhagen.

While Skou was in medical school, World War II broke out and Germany occupied Denmark. In an autobiographical essay posted on the Nobel e-Museum Web site, Skou recalled the difficult years of German occupation. "In May and June 1944, we managed to get our exams," he wrote. "A number of our teachers had gone underground, but their job was taken over by others. We could not assemble to sign the Hippocratic oath, but had to come one by one at a place away from the University not known by others."

Jens C. Skou

After earning his M.D., in 1944, Skou performed clinical training at a hospital in Hjøorring, in northern Denmark. There, Skou recalled in his essay, the "assistant physician . . . was very eager to teach me how to make smaller operations, like removing a diseased appendix. I soon discovered why. When we were on call together and we during the night got a patient with appendicitis, it happened—after we had started the operation—that he asked me to take over and left. He was then on his way to receive weapons and explosives which were dropped by English planes on a dropping field outside Hjøorring."

Skou completed his training at the Orthopedic Hospital in Aarhus, Denmark. In 1947 he accepted a position as assistant professor at the Institute of Physiology at the University of Aarhus. Meanwhile, he also worked to complete a doctoral dissertation. In 1954 he was awarded the degree of Doctor of Medical Sciences from the University of Aarthus. That same year, he became an associate professor at the university; in 1963 he became a full professor of physiology and chairman of the Institute of Phsyiology. In 1978 he became a professor of biophysics at the university.

The work for which Skou would earn the 1997 Nobel Prize in Chemistry, his discovery of the enzyme known as sodium, potassium-ATPase, began in the 1950s. As early as the 1920s, scientists had known that the ion composition within living cells is different from the ion composition of the cell's surroundings. Within the cell, the sodium concentration is lower and the potassium concentration is higher. In 1953, an important discovery was made by the British scientists Richard Keynes and ALAN HODGKIN. (Hodgkin won the 1963 Nobel Prize in Physiology or Medicine for this work.) Keynes and Hodgkin demonstrated that, when a nerve is stimulated, sodium ions pour into the nerve cell. The cell's original sodium level is restored when sodium is transported out of the nerve cell. From this discovery they inferred that this transportation process required the use of the cell "fuel" adenosine triphosphate (ATP); the process could be stopped by inhibiting the formation of ATP.

Skou set out to find an enzyme in the nerve membrane that was associated with ion transport. In 1957 he uncovered an enzyme that uses stored energy in ATP to move ions across the cell membrane. This enzyme, he showed, works in conjunction with ATP to regulate the concentration of sodium and potassium inside a cell. Skou published an article on the subject the same year, describing an ATPase that is activated by sodium and potassium ions—an ion pump that has become known as sodium, potassium-ATPase.

Skou performed his research on the finely ground nerve membranes of crabs. He found that an enzyme in the membranes breaks down ATP when both sodium and potassium ions surround a cell. He then began a series of tests in which he systematically altered the concentration of the ions. The ATP-degrading enzyme, found in the initial preparation of the nerve membranes, was stimulated when it came into contact with increasing amounts of sodium ions. Skou next determined that if small quantities of potassium ions were added to the membranes, further stimulation occurred. He discovered that maximum stimulation of the enzyme occurred when the concentrations of sodium and potassium were at the level that normally occur in the nerve, thereby indicating that the enzyme was directly related to the transportation of sodium and potassium ions in nerve cells. In short, this meant that an enzyme in the cell membrane pumps sodium out of cells and potassium in.

The electricity created through the sodium and potassium transfer across the cell membrane allows nerve stimulation to reproduce along a nerve fiber. Without the sodium, potassium-ATPase enzyme, nerve cells could not fire and important messages could not reach the brain. It has also been established that the enzyme is crucial for cell volume maintenance; in fact, if it fails, the cell swells and the organism's life is endangered.

The sodium, potassium-ATPase enzyme is estimated to use about one third of all the ATP that the body generates. Skou was the first person to publish information on an enzyme that promoted the transport of substances through a cell membrane, a process that is essential to all living cells. Since Skou's pioneering research, there have been other discoveries of enzymes that perform similar functions. For example, scientists have discovered an enzyme known as hydrogen, potassium-ATPase, which produces hydrochloric acid in the stomach. The discovery of this enzyme aided in the treatment of ulcers.

Although research continues to uncover more information about sodium, potassium-ATPase, the detailed workings of this ion transporting enzyme remain an enigma. Scientists now understand its amino acid sequence, and they also know which regions of it are embedded inside cell membranes and which are not. It has proven very difficult to determine the enzyme's three-dimensional structure, however. Without this knowledge, Skou told Robert F. Service in *Science* (October 24, 1997), "we still do not understand fully how this machine works."

The Royal Swedish Academy of sciences awarded Skou one half of the 1997 Nobel Prize in Chemistry for his discovery of the first ion-transporting enzyme; the other half was shared between the biochemists PAUL D. BOYER and JOHN E. WALKER for what the Academy called "their elucidation of the enzymatic mechanism underlying the synthesis of adenosine triphosphate," as posted on the Nobel e-Museum Web site. In the *Washington Post* (October 16, 1997), the biochemistry expert Kathleen J. Sweadner told Curt Suplee that Skou's insight "was really crucial, and not just for this one enzyme but for understanding a great deal about the physiology of the cell. It opened [researchers'] minds to studying a whole bunch of other processes."

Jens Skou married Ellen Margrethe Nielson in 1948; the couple has two daughters. Skou retired from active research and teaching at the University of Aarhus in 1988; he then taught himself how to program computers in order to create electronic models of ion pumps. He is a member of the Danish Royal Society, a foreign associate of the American National Academy of Sciences, and an honorary member of both the Japanese Biochemical Society and the American Physiological Society. In addition to the Nobel Prize, he has been awarded the Leo Prize (1959), the Novo Prize (1964), the Consul Carlsen Prize (1973), and the Anders Retzius' Gold Medal from the Swedish Medical Association (1977).

ABOUT: InSCIght (on-line) October 16, 1997; Nobel e-Museum Web site; Science October 24, 1997; Science News October 25, 1997; Washington Post October 16, 1997.

Courtesy of Stanford Graduate School of Business

Spence, A. Michael

(1943–) Nobel Prize for Economics, 2001 (shared with George A. Akerlof and Joseph E. Stiglitz)

The economist Andrew Michael Spence was born in 1943 in Montclair, New Jersey, and grew up in Canada. His father, who was

Canadian, had a Ph.D. in commerce and finance and worked as a teacher and businessman. The younger Spence enrolled at Princeton University, in Princeton, New Jersey, graduating in 1966 with a B.A. in philosophy and the Honors Thesis Prize in that subject. In an interview with Karen W. Arenson for the *New York Times* (April 1, 1984), Spence explained that although he believed that philosophy "was very useful intellectual training," he didn't want to pursue the subject further. "Some academics sit down with paper and pencil and just think," he said. "I wanted a field in which there was more diversity." After his graduation, Spence was named a Danforth Fellow and earned a Rhodes Scholarship to study at Oxford University, receiving a combined B.A./M.A. degree in mathematics in 1968. After returning to the U.S., Spence began his doctoral studies in economics at Harvard University, in Cambridge, Massachusetts. Spence told *Noble Prize Winners* that he became interested in economics because of "its theoretical rigor and its applicability to day to day things." His doctoral dissertation, which earned Harvard's David A. Wells Prize, explored the phenomenon of market signaling. The study broke new ground in the discipline, and would eventually earn him the Nobel Prize. Spence received his Ph.D. in 1972.

In 1971 he became an assistant professor of political economy at Harvard's John F. Kennedy School of Government. Two years later, he joined the faculty of Stanford University, in California, as an associate professor of economics. In 1975 he became an honorary research fellow in Harvard's economics department. After completing his fellowship, in 1977, he began teaching as a professor in Harvard's economics department and in the Graduate School of Business Administration. The next year, he was honored with Harvard's John Kenneth Galbraith Prize for excellence in teaching.

Throughout the 1980s Spence gradually assumed more responsibilities and leadership roles at Harvard. In 1981 he served as the chairman of the university's business economics Ph.D. program. Two years later he became the George Gund Professor of Economics and Business Administration as well the chairman of the economics department. In 1984 Spence was appointed the dean of Harvard University's Faculty of Arts and Sciences. "The deanship here came as

a complete surprise," he told Arenson. "But when I was offered the job, I thought it might be a once-in-a-lifetime chance, and there wasn't a realistic chance of saying no." In this position Spence became Harvard's second-highest executive, responsible for overseeing a $225-million budget, the campus museums and libraries, and 2,000 employees. In 1986 Spence helped change how Harvard hired professors. At the time the university recruited most of its faculty from other institutions. However, by the mid-1980s, increased competition from other Ivy League schools and the high housing costs in the Boston area made Harvard less attractive to scholars whose careers were already established. To avoid recruiting problems Spence called for greater flexibility in hiring decisions and for the increased promotion of members of the junior faculty.

In 1990 Spence left Harvard to serve as the Philip H. Knight Professor and the dean of Stanford University's Graduate School of Business. He stepped down as dean in 1999 to resume his scholarly research and pursue business projects as a partner with the firms Oak Hill Capital Partners and Oak Hill Venture Partners, both in California.

Spence's theory of market signaling built upon the work of GEORGE A. AKERLOF, who introduced the concept of information asymmetry in a 1970 article, *The Market for 'Lemons': Quality Uncertainty and the Market Mechanism*. Akerlof discussed the market for used cars, where the prospective buyer has less information than the seller about the quality of the vehicle. The buyer, fearful that the car will turn out to be a "lemon," will offer a low price—even if he or she would be willing to pay a higher price for a car that was in good condition. As a result those with high-quality cars opt to leave the market, keeping their vehicles rather than selling them at low prices. Only low-quality cars will come up for sale in such a market, a situation Akerlof termed adverse selection. In this situation, the free market has failed to allocate resources effectively: owners retain cars they should have been able to sell, and buyers are left with a market of lemons. Spence told Dan Ackman for *Forbes* (October 26, 2001, on-line) that this kind of information asymmetry is characteristic of many markets, particularly for "any complex product—consumer durables, financial products, job markets."

Spence's insight was to describe how market agents can overcome the information inequality. "There is a clear incentive for sellers of high-quality products to distinguish themselves, to signal the fact," he explained to Ackman. "So that's what led me to try to find out what could work as a signal." A common kind of signal is a warranty, offered, for example, by used-car dealers to assure customers of their cars' value. A warranty thus constitutes a "signal" to the less-informed party about the value of the goods being exchanged.

Spence coined the term "market signaling" in his article, "Job Market Signaling," published in the *Quarterly Journal of Economics* (August 1973), and later in his book, *Market Signaling: Informational Transfer in Hiring and Related Processes* (1974). "Market signals are activities or attributes of individuals in a market which, by design or accident, alter the beliefs of, or convey information to, other individuals in the market," he explained in the book. He provided the example of the job market, in which neither the employer nor the potential employee has any certainty about what the other party is offering. Spence argued that employers view educational achievement and professional recommendations as a sort of informal warranty against hiring unqualified or underperforming employees. If an employer had no means of judging an applicant's level of productivity, the market might devolve into a situation similar to Akerlof's "lemon market," in which only low-productivity workers are hired for low wages. This situation can be averted, according to Spence, because applicants can choose to signal their level of productivity to the employer by revealing a higher level of education or important job skills. One of Spence's more important insights was that education works as a signal because it is costly—in terms of effort, expenses, and time—and thus signals to employers the applicant's degree of productivity. Spence also examined how the relationship of education and productivity is construed differently among different races or genders.

Although Spence's work focused on the job market, the Nobel Prize Committee noted that his signaling theory has many applications. It helps explain, for example, how aggressive price cuts and costly advertising—moves that may convey little information about a product—can function as signals of a company's financial strength. A company that finances its operations through debt rather than issuing new shares signals the management's confidence in profitability. Signaling also seems to explain why some firms choose to pay dividends to their shareholders, even though dividends are subject to higher taxes than are capital gains. For firms with "insider information," paying dividends signals an outlook of strong profitability.

Spence was vacationing on the Hawaiian island of Maui when he was contacted about the Nobel Prize. "It's wonderful," Spence said of the award, as quoted in *Business Wire* (October 10, 2001, on-line). "It's an incredible honor to be recognized for something that people perceive as moving the ball down the field in one's academic discipline."

In addition to the Nobel Prize, Spence has received the 1981 John Bates Clark Medal, awarded biennially by the American Economic Association to an economist under the age of 40. Spence is a member of the American Economic Association. He served as chairman of the National Research Council Board on Science, Technology, and Economic Policy from 1991 to 1997, and is the author of numerous academic papers and the books *Signaling and Screening* (1976), *Competition in the Investment Banking Industry* (1983) with Samuel L. Hayes and David Van Praag Marks, and *International Competitiveness*, a collection of articles co-edited with Heather A. Hazard. His current work focuses on how information technology, particularly the Internet, affects markets and economies.

Spence and his wife, Monica, divide their time between a home on the Stanford University campus and a condominium in Maui.

ABOUT: Forbes (on-line) October 16, 2001; New York Times April 1, 1984, October 11, 2001; Nobel e-Museum Web site; Quarterly Journal of Economics August 1973; Stanford University Business School Web site.

Courtesy of Columbia University

Stiglitz, Joseph E.

(February 9, 1943–) Nobel Prize for Economics, 2001 (shared with George Akerlof and A. Michael Spence)

The economist Joseph Eugene Stiglitz was born on February 9, 1943 in Gary, Indiana, an industrial town near Lake Michigan. Stiglitz's father was an insurance agent, and his mother began teaching in public school at age 50. In an interview with Louis Uchitelle for the *New York Times* (May 31, 1998), Stiglitz described his parents as "liberal Democrats" who were "not revolutionary, but very dedicated." For the *Taipei Times* (December 11, 2000, on-line), Stiglitz wrote that while growing up in Gary, he "saw poverty, unemployment and discrimination. I entered economics because I wanted to understand and do something about these phenomena."

An excellent student, especially in mathematics, Stiglitz earned a scholarship to Amherst College, in Massachusetts. In his junior year he was elected president of the student body, and he participated in Dr. MARTIN LUTHER KING's historic 1963 march for civil rights on Washington, D.C. After graduating from Amherst, in 1964, Stiglitz enrolled at the Massachusetts Institute of Technology (MIT), in Cambridge, where he received his doctorate in economics in 1967. He later studied at Cambridge University, in the United Kingdom, earning an additional degree.

After completing his education Stiglitz embarked on an academic career. In 1970 Yale University, in New Haven, Connecticut, hired him as a full professor of economics. Four years later, he left Yale to teach at Stanford University, in California. From 1976 to 1979 Stiglitz served as the Drummond Professor of Political Economy at Oxford University's All Souls College, in the United Kingdom. In 1979 he joined the faculty of Princeton University, in New Jersey. He returned to Stanford University in 1988.

Stiglitz took a leave of absence from teaching in 1993 to serve as a member of President Bill Clinton's Council of Economic Advisers; he acted as the body's chairman from 1995 to 1997. While on the council Stiglitz advocated a number of policy initiatives, including raising the capital gains tax and reforming the Superfund program, which was created by Congress in 1980 to clean up toxic waste sites. Stiglitz also opposed the administration's plans to privatize the United States Enrichment Corporation, an agency that purchased uranium from the former Soviet Union and sold it in refined form for use in nuclear reactors. The economist argued that privatization in this case would not work. "When I was at the White House, in an environment dominated by lawyers and politicians, I often felt that I had arrived in another world," Stiglitz recalled, as quoted by Uchitelle. "I had expected lower standards of evidence for assertions than would be accepted in a professional article, but I had not expected that the evidence offered would be, in so many instances, so irrelevant and that so many vacuous sentences— sentences whose meaning and import simply baffled me—would be uttered."

In 1997 he was appointed chief economist of the World Bank, an international organization founded after World War II to help rebuild Europe, whose current mission is to alleviate poverty in developing nations. Stiglitz attracted some controversy in this position. In an article for the *New Republic* (April 17, 2000), he asserted that the policies of the International Monetary Fund (IMF) and the U.S. Treasury Department led directly to the economic crisis that affected many nations in East Asia in the late 1990s. During his tenure, Stiglitz lobbied the IMF to take measures to improve the economies of East Asia, but his efforts were rebuffed.

Several press accounts have reported that Stiglitz's outspoken criticism of the IMF, whose stated mission is to promote monetary cooperation and foster world economic growth, led the Treasury Department to have him removed from the World Bank.

In 1999 Stiglitz began teaching at Columbia University's Business School. In 2000 he helped co-found the Initiative for Policy Dialogue (IPD), an international group of economists and social scientists based at Columbia that helps developing nations explore alternative economic policies.

Even as a doctoral student at MIT, Stiglitz questioned what he was being taught about economics. "We were taught the perfect-market-competition model [which supposes that the economy is in perfect equilibrium], and then we were told that only at the University of Chicago, a center of conservative economics, did they take the model seriously," he recalled to Uchitelle. "We agreed with our professors that there was something wrong, but we were not given an alternative." The simplistic models that were being taught stated, for example, that if the demand for labor equaled the supply, there would be no unemployment—a situation that Stiglitz knew to be untrue in the real world. He concluded that markets do not always work perfectly or efficiently, as the models suggested, and believed that intervention by the government or other parties was occasionally necessary to improve their performance and address such problems as poverty and unemployment. He has pointed out, for example, that without the Securities Exchange Commission to guarantee full disclosure, investors might buy corporate stock without enough knowledge to determine their proper value. Management might know about hidden deficiencies in their companies, and if such an imbalance of knowledge took place too often, the stock market could break down.

GEORGE AKERLOF, a classmate of Stiglitz's at MIT, had pioneered the study of what he termed "asymmetric information" in markets in his paper, "The Market for Lemons," published in the *Quarterly Journal of Economics* (1970). Analyzing the used-car market, Akerlof observed that the seller in a transaction always knows more about the quality of the product than the buyer. If enough "lemons" were sold, then the used-car market could collapse because many buyers would be skeptical about the quality of the product and agree to pay only a low price for it, thereby negatively affecting honest sellers who offer good-quality products. Even minor imbalances of information could thus have profound effects on the economy. The economist A. MICHAEL SPENCE expanded on this work by examining what he called "market signaling," by which the better-informed party in a transaction can signal additional information to the other. For example, if the seller of a car offers a warranty, the signal is sent to the buyer that the vehicle is reliable.

In an article for the *Quarterly Journal of Economics* (1976), Stiglitz and a fellow economist, Michael Rothschild, analyzed the problem of asymmetric information in the insurance market, arguing that insurance companies cannot distinguish between high-risk and low-risk buyers. "For example, suppose that some persons occasionally drink too much, while the others almost never drink," they wrote. "Insurance firms cannot discover who drinks and who does not. Individuals know that drinking affects accident probabilities, but it affects different people differently. Each individual does not know how it will affect him." In an attempt to ensure profitability, insurance companies could charge the same high rate for all buyers regardless of their risk status. However, this would result in many low-risk customers declining coverage, and a company with only high-risk customers would often have to pay out claims. "What is required is that individuals with different risk properties differ in some characteristic that can be linked with the purchase of insurance and that, somehow, insurance firms discover this link," Stiglitz and Rothschild wrote. Instead of setting the same price for all customers, as the "price competition model" states, Stiglitz and Rothschild developed the "price and quantity competition" market model, which theorizes that companies offer differently priced insurance contracts with varying amounts of coverage to suit the needs of all buyers and maximize profits. Stiglitz has also explored asymmetric information in credit and financial markets. He has argued, for example, that banks could reduce losses from bad loans by rationing the volume of loans instead of raising lending rates.

In awarding the 2001 Nobel Prize in Economics to Akerlof, Spence, and Stiglitz, the Nobel committee acknowledged that the trio's findings have had enormous practical implications. As quoted by Uchitelle, the committee cited Stiglitz's work as the broadest of the three and stated, "[His] many contributions have transformed the way economists think about the workings of the market. Together with the fundamental contributions by George Akerlof and Michael Spence, they make up the core of the modern economics of information."

Stiglitz has written and co-written many academic papers and several books, including *Economics of the Public Sector* (1986), *Economics* (1993), *Principles of Macroeconomics* (1993), *The Economics of Rural Organization: Theory, Practice, and Policy* (1993), *Whither Socialism?* (1994), *Financial Liberalization: How Far, How Fast?* (2001), and *Globalization and Its Discontents* (2002). In addition to the Nobel Prize, he has earned many distinguished awards

and honors, including fellowships from the National Science Foundation, the Fulbright Scholar Program, and the Guggenheim Foundation. In 1979 he won the John Clark Bates medal, which is presented every two years to an American economist under 40 who makes important scholarly contributions.

Joseph Stiglitz is married to Jane Hannaway, a fellow professor. The couple has four children.

ABOUT: Chang, Ha Joon (ed.) Joseph Stiglitz and the World Bank: The Rebel Within, 2001; American Prospect July/August 1999; Contemporary Review October 2001; International Economy March/April 1999; New Republic April 17, 2000; New York Times May 31, 1998; Nobel e-Museum Web site; Taipei Times (on-line) December 11, 2001.

Courtesy of Horst L. Störmer

Störmer, Horst L.
STERM-er

(April 6, 1949–) Nobel Prize for Physics, 1998 (shared with Robert B. Laughlin and Daniel C. Tsui)

The physicist Horst Ludwig Störmer was born in Frankfurt, Germany, on April 6, 1949, the son of Karl-Ludwig and Marie

(Ihrig) Störmer. His parents owned an interior-design store in the town of Sprendlingen, south of Frankfurt. He and his younger brother, Heinz, were raised amid an extended family of aunts, uncles, and cousins who lived in a compound that included his parent's shop, two houses, barns, and sheds. "It was an ideal playground for two boys growing up," Störmer wrote in an autobiographical essay posted on the Nobel e-Museum Web site. "Constructing huge sand castles with moats and bridges, cardboard tents from the shop's packing material, building elaborate knight's armour from scrap floor-covering and intricate race tracks for marbles from curtain rails remain fond memories of childhood." As a boy Störmer enrolled in the Goethe Gymnasium, where he excelled in math and physics, thanks in part to an articulate and lively young teacher named Dr. Nick. Outside of school Störmer's innate curiosity led him to build steam engines and clocks and wire his home with speaker phones; once, a homemade bomb exploded in his hand, taking off part of his thumb.

In 1968 Störmer enrolled at Goethe University, in Frankfurt, studying mathematics and physics, and then completing thesis work under the supervision of Professor Eckhardt Hoenig. (GERD BINNIG, the 1986 Nobel laureate for physics, was another student of Hoenig's at the time.) In 1974 Störmer moved to Grenoble, France, to pursue his Ph.D. at a high-magnetic field facility run jointly by the German MAX PLANCK Institute for Solid State Research and the French National Center for Scientific Research. "Going to Grenoble was the single most important step in my life," he recalled in his autobiographical essay. "Leaving the familiar surroundings of home, diving into another culture, another language, meeting new people, making new friends was initially frightening, but eventually immensely educational and gratifying." At the laboratory in Grenoble, Störmer completed his doctoral research, on the properties of electron hole droplets in high magnetic fields, and was awarded a Ph.D. in 1977 from the University of Stuttgart, which had a relationship with the Grenoble facility.

Störmer then accepted a position at Bell Labs, the research wing of American Telephone and Telegraph (AT&T), based in Murray Hill, New Jersey. At the time, Störmer recalled in his essay, Bell Labs was the mecca of solid state research, his own field of interest. Initially a consultant, he was taken on as a permanent member of the technical staff of the Lab's physics department after one year, thanks to his contribution to the development of a process known as "modulation-doping," a technique used to increase the mobility of two-dimensional electron systems. In 1983 he was named head of the department for electronic and optical properties of solids. In 1991 he was appointed director of the Physical Research Laboratory, supervising some 100 researchers. In 1998 he became a professor of physics and applied physics at Columbia University, in New York City. He retained his affiliation with Bell Labs, now run by Lucent Technologies, as a part-time adjunct physics director.

Horst Störmer, DANIEL C. TSUI, and ROBERT B. LAUGHLIN were awarded the 1998 Nobel Prize in Physics for their "discovery of a new form of quantum fluid with fractionally charged excitations," as cited on the Nobel e-Museum Web site. Their research has demonstrated how electrons change their behavior in ways that seem to contradict previous subatomic theory. They found that, when placed in a strong magnetic field and cooled to near absolute zero, groups of electrons condense into composite particles that act more like a fluid than like individual particles. This "quantum fluid" can take many

forms, including liquid helium, and share such properties as a lack of energy resistance at extremely low temperatures. Störmer and his associates discovered a new form of matter, different than anything described in modern physics. Störmer and Tsui, a Chinese-born physicist from Princeton University, collaborated at Bell Labs in the early 1980s on the work that would eventually earn them the Nobel Prize. Robert B. Laughlin's major contribution was his elucidation of the main theory behind the research, which he released in published form in 1983.

Interest in this particular field of quantum physics began as early as 1879, when an American college student named Edwin H. Hall was the first to observe an unusual electrical phenomenon. Hall found that, when a magnetic field is applied at a perpendicular angle to the plane of a metal strip, the electrons accumulate on one edge of the strip, causing the electrical charge to build up. The strength of the charge is determined by the strength of the magnetic field. The phenomenon became known as the "Hall effect" and was the object of study by scientists for more than a century. It has been used as a method for measuring the density of charge carriers in conductors and semiconductors.

A German physicist named KLAUS VON KLITZING studied the Hall effect at the Max Planck Institute for Solid State Research. Scientists had observed that new phenomena occur when electrons are confined to two dimensions, an artificial environment created in laboratory conditions in which electrons are made to move in an extremely thin layer. In 1980 von Klitzing discovered that, under these conditions, the Hall conductivity varies at distinct levels, or "quanta," in proportion to integer numbers. In 1985 von Klitzing won the Nobel Prize for physics for what became known as the "integer quantum Hall effect."

Störmer and Tsui studied this effect in the course of their research into the way electrons travel through semiconductors—the basis for today's high-speed computers, among other important technologies. They created extremely thin layers of a gallium-arsenide semiconductor in which electron movement occurred in two dimensions rather than three. Making use of a powerful magnet at the Francis Bitter National Magnet Laboratory at the Massachusetts Institute of Technology (MIT), Störmer and Tsui exposed this semiconductor to extremely low temperatures and strong magnetic fields. The electron motion they observed surprised them: they discovered more levels, or quanta, within the integer levels that von Klitzing had observed—an apparent exception to the long-held theory that every electron has the same charge. Since these new levels carried exact fractions of electrical charges, this new quality was named the "fractional quantum Hall effect."

One year after this experiment, Robert Laughlin, who was then working at the Lawrence Livermore National Laboratory, theorized that the fractional quantum Hall state had to be a new kind of fluid. The mobility created by the semiconductor under low temperatures and a powerful magnetic field freed the electrons to behave in new ways, forming a kind of matter known as a quantum liquid. "The electron is not falling apart," Störmer explained of this effect on the Lucent Technologies Web site. "Instead, many electrons working together create something smaller than the electron itself. Now you start wondering which is the whole and which is the part. Could this also be true in other areas of physics? Is what we see really what is?"

"The contributions of the three laureates have thus led to *yet another breakthrough in our understanding of quantum physics* and to the development of new theoretical concepts of significance in many branches of modern physics," the Royal Swedish Academy of Sciences stated in a press release archived on the Nobel e-Museum Web site. Among other things, the physicists' research can be applied to develop microelectronic devices, including smaller and faster computer chips. Physicists are still digesting the import of this work, but many speculate that it will prove very significant in years to come.

In addition to his Nobel Prize, Störmer has received the 1984 Oliver E. Buckley Prize from the American Physics Society, the 1985 Otto Klung Prize, presented by his native country, and the 1998 Medal of the Franklin Institute. He has been named a fellow of Bell Labs, the American Academy of Arts and Sciences, and the American Physics Society.

Störmer married the former Dominique Parchet in 1982.

ABOUT: Lucent Technologies Web site; New York Times October 14, 1998; Nobel e-Museum Web site; Salt Lake Tribune (on-line) October 14, 1998; Scientific American (on-line) October 19, 1998; (Singapore) Straits Times (on-line) August 10, 2001; Washington Post October 14, 1998.

Courtesy of Spinoza Institute/ITP

't Hooft, Gerardus

(July 5, 1946–) Nobel Prize for Physics, 1999 (shared with Martinus J. G. Veltman)

The physicist Gerardus 't Hooft was born July 5, 1946 in Den Helder, the Netherlands. He attended high school at the Dalton Lyceum in The Hague, graduating in 1964. He pursued advanced studies at the University of Utrecht, the Netherlands, majoring in physics and mathematics. As an undergraduate he took several part-time jobs as a student assistant at Utrecht, beginning in 1965. 't Hooft received his degree in 1966 and remained at Utrecht for his doctoral work. In 1969 he became a full-time staff member at the University of Utrecht's Institute for Theoretical Physics. He completed his Ph.D. thesis, "Renormalization Procedure for Yang-Mills Fields," in March 1972. The following September 't Hooft was made a fellow at CERN, the European laboratory of particle physics in Geneva, Switzerland. His fellowship lasted two years, after which 't Hooft returned to the University of Utrecht as an assistant professor. He temporarily departed Utrecht in the winter of 1976, teaching as an assistant professor for one semester at Harvard University and another at Stanford. In February 1977 he resumed his career at the University of Utrecht as a full professor.

The groundbreaking work done by 't Hooft and fellow Nobel Prize–winner Martinus J. G. Veltman was in the field of particle physics theory. The modern form of this discipline took shape in the 1950s, when it became possible for scientists to observe matter at its most minute level using large particle accelerators, which stimulate subatomic activity. One of the early theories put forth in particle physics helped establish what is called the "standard model," a framework that categorizes all elementary particles into three groups that interact through a number of "exchange" particles, such as protons. Particle interactions produce strong nuclear, weak nuclear, and electromagnetic forces. These forces, along with gravity, govern physical matter.

Before the work of 't Hooft and Veltman, the theoretical basis for the standard model was incomplete, because scientists could not mathematically substantiate it. Many doubted if it was possible to make use of the theory for calculating actual subatomic physical quantities. The theoretical foundation provided by 't Hooft and Martinus further illustrated the standard model in mathematical terms, thus allowing researchers to use it to predict the properties of new particles. One of the major benefits of 't Hooft and Martinus's mathematical foundation is that it proves there is a connection between electromagnetism and weak nuclear force, which has long been postulated by physicists as the electroweak theory. The ultimate goal is to prove that all the forces are actually properties of a single "unified field." By proving the connection of two forces, 't Hooft and Martinus have helped modern physics take a bold step toward the unified field.

In 1969 't Hooft began working with Veltman, then a newly appointed professor at the University of Utrecht. As a particle physicist working on the standard model, Veltman found that the theory of electroweak interaction was proving unreliable in calculating the properties of particles. Since com-

puters were not yet a mainstay of scientific research, many of the calculations were too complex and time-consuming to solve by hand. When solvable, the calculations often produced baffling impossibilities such as negative masses and negative probabilities, and in some cases even infinite values, which were obviously meaningless. Many researchers questioned the value of pursuing the theory any further.

Veltman, who had developed a computer program to deal with the complex calculations, accepted 't Hooft as his research assistant and assigned him the task of working out the mathematical properties of the standard model, known in physics as a non-Abelian gauge theory. Succeeding beyond even his mentor's expectations, 't Hooft helped develop a feasible calculation method. He published two breakthrough articles on the subject in 1971. "He could solve problems that seemed unsolvable in a way so elegant that you could only sit in absolute stupefaction," Dr. Peter van Nieuwenhuizen, a former colleague of 't Hooft's, commented to George Johnson for the *New York Times* (October 17, 1999). The door had been opened for performing precise computation using the non-Abelian gauge theory of electroweak interaction.

Using Veltman's earlier work as a starting point, 't Hooft had succeeded in eliminating the infinite values and other statistical impossibilities from the equation. He also postulated that what might have separated the electromagnetic and weak nuclear forces in the first place was an as-yet-undiscovered particle known as the Higgs particle. Named after the English physicist Peter Higgs, who first hypothesized its existence, the Higgs particle is thought by many physicists to be responsible for endowing other particles with mass through its interaction with them. Veltman disagreed with his pupil regarding the Higgs particle, and this created a rift between the two scientists. The elder physicist also felt that his protégé was getting an inordinate amount of credit for the breakthrough. Over time Veltman and 't Hooft drifted apart.

Gerardus 't Hooft and Martinus J. G. Veltman were jointly awarded the 1999 Nobel Prize in Physics for their achievement. "What 't Hooft did, under the guidance of his supervisor, Veltman, was to prove that the theory made sense. It may have been a lot of tosh," said Dr. Graham Farmelo of

London's Science Museum to Tim Radford of the *Manchester Guardian Weekly* (October 13, 1999). "When I was a graduate student 't Hooft was the megastar and many people, when [Steven] Weinberg, [Sheldon] Glashow, and [Abdus] Salam won the prize [in 1979], thought 'What about 't Hooft?'" (Weinberg, Glashow, and Salam were the original developers of the electroweak theory in the 1960s.)

't Hooft served as a guest professor at Boston University in 1988 and Duke University in 1989. He has been a member of the Dutch Academy of Sciences since 1982, the American Academy of Arts and Sciences since 1986, and the U.S. National Academy of Sciences since 1984. The numerous honors he has received for his work include the Winkler Prins Prize (1974), the Akzo Prize (1977), the Dannie Heineman Prize (1979),

honorary doctorates from the University of Chicago and the University of Bologna (1981 and 1998, respectively), the Wolf Prize from the State of Israel (1982), the Vatican's Pius XI Medal (1983), and the Franklin Medal (1995).

Gerardus 't Hooft married Albertha Anje Schik, an anesthetist, on July 1, 1972. Their first daughter, Saskia Anna, was born in 1976, and their second, Ellen Marga, was born in 1978. On his professional Web site, 't Hooft explained his fascination with physics by stating, "To me, Nature is a big jig-saw puzzle, and I see it as my task to try to fit pieces of it together."

ABOUT: Guardian Weekly October 13, 1999; New York Times (on-line) October 17, 1999; Nobel e-Museum Web site.

© The Nobel Foundation

Trimble, David

(October 15, 1944–) Nobel Prize for Peace, 1998 (shared with John Hume)

The politician David Trimble was born on October 15, 1944 in Bangor, a seaside resort town east of Belfast, Northern Ireland. He is the son of William Trimble, a civil servant, and Ivy Trimble, whose family was involved in the building business. The Trimble fami-

ly were Protestants who enjoyed a comfortable middle-class lifestyle. David Trimble attended Bangor Grammar School and earned a law degree from Queen's University, Belfast, in 1968. He was called to the Bar of Northern Ireland in 1969, and worked as a lecturer in the school of law at Queen's University from 1968 until 1980.

Trimble joined the hard-line Vanguard Party, which supported the goal of a British-ruled, semi-independent Ireland, in the early 1970s. In 1975 he was elected to the Northern Ireland Convention of South Belfast as a representative of Vanguard. He served briefly as Vanguard's deputy leader. By 1978 his views had become more moderate, diverging from the extremist Vanguard leaders, and he joined the Ulster Unionist Party (UUP), which favors British rule and wants Northern Ireland to remain part of the United Kingdom. "The Unionists have a culture distinct from, and in many ways alien to, that of the rest of Ireland," a writer for the *Economist* (September 20, 1997) explained. "They have different loyalties, traditions, and heroes. . . . They have fought and died for Britain in two world wars. They cannot imagine feeling comfortable as a permanent minority in a unified Ireland." Trimble was soon named honorary secretary of the UUP. He also served from 1985 to 1990 as the chairman of both the Lagan Valley Unionist Society and the Ulster Society, right-wing organizations that had fought against the

Anglo-Irish Agreement of 1985, which gave the predominantly Catholic Irish Republic more political representation in Northern Ireland. In 1990 Trimble was elected to the British Parliament. Trimble's manner during this time was described by a writer for *Newsmakers* (1999): "He was not known for his charm or compromising ways; he became known as a forthright and rather undiplomatic personality who was prone to rises in temper."

In 1993 British prime minister John Major and Irish prime minister Albert Reynolds signed the Downing Street Declaration; one of its provisions allowed Sinn Féin, a group founded in 1895 with the aim of winning Irish independence from Britain, to participate in the discussion of Northern Ireland's future. The agreement required the IRA, Sinn Féin's military counterpart, to renounce violence. Soon afterward the IRA, which seeks to unite the British province with the Republic of Ireland, declared a cease-fire. In 1995 the UUP chose the militant Trimble as their new leader, over the more moderate John Taylor. Some Unionists were upset because Trimble was not Anglo-Irish, the traditional background of the organization's leaders. Trimble was seen by Irish nationalists as a bigoted, anti-Catholic individual. Many of his colleagues in the British Parliament, too, opposed his appointment because they considered him an extremist.

Some speculated that Trimble's involvement in what had become known as "the siege of Drumcree" (named for the church where Protestants began large protest marches) had sealed his election. Trimble had helped to organize opposition to a ban preventing the Orange Order (a coalition of various Protestant factions) from holding its annual march through the Catholic district of Portadown, in Armagh County, in 1995. (The march commemorated the Protestant King William's victory over Roman Catholic James II in the region in 1690.) In 1996 Trimble once again attended the march, and again the police tried, but failed, to prevent it. He was seen on television marching down Garvaghy Road as police beat Catholic protestors, an act that proved his loyalty to the UUP's cause but also made him appear to many observers in a negative light. The IRA reversed its cease-fire soon thereafter. The United States then sent Senator George Mitchell (believed by some to be pro-Catholic) to Ireland to mediate peace talks.

The cease-fire resumed in July 1997, and the talks began in earnest in September, in spite of the August bombing of the Protestant neighborhood of Omagh, attributed to a splinter group called the "Real IRA." The bomb attack killed 29 people and injured more than 200 others.

The peace talks brought Trimble into contact with one of his oldest enemies, Gerry Adams, the leader of Sinn Féin. Adams, a high-school dropout, grew up in a family with a history of armed resistance to British rule. Believed to be a former leader of the IRA, he was considered influential enough to be flown, in 1972, from prison in Northern Ireland to secret cease-fire talks in London. Adams was known for his sense of humor as well as his knowledge of Gaelic, which he had studied while in prison. In 1985, after his release, Adams took control of Sinn Féin, advocating a peaceful settlement to the conflict without denouncing the IRA's history of violence. Although elected to the British Parliament as a representative of West Belfast, he had refused to take his seat in the House of Commons, as that would have required him to swear allegiance to Queen Elizabeth II, the British monarch.

As the historic peace talks with Trimble, Hume, and Adams began, Mitchell became concerned about assassination attempts; he and Prime Minister Tony Blair thus set a deadline of Easter (which fell in mid-April that year) for the completion of a settlement. Both Trimble and Adams were heavily guarded throughout the talks. The meetings got off to a less than auspicious start, when Trimble refused to accept Adams's assertion that Sinn Féin was not closely tied to the IRA and declined to look his adversary in the eye. The *New York Times* (September 24, 1997) quoted Trimble's deputy, Ken Maginnis, as saying that Sinn Féin had "diminished democracy, sacrificed the freedom of the people of Northern Ireland to the terrorist and elevated an evil mafia to a status that would shame any other country in Western Europe."

A new deadline of April 9 was established, but the negotiations stretched 17 hours past that date. U.S. president Bill Clinton made last-minute phone calls to the leaders of both parties, and both Tony Blair, and the Irish prime minister, Bertie Ahern, acted as mediators in the final hours of the talks. On April 10 (the Christian holiday of

Good Friday), a landmark compromise was reached. The Good Friday Agreement called for a new assembly for Northern Ireland, allowing the region to govern itself while remaining a province of Great Britain. The treaty was approved on May 22, 1998 by 94 percent of the voters from the Irish Republic and 71 percent of the voters in Northern Ireland.

At the assembly's first meeting, Trimble was named leader of Northern Ireland's new governing body. Trimble's party retained 28 seats when voting for the new assembly took place in June, but many turned against him and voted for members who were opposed to the power-sharing agreement. Although the many members of Trimble's own party who were against the Good Friday Agreement labeled him a sellout, he remained dedicated to the Unionist cause. Trimble effectively brought the treaty to a halt when he proclaimed that Sinn Féin would not be allowed to participate in the assembly until the IRA began decommissioning its weapons arsenal. Although Adams reiterated that his organization had little or no control over the IRA, and pointed to the cease-fire as evidence of the Catholics' commitment to nonviolence, Trimble was persistent in his demands. The result was a stalemate that would stall the peace process for more than a year.

In September 1998 Trimble agreed to meet and speak to Adams face-to-face. Although this latest attempt at establishing lasting peace gave hope to some, Trimble refused to shake hands with Adams when the meeting came to an end. "The question for you when Mr. Adams comes out is whether his dirty squalid little terrorist war is over," Trimble said, according to John Murray Brown, writing for the *Financial Times* (April 11, 1998, on-line). "When he accepts the democratic process, we'll see [about shaking hands]."

In October the Nobel Committee awarded the Nobel Peace Prize to Trimble and JOHN HUME, the head of Northern Ireland's Roman Catholic Social Democratic and Labour Party. Hume had argued for nearly 25 years for a plan very similar to the Good Friday Agreement. (Adams was not considered for the prize.) The Nobel Committee cited Trimble for his "great political courage" in taking the first steps toward peace. It was not the first time that the Nobel panel had attempted to encourage peace in the region; in 1976

it had awarded the prize to BETTY WILLIAMS and MAIREAD CORRIGAN of Northern Ireland, for their efforts in creating the International Peace Group, which later disbanded.

Meanwhile, the stalemate continued into the late months of 1998. Many of those in favor of an Irish Republic felt that the decommissioning of the IRA's weapons arsenal would be tantamount to surrender, and regarded the entire peace process with suspicion. Although the treaty gave Sinn Féin and the IRA two years to begin disarmament, Trimble would not yield in his demand that the process begin immediately. At the suggestion of Paul Doris, national chairperson of the Irish Northern Aid Committee, a letter-writing campaign was launched in the U.S., urging Prime Minister Tony Blair to intervene to find a solution to the problem. "If republicans can accept the fact that loyalists do not intend to disarm prior to setting up the Executive, the Unionists must have the backbone to accept that the IRA will decommission only when it is practical to do so," Doris said in his statement, which was reprinted in the *Irish People* (November 21, 1998, on-line).

The war of words continued throughout 1999, rendering the new ruling body powerless. As the debate dragged on, violence began to increase on the streets of Northern Ireland, as members of both sides of the conflict engaged in what became known as "punishment beatings"—sudden attacks by paramilitary forces on unsuspecting civilians, to exact revenge. Trimble used these beatings as a point of argument, claiming that they violated the cease-fire and thus proved that the IRA was not interested in abiding by the Good Friday Agreement. Many Protestants were also angered by the release—as promised by the treaty—of 277 Republican national prisoners.

By early summer it began to look as if the assembly might be shut down entirely. In an article for the *New York Times* that was reprinted in the *Economist* (June 26, 1999), Trimble warned that closing the assembly would put an end to the peace process: "Abandoning the Agreement at the beginning of the summer would be simply irresponsible. Worse, it will be the government resolving the decommissioning issue in favor of the terrorists." According to the Good Friday Agreement, a 10-person cabinet (on which Sinn Féin was slated to hold two seats) was to be established for the Northern

Ireland assembly, but Trimble delayed forming the cabinet while disarmament talks continued. In spite of its own deadline, the British government rushed amendments through Parliament that would have expedited disarmament, hoping to appease Trimble and the UUP. On July 15 Trimble and 28 other members of the UUP boycotted the meeting in which cabinet members were to be chosen. This move automatically subjected the agreement to a review by the British government, a process that was expected to last for the rest of the summer. Seamus Mallon, the deputy first prime minister and a member of the Northern Ireland Assembly and of the Social Democratic and Labour Party, was infuriated by the party's actions and resigned, calling on Trimble to follow suit. The assembly adjourned without deciding on a date to return.

George Mitchell was called in again, and after 11 weeks of negotiating, both parties released statements that seemed to point toward a compromise. Gerry Adams declared that his party would agree to paramilitary disarmament and would appoint one of its members to the International Commission on Decommissioning. The New York Times (November 28, 1999) reported that "in exchange for relaxing their demand for immediate IRA weapons turnover, the unionists were gaining self-rule, the right to keep Ulster British as long as its residents wished it, the end to the 1985 Anglo-Irish Agreement that gave Dublin joint authority with Britain in some of the North's affairs, and the withdrawal of the clauses in the Constitution of the Irish Republic that make a territorial claim on Northern Ireland." Encouraged by the talks, Trimble made a surprising statement in favor of peace and equality. "For too long, much of the unrest in our community has been caused by a failure to accept the differing expressions of cultural identity," he said, according to Warren Hoge in the New York Times (November 17, 1999). Under the terms of the new agreement, disarmament was scheduled to begin January 31, 2000.

But in mid-February 2000, after the IRA had failed to make what the government saw as sufficient progress toward disarmament, the Northern Ireland assembly was shut down by the British government; the historic experiment had lasted a total of 72 days. Britain had acted in the hope that it could head off the resignation of Trimble, who had pledged to step down if disarmament was not achieved—and without whom the peace agreement would likely cease to exist. Soon after the new government had been suspended, the IRA released a statement indicating that it was willing to cooperate with disarmament plans. The International Commission on Decommissioning also issued a report, reprinted in part in the New York Times (February 13, 2000), which stated, "We find particularly significant, and view as valuable progress, the assertion made to us by the IRA representative that the IRA will consider how to put arms and explosives beyond use."

"The Unionists, the Irish nationalists, Britain, and Ireland are all paralyzed, seemingly unable to get themselves out of a potentially tragic situation," Terry Golway wrote for Newsday (March 6, 2000). As reported on CNN.com (February 24, 2000), Britain's Northern Ireland secretary, Peter Mandelson, spoke to reporters at the White House about the need for continued negotiation: "We need to get people talking again. We need to get ideas back on the table so that we can get the executive and the institutions back on track." In March 2000 Trimble narrowly defeated Martin Smyth, a Presbyterian minister and former leader of the Orange Order who had announced his candidacy less than a week before the vote.

Over the next two years, Trimble continued to battle challenges to his leadership by hard-line Protestants and press both the IRA and Sinn Féin on disarmament. In an effort to quell a rebellion in his own party, Trimble announced that he would resign as Northern Ireland's first minister if the IRA did not begin disarming by July 1, 2001. "The time has come for people to honour their obligations," he said, as quoted by Oliver Wright for the London Times (June 25, 2001). "We want both devolution and decommissioning. There will be a problem as a result of me stepping down, and it does put things at risk, but all I am asking [the IRA] to do is to implement the [Good Friday] agreement. They haven't kept their promise to disarm." With no signs of cooperation from the IRA, Trimble carried out his threat on June 30. His resignation was met with widespread disapproval by Prime Minister Tony Blair and President George W. Bush. Trimble was widely considered the only leader who could keep Northern Ireland's joint Catholic-Protestant administration alive. Trimble, however, said he would consider resuming his post if the IRA agreed to disarm. In October, the IRA announced it would put some of its arms "beyond use," as quoted by the *BBC News* (November 2, 2001, on-line), and Trimble returned as first minister. In November 2001 Trimble was re-elected first minister by the assembly, with the unanimous support of Catholics and a razor-thin majority of two votes among the Protestant members. (According to the assembly's rules, a majority vote in both camps was needed for the first minister to be re-elected.) In December 2001 Trimble defeated another challenge to his leadership as the head of the UUP by hard-liners.

Trimble and his second wife, Daphne Orr, were married in 1978. They have two sons and two daughters. In his leisure time Trim-

ble reads and listens to opera, especially the music of Strauss, Verdi, and Wagner.

ABOUT: BBC News (on-line) November 2, 2001; CNN.com February 24, 2000; Economist February 13, 1999, June 26, 1999; Financial Times (on-line) April 11, 1998; Irish People (on-line) November 21, 1998; New York Times September 24, 1997, March 31, 1998, April 19, 1998, April 20, 1998, June 28, 1998, February 1, 1999, July 13, 1999, November 17, 1999, November 20, 1999, November 28, 1999; Newsday March 6, 2000; Newsmakers 1999; Nobel e-Museum Web site; (London) Times June 25, 2001.

Courtesy of Princeton University

Tsui, Daniel Chee

(1939–) Nobel Prize for Physics, 1998 (shared with Horst Störmer and Robert B. Laughlin)

The physicist Daniel Chee Tsui was born in a small, isolated village in the Chinese province of Henan, in 1939. In an autobiographical essay posted on the Nobel e-Museum Web site, he recalled: "My childhood memories are filled with the years of drought, flood and war which were constantly on the consciousness of the inhabitants of my over-populated village, but also with my parents' self-sacrificing love and the happy moments that they created for me." Tsui's parents, like most of the people in his village, had no education and were unable to read or write; nevertheless, they worked hard to ensure that their own children had access to an education. In 1951 Tsui's parents sent him to Hong Kong, where he began formal schooling at a sixth-grade level. After one year, Tsui entered Pui Ching Middle School, which was known for its exceptional program in the natural sciences. In his essay he described his teachers at Pui Ching as "the brightest graduates of the best universities in China and under normal circumstances would have been highly accomplished scholars and scientists." He continued, "The upheaval of the war in China, however, forced them to hibernate in Hong Kong teaching high school kids. . . . Their intellects and their visions inspired us."

After graduating from Pui Ching in 1957, Tsui began a two-year program designed to prepare Chinese students for the University of Hong Kong. However, one year into his program, he learned that he had received a full scholarship to attend Augustana College, a Lutheran college in Rock Island, Illinois, that Tsui's Lutheran pastor had attended. At Augustana, Tsui enjoyed the opportunity, as he described, "to read, to learn and to think through things at my own pace." Yet from the start he knew that he intended to pursue post-graduate work, and had chosen the subject. "C. N. Yang and T. D. Lee [two Chinese-born physicists] were awarded the Nobel Prize in Physics in 1957 and they both went to the University of Chicago," Tsui explained in his essay. "Yang and Lee were the role models for Chinese students of my generation and going to the University of Chicago for graduate school was the ideal pilgrimage."

Soon after completing his degree at Augustana, Tsui began a Ph.D. program at the University of Chicago's Department of Physics. He worked as a research assistant for Royal Stark, a physics professor whose research focused on solid state physics experimentation. In Stark's laboratory, Tsui developed his hands-on technical research skills. Tsui focused his own experiments on Fermi surfaces and the band structure of ferromagnetic metals. (Fermi surfaces are energy surfaces that encase all of the electrons in a crystal at absolute zero, which is the lowest theoretical temperature. Ferromagnetic metals are metals in which the electron spins are aligned to form microscopic groups, or domains, with a common magnetic orientation.)

After obtaining his Ph.D. in physics, in 1967, Tsui worked as a research fellow at the University of Chicago. In the spring of 1968 he joined the technical staff of AT&T's research wing, Bell Laboratories (now part of Lucent Technologies), in Murray Hill, New Jersey. He explained his move in his autobiographical essay: "Since I could always fall back on a job using my technical skills, I reasoned, why not then take a risk and try a research position doing something entirely novel and at the same time intellectually challenging." At Bell Labs, rather than focusing on the traditional areas within semiconductor research, Tsui became interested in the emerging study of the physics of two-dimensional electrons. During his 13 years at Bell Labs, Tsui worked on the particular field of quantum physics that explores the "Hall effect," a phenomenon discovered in 1879 by the American college student Edwin H. Hall. Hall observed that, when he placed a thin gold plate in a magnetic field at right angles to its surface, a stream of electrons developed with an excessive electrical charge. The electrons, affected by the magnetic force, accumulated on one side of the strip and deflected laterally. Hall found that this resulting voltage drop was directly proportional to the force of the magnetic field. His contribution has enabled a better understanding of conductors and semiconductors, as well as the field of quantum physics.

Nevertheless, Hall's initial observations remained limited—and unexplained—for more than 100 years, in part due to the limited scope of his experimentation. Hall performed his tests at room temperature and with moderate magnetism. As scientists began to experiment with extremely low temperatures—nearing absolute zero—and powerful magnetic fields, they began to observe new properties of the Hall effect. In one such experiment in 1980, the German physicist KLAUS VON KLITZING achieved the Hall effect using high-quality silicon; this time, however, a modified effect emerged: As the magnetic field was applied to the silicon material, the electrons exhibited a voltage drop that changed in steps proportional to integer numbers. At these distinct levels, or "quanta," von Klitzing could then measure the resistence of the electrons' orbits in relation to the strength of the magnetic field. For his work on what was termed the "integer quantum Hall effect," von Klitzing won the Nobel Prize for Physics in 1985.

Just two years after von Klitzing's major experiment, Tsui and Störmer used a gallium-arsenide-based semiconductor and an ultra-powerful magnet at the Francis Bitter National Magnet Laboratory of the Massachusetts Institute of Technology to observe an entirely new level in the Hall effect. As Tsui told Bertram Schwarzschild for *Physics Today* (December 1998), "We wanted to look at this unexplored extreme quantum limit, where the flux quanta outnumbered the electrons." When they reduced the temperature even closer to absolute zero, Tsui and Störmer found that the electrons within the gallium-arsenide layer did not just divide into steps proportional to integers but into *thirds* of steps. Moreover, the electronic charges of these condensed, fluid-like particles were fractional to the charge of one electron—a condition that seemed to contradict subatomic theory, which maintains that all electrons share the same charge. Due to the fractional nature of the quantum, the effect was dubbed the "fractional quantum Hall effect."

One year after Tsui and Störmer's discovery, the physicist ROBERT LAUGHLIN offered a theoretical explanation for the fractional quantum Hall effect. He speculated that the extremely low temperatures and the high magnetic field forced the electrons to condense into composite particles that behave more like a fluid than like individual particles. According to the Nobel Committee, these fluids are important because of their potential to instruct scientists on the dynamics of matter. As stated in an October 13, 1998 press release posted on the Nobel e-Museum Web site, "The contributions of these three laureates have thus led to *yet another breakthrough in our understanding of quantum physics* and to the development of new theoretical concepts of significance in many branches of modern physics."

Shortly after the discovery of the fractional quantum Hall effect, Tsui left Bell Laboratories for a professorship in the Department of Electrical Engineering at Princeton University, in Princeton, New Jersey. He focused his research on the electrical properties of semiconductors and solid state physics. Tsui is particularly interested in expanding his research of the quantum physics of electronic materials in strong magnetic fields and low temperatures. He is currently the Arthur LeGrand Doty Professor of

Electrical Engineering at Princeton. Of his decision to leave Bell Labs, he reflected in his autobiographical essay, "Perhaps it was the Confucius in me, the faint voice I often heard when I was alone, that the only meaningful life is a life of learning. What better way to learn than through teaching!"

In addition to the Nobel Prize, Tsui has been honored with the Buckley Prize for condensed matter physics (1984) and the Benjamin Franklin Award in physics (1998). He is a fellow of the American Association for the Advancement of Science and the American Physical Society, a member of the National Academy of Science, American Academy of Arts and Sciences, Academia Sinica, the Third World Academy of Sciences, and a foreign member of the National Academy of Sciences in China.

In 1964 Tsui married his wife, the former Linda Varland, whom he met at the University of Chicago; they have two children. Tsui is now a U.S. citizen.

ABOUT: Economist October 17, 1998; New York Times October 14, 1998; Nobel e-Museum Web site; Physics Today December 1998; Science October 23, 1998.

United Nations

(founded in 1945) Nobel Prize for Peace, 2001 (shared with Kofi Annan)

The United Nations was created in 1945, the brainchild of President Franklin D. Roosevelt and other World War II–era Allied leaders, who sought to create an international body that would not only replace the disbanded League of Nations, but would also do what the League had been unable to—prevent another world war. Since 1945 the United Nations has helped to keep the peace, and since the end of the Cold War, it has been able to conduct itself in the way it had originally been conceived—by actively enforcing peace and security, by settling disputes between nations, and by authoring international accords to combat the world's environmental, economic, and social problems. For these reasons, the Nobel Committee presented the organization, in equal

parts with its secretary-general, KOFI ANNAN, the Nobel Peace Prize for 2001.

With the outbreak of World War II in September 1939, the need for a new and more powerful world body became apparent. The League of Nations had been unable to prevent the toppling of European countries by Hitler's war machine, and equally unable to stop the rearmament of countries, who only 20 years earlier, had pledged to do all they could to prevent the onset of another world war; instead, the League had fallen apart with the outbreak of World War II. President Roosevelt, then watching this new war unfold from inside a predominately isolationist America, began to quietly consider a new international league, which he called the United Nations. He believed that in order for such an organization to succeed, it would need the total support of the United States, which had bowed out of joining the League. Roosevelt began setting in motion plans to ally the United States with other like-minded nations in order to establish rules for international collaboration. His first overtures were two documents—the Inter-Allied Declaration and the Atlantic Charter—signed jointly with British prime minister WINSTON CHURCHILL in the summer of 1941; both documents promised bilateral collaboration. However, since the United States had not officially entered World War II that summer, all references to a new international body had to remain covert.

This all changed after the Japanese attack on the American military base in Pearl Harbor, on December 7, 1941. With the United States now facing attack by both Japan and Germany (Hitler declared war on America shortly after the Japanese attack), Roosevelt began to speak openly about the need for an international organization to maintain the peace, knowing that it needed to begin among the Allied nations. On January 1, 1942, representatives of the 26 nations allied against the Axis powers of Germany, Italy, and Japan met in Washington, D.C. to sign the Declaration by United Nations, which showed their support of the Atlantic Charter. This was also the first public use of the term United Nations.

The idea of a new international body began to pick up steam with the Moscow Declaration of October 30, 1943, issued by the governments of the United States, the Soviet Union, Great Britain, and China. This document officially called for the creation of such an organization. The first blueprint of the United Nations was then mapped out at a conference in the Dumbarton Oaks mansion in Washington, D.C. during September and October 1944. At the Yalta Conference in February 1945, the "Big Three" Allied leaders—Roosevelt, Churchill, and Soviet premier Joseph Stalin—called on all nations who had signed the 1942 Declaration by United Nations and all those who had declared war on Germany or Japan by March 1, 1945 to meet at the organization's founding conference, which would be held that April in San Francisco, California. At that inaugural meeting, which lasted from April 25 to June 26, 1945, delegates of 50 nations drew up and adopted the U.N. Charter, composed of 111 articles, establishing the organization's principles and outlining its main components: the General Assembly, the Security Council, the Economic and Social Council, the Trusteeship Council, the International Court of Justice, and the Secretari-

at. The charter was then ratified by the five permanent members of the U.N. Security Council—the United States, Soviet Union, Great Britain, China, and France—on October 24, 1945, officially celebrated annually as United Nations Day.

The first U.N. General Assembly met on January 11, 1946 in the Central Hall of Westminster in war-ravaged London. Representatives of 51 member nations agreed that the organization's headquarters should be located in the eastern portion of the United States and elected Belgian foreign minister Paul-Henri Spaak as president of the first General Assembly. Later in the year the General Assembly accepted an $8 million gift from John D. Rockefeller, Jr. to build its headquarters on a piece of land along the East River in New York City. (The Secretariat and General Assembly buildings were completed in 1952; the library, dedicated to a future secretary-general, Dag Hammarskjöld, was finished in 1961.)

In its early years, the United Nations focused on eliminating nuclear weapons and other weapons of mass destruction. However, the Cold War rivalry between western nations, led by the United States, and eastern nations, led by the Soviet Union, prevented any unanimity on the subject. Accords were further hampered by the veto power of the Security Council, which prevented action on any resolution if one of the permanent members dissented. (By 1955 the veto had been used 78 times in the Security Council, 75 times by the Soviet Union.) However, East and West often joined forces in U.N. efforts to secure peace: in 1946 the U.N. settled Syria and Lebanon's complaint that France and Great Britain were occupying their territory; in 1949 the U.N. brokered a cease-fire between the newly created Israeli state and its Arab neighbors. During the same period the organization also settled a dispute between India and Pakistan over the contested territory of Kashmir.

In 1950, shortly after the Communist takeover of mainland China, the Soviet Union boycotted the Security Council for refusing to seat the new Chinese government. With the Soviets—and their veto power—absent, the Security Council voted to organize member states into an armed force, directed at repelling Communist North Korea's recent invasion of South Korea. Just as the U.N. had begun to seem weak, the organization embarked on the most far-reaching collective security action in history, with the U.S. providing the lion's share of personnel and weapons. The cease-fire between the two Koreas, which effectively divided the peninsula, was signed on July 27, 1953 by the U.N. Command and the Chinese–North Korean Command.

Throughout the 1950s the role of the secretary-general, and of the United Nations itself, was evolving. In 1952, after the election of Dag Hammarskjöld to the secretary-generalship, the organization became considerably more activist in nature and sought peace at any cost, in spite of the deadlock in the Security Council. Hammarskjöld achieved this through what has been called "quiet diplomacy." He expanded the powers of the secretary-general by bypassing the deadlocked Security Council and working directly with the General Assembly. Though he was unable to persuade the Soviet Union to remove its troops from Hungary after a revolt in 1956, he was able to broker a resolution in the General Assembly that same year, calling for an immediate cessation of hostilities during the Suez Canal crisis and overseeing a removal of British, French, and Israeli forces from the newly nationalized Egyptian canal. Two years later, over the veto of the Security Council but supported by the General Assembly, he sent a force of U.N. observers to Lebanon. In 1959, over the protests of the Soviet Union, he went on a mission to Laos and later sent a special U.N. ambassador to that country. On September 18, 1961, Dag Hammarskjöld was killed in a plane crash while on route to a peace mission in Congo.

In the 1950s and 1960s the United Nations was also changing in response to its growing membership. Though conceived as merely an alliance of "freedom-loving" nations, the organization began to move toward the idea that its membership should include every nation in the world. As more African and Asian countries gained independence from European colonial powers, they began to join the U.N. and form a new voting bloc in the General Assembly. Together with Latin American countries, many of which had broken from their pro–U.S. stance, newly created African and Asian nations demanded that the U.N. attend to the problematic legacies of colonialism. In 1960 the government of Congo invited U.N. troops to settle the dispute with the breakaway Katanga province, which three years later reinte-

grated itself with Congo. The U.N. also sent peacekeeping forces to Cyprus, again to deal with internal problems, as well as to prevent violence from spilling over to neighboring countries. Finally the organization sought to change the racist policies of South Africa, first by placing a voluntary arms embargo on the country in 1963 and then stripping that country of its mandate to govern Southwest Africa, now known as Namibia. They also condemned racist policies in Rhodesia and the colonial policies in Portugese colonies. Unfortunately, these U.N. resolutions had little immediate effect on such policies and signaled a weakening influence of the United Nations in international affairs.

The U.N.'s diminishing influence in the late 1960s and 1970s was a direct result of the United States joining forces with its rival, the Soviet Union, in order to keep major issues within the confines of the Security Council. The Soviets, in turn, wanted to restrict the powers of the secretary-general by replacing that single office with a three-man body, made up of Western, Eastern, and neutral members. Though that plan was defeated, the combination of the great powers controlling major issues from the Security Council, the desire to see a less activist secretary-general, and financial burdens (the Soviets refused to pay for certain U.N. actions; the Americans refused to contribute any more to the organization's budget) made the U.N. a considerably weaker body during this period. Thus, while the organization had some successes, including an agreement to use atomic energy peacefully, a mandatory arms embargo against South Africa, and the successful elimination of smallpox, the U.N. had little influence on major negotiations or peace accords. Such settlements, including the peace accords for the Arab-Israeli Wars of 1967 and 1973, the India-Pakistan War of 1971, and the Vietnam War, were therefore done on a bilateral basis.

Locked out of treaty negotiations between the great powers during the 1970s and 1980s, the United Nations turned its attention to developing countries. The organization made significant contributions to aiding refugees, administering vaccinations and preventing the spread of disease, granting relief from natural disasters, and providing technical innovations. The U.N. acted as a go-between for wealthier countries to provide aid, money, and resources to countries in need. At the same time, the U.N. organized conventions to adopt standards for human rights, the elimination of racism, the end of discrimination against women, the establishment of labor standards, and the protection of the ozone layer and other environmental resources.

With the end of the Cold War and the collapse of the Soviet Union, in 1991, the United Nations was able to assert itself as a major player in international affairs. Beginning with the 1991 Persian Gulf War, the organization has shown its ability to function as it was intended—as broker for global agreements, a peacekeeper, and a promoter of international cooperation and peace. During the Gulf War, the U.N. approved the use of military action to push Iraqi forces from neighboring Kuwait, oversaw the cease-fire agreement, and sanctioned the embargo on Iraqi goods until the government complied with the U.N.–mandated removal of weapons of mass destruction.

In the decade since the Gulf War, the U.N. provided supervision to elections in such places as Eritrea, Cambodia, South Africa, and Mozambique. The organization oversaw historical accords on preserving the environment in Rio de Janeiro in 1992 and in Kyoto in 1997. It also aggressively pursued disarmament work by extending it to include the elimination of land mines and the reduction of small arms. It adopted the Comprehensive Test-Ban Treaty in 1996; signers to the treaty have vowed not to test their nuclear weapons.

The U.N. has come under criticism at different points in history for failing to act, or for acting in a way that is perceived to be ineffective or unfair. Many have criticized the organization for failing to stop the genocide in Rwanda, in 1994, and have accused the organization of ignoring African countries. During the 50th-anniversary celebration of the United Nations, in 1995, critics derided the organization for doing nothing to broker a peace accord in the civil war in Bosnia.

With the collapse of the Soviet Union, countries once under Soviet control began applying for membership to the United Nations, bringing the current number of official member countries to 189. The U.N. is now closer than it has ever been to being a universal body, but much work remains: in addition to its regular activities, the organization had 15 ongoing peacekeeping mission as of December 2001. For the central role it plays in settling disputes and working for

justice, the United Nations, together with its current secretary-general, Kofi Annan of Ghana, was awarded the Nobel Peace Prize for 2001. The Nobel committee noted in its press release: "The U.N. has in its history achieved many successes, and suffered many setbacks. Through this first Peace Prize to the U.N. as such, the Norwegian Nobel Committee wishes in its centenary year to proclaim that the only negotiable route to global peace and cooperation goes by way of the United Nations."

ABOUT: New York Times (on-line) January 11, 1946; Nobel e-museum Web site; U.N. Chronicle December 1995; United Nations Official Web site; U.S. News and World Report October 23, 1995.

Courtesy of Mertinus Veltman

Veltman, Martinus J. G.

(1931–) Nobel Prize for Physics, 1999 (with Gerardus 't Hooft)

The physicist Martinus J. G. Veltman was born in the Netherlands in 1931. Little has been written about his early life, though it is known that he attended the University of Utrecht, in the Netherlands, where he received his Ph.D in theoretical physics in 1963. Upon receiving his degree Veltman was given a fellowship at CERN, the European laboratory for particle physics in Geneva,

Switzerland. At the time, the study of particle physics was a fairly new discipline; its modern form had only developed in the 1950s, when researchers were first able to study matter at the subatomic level by using large particle accelerators, which stimulate such microscopic activity. The "standard model" of particle physics was formulated at this time and suggested that a framework could be devised to catagorize all elementary particles into three basic groups. With the help of exchange particles, such as protons, these groups of elementary particles of matter interact to produce three types of forces: electromagnetic, strong nuclear, and weak nuclear. These three forces, along with gravity, control matter and bind the universe together. Unfortunately, throughout the 1950s and 1960s, the standard model's theoretical basis could not be proven mathematically. Although American physicist and Nobel laureate RICHARD FEYNMAN had by this time systematized computational rules for particle interactions, physicists had to work out the complex and time-consuming calculations by hand. In order to help with such calculations, Veltman developed the first general purpose computer program that could perform algebra. The major principals of this computer program have since been further developed and are now part of software used by scientists across the globe.

In 1966 Veltman joined the physics department at the University of Utrecht, where he began his breakthrough work on proving the standard theory. As a gauge theorist he believed that all forces affecting particles— weak and strong nuclear forces, electromagneticism, and gravity—were connected, and that by precisely understanding such connections, one can better understand the workings of the universe. By this time physicists had developed a theory blending weak nuclear force with electromagnetism, yet they were unable to prove it. Often, when they tried to prove it mathematically, their proofs generated infinite quantities or negative probabilities, which were meaningless. In 1968 Veltman began developing the proof needed to link weak nuclear force with electromagnetism, using his computer program to perform the calculations.

In 1969 Veltman was joined on his quest by Gerardus 't Hooft, a 22-year-old graduate student at the University of Utrecht. As Veltman's research assistant, 't Hooft was assigned to work out the mathematical properties of the standard model and search for a way to renormalize gauge theory to eliminate meaningless answers. In short order he not only worked out the mathematical properties but also developed a feasible calculation method. In 1971 the pair published two papers that provided the mathematical proof that solved the standard model theory (or the non-Abelian gauge theory, as it is also known) and, more importantly, showed a connection between weak nuclear force and electromagnetism. The significance of this work is that it provides proof of a concrete connection between two of the four natural forces acting on particles (the other two being strong nuclear force and gravity). Ultimately the work conducted by Veltman and 't Hooft has served as a building block to physicists who would like to prove that all four forces are part of single "unified field."

In addition to proving the theory, Veltman and 't Hooft helped to create a better understanding of how these four forces might have once been part of a single "superforce" that existed in the earliest stages of the creation of the universe, as it has been explained by the Big Bang theory. 't Hooft believed that this breaking was caused by a still undiscovered particle scientists call the Higgs particle, named after the English physicist Peter Higgs, who postulated its existence. Many physicists believe the Higgs particle responsible for endowing other particles with mass through its interaction with them. Veltman, however, disagreed with his student on the Higgs particle theory and the two eventually began to drift apart due to such differences. In subsequent years Veltman made significant contributions to the theory of radiative corrections, which are used to make reliable theoretical predictions in quantum field theories. He helped develop the Sutherland-Veltman algebraic theorem, which deals with the decay of the pi meson particle, and made very important donations to the study of formal field theory, for which he created the "Veltman cutting rules," a working method of implementing probability conservation. Currently, he is working to prove or disprove the existence of the Higgs particle.

Veltman and 't Hooft were announced as the winners of the 1999 Nobel Prize in Physics on October 12, 1999. The Academy's citation noted that they were receiving the award "for elucidating the quantum structure of electroweak interactions in physics." Paul Guinnessy, editor of *Physicsweb*, told *BBC News* (October 12, 1999, on-line), "It is not a surprise that 't Hooft and Veltman have won the prize, they have done some outstanding work in particle physics. It has been suggested for some time that they should win and a lot of people will be very happy that they did." Both Veltman and 't Hooft agreed that their theory had little practical purpose in the everyday world. "The social benefit of my theory is absolutely nil you won't eat any more or less as a result," Veltman was quoted as saying by the *Online NewsHour* (October 12, 1999). In the same article he was also quoted as saying that he has always had difficulty explaining the nature of his work: "It is a difficult and abstract subject and something that I have never been able to explain to my wife and children."

In addition to his post at the University of Utrecht, Martinus J. G. Veltman has held posts at the University of Michigan, in Ann Arbor, from 1981 to 1989, and the University of Leiden, in the Netherlands, in 1989. Though he lives in Bilthoven, the Netherlands, he holds the title professor emeritus from the University of Michigan. He has been a member of the Dutch Academy of Science since 1981 and a fellow of the American Physical Society since 1984. He has received numerous honors for his work, including: the Alexander von Humbolt Award from Germany, in 1989; an honorary doctorate from the State University of New York at Stony Brook, in 1989; the Fifth Physica Lezing from the Netherlands, in 1990; and the High Energy Physics Prize from the European Physical Society, in 1993. In 1992 Veltman was knighted into the Dutch Order of the Lion in honor of Queen Beatrix of the Netherlands.

ABOUT: BBC News (on-line) October 12, 1999; New York Times (on-line) October 13, 1999, October 17, 1999; Nobel e-Museum Web site; Online NewsHour October 12, 1999.

Walker, John E.

(January 7, 1941–) Nobel Prize for Chemistry, 1997 (shared with Paul D. Boyer and Jens C. Skou)

The biochemist John Ernest Walker was born on January 7, 1941 in Halifax, England, to Thomas Ernest Walker and Elsie (Lawton) Walker. He attended the Rastrick Grammar School in West Yorkshire and earned a B.A. and M.A. from St. Catherine's College, at Oxford University. In 1969 he earned a doctorate in chemistry, also from Oxford.

After graduating Walker embarked on a series of research fellowships. In 1969 he began a two-year fellowship as a visiting researcher at the University of Wisconsin. He then accepted a fellowship as a North Atlantic Trade Organization (NATO) researcher at the Centre National de la Recherche Scientifique (CNRS), in Gif-sur-Yvette, France. The following year he left CNRS for another fellowship, given by the European Molecular Biology Organization (EMBO), to conduct research at the Pasteur Institute in Paris. When this work concluded, in 1974, Walker returned to England and joined the Medical Research Council Laboratory of Molecular Biology at Cambridge University.

© The Nobel Foundation

In 1980 Walker began working with the organic compound adenosine triphosphate, or ATP. He was promoted to senior scientist at the Lab in 1982, a move that allowed him to devote himself to ATP research and to assemble a staff to aid him in his work—work that would eventually earn him the 1997 Nobel Prize in Chemistry, alongside JENS C. SKOU and PAUL D. BOYER. Walker and Boyer shared half the prize for what the Royal Academy of Sciences termed the "elucidation of the enzymatic mechanism underlying the synthesis of adenosine triphosphate," as archived on the Nobel e-Museum Web site. (Skou was awarded the other half for his discovery of the enzyme that regulates the concentration of sodium and potassium in cells.)

ATP is one of organic life's most essential compounds, often described as the "energy currency" of the cell. It captures the chemical energy created by the combustion of nutrients and then releases that energy where it is needed—to build proteins, contract muscles, or transmit nerve signals. The German chemist Karl Lohmann discovered ATP in 1929, and determined that it both captures the energy released by the breakdown of nutrients, and diverts that energy to important biochemical reactions. ATP's structure was later clarified by the Scottish scientist ALEXANDER TODD, who won the 1957 Nobel Prize in Chemistry. The 1953 Nobel laureate in medicine, the American researcher FRITZ LIPMANN, was the first to show that ATP is the primary bearer of chemical energy within cells.

Produced and utilized every day in the human body in large quantities, ATP is composed of the compound adenosine and three phosphate groups. When the outermost phosphate group is removed from ATP, adenosine diphosphate (ADP) is formed and energy is released. The opposite also occurs: when energy is used by the enzyme ATP-synthase to bond ADP to a phosphate group, it forms ATP. ATP-synthase is the enzyme that drives this back-and-forth process.

The American scientist Efraim Racker discovered ATP-synthase in 1960. Then Paul Boyer theorized that hydrogen ions drive ATP-synthase to create ATP. After a series of experiments in the 1970s, Boyer concluded that the ATP-synthase enzyme looks like a cylinder, which a passing stream of hydrogen ions causes to rotate. This rotating cylinder is the "engine" that drives the synthesis and release of ATP.

In his research into ATP-synthase during the 1980s, John Walker mapped out the amino acid sequences in the proteins that make up the ATP-synthase enzyme—a task that Richard L. Cross, of the State University of New York Health Science Center, described for C. Wu in Science News (October 25, 1997) as "Herculean." Walker believed that, in order to understand how the enzyme functions, it was first necessary to uncover its chemical makeup and structure. His later work in the 1990s clarified the three-dimensional, rod-and-cylinder structure of ATP-snythase, thus lending support to Boyer's theory. Using samples of the enzyme taken from cows, Walker detailed the cylindrical structure. Collaborating with crystallographers—who specialize in describing the forms and structures of crystals—he bombarded the enzyme samples with x-rays to produce an atomic-scale map. This allowed Walker to see exactly how the enzyme functions. In particular, he discovered a catalytic portion of the enzyme that resembled a pumpkin, with a stalk protruding from its center. The cylindrical portion, Walker revealed, functioned like an electrical wire, guiding the flow of hydrogen ions necessary to maintain the rotation of the entire structure. In recognizing such findings, the Royal Swedish Academy of Sciences stated that "Walker's work complements Boyer's in a remarkable manner, and further studies based on this structure demonstrate the correctness of the mechanism proposed by Boyer," as archived on the Nobel e-Museum Web site. The "$64,000 question," the biochemist Robert Fillingame told Robert F. Service for Science (October 24, 1997), is to next determine precisely how the flow of hydrogen ions causes the enzyme to spin like a wheel.

Walker made the results of his research public in 1994. After hearing about the awarding of the Nobel Prize to Walker, Boyer, and Skou, the biochemist Steven M. Block, of Princeton University, told C. Wu that these three men "are richly deserving of the prize," noting that "man, in his hubris, thought that he had invented the wheel. In fact, the wheel was one of nature's earliest inventions. It wasn't until the 1970s that we discovered that rotary mechanisms exist in biology."

John E. Walker has been a senior scientist at the Laboratory of Molecular Biology since 1982. He has received numerous recognitions during his career, including admittance to the European Molecular Biology Organization (1983) and the Royal Society of London (1995). He has been awarded the Johnson Foundation Prize from the University of Pennsylvania (1994), the Ciba Medal from the Biochemical Society (1995), and the PETER MITCHELL Medal at the European Bioenergetics Conference (1996).

Walker married Christina Jane Westcott in 1963; the couple has two daughters and resides in Cambridge, England.

ABOUT: Nobel e-Museum Web site; Science October 24, 1997; Science News October 25, 1997; Scientific American (online) October 20, 1997.

Courtesy of The University of Colorado at Boulder

Wieman, Carl

(March 26, 1951–) Nobel Prize for Physics, 2001 (shared with Eric Cornell and Wolfgang Ketterle)

The physicist Carl Wieman was born on March 26, 1951 in Corvallis, Oregon. After high school, he attended the Massachusetts Institute of Technology (MIT), in Cambridge, where he studied with the physicist Daniel Kleppner, a specialist in atomic, molecular, and optical physics. As Kleppner recalled to David H. Freedman for *Discover* (February 1993), as an undergraduate Wieman was so interested in lasers and atomic physics that he would often ask to be excused from his classes to conduct lab research, even opting to sleep in the lab some nights; he frequently focused on building la-

sers. Wieman worked with fluorescent dye to produce a new type of laser that would release large amounts of photons (the particles that create light beams) and thus stronger beams. After earning his B.S. degree in 1973, Wieman continued his research with lasers at Stanford University, in Stanford, California, earning his Ph.D. in 1977. He then spent seven years, first as an assistant research scientist and later as an assistant professor of physics, at the University of Michigan, where his research confirming the theories of "parity non-conservation" earned him a reputation as one of the most important new scientists in the country. Parity non-conservation, or violation, has to do with the idea that nuclear and sub-nuclear particles do not obey classical physical theories of conservation and, when it comes to theories of classical optics, would not produce lasers whose angles of incidence equal the angles of reflection when bounced off a mirror. Malcolm W. Browne for the *New York Times* (May 28, 1991) explained: "A peculiarity of nuclear and sub-nuclear particles is that they exhibit a kind of uneven 'handedness' that scientists call parity violation. The discovery in the 1970s that the electromagnetic force is directly related to the weak nuclear force through a carrier called weak neutral current involves just such a parity violation, and a very successful theory precisely predicts the size of this uneven handedness." Wieman's research in this field led to new discoveries about scientists' capabilities for measuring types of parity non-conservation with precision; he conducted numerous experiments testing new physical theories as well as investigating older models.

In 1984 Wieman joined the staff of the University of Colorado at Boulder as an associate professor of physics, becoming a full professor in 1987 and a distinguished professor in 1997. He became a fellow in 1985 for JILA, formerly known as the Joint Institute for Laboratory Astrophysics, a joint center for research and education for the National Institute of Standards and Technology (NIST) and the University of Colorado; he served as JILA's chairman from 1993 to 1995.

When Wieman moved to Boulder, he explored the idea of adding new lasers to his lab to improve the accuracy of his work; but when he found that the dye lasers he would require cost nearly $80,000 each, he began to consider alternatives. He ultimately settled on the tiny mass-produced "diode" lasers used in CD players, which cost only about $200 each. Wieman concluded that, despite having weaker beams, these diode lasers would be sufficient for the applications he intended; he even found that he could tune and "de-tune" these lasers, thus more easily shifting the wavelength of the light, depending on the atoms with which he was working. In 1986 Wieman shifted the focus of his work to laser cooling and began using his diode lasers to obtain temperatures close to absolute zero (-459.67 degrees Fahrenheit or -273.15 degrees Celsius), the lowest theoretical temperature. Physicist STEVEN CHU and his team at AT&T Bell Labs had already begun conducting research on laser cooling using more expensive dye lasers and had reached temperatures as low as 240 microkelvin, or millionths of a degree on the Kelvin scale, where absolute zero is simply zero. Using his diode lasers, Wieman matched Chu's work within a year, and the two physicists were soon engaged in a friendly competition to see who could achieve the lowest temperature on record. Over the next several years, Wieman's group, Chu's group, a team led by WILLIAM PHILLIPS at the NIST, and a team led by CLAUDE COHEN-TANNOUDJI at the École Normale Supérieure in Paris were all engaged in research on laser cooling, making regular breakthroughs and essentially taking turns in breaking the lowest temperature records. In 1990 Claude Cohen-Tannoudji's team achieved a temperature of only two microkelvin; just three weeks later, Wieman's group announced that it had produced a temperature slightly above one microkelvin, which remained the record for years. Over time, the remaining teams reduced the lowest temperature record even more, achieving temperatures measured in nanokelvins, or billionths of a degree Kelvin. For their achievements in developing new methods for cooling and trapping laser light, Chu, Phillips and Cohen-Tannoudji were jointly awarded the 1997 Nobel Prize in Physics. By that time, however, Wieman had shifted the focus of his research once again, this time toward achieving Bose-Einstein condensation (BEC). "There is some good, exciting physics in the interaction of atoms at low temperatures," Wieman had told David H. Freedman. "But the really big payoff will be if we can get to Bose condensation. That's the sort of experiment that wins a Nobel Prize."

The theories behind BEC began in 1924, when a young Indian physicist, Satyendra Nath Bose, sent ALBERT EINSTEIN a paper in which he had made some important theoretical calculations about light particles, or photons. In their article on BEC for *Scientific American* (March 1998), Cornell and Wieman explained the theoretical construct: "At ordinary temperatures, the atoms of a gas are scattered throughout the container holding them. Some have high energies (high speeds); others have low ones. Expanding on Bose's work, Einstein showed that if a sample of atoms were cooled sufficiently, a large fraction of them would settle into the lowest possible energy state in the container. In mathematical terms, their individual wave equations—which describe such physical characteristics of an atom as its position and velocity—would in effect merge, and each atom would become indistinguishable from any other." In other words, as these atoms were cooled to temperatures nearing absolute zero, Einstein predicted they would form a "condensate," or a gas of atoms, in which all motion would essentially stop. Scientists named this theoretical state of matter Bose-Einstein condensation (BEC), though it remained little more than a prediction for more than 70 years. BEC was such a unique theory, Wieman told Curt Suplee for the *Washington Post* (July 14, 1995) that "if it hadn't been Einstein, it would have been laughed off as a ridiculously far-out idea."

Working with another physicist, ERIC CORNELL, who joined JILA's staff in 1990, Wieman began experimenting with alkali atoms, such as cesium, rubidium, and sodium rather than hydrogen, because, he theorized, the atoms were larger and would be able to bounce off each other more frequently, thus sharing their energy and allowing the formation of a condensate before freezing could occur. More than five years into their research, on June 5, 1995, Wieman and Cornell achieved their goal, when they cooled rubidium atoms to less than 170 billionths of a degree above absolute zero and observed the first creation of a super-atom condensate performing as a single entity. Under Wieman's method, the physicists first slowed and trapped approximately 10 million rubidium atoms using diode lasers by bombarding the gas with a steady stream of photons from all directions. In a JILA press release (June 13, 1995), Wieman told the institute's press representative, "It's like running in a hail storm so that no matter what direction you run the hail is always hitting you in the face. So you stop." Then, after trapping the atoms by the force of the lasers' light—at a temperature of about 40 millionths of a degree above absolute zero—Wieman turned off the lasers and activated a second stage of cooling using magnetic trapping and evaporative cooling. The theory behind magnetic trapping relied upon the magnetic property inherent within all atoms that would subject them to a force when placed in a magnetic field. Once held securely in place within this magnetic field, the atoms cooled further through evaporative cooling, a process in which the most energetic atoms would escape from the magnetic bowl, carrying away their energy and leaving the remaining atoms colder. This process worked much the same way as cooling a cup of hot coffee, in which the hottest atoms leap out of the cup as steam. The last hurdle for Wieman's research team involved finding a way to hold enough atoms within the magnetic field to allow the formation of BEC. In response, Cornell designed a technique to improve the magnetic trap, which he called "a time-averaged orbiting potential trap," in which the hole through which atoms could escape was continually revolving. Cornell told the institute's press reporter, "It's like playing keep-away with the atoms because the hole kept circulating faster than the atoms could respond." Ultimately, with about 2,000 rubidium atoms remaining in the trap, Wieman and Cornell used a laser to cast the shadow of a dense droplet of overlapping atoms, observing their results through a magnified video camera lens. In a March 1998 article for *Scientific American*, they recalled, "We caused the atoms to lose for a full ten seconds their individual identities and behave as though they were a single 'super-atom.' The atoms' physical properties, such as their motions, became identical to one another. This Bose-Einstein condensate (BEC), the first observed in a gas, can be thought of as the matter counterpart of the laser—except that in the condensate it is atoms, rather than protons, that dance in perfect unison."

The project's success earned national attention, as Wieman and Cornell had not only proved Einstein's theory but, in the process, created the coldest place in the universe and achieved a truly new state of matter. The results held great potential for the enhanced study of quantum mechanics: As Wieman and Cornell explained, physicists rarely have the opportunity to examine the wave properties of matter through macroscopic particles—those large enough to be observed with the naked eye. In BEC, as the atoms' wave packets grew and eventually condensed with those of other atoms, the overall wave packet that extended across the sample of condensate became large enough to be seen by the naked eye, thus giving physicists new opportunities to study the structure and interactions of matter. Because of Wieman's dedication to using affordable lasers, his team achieved BEC using only about $50,000 worth of equipment, a reasonable expense that most university laboratories could easily afford. "It's not impossible that in a few years this could be the stuff of an undergraduate thesis," Wieman told David H. Freedman in a January 1996 *Discover* article. On October 9, 2001 the Royal Swedish Academy of Science awarded the Nobel Prize in Physics to Wieman, Cornell, and WOLFGANG KETTERLE, a German physicist who independently achieved Bose-Einstein condensation using sodium atoms. The academy speculated that this work could bring "revolutionary applications in such fields as precision measurement and nanotechnology," as stated on the Nobel e-museum Web site, with practical applications for the creation of new atomic lasers, atomic clocks, molecular motors, and advanced microcomputers.

While scientists still do not know all there is to know about BEC, Wieman and Cornell continue to explore its properties, and in July 2001 they published new research on their success in collapsing and exploding the condensate by manipulating its magnetic fields. In August 2001 the National Science Foundation announced it would grant JILA $15 million over five years to further the study of atomic and molecular physics.

In addition to the Nobel Prize, Wieman has earned numerous honors and awards for his contributions to science and education, including the E. O. Lawrence Award in Physics (1993), the Davisson-Germer Prize of the American Physical Society (1994), the Einstein National Medal for Laser Science from the Society of Optical and Quantum Electronics (1995), the Richtmyer Memorial Lecture Award from the American Association of Physics Teachers (1996), the Fritz

London Award in Low Temperature Physics from the International Union of Pure and Applied Physics (1996), the Lorentz Medal from the Royal Netherlands Academy of Arts and Sciences (1998), the R.W. Wood Prize from the Optical Society of America (1999), the Schawlow Prize for Laser Science from the American Physical Society (1999), and the Benjamin Franklin Medal in Physics from the Franklin Institute (2000). In 2001 Wieman was awarded the National Science Foundation Director's Award for distinguished teaching scholars, an honor that recognizes scientists who have "advanced the frontiers of education." He has received an honorary doctorate of science from the University of Chicago and is a member of the Optical Society of America, the American Physical Society, and the American Association of Physics Teachers. Wieman contributed to the physics textbook *Laser Physics at the Limits*, published in November 2001. He currently lives in Colorado with his wife, Sarah Gilbert, a physicist at NIST.

ABOUT: Discover February 1993, January 1996; JILA Web site; New York Times May 28, 1991; Nobel e-Museum Web site; Physics Today August 1996; Scientific American March 1998; Washington Post July 14, 1995.

International Capaign to Band Landmines

Jody Williams

Jody Williams and the International Campaign to Ban Landmines

(International Campaign to Ban Landmines founded in 1992; Jody Williams born in 1950–) Nobel Prize for Peace, 1997

The peace activist Jody Williams was born on October 9, 1950 in Rutland, Vermont, and grew up in Brattleboro, Vermont. She was the second of five children. Her father was a county judge; her mother oversaw housing projects. Through defending her deaf brother, Stephen, from the taunts of other children, Williams learned to speak out on behalf of others. "Anybody who didn't know how to speak for themselves, I thought, 'I know how. I'll speak for you,'" she told *People* (October 27, 1997). In 1972 Williams earned a B.A. degree from the University of Vermont at Burlington. Four years later she received an M.A. degree in teaching both English as a second language (ESL) and Spanish from the School for International Training, in Brattleboro. She then spent some years teaching ESL in Mexico, the United Kingdom, and Washington, D.C. In 1984 she earned a second master's degree, this one in international relations from the Johns Hopkins School of Advanced International Studies, in Washington, D.C.

Williams spent the next dozen years working on projects to increase the American public's awareness of the U.S. government's activities in, and policies connected with, Central America. For two years she served as the co-coordinator of the Nicaragua-Honduras Education Project. In that capacity she led fact-finding missions to Nicaragua (where the United States was supporting a counterrevolutionary military force, called the Contras, to oppose the left-wing, Sandinista government), and Honduras (which the Contras were using as a base of operations). In 1986 she became the deputy director of Medical Aid for El Salvador, a Los Angeles–based organization, for which she helped to develop and direct projects to aid the civilian population, which was suffering the terrible effects of a civil war between the U.S.–backed, repressive right-wing government and leftist guerrillas. During her half-dozen years with the group, she recruited 20 U.S. hospitals to donate medical care to Salvadoran children injured by war. She herself witnessed the devastating damage that land mines can wreak on noncombatants of all ages.

For countries at war, minefields are a relatively inexpensive way of defending territory. The cheapest land mines cost as little as $3, and unlike soldiers, they need neither lodging nor sustenance. Ever-ready to discharge, they are vigilant, unfeeling, unthinking sentries—so unthinking, in fact, that they often kill and maim long after hostilities have ended. In the North African desert, people still occasionally find active mines that were planted during World War II. In areas where more recent conflicts have been waged—Laos, Cambodia, Afghanistan, Iraq, Bosnia and Herzegovina, Somalia, Nicaragua, to name a few—land mines represent an even greater threat. Many a farmer plowing a former battlefield has unwittingly triggered a forgotten mine. The result, much of the time, is shredded limbs; other times, the result is death.

The UNITED NATIONS has estimated that about 100 million land mines are currently deployed across the globe—one for every 60 people—and more are laid each day. (In Afghanistan, for example, according to various sources, during the decade that followed the Soviet Union's invasion of that nation, in 1989, Afghan forces and Soviet troops planted an estimated eight million to 10 million land mines.) There are two types of land mines. One of them, the antitank land mine, normally explodes only when exposed to the pressure of very heavy objects, such as tanks or automobiles. As little as six pounds of pressure can set off the second type, the antipersonnel mine. Land mines kill or maim an estimated 26,000 people a year, and most of these victims are not soldiers at war but civilians in peacetime. Indeed, some observers claim that land mines have inflicted more damage than certain weapons associated with mass destruction. "People were rightly outraged when [Iraqi president] Saddam Hussein used chemical weapons against the Kurds," Senator Patrick J. Leahy of Vermont told the *Washington Post* (August 8, 1993). "But how many people realize that all the deaths from chemical, biological and even nuclear weapons are only a fraction of the number who have been killed or maimed by land mines?" The cost of finding, deactivating, and discarding a single deployed land mine has been estimated at between $300 and $1,000. If, as the United Nations has estimated, 100 million land mines remain deployed, getting rid of every one of them would cost at least $30 billion.

On a Sunday afternoon in November 1991, Bobby Muller, the president of the Vietnam Veterans of America Foundation, called a meeting of a small group of activists, including Jody Williams, to discuss the problem of land mines; the ICBL came into being the following year. The veterans foundation subsequently hired Williams to coordinate a campaign against the use of land mines. "For sure, none of us thought we would ever ban land mines," she recalled to Raymond Bonner for the *New York Times* (September 20, 1997). In addition to the Vietnam Veterans of America Foundation, the members of ICBL initially included the groups Human Rights Watch, which is based in New York City; Physicians for Human Rights (Boston); Medico International (Germany); Handicap International (France); and the Mines Advisory Group (England). One of ICBL's earliest supporters was Lloyd Axworthy, the foreign minister of Canada, who proved to be influential in lobbying other nations to ban land mines. The first U.S. politician to join the ICBL's cause was Senator Leahy, who, in 1992, persuaded the U.S. Congress to pass a bill prohibiting the United States from exporting land mines for one year. George Herbert Walker Bush, who was then the president, signed the bill into law. A year later Leahy successfully engineered a three-year extension of the moratorium. Another influential voice was the INTERNATIONAL COMMITTEE OF THE RED CROSS. "It was the first time that the Red Cross, [traditionally] fearful of offending governments lest it lose its neutrality and effectiveness in the field, had engaged in vigorous advocacy," Raymond Bonner wrote for the *New York Times*.

By 1997 more than a thousand organizations from 60 countries had aligned themselves with the coalition. (As of early 2002, more than 1,300 organizations from more than 90 countries, ranging from arms-control and development groups to women's organizations, are affiliated with the ICBL.) Celebrities, among them Princess Diana of Great Britain, also publicly supported the cause. Williams kept in touch with her fellow activists largely through e-mail, thereby demonstrating the usefulness of the Internet for social activism. "From day one, we recognized that instant communication was critical," she told the *Washington Post* (October 11, 1997). "It made people feel they were part of it."

In September 1997 the movement to ban land mines took a giant leap forward. That month approximately 90 countries drafted a treaty to ban antipersonnel land mines completely, and on December 3, 1997, in Ottawa, Canada, 122 countries signed the Mine Ban Ttreaty. Since then, the number of signatories has increased to 142. Signatories to the treaty, which went into effect after 40 countries ratified it, must destroy stockpiles of land mines within four years of ratification and remove all deployed land mines within 10 years of ratification.

The Mine Ban Treaty was historic not only in its intent but also because never before had a group of small, nongovernmental organizations successfully pressured the worldwide community to enact such a global ban so quickly. Indeed, Williams and her fellow activists were surprised at their own success. Coordinated partly via the Internet, the ICBL may prove to be an excellent model for social movements in the Information Age. At the Nobel Peace Prize acceptance ceremony in Oslo, the Norwegian Nobel Committee stated, "As a model for similar process in the future, it could prove of decisive importance to the international effort for disarmament and peace."

The ICBL considers the Mine Ban Treaty a stunning achievement but by no means the complete answer to the problem of land mines. That is because some of the world's biggest producers of land mines—Russia, China, and the United States—were conspicuously absent from the signing in Ottawa. President Bill Clinton opted against having the United States sign the treaty because, he stated, he believed that so-called smart mines, which are designed to self-destruct after a predetermined period of time, pose no threat to civilians after a war is concluded. Moreover, in his opinion, the land-mine ban should not include South Korea, whose border with North Korea is one of the most heavily militarized regions on the planet. While experts generally agree that South Korean and U.S. forces would be able to defeat a North Korean invasion of South Korea, they believe that the allied

troops would incur greater casualties if the nearly one million land mines that the U.S. has deployed along the border were not in place.

Williams has dismissed such arguments; she accused Clinton of being against "the tide of history." "France, U[nited] K[ingdom], Germany have decided that they do not need this weapon and they can destroy it now. Why does the one remaining superpower with the most advanced war weapons in the world still need to rely on the land mine?" she asked in an interview with Phil Ponce for the *Online Newshour* (October 10, 1997). Williams's position has been endorsed by 14 retired American generals (including General H. Norman Schwarzkopf, the leader of the coalition forces against Iraq in the 1991 Persian Gulf War), who in 1996 signed a statement expressing their opposition to the continued use of land mines.

Perhaps influenced by the efforts of the ICBL, President Clinton announced his own timetable for the elimination of land mines. In May 1996 he announced that the U.S. would stop using "dumb" mines (mines that remain live for years, or even decades). Later, he stated that by 2003, the U.S. would stop using antipersonnel mines except in South Korea. He also directed the Pentagon to investigate alternatives to land mines so that by 2006, they can be eliminated in South Korea as well. As of early March 2002, the administration of President George W. Bush, who succeeded Clinton in the White House, had made no public statement regarding its position on the land-mines issue.

Williams currently serves as the ICBL's campaign ambassador, in which capacity she speaks all over the world on the movement to ban land mines. When Phil Ponce asked her in 1997 what receiving the Nobel Peace Prize meant to her, she responded, "Very few people are allowed the luxury to decide that they want to do something out of the mainstream. Most people tend to pretty much go to college and get a job and buy a house and pay the mortgage. For whatever reason, I've had the luxury of deciding to do things a little bit differently. And I consider much of my life to be a privilege, and this is sort of the most amazing part." A few months later, at the signing of the Mine Ban Treaty, she made the point that many voices speaking out together can successfully challenge not only schoolyard bullies but also the governments of the world's most powerful nations. "Together we are a superpower," she said. "It's a new definition of superpower. It is not one, it's everybody."

Williams lives in a farmhouse in Putney, Vermont.

ABOUT: Ms. January/February 1998; New York Times September 20, 1997, October 11, 1997, December 4, 1997, February 20, 1998; New York Times Magazine January 23, 1994; Nobel e-Museum Web site; Online NewsHour October 10, 1997; People October 27, 1997; Time October 20, 1997; Washington Post October 11, 1997.

Courtesy of California Institute of Technology

Zewail, Ahmed H.

(February 26, 1946–) Nobel Prize for Chemistry, 1999

The chemist Ahmed H. Zewail was born on February 26, 1946 in Egypt. He began his professional career in 1966 as an undergraduate trainee at the Shell Corporation in his native country. A year later he received his bachelor of science degree from Alexandria University, in Egypt. He continued his studies at Alexandria, earning a master's degree in 1969, while working there as a chemistry instructor and researcher. In the early 1970s Zewail traveled to the United States to study at the University of Pennsylvania in Philadelphia, where he earned his Ph.D. in chemistry in 1974. From 1974 to 1976 he worked at the University of California at Berkeley on an IBM postdoctoral research fellowship. In 1976 he joined the California Institute of Technology (Caltech) as an assistant professor of chemical physics. Here, over the next two decades, he would conduct his pioneering research in the field of femtochemistry—the study of chemical acts that occur in a femtosecond, or one-quadrillionth of a second. (A femtosecond is equal to 0.000000000000001 of one second, which is to a second what a second is to 32 million years.)

Femtochemistry was once a rarely explored field. Before Zewail began his work, scientists were unable to watch the breaking or making of molecules, since no camera was fast enough to capture these actions. All cameras were limited by the time an electric current could travel through the wire and semiconductor materials that comprise switches. No electronic circuit could be built that could turn the flash circuit off and on faster than one-hundredth of one-billionth of a second—far slower than a femtosecond. Knowing these limitations, scientists had to settle for before-and-after pictures of the creation or destruction of molecules, which left the actual point of bonding or cleaving unrecorded. In order to capture that moment in which molecules bond or cleave, Zewail had to rethink the way in which that instant could be visually recorded.

Zewail found his answer in mode-locking, a technique developed by physicists at Bell Laboratories in the early 1980s that worked at the femtosecond level. According to Gary Taubes, who wrote about Zewail's work for *Discover* (February 1994): "To understand mode-locking . . . start with a light bulb. The light emitted is composed of electromagnetic waves, all with random wavelengths and out of phase, meaning that they're oscillating up and down out of step with one another. The result is the familiar beam of white light. A laser beam, in contrast, generates all the light waves at virtually a single wavelength, or color, and all in phrase, which is to say they're 'coherent,' all oscillating in more or less perfect step." However, an ordinary laser produces a continuous electromagnetic wave, which is unsuitable for what Zewail wanted to accomplish. He needed something more akin to a strobe effect: coherent pulses of light flashing in a femtosecond.

Zewail's solution was to generate light at more than one wavelength—10,000 different wavelengths, in fact. Each wavelength would be evenly spaced but out of phase 99.996 percent of the time. In phase the other .0004 percent of the time, the wavelengths would line up exactly, with all the peaks and troughs level. A single pulse of laser light would thus be created, enabling the movement of the molecule to be photographed as if with an incredibly fast shutter. By the late 1980s his research group was able to create a kind of motion picture of chemical reactions by taking a series of frames of the reaction.

One of the earliest discoveries Zewail's work uncovered, according to a report in *BBC News* (October 12, 1999, on-line), "was the realisation that as chemical reactions proceed intermediate products are formed that are quite distinct from the reactants and final products." Since their first experiments, Zewail and his associates have studied more than 50 molecular reactions and are branching out into different fields. In the subbasement of Noyes Hall on the Caltech campus, the group works in an area dubbed "Femtoland," in which five laboratories are devoted to different types of chemical reactions, examining everything from the simple breaking and bonding of molecules to how the dynamics of a tangle of forces on a complex molecule affect it. Zewail's work has greatly altered academic research in chemistry labs across the United States, moving it away from Bunsen burners and beakers and toward advanced laser technology on a microscopic level. Such labs are busy experimenting on the dynamics of proteins, as well as the mechanics of human eyesight. The significance of this work is not lost on the man who has been dubbed the "father of femtochemistry" by the American Chemical Society. "Look at the world," Zewail told Gary Taubes. "Everything around us is chemical reactions. Everything—inside you and me, the atmosphere, everything we breathe, we touch. Everything is a chemical reaction. So we have to develop a unified theory of how chemistry takes place. We can't understand this unless we really have a coherent understanding of how atoms and molecules like or dislike each other. That's our ultimate goal."

As the pioneering figure of femtochemistry, Ahmed Zewail has been greatly honored for his work, both in the United States and abroad. In addition to winning the 1999 Nobel Prize for Chemistry, Zewail has won the Buck-Whitney Medal from the American Chemical Society (1985), the King Faisal International Prize in Science (1989), the Nobel Laureate Signature Award (1992), the 1993 Earl K. Plyler Prize from the American Physics Society, the 1993 Wolf Prize in Chemistry, and the 1993 Medal of the Royal Netherlands Academy of Arts and Sciences, among others. In 1990 he was named Caltech's first LINUS PAULING Professor, a position established in memory of the two-time Nobel laureate. Zewail has been twice honored by the country of his birth: first in 1995 by Egyptian President Mubarak, who presented him with the Order of Merit, First Class, and again three years later when the Egyptian government issued two postage stamps with Zewail's portrait.

Ahmed H. Zewail, who holds citizenships in the United States and Egypt, lives in San Marino, California, with his wife Dema Zewail, a physician in public health at the University of California at Los Angeles. They have four children.

ABOUT: American Men and Women of Science, 1998–99; BBC News October 29, 1999; Columbia Dispatch (on-line) October 31, 1999; Discover February 1994; New York Times (on-line) October 13, 1999; Nobel e-Museum Web site; Scientist March 5, 1990.